CONQUISTADORS
OF THE USELESS
· · · · · ·

D1714979

CONQUISTADORS
OF THE USELESS

• • • • • •

FROM THE ALPS TO ANNAPURNA

BY LIONEL TERRAY

Translated by
GEOFFREY SUTTON

Foreword by
DAVID ROBERTS

LEGENDS AND LORE SERIES

MOUNTAINEERS
BOOKS

To my friends killed climbing

**MOUNTAINEERS
BOOKS**

Mountaineers Books is the publishing division of The Mountaineers, an organization founded in 1906 and dedicated to the exploration, preservation, and enjoyment of outdoor and wilderness areas.

1001 SW Klickitat Way, Suite 201, Seattle, WA 98134
800.553.4453, www.mountaineersbooks.org

Original French-language edition *Les Conquérants de l'Inutile*
© Editions GALLIMARD, Paris, 1961
English-language translation © 1963 Victor Gollancz Ltd and © 2001 Gollancz
(Orion Publishing Group)
Foreword © 2001 by David Roberts

Printed in the United States of America
19 18 17 16   1 2 3 4 5

Layout: Jennifer Shontz, www.redshoedesign.com
Series Design: Karen Schober
Cover photograph: *Lionel Terray and Jacques Soubis on Mount Huntington in 1964*
Frontispiece: *Young Lionel Terray formally dressed, even for a walk* (courtesy of Antoine and Nicolas Terray)

A catalog record for this book is available at the Library of Congress.

Mountaineers Books titles may be purchased for corporate, educational, or other promotional sales, and our authors are available for a wide range of events. For information on special discounts or booking an author, contact our customer service at 800-553-4453 or mbooks@mountaineersbooks.org.

♻ Printed on recycled paper

ISBN (paperback): 978-1-59485-111-7
ISBN (ebook): 978-1-68051-084-3

CONTENTS

FOREWORD

BY DAVID ROBERTS

OF THE FOUR GREAT FRENCH mountaineers who were in the vanguard of the legendary first ascent of Annapurna in 1950, three would never go on another expedition. Maimed by frostbite, Maurice Herzog and Louis Lachenal would find returning to the mountains a painful challenge. Lachenal, haunted by the loss of his matchless grace, threw himself back at the world with reckless abandon, and died in 1955 when he skied unroped into a crevasse on the Vallée Blanche. Gaston Rébuffat would continue to perfect his craft in the Alps, winning the status of the most famous guide in Europe, yet he never returned to the great ranges.

The fourth Annapurna stalwart, however, became, in my view, the greatest expeditionary mountaineer of all time. Others—most notably Reinhold Messner—might lay fair claim to that honour. Messner, like some of his rivals in the 1980s, emerged as a specialist in oxygenless ascents of eight-thousand-meter peaks. For Lionel Terray, nicknamed 'the strong sahib' by the Sherpas, what mattered most was seeking out the hardest, most beautiful mountains in the Andes, the Himalayas, and Alaska, and throwing all his energy and daring at their first ascents. From FitzRoy in 1952 to Mount Huntington in 1964, Terray succeeded on nine of the most stunning mountains on earth.

Almost always, Terray led not only as titular chief of the expedition, but on the sharp end of the rope as well: not once did a summit party fail to include him, even, as on Huntington, when he was crippled by a dislocated elbow suffered in a near-fatal fall.

One day in 1963, a college friend lent me a copy of *Conquistadors of the Useless*. Terray I knew from Herzog's *Annapurna*, but only as the man who had given up his own chance for the summit to carry loads to high camps in support of his teammates. In his own autobiography, however, Terray sprang forth as a fully rounded character, gruff, impetuous, visionary; he climbed like a bull, but wrote with a unique, homespun lyricism. What moved me most of all was Terray's account of the magical partnership he had forged with Lachenal culminating in their second ascent of the Eiger Nordwand in 1947.

Don Jensen and I were both so transported by the book that we began to identify with that great *cordée*. On our own Alaskan expeditions, we got so carried away as to address each other as 'Louis' and 'Lionel'. Stocky and strong, Don 'was' Terray; skinnier, more impatient and mercurial, I became Lachenal. In 1974, in a critique of climbing memoirs I wrote for *Ascent*, I argued that *Conquistadors* was the finest example of the genre ever written. More than a quarter of a century later, I see no reason to revise that judgment. Terray's book has its faults, but it conveys more of the truth of mountaineering than any other climber's autobiography I know of.

Two years ago, then, it came as a shock to be told by several French experts that Terray had not, in fact, written the book—it had been ghostwritten by Roger Nimier, his editor at Gallimard. The wife of one of his climbing partners seemed to confirm this. 'He was a bit of a country bumpkin,' she claimed. 'His writing, even in letters, was only semi-literate.' While researching for my own book about Annapurna,* my French editor, Michel Guérin, asked Marianne Terray for the key to the family home, a hillside château in Grenoble. In 1965, Terray had been using a room there as a study. It was from here that he set out for that final climb in the Vercors with Marc Martinetti. Neither returned alive.

The key opened a creaky door on the third floor. Everything was covered with dust; the wallpaper hung peeling from the walls; old mirrors had grown cloudy and speckled. Michel had been given permission by Marianne to look for old letters. There were piles and piles of papers on tabletops, in closets, inside desk and bureau drawers. There was something claustrophobic and oppressive about the place. It was hard to imagine the blithe mountaineer living even temporarily in such squalor. We were about to go, when Michel, poking through another closet, found a bulging folder with a sheaf of loose pages.

* *Publisher's note. True Summit: What Really Happened on the Legendary Ascent of Annapurna* by David Roberts (Simon and Schuster, New York, 2000).

'That's Terray's handwriting,' he said, scanning the lines. I peered over his shoulder as he leafed through the carefully written manuscript. A moment later, he let out a curse under his breath. 'It's the manuscript of *Les Conquérants*', he said softly.

Later, back in Chamonix, we studied this lost relic carefully. It was word-for-word what Gallimard published. So much for Roger Nimier!

Among the many revelations of my research none was more gratifying than this chance find. The authorship of *Conquistadors of the Useless* belonged fully to the man who not only had performed those great deeds in the mountains, but had found, with no help from another, the right words to memorialize them. Thus it is a deep pleasure now to invite a whole new generation to read *Conquistadors* and discover Terray's truth, which shines forth four decades later with all the dazzling brilliance of his finest climbs.

| 1 |

DISCOVERY

I HAVE GIVEN MY WHOLE LIFE to the mountains. Born at the foot of the Alps, I have been a ski champion, a professional guide, an amateur of the greatest climbs in the Alps, and a member of eight expeditions to the Andes and the Himalayas. If the word has any meaning at all, I am a mountaineer.

In apparent contradiction to this way of life, it so happens that I have had to give a great many lectures illustrated with slides. One evening, after one of these lectures, I was invited for a drink to the home of some local celebrity. A dark-suited professional man came up, looked me intently in the face, and said quietly:

'You interested me very much, monsieur.'

As I muttered my thanks in some conventional phrase or other, he went on:

'But what do you normally do for a living? An engineer, a teacher . . . ?'

The good man could not hide his surprise when I replied:

'Not at all, monsieur. I am a mountain guide pure and simple.'

Later, in my bleak hotel room, trying with difficulty to sleep after the nervous excitement of two hours of intense concentration in front of an audience, the man's words came back to me. I began to realise that the rather storybook life I had led had made me into a person of unusual duality. I saw that for anyone seeing me for the first time, in collar and tie and lounge suit, giving a lecture on the human geography of the Himalayas, I bore no resemblance to the real man behind this worldly façade—the mountaineer, that figure which a conventional literature has fixed in everybody's mind as a rough, crude-mannered peasant. And so for the first time I appreciated the full strangeness of the fate which had turned a child born to a family of middle-class intellectuals into a conqueror of the highest and most difficult mountains in the world.

The story begins at Grenoble, in a sort of château covered with Virginia creeper, built on the side of a hill above the town. There I was born, and one of my first sights must have been the shining barrier of the snowy peaks of the Belledonne range opposite our large, comfortable family seat.

My parents came of what the world calls a good family, in other words comfortable bourgeois, magistrates, owners of businesses, and high-ranking officers. Actually the family hid under its bourgeois appearance rather more originality and imagination than one might have expected at first sight. My ancestors on both sides included a considerable number of unusual men, enterprising men of affairs, travellers in search of fortune and adventure, daring soldiers and politicians. Such forebears gave my parents a broader-minded outlook than is usual in their walk of life.

Tall, powerful, large-headed and heavy-jowled, his bright blue eyes almost hidden behind thick spectacle-lenses, my father was of definitely Nordic type. Though violent, passionate, ascetic and stubborn, he was also kindly and constantly bubbling with wit. Exceptionally gifted intellectually, his memory in particular was almost phenomenal. His life was nothing if not eventful: after qualifying brilliantly in chemical engineering, he set out to found a company in Brazil and had achieved assured success when suddenly the 1914 war broke out. Throwing up everything without hesitation, he went straight back to France to do his duty as a soldier. At the age of forty, fed up with business, he was not afraid to exchange industry for medicine, and after five years of study he qualified as a doctor. In his youth he had shown sporting interests of a kind unusual at that time, among them free ballooning and motor racing. In particular he was one of the first Frenchmen to take up skiing, and the very first to master the elegant telemark technique, the only method of turning known in those heroic times.

By contrast, my mother was Italian in style: small, with classical features, very dark eyes and hair the colour of jet. Of artistic temperament, she had studied painting She was an interested and active person, and showed a good deal of originality for her time, driving cars in 1913 and being the first French-woman sufficiently daring to don trousers for skiing. The great passion of her youth had been riding, at which she excelled, especially at point-to-point. In

Brazil she made journeys of several weeks on horseback, visiting wild areas where very few white women had ever been.

Although the adventurous and sporting instincts of my parents were quite strong they were never extreme, and particularly in the case of my father they never took an important place in his scheme of life. If it is true that my antecedents and education must have inclined me towards sport and the career of a man of action, it would be exaggerating to see in them auguries of a life completely devoted to adventure. One thing is certain: it was not from my parents that I derived any taste for climbing. Despite having passed the greater part of their lives among mountains, they had never mountaineered to any greater extent than tramping up one or two easy summits which required no climbing in the real sense. Indeed they disapproved of the sport and thought of it as madness. I remember quite well, one day when I was a little boy of seven or eight, my mother saying to me:

'I shall be very happy for you to go in for any sport except motorcycling and climbing.'

When I asked her the meaning of this last word, she added:

'It's a stupid sport which consists of dragging yourself up rocks with your hands, feet and teeth!'

If my mother disapproved of climbing mainly out of lack of knowledge, my father, on the contrary, heaped sarcasm and contempt upon it. Sport, for him, was mainly a way of keeping oneself fit to do the work necessary to social and financial success, and perhaps to advance oneself directly in life into the bargain. To go in for an activity as exhausting, dangerous and unknown as mountaineering seemed to him the height of absurdity, and I heard him say a hundred times if I heard him once:

'A man must be completely crazy to wear himself out climbing a mountain, at the risk of breaking his neck, when there isn't even a hundred franc note to be picked up on the summit.'

One of my cousins who had been crippled as a result of a climbing accident was constantly held up to me as a living example of the wretched consequences of such madness. Sometimes, in the street, my father would point contemptuously to the German students who frequently made the headlines in our local papers with their mountain accidents, and would not miss the chance of pointing to the moral at the same time.

'Take a good look at those idiots. A lot of good they'll have done themselves when they're walking on crutches like your cousin René!'

Family tradition has it that from the beginning I was a child of exceptional energy. I weighed about eleven pounds at birth, and the story runs that I had so much hair that they had to take me to the barber's at the age of four days. Those who know that at the age of twenty-one I was already as bald as a billiard ball can measure the injustice and irony of fate!

My character in childhood was, it seems, of almost unhealthy independence, and my exploits provide to this day an inexhaustible source of tales for winter evenings over the hearth. One of these seems to me worth relating. When I was four or five years old, my mother loved to dress me in elegant little black velvet costumes with white collars. Every time I was forced to wear one of these outfits, so ill adapted to my turbulent tastes, I used to get into a terrible temper. One day at the seaside, I refused completely to go in paddling. In the end my mother got bored, and ended up by dressing me again in one of these little Lord Fauntleroy suits which I so detested. No sooner was I dressed than I hurled myself with joy into the surf . . . Some people may think I was not only independent, but had very bad manners.

I was three and a half when my father put me on skis for the first time. Family tradition is contradictory about the results. Some say I did brilliantly, others the reverse. Objectivity forces me to suppose that my beginnings were similar to those of most children of that age, in other words that they consisted of a few short slides punctuated by bumps and tears. Be that as it may, I quickly began to adore the sport, and up to the age of twenty it was to absorb the larger part of my time, my energy and dreams.

Our house was set in spacious grounds comprising, as well as vineyards and kitchen gardens, a thick woodland with thorny brakes, ruins and rocks. This wild place formed a perfect world in which to realise the dreams of a child possessed with freedom and the wonders of nature. I grew there almost without constraint, running through the woods, clambering the rocks, trapping rabbits, foxes and rats, shooting blackbirds, thrushes, sparrows and sparrow hawks. Except in winter, when I passed every spare minute skiing, I used to spend more or less all my spare time from school in this park. For me there was little or no cinema-going, football, or afternoons at my friends'. Not only did I go there every Thursday and Sunday, whatever the weather, but also in the morning before school and when I got home in the evening. Sometimes even, in spring, when the air was warm and charged with a sense of excitement, I used to escape out there at night. Wandering through the fields and woods, I tried to penetrate the mysteries of their life when all nature was in shadow and silence. Hidden in the bushes I stayed motionless for hours together listening for the crack of twigs, the cries of owls, the blackbirds' clucking, the thousand almost inaudible sounds which revealed the intense activity of a nocturnal world. These years of boyhood passed in intimate contact with nature profoundly affected my physical and mental being.

Like almost all children, I adored playing at trappers or at cowboys and Indians. But unlike most others I had not the trappings but the reality. I had no Stetsons, flamboyant shirts, coloured feathers or sheriff's star; I had real guns, real hunting knives, a real forest containing wild animals. The house was full of weapons inherited from generations of hunters or brought back from Brazil, and with almost incredible carelessness my parents let me use most of them. From the age of nine I had my own rifle, for which I soon learnt how to make my own cartridges. One of my playmates and I invented a new game. The estate was infested with enormous rats which came out of the sewers of the nearby town, and we caught large quantities of them with the aid of special traps. Instead of just killing off the repugnant beasts in a simple way, we gave them one last chance. The trap was placed at one end of a sort of runway made of planks. One of us then opened the trap, and it was up to the other to get the rat with a bullet as he ran at top speed through the last two yards that led to freedom. The rats thus killed were then skinned and their hides dried in the sun until they were ready to be quickly tanned and sewn into picturesque costumes which, we hoped, resembled those of Attila's Huns, of whom we had read that they went clothed in rat skins!

This little savage's life had a disastrous effect on my school record. I was a very bad student. I had a normal respect for discipline and, without being very intelligent, showed no signs of unusual stupidity. No, the trouble came from a complete incapacity to concentrate: I was at the school physically, but my mind could not succeed in settling there. The same thing happened every day. With all the goodwill I could muster, I would listen for several minutes to the voice of my teacher. Then, as though by enchantment, the dreary world of blackboards, black desks, black aprons and black inkwells would fade away, and I would be madly flying down some endless snow slope, or tracking through a green wood full of whistling blackbirds, malicious squirrels and terrifying serpents.

My mother surrounded her two sons with the warmest affection, and if I had not been of such an independent nature I would have grown up in cotton wool. Her optimistic and easygoing nature did not seem too put out by my poor school reports. My father, on the other hand, much absorbed in his work and not normally giving too much attention to his children, could not help remembering with pride his own brilliant academic successes, and his vanity would have been greatly flattered to see me repeat them. Thus he was devoured with rage to find he had begotten such a dunce. In spite of outcries, spankings and extra classes, I continued to grow up between the bleak, black world of the school and that other, how much more thrilling, of our sunlit and mysterious park. I remained an immovable dunce and became a lively, robust boy, full of initiative and practical intelligence: at once enthusiastic and high-spirited, melancholy and secretive.

Most children instinctively like to climb trees, walls and rocks. Thus the little limestone crags around our grounds were a perfect playground for me, and thanks to them I learnt very early on the rudiments of the technique of rock climbing. Indeed I was only five years old when I had my first accident, which still remains the most serious I have had. While climbing some rocks in the park I fell, gashing my forehead deeply. Legend relates that I entered the house covered in blood but without a single tear—but we all know how these sort of legends grow up. To scramble around on a few little rocks, however, is not the same thing as mountaineering. If only by virtue of his size, a child cannot be expected to begin the sport before the age of eleven or twelve. My own interest in climbing mountains as such began to be aroused when I was about ten; but it should be noted that my physical development was exceptional and that, in spite of my mediocrity at school, my character was mature for my age. Far from putting me off, my parents' aversion for mountaineering, and the fact that they had forbidden it, made it particularly fascinating: as everyone knows, there is no fruit like forbidden fruit.

Odder still, the sheer violence of my father's repudiation of the sport struck against some hitherto hidden fibre in my heart to such a degree that, whenever he heaped his sarcasms on mountaineers, I felt a violent hatred rising in me. It seemed to me in a confused sort of way that such virulent hatred of an apparently rather unimportant activity implied more than the reaction of a balanced being to a silly game. It was rather the indignation of a man deeply attached to a particular view of the world face-to-face with a force which was in contradiction to his whole scheme of things. Today, with the passing of time, I realise that he abused certain forms of art, certain political and social ideals, with exactly the same kind of passion.

But to tell the truth, although at this very young age I already had an interest in mountains remarkable for its spontaneity, I only had the most muddled ideas about what they were really like. In a town like Grenoble, situated in the heart of the Alps, there are lots of climbers. There were even a few among our neighbours and relations; but with the exception of Dr Couturier, well known not only for his hunting exploits and books on alpine game but also for first ascents in the Mont Blanc range with the guide Armand Charlet, none of them had ever carried out any really big climbs. Having no means of comparison, I listened with the most fervent passion when these heroes related their exploits, and my spirit was exalted by their fabulous courage and strength. Furthermore I had discovered in our library a number of climbing books containing adventures which seemed to me of unexampled heroism. Without always understanding them very well, I devoured the lot in a frenzy. An imaginary world began to form in my childish mind, made up of terrible peaks constantly shaken by giant avalanches, of labyrinths of ice where crevasses kept opening with appalling crashes all around, of supermen who triumphed over all these obstacles in a series of nonstop adventures. Such a mass of grandeur, mystery and danger almost turned my young head, full of its dreams of adventure. Though I never imagined for a moment that I could ever join the select band of alpine heroes, it seemed that there could be no more marvellous destiny than to become one of the least of their accomplices.

Our baker's son had done a few climbs in the foothills around Grenoble. Boastful and talkative, he liked telling about his exploits and enlivened them a bit in the process. Carried away by his fluency, I literally worshipped this perfectly insignificant youth. He seemed to me a sort of demigod, and I spent hours listening to his tall tales. When I begged him to take me with him on one of his outings, he replied with disdain:

'Certainly not, you're nothing but a kid. You've got to be tough to go climbing, and have nerves that'll stand up to anything.'

I was also great friends with Georgette, our housekeeper's daughter. She was fifteen or sixteen, and went out each Sunday with a group from the Société des Grimpeurs des Alpes. The expeditions of this group were limited to local minor summits, which they reached by routes really little more difficult than steep paths. No doubt because there was not much danger about them, I had little difficulty in persuading Georgette to take me along with her on one of these trips, unknown to my parents. Thus it was under the pretext of innocent bicycle excursions that I climbed my first peaks. These ascents enraptured me, and the impression they made on me was so deep that even today the memory of those enchanted hours is fresh and alive.

For all that, the summits themselves were about as modest as they could be while still meriting the term. The first was the Aiguille de Quaix, a little limestone spire. A Rabelaisian legend had it that it was in fact no more than one of the droppings of Gargantua. Nevertheless the ascent kept me interested from beginning to end. On the way up we got into the wrong gully, and we floundered about for a long time among screes and brushwood. My life in our family park had made me a master of this art, which I showed off to my companions with naive pride. The climbing itself did not strike me as very difficult, but terribly vertiginous. One young girl almost fainted from giddiness and had to be revived with a cordial. On the way down our leader conducted us with hardly a mistake through what seemed to me a maze of smooth walls, ledges and chimneys. I was filled with admiration for his skill in routefinding. The imagination of an eleven-year-old can turn the simplest climb into the most gripping adventure.

I was twelve years old when something happened that was to play a crucial part in the development of my half-formed mountain vocation. My young brother fell ill, and the doctor recommended a holiday in the mountains. My mother decided to take us off to spend our school holidays in the Chamonix valley, where she had already stayed some years before. Up to that time the only mountains I had known had been the Préalpes, with their walls of grey rock dominating cultivated valleys. Only from afar had I admired the eternally white summits of Belledonne and the Oisans. This first contact with really big mountains was a revelation: to this day I keep absolutely intact the memory of my wonder at the sight of those masses of ice, shining against a sky of unearthly purity, and those rock needles which seemed to fling down a gauge to the daring of men.

At this time I was a boy of such size and energy that one might easily have taken me for fifteen or sixteen. Under this athletic exterior, however, was hidden an extreme sensitivity and a spirit in torment. The meanness, vulgarity and monotony of the world were already painfully obvious to me, and I dreamed passionately of a nobler, freer and more generous existence. At the first sight of the high mountains, 'I sensed at once all that they offered of joys to taste, of dreams to hoard, of glory to be won.'* In a way at once undefined and yet quite definite I divined every possibility of this world of ice and rock where there was nothing to be plucked but weariness and danger; I was the measure of the full savour which these useless fruits, plucked not from the mud but from a garden of beauty and light, could hold.

As soon as the first vision was over, I began to cast about for ways of getting closer to the marvel. In company with some boys of my own age I clambered up several of the belvederes of the Aiguilles Rouges, then crossed the Mer de Glace in the charge of one of the old guides, who, in those days, used to tout around the edges of the glacier, offering to take tourists to the other side. But on the Bossons glacier, emboldened by experience, I disdainfully rejected the services of the moustachioed and bemedalled 'pirate' who insistently warned us against the dangers to which we would be exposed in crossing the ice without his aid.

These gentle afternoon strolls hardly satisfied my appetite for adventure or my growing ambition. With all my soul I longed to penetrate to the very

* *Publisher's note.* Guido Lammer

heart of these mountains, and to tread their summits. The passion with which I pleaded my cause must have helped to convince my mother, who eventually let me go on the collective parties organised by the Compagnie des Guides de Chamonix. My first expedition was to go up to the Couvercle hut via the Paroi des Egralets, returning by the Talèfre Glacier and the Pierre a Béranger. The emotions I felt in jumping my first crevasse and crossing my first snow-bridge were hardly less intense than those with which I later stood on the virgin summits of the Pico FitzRoy or Makalu. And with what pride I showed my mother, on my return, a postcard of the Paroi des Egralets which I had just conquered, though in fact it was as banal an exploit as you could hope to find, since all the steep bits are equipped with cables and ladders! But quite soon these collective courses in their turn began to seem too tame to appease my aspirations. What I wanted was real climbs with ropes, crampons, ice axes, rappels—the lot.

But for all her usual kindness, my mother obstinately refused to let me risk my life on such adventures. Fortunately one of my cousins, who was a regular officer, happened to be stationed at this time at the École Militaire de Haute Montagne. He was a good climber with a reputation for being safe and sound. My mother was reassured by the guarantee offered by such a guide, and ended by letting me accompany him in the ascent of the Aiguillette d'Argentière. On this infinitesimal point, which hardly merits the name of a summit, I did my first rappel.* Although physically easy, this exercise is impressive to a beginner. At the moment of letting themselves slide towards the abyss, quite a lot of women and children cannot restrain themselves from whimpering with fear. Although I didn't whimper, my heart was in my mouth and my muscles were paralysed with fear. For the first of a great many times, my will drove me where my body was unwilling to follow. In view of the evident and profound joy I got out of these climbs, my cousin soon realised that nothing was going to change my passion for the mountains, and that it would be wiser to educate it than forbid it. On his advice my mother eventually decided to entrust me to a good professional guide, who took me for a first trial on the Clocher and Clochetons de Planpraz. As we completed this short but quite difficult climb very quickly, he took me the same day up the giddy south-east face of the Brévent. During this first alpine season, I also climbed the Grands Charmoz and the Petite Aiguille Verte.

* *Publisher's note.* A method of descending steep rocks. The climber slides down a rope which has been doubled round a spike hammered into the rock, then recovers it by pulling one of the ends. It is also known as abseiling.

Back in Grenoble after these promising beginnings, I reckoned I was fit to lead climbs for myself without the help of any guide. As soon as spring came along, I managed to persuade my friend Georgette to come with me to try and climb the Dent Gérard, in the Trois Pucelles, by the 'Grange Gully' route. Now without being really difficult, this climb, situated in a range of foothills near Grenoble, does demand a certain technique which I had not yet sufficiently mastered. It turned out to be one of the most dramatic of my career, and perhaps I have never come so close to death as I did on that day. We were very badly equipped, and one particular aspect of this state seems quite inexplicable to me today: although the Vercors range is formed of an extremely smooth and slippery limestone, we climbed in boots shod with clinker nails. This amounts to saying that we had about as much adherence to the rock as a horse trying to get up a very steep cobbled street!

The first bit, a traverse, was effected amid horrible scrapings of nails, which struck sparks from the rock as they skidded. Several times I was left hanging by my hands, and it was a miracle that I did not fall to the screes some sixty feet below me. When I finally arrived out of breath on a welcome ledge, a group of five climbers had been watching me with their hearts in their mouths offered to let me join on to their rope, no doubt thinking that it would be better to drag living bodies to the top of the mountain than to have to carry down dead ones. My vanity was somewhat wounded by this proposition, but when I thought how risky the first bit had been, discretion seemed the better course. After this, with the assurance of the rope above me, I followed the others quite easily. Unfortunately their party, which was too big in the first place, contained three girls who were almost beginners. The leader was obliged to hoist them like sacks up each rope's length or, as climbers say, 'pitch'. All this haulage took up a lot of time, and our centipede of a party advanced very slowly. It was already well on in the day when we arrived at the foot of two vertical cracks. The leader tackled the left-hand one, known as the 'Dalloz' crack, which was reputed to be quite difficult. He was a good climber, and aided by his gym shoes a few catlike movements brought him to the top of the pitch. But things took a turn for the worse when it came to getting up his heavy and clumsy companions. The crack went diagonally up across a vertical slab of rock as polished as a dance floor. The first girl did not know how to jam her hands and feet in the crack, and lost her hold as soon as she started to climb, swinging across the wall. After flailing around like a carp on a line for a few seconds, she let herself hang with limply swinging arms so that the leader had to hoist a dead weight of 125 pounds. After some minutes of sweating blood the poor fellow succeeded in getting the girl up to him, but was so exhausted by the exploit that he proved quite incapable of pulling up the next, whose abundant bosom and backside gave promise of a weighty matter. So the other man had to be got up to lend him a hand. All this took up so much time that the leader began to realise the risk of being caught by night on the crags.

Hoping to gain time, he asked me if I could climb the right-hand crack alone. This was called the 'Sandwich' crack, and he assured me it was less difficult than the Dalloz. This sign of confidence in my abilities was balm to my pride, and without hesitating a second I started up the narrow, vertical chimney, without a rope from above. This pitch, though not really very difficult, none the less needs a bit more technique than I possessed at that time, and I was terribly impeded by my nailed boots, which kept slipping. However by means of desperate energy and grim determination I succeeded in wedging my way slowly upwards, panting like a seal, amid the horrid scraping of my boots. In this way I got quite close to a ledge, but unfortunately at this point the crack, which had been vertical, became slightly overhanging. In order to get up the last few feet I had to free my body from the crack as much as possible, and give up the relative safety of my wedging, in order to reach holds which would make possible the final move onto the ledge: what climbers call a 'mantelshelf' movement. Pretty well exhausted by my efforts, I hesitated a long time before making up my mind. Finally, summoning up all my determination, I went at it with the energy of despair . . . but at the very moment my fingers gripped the coveted holds, my feet shot out from under me and left me swinging from my hands. Never since that day have I experienced so vividly the feeling that my fingers would open, that I would inexorably be dashed to death on the rocks below. Only those unsuspected reserves that one learns of in the most desperate situations enabled me to make that saving mantelshelf.

Well, so I had got up: but we weren't much better off as a result. When you play at being guides, you've got to get your clients up too. How was I going to help my heavy, clumsy companion, who would not be able to climb an inch of the pitch on her own? It was a horrifying problem for an exhausted boy of less than thirteen.

Very fortunately for us, a small tree had been so good as to grow close to the top of the crack, and thanks to this we were able to get ourselves out of a scrape which otherwise had no apparent solution but a bivouac and a rescue party. Each time I managed to hoist Georgette a few inches by a ferocious burst of strength, I was able to block the rope from slipping back round the trunk of the tree. This would give me sufficient rest to recover the energy for another pull of a few inches, and so, inch by inch, despite the sobs and protests of my half-suffocated companion, I finally got her up to me. The difficulties were now all over, the other party was joined, and the descent effected uneventfully.

This depressing experience as leader of a rope left me with a lack of self-confidence which hindered my climbing career for a long time. I came to the conclusion that mountaineering was reserved for a few athletes of superhuman courage, strength and agility. Perhaps my lack of aptitude was due to insufficient strength? I therefore set myself to intensive daily physical culture, acquiring enormous arms for a boy of my age without, however, being able to climb any better as a result.

A second try at the Grange Gully turned out as much of a fiasco as the first. This time I was accompanied by my cousin Michel Chevalier, later to become an excellent mountaineer. At this time he had done no climbing at all, and so, although I was the younger by three years, I found myself again in the lead. This time the first pitch went without any excitement, but I didn't seem to be able to get up the last few feet of a chimney which followed. In order to get the better of this bit we had to perform some acrobatics, in which my cousin jammed himself across the chimney between its two walls and I climbed up onto his shoulders. My boot-nails bit into his flesh as I searched around for the holds above, wringing groans of suffering out of him. Once we were safely up this chimney Michel would not hear of continuing such a doubtful enterprise, and I returned to Grenoble sulky and disappointed at this new setback.

On my next visit to Chamonix I did some more climbs with a guide, but unfortunately the one I employed was completely lacking in imagination or any spirit of enterprise, sticking the whole time to conventional routes of little difficulty. Furthermore he entertained a strong interest in the waitresses in the alpine huts, whatever their age and appearance. In order to return as quickly as possible to these dreams of delight, we almost ran up our climbs, and where I didn't climb fast enough for his taste he would drag me with the rope. In conditions like this it was difficult to perfect one's technique, and in fact I made hardly any progress that season.

The following winter, however, the gift for skiing which I had had since early childhood began to mature. In the regional competitions of the Dauphine no boy of my own age could keep up with me anymore, and for this reason I was allowed to compete with the juniors and even the seniors. Despite this I still managed to carry off some of the prizes. Some people began to say that I had the makings of an international champion, and what was more serious, I began to believe them. From this time on, skiing occupied an always larger place in my life. After the winter was over I continued to go out every Sunday to practise skiing at high altitude up in the hills.

With the return of summer I went back to the Chamonix valley, where my mother had had a modest chalet built close to the charming Hameau des Bois. During the course of this season, I persuaded my guide to take me on the traverse of the Grépon—to 'traverse' a peak in climbing parlance means to go up one side and down another. Now in those days equipment was still quite rudimentary, and, in particular, people still climbed in nails. The mental approach to mountains was also quite different from what it has become today. The traverse of the Grépon was still considered a very serious undertaking, for proven climbers only. Even with a guide, it was most unusual to do such a thing at the age of fourteen. I had read all the stories about the climb, especially that of the first ascent by Mummery, with passionate enthusiasm, and my youthful aspirations had fixed on it more than all others. For months I had dreamed of the day when I might tread its famous battlemented crest, composed of gigantic, geometrically shaped blocks of granite.

As the price for an enterprise of this kind was relatively high, I asked one of my friends, Alain Schmit, to share it with me. Alain was little older than myself, but he was a most gifted climber who had already done a number of classic routes. My guide knew all about him and had no objection to him coming along with us.

And so, one clear starry night, towards three o'clock in the morning, we set out from the old Montenvers Hotel which is the usual base for the Grépon. I was radiant with joy at the thought that, at long last, I was going to face one of the great Alpine routes. I felt bursting with energy and fitness. The day dawned magnificently fine, and it seemed that nothing stood between us and the enchanted hours of a good climb perfectly executed. I had forgotten one important detail, however: the Montenvers had not just one or two waitresses like the high huts, but at least a dozen. I shortly began to understand that the pace of my guide was directly proportional to the number of waitresses awaiting his return. Instead of contenting himself with his usual very fast walk, he was literally running! Alain and I were both good goers, and in training. We were also vigorous boys, and conscious of being so. Out of pride, therefore, we tried to keep up with the furious pace of our guide, but it was our pride that was our undoing.

Everything went quite well on the path, and even on the earlier part of the climb. After a few hours, however, we began to feel tired, and somewhere about the middle of the Charmoz-Grépon Couloir I started to weaken and asked the guide to slow up a little. He would hear of nothing of the sort.

Despite the complete absence of clouds he declared a storm to be imminent, and averred we ought to hurry up. It was only very much later that I learned how useful rumours of storms could be to a guide!

At the foot of the Mummery crack, Alain and I, pretty well asphyxiated by our frenzied efforts, were at the end of our tether. Not far from tears, I begged the guide for a moment's rest and a little food, but he remained inflexible. He was an excellent climber, and a few seconds later he was at the top of the famous pitch: at once I felt myself being hoisted into the air as though by some mistake I had got attached to a crane. Hardly had I arrived on the platform at the top of the crack when I saw Alain come surging upwards out of the depths like a carp on the end of a fisherman's line. The rest of the climb remains a confused memory. Suffocated by the drag of the rope, groggy with fatigue, terrorised by the cries of the guide, everything after that seemed a sort of nightmare, and I only recovered consciousness in front of a glass of beer back at the Montenvers, well before noon, under a sky as marvellously blue as ever.

Like a good many others who have been the victims of the various playful little tricks which some professionals, luckily getting fewer and fewer, use to keep their clients moving, I was completely put off guided climbing by this meteoric experience, and indeed very nearly put off climbing altogether. However I did not attribute my miseries to any brutality or impatience on the part of my mentor; I simply decided that I was not cut out for climbing, and that big routes would always be out of the question. This loss of confidence in my abilities became a positive complex, and it was a good five years before a happy chance made me aware of my real potentialities.

For some time now my parents had been separated from each other, due to completely incompatible temperaments, and about this time they took the final decision to get divorced. I was entrusted to my father, who decided to send me to boarding school. The highly respectable institution he chose was a small seminary which, owing to its proximity to Grenoble, had got gradually diverted from its original purpose into a more or less open type of school. The rules and traditions had not changed accordingly, but remained rigid, harsh and anachronistic. The buildings of the college consisted of an old monastery which had been built in a magnificent position on a hill above the valley of the Isere, and the old walls surrounded with great trees were not without charm. From the outside, indeed, the establishment was positively attractive, but one was disillusioned the moment one set foot across the doorway.

Lacking even the most elementary comforts, the interior was dreary and dusty. Only the classrooms had any heating, which took the form of ancient stoves which smoked copiously. The enormous dormitories contained forty or fifty pupils at a time. The sole sporting facilities consisted of two medium-sized and almost unequipped yards. In this barrack-like place life was about as spartan as it could be. The half-cooked food was eaten off metal plates which were never washed. Hygiene existed as a quick rinsing of the hands and feet in cold water—there was apparently a room where students could hose each other down, but I never heard of anybody using it. On the whole a spartan life is not a bad thing, and even the bleakness of the place and the toughness of its ways might have been bearable if the pupils had not been submitted to an overloaded timetable, imposed with military discipline. To some ten hours of study were added a couple more of religious observances. Exercise was limited to one hour of recreation a day, one hour of physical jerks a week, and a short afternoon walk on Thursday and Sunday.

Used as I was to a life of liberty and intense physical exercise in permanent contact with nature, I was particularly ill-prepared for living in this sort of juvenile prison. From the moment I went there I felt as wretched as a caged nightingale. Nevertheless I hoped that the monastic regime would help me to catch up on my neglected studies, and I made up my mind to have an honest try at sticking it out. For two months I forced myself in praiseworthy fashion to respect the discipline of the place and to absorb the massive dose of knowledge which was administered to me. But the sedentary life we led, surrounded by an atmosphere of boot-licking, petty intrigue and dirty little secrets, seemed more intolerable to me with every day that went by. Finally I recognised that I was physically incapable of remaining shut up like this for months at a time, and wrote to my father asking him to take me away. I added that since my lack of scholastic aptitude became daily more obvious, I would like to give up this senseless waste of time and learn some kind of manual craft. My father, however, blinded by his pride as a middle-class intellectual, was quite unable to see that his son was incapable of pursuing higher studies. As might have been expected he took my letter in the worst possible way, and roundly informed me that I would remain at college, and that there could never be any question of my learning a trade. I replied that if he would not withdraw me from college of his own free will, he would be forced to by circumstances.

The following Sunday, having got permission to visit the town, I bought a blank-cartridge pistol and some ammunition. At midnight the first detonations resounded through the arches of the enormous dormitory. Others followed, creating an uproar quite unprecedented in the annals of the venerable establishment. The following morning at ten o'clock I was summoned to the headmaster's study, where my father was waiting for me, apoplectic with anger, and expelled from the college.

After this bombshell I feared the worst. Perhaps I would even be sent off to a reformatory? Nothing of the sort. On the contrary, my father, showing rather more insight than usual, went from one extreme to the other; after this unhappy experience of the effect of old-fashioned methods, he now placed me in a college where their methods were ultramodern. The one he chose was situated at Villard-de-Lans, a resort some three thousand feet up in the Vercors range. There, he reckoned, I would get the skiing and climbing which seemed necessary to my physical and psychological balance, while still getting on with my studies.

This establishment, which was quite small, was run by a woman of great intelligence and culture. Despite a relatively light timetable and an atmosphere of friendly gaiety, she had had the ability to arrange things so that we got excellent teaching. The classes were of eight or ten students, who were all able to practise open-air sports every afternoon from two to half past four. Thanks to this arrangement I was able to train at skiing daily throughout the winter, and every Sunday I could go in for competitions. Thus at the age of sixteen I first won the junior championship of the Dauphine, and came third in the senior category.

During the autumn and spring, skiing was replaced by walking in the woods and lower hills. As my walking capacities were much greater than the majority of the other students, the headmistress let me select a small group to take on much longer walks and even easy climbs, on my own responsibility. She even authorised me to go climbing properly, with one of the masters. By a lucky chance this man was an excellent climber and a member of the Groupe de Haute Montagne (or G.H.M.), a select association consisting of the majority of the best French mountaineers. I owe him a great deal, and it was with him that I was finally able to do the Grange Gully on the Trois Pucelles in satisfying circumstances.

Conditions in this school were perfectly suited to my tastes and temperament, and I spent two exceptionally happy years there, growing considerably in body and mind. As far as my studies went, I was never able to catch up sufficiently in some subjects to have any chance of passing my *baccalauréat*, but I did succeed in raising my intellectual level quite considerably, and even acquired a breadth of literary culture greater than normal for my age. When I sat the examination, however, my marks were so bad in all subjects except English and French that it should have been obvious to anyone that it was no good my going on trying. For all that my father decided that I should repeat the year and, in order that I should also be able to see more of my mother, who had been living in Chamonix for some time now, he sent me to be a boarder in a deluxe establishment in that capital of the mountaineering world. Unfortunately this school was much less well run than the one at Villard-de-Lans, and the atmosphere was not at all pleasant. In any case I had no further illusions as to the utility of the studies I was forced to pursue.

In these circumstances I soon lost all interest in my work, and all my energies went into the one activity that gave me any satisfaction in life: skiing. Happily for me the school's timetable, though fuller than the one at Villard, made it possible for me to train every Thursday and to take part in Sunday competitions. As I could not get away until Sunday morning, I was, however, limited to the events held in the valley, and anything more than local was out of the question. This restriction of my freedom of movement led to some rather comic events. Having been selected to go in for the championships of France at Luchon, in the Pyrenees, I asked permission to be absent from school for a week in order to compete. As was quite normal, my request was rejected. At that time nothing seemed more important in my eyes than to compete in the championships, so I made up my mind to run away from school. For several days I was busy making preparations for my escape. On the night itself there was nothing more to it than to leave a message on my bunk, to open a first-storey window and throw out my sack, then to jump after it into the snow. A quarter of an hour later I was in the train, and by the time my absence was noticed the next morning I was far away on the plains, rolling swiftly towards the distant Pyrenees.

My father telephoned to Luchon to say that for this once he threw in the sponge, but that he relied on me to return promptly as soon as the competitions were over. I did very well in the event, and was asked to compete, all expenses paid, in the Grand Prix de Provence at Barcelonnette. Without a moment's hesitation I went straight off to this jolly little southern resort, where I skied brilliantly and carried off third place in the overall classification. But just as I was joyfully getting ready for the prize giving, I saw two rather embarrassed-looking policemen arriving. With strong local accents they explained that, my father having alerted the police, they had no choice but to put me on the next train.

After this escapade the college refused to take me back, and my father, no doubt by now completely dispirited at having engendered such a monster, seemed not to take much further interest in my fate. Finding myself free as the air and haloed with the glory of a star in the ascendant, I was in a position to reply to the numerous invitations I received from organisers of ski events. I took part in all the main occasions towards the end of the season and scored some gratifying successes, notably the downhill from the Brèche de la Meije, where I triumphed over a field which included the world champion James Couttet and several other members of the national team.

Reading these tales of a naughty boy, it would be easy to suppose that I was a typical playboy son of a rich father, spoiled by having too much money, imagining he could do anything because his parents were comfortably off, giving himself up to a life of laziness and pleasure. In fact nothing could be farther from the truth. I had so little money that to break a pair of skis was practically a disaster. If, moreover, the differences between my parents made possible a degree of liberty of which many boys would have taken advantage to have a gay time, the opposite was true in my case. My nature was so shy and reserved that I led an almost ascetic life, taking little part in the typical pleasures of my age despite the easy successes my physique could have ensured me. I devoted myself to skiing almost with mysticism, and far from going a round of gaiety I was acutely worried about my future, which appeared to me in the most sombre light.

During the summer of 1939 the thing happened which a whole world had believed impossible: war. Throughout the following months I found myself very much alone and my situation was, in sober fact, critical. My father seemed to have lost all interest in me, and I could expect no further help from this quarter. My mother, who had considerably reduced her fortune in a number of unfortunate speculations, could no longer support me without difficulty, and lacked the means to make me independent. After my ill-starred record at school I had no chance of earning my living in an intellectual profession; and since I had not been allowed to learn a trade nothing of that sort was open to me apart from simple labouring. The only activity through which I could reasonably hope to find a way out of this maze was skiing, and in those days a skiing instructor's life was far from being as lucrative as it is today. I was painfully aware that it provided one with a poor sort of livelihood for the winter months alone, and that the only way to make a decent thing out of it was to be an international champion. My recent successes gave me some slight hope of one day joining the elect, but a career built on such a dubious speculation seemed about as uncertain as could be. To cap everything, the war had reduced all skiing activity to virtually nil. Nine-tenths of the money had gone out of it, and all competitions had been forbidden.

I spent the first part of the winter at Luchon, working in the sports shop of a friend, repairing skis, putting on bindings and edges, and helping to sell. But there was practically no business, and I was soon forced to go back to

Chamonix. There I could at least go on training, and I had the rather slender satisfaction of winning the only race held that melancholy winter. I was about to volunteer for the army when the disaster of 1940 occurred. My personal decisions were deferred for a few more months.

Since my unfortunate traverse of the Grépon I had given up any idea of the really big climbs without, however, giving up mountaineering altogether. At Villard-de-Lans I had done a lot of hill-walking and a number of short climbs, some of which were quite difficult. At Chamonix, apart from some easy scrambles, I had done a lot of spring and summer skiing, which often amounts to more or less the same thing. I would have liked to do bigger climbs, but did not believe myself able to lead them, while the few friends I had who could have taken me along as a second were naturally not too keen to load themselves down with a semi-beginner. Such was my general state one fine morning in July 1940 when the mountains shone in their perfect beauty through the crystal-clear air. I was reading in my room, my open window giving on to Mont Blanc, when I received a visit from a recently demobilised climber who wanted to forget among the mountains the disgrace of an inglorious defeat. He was looking for a companion, and a mutual friend had put him on to me. Only too happy to escape from my frustrations into the ecstasy of action, I accepted his invitation with enthusiasm.

We immediately began to discuss plans. To my dismay, my visitor suggested doing the Mayer-Dibona ridge on the Dent du Requin as our first climb. This had the reputation, in those days, of being very difficult, and only strong parties dared to attempt it. I was so afraid of launching out into an adventure which seemed so far above my standard that the newcomer was forced to point out that he was a member of the G.H.M., and that in his company I could try anything. I continued to refuse to have anything to do with such a harebrained scheme, and suggested instead the much easier south ridge of the Moine. Being unable to budge me, the member of the G.H.M. ended by resignedly agreeing to take me up this somewhat inglorious ridge.

I had now had several years of intermittent climbing, hill-walking and high-level skiing, and although these had not given me a refined rock-climbing technique, they had made me very sure-footed on mixed ground, by which I mean easy but loose rocks, and medium-angled snow slopes and glaciers. As I had thus no difficulty in following my companion up the first part of the Moine ridge, we got on very fast. However, when we got to the corner which is the hardest part of the climb, he found it too much for him, partly through lack of training and partly because he had forgotten his gym shoes. He made several courageous attempts, trembling frantically the while; and each time I watched with dilated eyes, expecting to see him fall off. After the third try he was completely out of breath and told me, apologetically, that as he could not get up the pitch: we would just have to climb down again. I was most upset at the idea of this premature retreat, and felt a surge of revolt mounting inside me. The day was too fine, and I felt too much life boiling through my muscles, to let myself be beaten quite so easily. With some astonishment I heard myself asking if I might have a try at the pitch.

The first long stride out over space seemed the more disagreeable for a sharp blade of rock some way below, which seemed to have been put there by nature to punish the foolhardy. Unwilling to be impaled like an oriental criminal, I felt a surge of energy, and in a few quick moves I stood at the top of the pitch. Emboldened by this success, I continued at the front of the party. Higher up I had a bit of trouble with a vertical wall of some fifteen or twenty feet which seemed practically hold-less, but I eventually got up thanks to the adhesive qualities of the clothes covering my chest and stomach! Soon after this, my face shining with joy, I reached the modest summit of the Moine. Not a cloud marked the vivid blue of the sky. It seemed impossible a day so clear could ever deaden into twilight. We rested a long time, gazing at the savage walls, hemmed with lace of snow, that ringed us round from the Dru to the Charmoz in a cirque without rival in the whole of the Alps. At a time when France was just beginning to recover some sort of unstable balance from one of the worst convulsions in her history, we were alone in the mountains. A mineral silence entered into us. In that enormous peace, I felt that some-how, henceforward, nothing would truly count for me beyond this world of grandeur and purity where every corner held a promise of enchanted hours.

This ascent of the Aiguille du Moine had a decisive influence on the course of my life. Like Guido Lammer, 'Having been a prey from childhood to every cruel division, conflict and disorder of thought and of modern life, I stretched longing arms towards inner peace and harmony, which I found in the solitudes of the Alps.'

My easy success on this climb had given me back the confidence in my own will and physical powers which is sine qua non to undertaking the really great climbs, outside of which, in my opinion, mountaineering is only a sporting form of tourism. For 'Although from my childhood I have found pleasure in the many aspects of nature's mysteries at high altitudes, and tried with ever-increasing fervour to catch the meaning of her silent language, the bitter-sweetness and the best of mountaineering have always been for me in the rough adventure, the conquest of danger, of the climbing itself. . . . If all one sought were a few moments of rest and peaceful reflection, how absurd it would be to reach the summit at the cost of so much fighting and suffering, amid so many mortal dangers, and by such extraordinary routes, when a cable-car could carry us to the same spot by the shortest possible line. No, from my earliest ascents I have recognised that a passionate involvement in the act of mountaineering, and the constant menace of danger disturbing the very depths of our being, are the source of powerful moral or religious emotions which may be of the greatest spirituality'—thus Guido Lammer.

That summer I did a lot of climbing, mostly with my companion of the Moine. I gave myself up to a life of adventure and action for its own sake and found in it perfect happiness, for, to quote Lammer once more, 'on summits haunted by the unfettered elements, you may take long draughts of the foaming cup in the headiness of action which admits no obstacles.'

But to be truthful, though I read Lammer between climbs, finding in his romantic style a clear expression of what I also felt in my confused way, there was nothing of the intellectual climber about me. I was rather an ardent young animal, bounding from summit to summit like a kid among the rocks. I had no thought of reputation, and the simplest climbs made me crazy with joy. The mountains were a sort of magic kingdom where by some spell I felt happiest.

By virtue of all this experience I began to make progress in technique, going through alternate stages of the most promising ease and the most paralysing fear. On the north ridge of the Chardonnet, for example, we found the final slopes consisted of bare ice. My companion cut very small steps which were also inconveniently outward-sloping. Taking these to be quite normal, I walked up them without any bother on the front two spikes of my crampons.* I would certainly have continued on to the summit in the same blissful state if I had not, at that moment, noticed a party of famous climbers behind us hacking away furiously to triple the area of our steps. A certain doubt found its way into my soul, which turned to worry. Suddenly I realised the full peril of our position on these tiny steps, up which we were gaily walking without any precautionary measures. It only needed one false move on the part of either of us, or one of the steps to give way, and we should be sliding inexorably towards the abyss which yawned beneath our heels ... in a moment I was paralysed with giddiness, and refused to move hand or foot in such unsafe circumstances. My companion had to cut real 'buckets' to give me sufficient confidence to finish the climb.

* *Translator's note.* Crampons are frameworks of steel spikes bound to the foot by climbers when they walk on steep ice or hard snow.

At that time the outlook of the majority of French climbers was very different from what it is today. The traverse of the Grépon was still considered a serious matter, calling for considerable natural aptitude and some years of experience. No one would then have dared to try this ascent without leading up to it carefully, a thing which is quite common today. The Mer de Glace face of the Grépon, the Mayer-Dibona ridge of the Dent du Requin, the Ryan-Lochmatter route on the Aiguille du Plan, the traverse of the Aiguilles du Diable, were all considered to be *grandes courses,** and the ambition to do them one day began to stir in the bottom of my mind. The north face of the Grandes Jorasses and even that of the Dru were generally considered to be quite out of the question for a normal human being. It was reckoned that to attack a face of this sort you either had to be a fanatical lunatic (a quality attributed in particular to the great German and Italian climbers) or one of those phenomenal supermen who turn up in every sport perhaps once or twice in ten years.

Feeling in no way fanatical and not taking myself to be in any way exceptional, the idea of trying such climbs never crossed my mind for a moment, and I used to think of the rare individuals who went in for this sort of thing with just the same kind of admiring pity that I sometimes see today on the faces of my own interlocutors.

By the end of the summer of 1940 I had done a respectable number of classic routes. If I had not been so impressed with the aura of legend which at that time surrounded the least little climb and the least little climber, I could already have been doing much harder and bigger things. I had amassed a fair amount of experience and possessed an excellent sense of direction. I was also very quick over mixed ground, but my rock and ice technique was by comparison still rudimentary. To be honest, I was held back more by the subjective aspect of difficulty than by the difficulties themselves. The very thought of climbing a pitch with a reputation for delicacy made me as tense as a gladiator entering the arena, and I had to stretch my willpower to the utmost in order to overcome this apprehension. Thus, due to a careless reading of the guidebook, I several times got up the 'crux' of a climb with no bother at all, whereas on an easier pitch, which I *thought* to be the crux, I trembled like a leaf.** I had occasional flashes of daring which astonish me when I remember them today,

* *Translator's note.* The phrase 'grandes courses', meaning the climbs which in any era are outstanding for length, seriousness and sustained difficulty, has no exact equivalent in English and is often used untranslated by British climbers.

** *Translator's note.* In climbing parlance the crux of a climb is its hardest pitch. The crux of a pitch is its hardest moves, and so on.

and when I think about the way I got up certain pitches shivers run up and down my spine.

During one ascent of the Cardinal, for example, I got by mistake into a smooth, overhanging chimney. I overcame the problem by pulling up on a blade of rock that I had managed to jam between the two walls. Many years later I found myself by chance on the same mountain and went a bit out of my way to have a look at the well-remembered chimney. Despite my modern moulded-rubber soles and ten years' experience of the hardest routes in the Mont Blanc range, I was quite unable to climb the last few feet. The most dangerous thing in mountaineering is certainly the carefree confidence of youth!

During the months which followed, some order seemed to come back into the world. For those living in the valleys of the Alps nothing seemed to have changed: the tourists were back, the joyous chinking of flowing money was heard again. Youngsters avid of sensations and fugitive glory were grouped again around the chronometers at the Sunday ski competitions, which were being contested with the old ardour. That winter was the apogee of my skiing career. In December I was selected to train for the national team. My summer season had put me into a state of exceptional fitness, and had given me the self-confidence essential to clearing the path of victory. I seemed highly likely to qualify when, in an unlucky fall, I badly injured my knee, and barely recovered in time to go in for the Dauphine championships for which I was still eligible. Nevertheless I won the downhill, the slalom, and the combined classification for the four events—for in those days they had the crazy notion to make the same men compete not only in the downhill and slalom but also in specialised events whose techniques were as far apart as the cross-country race and the jumping.

A few days later, by a stroke of luck, I came second in the 'combined downhill and slalom', and third in the overall classification in the national championships of France. Later in the season, at the Grand Prix de l'Alpe d'Huez, fate took a hand to redress matters. A hundred yards from the finishing post I was several seconds up on the whole of the French national team when some spectators got in my way and I lost first place by a fifth of a second.

By the time the last snows gave place to the delicate corolla of the crocus in the saturated fields, I had good reasons for thinking that my old vision of reaching the highest ranks of the sport were not just the daydreams of a silly child. How I would have laughed in the face of anyone who predicted that it would be many years before I was to know again the enraptured feeling of more than human force that comes from the utter concentration of the fight against the clock.

At my mother's house I had bed, board and a little pocket money, so that for months I was as free as a mountain goat. I had no place in society to fulfil, no other task than what I saw fit to set myself. Animated by an appetite for physical exercise which amounted almost to frenzy, I led a life of intense activity and virtual asceticism. From the beginning of December to the end of May my ski training, and the many competitions in which I usually entered for all four events, left me almost no spare time. I even grudged the time taken out to give skiing lessons for a bit of extra money. In summer I accumulated climbs at the speed of a professional guide, and in the midst of all this intense activity I still found the energy for enormous cycling trips and to go in for swimming, athletics and gymnastics.

It has to be admitted that my intellectual activity was very much less, being limited to a few books whose serious nature contrasted oddly with the physical preoccupation of my life. About this time I read almost the whole of Balzac, Musset, Baudelaire and Proust.

Had I been less acutely aware of the fragile bases on which my way of life, so rich in action, reposed, it would have satisfied me so completely that the future would not have worried me at all. I have never thought an occupation any the better for being lucrative: on the contrary, money has a way of soiling everything it touches. Then as now, what mattered for me was action and not the price of action. The value was in the acting itself. My whole life has been a sort of tightrope walk between the self-justifying action in which I have pursued the ideals of my youth, and a more or less honourable prostitution to the necessity of earning my daily bread. Could any mind be vulgar enough to suggest that the prostitution was worth more than the gratuitous act? In any case, outside of primitive societies where every gesture springs from the instinct for survival of the species, what in fact is a 'useful' action? If, in order to forget the emptiness of their existence, many people become drunk with words and speak of their place, their mission, their social utility, how meaningless and conventional their words really are! In our disorganised and overpopulated world, how many people can honestly say they are useful today? The millions of dignified go-betweens who encumber the economy, the titled pen pushers in their sinecures which drain society and frustrate the administration, all the hoteliers, journalists, lawyers and other such who could disappear tomorrow without anyone being a penny the worse? Can you even call the majority of doctors useful, when they fight like famished dogs for patients in the big cities, while all over the earth men are dying for the lack of their care? In this century when it has been shown a hundred times over that a rational organisation can vastly reduce the number of men needed for any task, how many can be quite certain that they are genuinely necessary cogs in the huge machine of the world?

By the end of the winter of 1941 I realised that the foundations of my free and wonderful life were becoming daily more uncertain. Despite her unending kindness, it was obvious that my mother could not go on keeping me like a racehorse forever. At this crucial moment a way suddenly opened up in front of me.

FIRST CONQUESTS

THE TRADITIONAL MILITARY SERVICE had now been replaced by a kind of civilian service aimed at the virtues of manliness, industriousness, and public and team spirit, much extolled by the national leaders of the day. An institution called Les Chantiers de la Jeunesse was set up to put young men of twenty-one through an eight months' training. A similar but much smaller organisation called Jeunesse et Montagne, or J.M. for short, was formed on parallel lines. Only volunteers could serve in this corps d'élite, the idea of which was to inculcate qualities of service and leadership among youth by the practice of mountaineering, skiing and a rough life among the mountains generally. The J.M. was endowed with a body of instructors consisting of professional guides and skiing instructors plus a few amateurs who were admitted after a difficult entrance examination. The pay was poor, but the life, dedicated entirely to mountains, seemed fascinating.

I possessed all the necessary skills to pass these examinations without much trouble, and I realised that in this way I could find a method of supplying my material needs while pursuing my true ambitions. Since I was bound to get called up soon in any case for the Service Civile, I decided to anticipate matters by volunteering for the J.M. I went in at Beaufort around the beginning of May.

In all walks of life during wartime there was a certain degree of disorganisation, or rather improvisation, which lent to things an element of fantasy which we quite miss in these productive days. The J.M. was still in the early stages of its formation, and a general chaos reigned quite happily side by side with rigid military discipline. For some days after my arrival I spent my time, in company with some thirty other recruits, in planting potatoes. Then, by one of those mysterious dispensations which always seem to occur in organisations of this sort, despite the fact that a good third of the new personnel were farmers' boys, I was designated to be a muleteer!

I had been quite used to cows from childhood, but had never come close to a mule in my life. Worse still, I entertained a wholesome terror for them, having heard that they were vicious, stubborn and endowed with a most redoubtable capacity for kicking. When our group leader announced my new profession I asked him, my features tense with fear, just what I would be expected to do. He replied with the succinctness which characterises all great leaders of men:

'Nothing to it. You go to the stable, you take the mules to drink at the trough, you give them one truss of hay per four mules and you clean out the stable. That's all for the moment.'

The only thing he forgot to tell me was that, owing to a short admin course, no one had appointed a new muleteer, and consequently the animals hadn't eaten for two days. I went into the stable with all the innocence of the newly converted going to his baptism, and if the animals seemed a trifle agitated I hardly noticed it.

'It's because they don't know me yet', I said to myself.

Dodging a kick vigorous enough to propel me into the next world, I squeezed in between two of the beasts in order to set them loose, then did the same for four others. Only then did it begin to dawn on me that I had done something rasher than climbing the Whymper Couloir at four o'clock in the afternoon.* Wild with hunger and thirst, the mules stampeded in all directions, and one of them, baring his long yellow teeth, tried to bite me in the most uncivilised fashion. Only the agility which enabled me to climb like a flash into the hayrack saved me from being trampled to death. I would probably have been stuck there for hours if, finding the door open, the mules had not burst out into the village in an unbridled cavalcade. Fortunately I was speedily relieved of my duties as a muleteer, and sent off to be part of a team building new military quarters about five thousand feet up in the high pastures of Roseland.

The chalet in which we had to install ourselves was primitive in the extreme. Everything normally considered necessary to the maintenance of a group of men, even in the hardest sort of conditions, was lacking—camp beds,

* *Translator's note.* The Whymper Couloir is a gully on the Aiguille Verte notorious for stone falls late in the day.

mattresses, blankets, even a stove. All these things needed to be got up as quickly as possible, but, the season being very late that year, Roseland was still half-buried in snow, and the last two or three miles of the road were unusable. The only method of transport was our own backs. The work of my own team consisted mainly of doing all this carrying. We had to do just one trip a day which, with a load of about a hundred pounds, took around three hours for the return journey. The hours were thus short, but the work required more than average energy, particularly inasmuch as, sleeping on the bare ground and eating inadequate food, simply to survive demanded a constant output. For this reason the team was made up of the stronger men. Used to working with mules, I was perfectly designed to replace them when the need arose!

The rough life we led at Roseland suited me ideally, except that three hours of work, however laborious, were not enough to appease my energies, so that I had to look around for other methods. With a few friends of similar tastes, I used to get up before dawn every day and climb the two thousand feet to the Grande Berge, a peak overlooking Roseland, on skis. After a swift downhill run came breakfast, then I would do a first carry, and in the afternoon another. Then the loads began to seem too light, so I started taking a little more each day. Some of the other porters joined in the game, which became a daily competition, until we were carrying up to a 130-odd pounds at a time.

It should be added that in those early days of the J.M. there reigned a wonderful team spirit and good humour. Our ideal may have been rather too simple, but most of us really did have an ideal for which we were willing to give our utmost strength. It was all very inspiring. In this atmosphere of shared high spirits and exhausting labour I passed days of intense and utter happiness. In the words of Schiller, 'In giving of itself without reserve, unfettered power knows its own joy.'

Once the snow had melted, the life of our troop changed completely. Our time was divided between forestry, ski-mountaineering, physical culture and, in a milder sort of way, climbing. The professional guides and instructors played a purely technical role, and the disciplinary side was looked after by the various grades of 'leaders'. These were mostly officers or noncommissioned officers from the disbanded air force. Most of them knew little about mountains and their lore, and some of them loathed the whole business. For this reason mountain activity was not always taken as far as it should have been, despite the enthusiasm of both the instructors and the volunteers.

The activity of each group depended a lot on the tastes of its leader, who might give priority according to his preferences to skiing, climbing, hill-walking, manual labour or cultural activities. By a stroke of luck our leader was an ex-N.C.O. of alpine troops, an experienced mountaineer and a one time *Bleausard*.* Thanks to him our time was mainly spent on long ski excursions along the high ridges of Beaufortin, or else in rock climbing. We worked out a number of practice grounds along the foot of the limestone pinnacles and crags above Roseland. At least twice a week we had to undergo half a day's climbing. I had no trouble in outclassing most of the others on these occasions, but one, named Charles, sometimes outdid me. Tremendous competitions resulted when, our safety ensured by a rope from above, we would strive to surpass each other by means of the most spectacular rock-gymnastics.

It was now that I first met Gaston Rébuffat. He was attached to a troop quartered in the picturesque Arêche valley, with its dense pine forests and lush pastures dotted with old rustic chalets. There being no rocks to climb in that pastoral area, this troop was forced to come up to Roselend for the purpose. Caught by the rain one day, they took shelter in our chalet, and somebody told me that among them was a young fellow from Marseilles who claimed to have done some big climbs. I had often heard about the wonderful training ground formed by the *calanques*, the rocky coast near Marseilles, and I excitedly got myself introduced to the new phenomenon.

In those days Rébuffat was of rather startling appearance at first sight: tall, thin and stiff as the letter *I*. His narrow features were animated by two small, black, piercing eyes, and his somewhat formal manners and learned turn of phrase contrasted comically with a noticeable Marseilles accent. All this took me a bit by surprise, but after a slightly strained beginning a mutual sympathy grew up quickly, and we spent the whole afternoon walking around in the rain talking climbing. As you would expect, each asked the other what he had done. I was astonished to learn that, without any other experience than the rock-gymnastic technique learnt in the Calanques, Rébuffat had done high mountain routes equivalent to my ultimate ambitions. The conversation came round to our future projects next, and again, his seemed completely extravagant to me. His whole conception of mountaineering, normal enough today, was far in advance of its time and entirely novel as far as I was concerned.

Among all the climbers I had met up to that time mountaineering was a sort of religious art, with its own traditions, hierarchies and taboos, in which

---

* *Publisher's note.* The term 'Bleausard' is applied to a habitué of the rocks in the forest of Fontainebleau, the closest climbing to Paris. The rock is a compact sandstone lending itself to the most acrobatic climbing, and the more so because the climbs are rarely so high that one cannot jump for it if in difficulty.

cold reason played quite a small part. Having grown up among the priesthood, I had blindly observed all the rites and accepted the articles of the creed. To Rébuffat this was all a lot of outdated rubbish. His sceptical mind was free of all prejudices: in his view what mattered was to be a really good rock climber, and willpower and courage would look after the rest. In support of his theory he cited examples of well-known German and Italian climbers who, with no other experience than what they had gained in the Dolomites and other lower limestone ranges of the eastern Alps, had put up some of the hardest high mountain routes. With implacable logic he drew the conclusion that what was possible for Germans and Italians was possible for Frenchmen too. Pushing his argument to its end, he reasoned that since he considered (rightly) that he was a really good rock climber, and had plenty of willpower and courage, he would shortly climb the fiercest faces in the Alps, even including the north faces of the Eiger and the Grandes Jorasses, then ranked as the 'top two'.

For one who, like myself, climbed instinctively because, when the glaciers were shining in the sun and the rock needles picked out against the blue of the sky, he felt an impetuous need of action surge through his muscles, this methodical will, these carefully worked-out theories, this self-confidence and cold ambition were quite bewildering. As I listened to him I was plunged into an indefinable mixture of amused scepticism, respectful admiration and vague desire.

Some time after this encounter I was chosen to go on a leader's course at the J.M. Central School at La Chapelle-en-Valgaudemar, in the south of the Oisans range. My rival Charles and Rébuffat were both going along too. At Roseland our leader had been changed, and all the pleasantness of our life went with him. Commanded by a narrow-minded brute, set to work on boring and ill-organised projects, we led a pointless existence which began to weigh heavily on me. The news of my departure for the mountains made me happy again, and some of my comrades told me that when the order was read out by the leader my face was so lit up with joy that nobody could help noticing it despite the fact that we were standing rigidly to attention.

I had now lived for some years in the over-civilised Chamonix valley where cable cars, rack railways and comfortable refuges combine to make climbing a less rugged pastime. I was used to the elegant majesty of rock spires, to the splendour of Mont Blanc's masses of hanging ice, and to the charms of the green pastures of Savoy. When I got to La Chapelle-en-Valgaudemar, I felt as much out of my own world as if I had suddenly been transported to Tibet. Everything in this valley was new to me, both man and nature. There were no elegant rock spires soaring into the sky like flames, no imposing glaciers to gladden the heart with the contrast of their whiteness against the blue of the sky and the green of the meadows. There were no fat pastures speckled with flowers; no prosperous-looking herds with bells tinkling among the peace of nature; no big chalets with wide, pine-shingled roofs looking as though built to last forever; no noisy bands of tourists; no mechanical contrivances disturbing the solitude of the summits.

Here nature was in a harsher mood, but remained almost unspoiled. The inhabitants seemed to be living in another century. The mountains with their rounded crests resembled ruined castles, their dark walls mouldering into vast screes and arid patches of scraggy grass. Only a few dirty snow gullies and moraine-covered glaciers relieved the sternness of the scene. At the foot of these somewhat unattractive summits was squeezed the valley, where men, apparently hardly out the Middle Ages, lived wretchedly in moss-thatched hovels, fighting with a hostile nature for every inch of cultivable earth. Right up to the very edge of the mountain little fields of low grass and thinly sown corn showed among the wastes of boulders like a green-and-yellow patchwork quilt.

In the village of La Chapelle the tarmacked road and a few small hotels formed the outpost of the modern world, but as one went farther up the valley the signs of civilisation gradually faded out. At the very end was the hamlet of Rif-du-Sap, perched between two avalanche gullies, where life was as primitive as in many parts of the Himalaya. Nevertheless the bareness and rusticity of Valgaudemar did have a certain austere poetry about them. They gave just the same kind of feeling of being at the ends of the earth that I recognised again with delight when, years later, I visited the remote mountains of Asia and America.

The J.M. Central School occupied a few old buildings in the middle of La Chapelle. Since we were going simultaneously through the courses for team leaders and rope leaders, we led a life so hard and active that if I did not still possess notes made at the time, I would be tempted to think my memory guilty of exaggerating.

The ascents that we did every week were in a different style from what I was used to in the Mont Blanc range. There was comparatively little rock climbing about them, and what there was was seldom very difficult. These great rubbish heaps of mountains were more a question of unending trudges among steep, slippery grass, rabbit warrens, and moraines of loose boulders. The habit of the school was to send us up to remote huts loaded like mules and at competition speed. In the same way, climbs were carried out at such speed that the majority of students ended up in a state of complete exhaustion. Given the fact that in those days there was very little food around, these mountain trips were profoundly tiring even for the toughest, and when we got back to the Centre after three or four days we were all more or less done in.

But we were far from being allowed to rest for the remainder of the week. An iron discipline imposed ten to fourteen hours of work every day. We were up at six, and it was usual for us to get back to our beds at midnight without having had any other time off than what was necessary for meals—if one could so term the absorption of a few ill-cooked vegetables, whose main nutritive value came from the innumerable flies stuck to the plate.

The day would begin with perhaps three-quarters of an hour of high-speed physical training. The rest of the morning would be spent at some kind of manual labour, wood fatigue or improving mountain tracks. The afternoons began with a rock climbing session on a small local crag, followed by lectures or study. After the evening meal we still had to attend cultural classes or rehearsals for a sort of music hall act called 'passing out' with which each course ended. Naturally all the activities were carried on at top speed, and the least little movement from one place to another was carried out at the double, and singing.

The method of character training at the J.M. Central School was, it appeared, modelled on that of the military colleges, and every day we had the opportunity of measuring its full excellence. However unexpected the ideas may be which germinate in the brain of the brass-hatted pedagogue, anyone would at least agree that they were formulated at a time when there was enough to eat to support such a painful existence. But in those days, when the whole of France was starving, this was decidedly not the case. After three weeks about half the course were at the end of their strength, and the rest were more or less run-down. Probably due to the inadequate nourishment we were nearly all suffering from a painful illness. The smallest scratches would turn into festering wounds which grew larger every day and resisted all attempts at medication. In varying degrees, we all had our hands, forearms, calves and feet covered in these agonising sores.

The course, which had begun in enthusiasm, turned into a sort of hell as the days went on. Without the impulsion of the ideals which remained in us like the voice of conscience and gave an unguessed-of endurance, such trials would have been insupportable. We told ourselves that anyone who could not take it was unworthy to be called a man. Had it been otherwise, there would have been no motive to resist the temptation of the sick bay, or even of the liberty of desertion. One might suppose that the leaders who imposed such an inhuman regime were mere bloodthirsty brutes, Nazis worthy of service in the S.S. Nothing could be farther from the truth, because in reality the great majority of them were likeable and intelligent men, frequently quiet and even sensitive. By what collective aberration these sensible beings could have been led to apply such stupid methods of education will always remain a mystery to me. Fortunately, after the first year, the excesses began to be understood, and the courses were subsequently humanised even to the point where enthusiasm gave way to a certain slackness. But this cannot change the fact that as a result of those first courses a number of young men contracted grave heart and lung ailments which will handicap them for the rest of their lives.

As for me, although I was one of the few to finish in reasonable physical condition, those five weeks have left a memory of exhaustion greater than any I have known since. I have no doubt that the ordeal had a permanent effect on me, and if later, on big expeditions, I have sometimes surprised my comrades by the ease with which I could undergo what seemed unusually exhausting and painful experiences, it has been because they seemed nothing to what I endured at La Chapelle.

At last the course came to an end. I had done little climbing, and learnt nothing new about it. But despite it all, I did not regret my time in Val-gaudemar. I had widened my horizons, met new men and new mountains, and had been enriched by an extraordinary experience which I was happy to have stuck out to the end. 'Ah, do not beg the favour of an easy life—pray to become one of the truly strong. Do not pray for tasks proportionate to your strength, but for strength proportionate to the task.'* I also had the lesser satisfaction of graduating first in the technical tests and second in the overall classification, the more studious Rébuffat having beaten me by a few points.

In the course of these five tough weeks which we had gone through shoulder to shoulder, Gaston and I had got to know each other and, despite profound differences of temperament, had become great friends. The trials of the course had not abated our love of the mountains or our desire for the great climbs. No sooner were the results published than Gaston wanted to drag me off to the famous northwest face of the Olan. It would make us A.W.O.L., but provided we accepted this and the punishment which would ensue on our return to our centres, we had the chance of doing the climb. Rébuffat's proposition was extremely tempting, and I wasn't very worried about the J.M. brand of punishment, which consisted of making us carry an eighty-pound sack of stones for twenty or thirty kilometres. But I was not yet ripe for climbs of this

* *Publisher's note.* Phillip Brooks

class, and had been over-impressed by the tale of the first ascent. Discretion won the day and I declined the offer.

Passing through Grenoble on the way back to Beaufort the temptations of civilised life were too strong, and we decided to stop over for twenty-four hours to get a bit of rest and Christian nourishment. After a copious meal and a good night we were once more bursting with energy and enthusiasm. Despite the prospect of stone carrying we put off our departure for Beaufort for another day, not for the sake of the fleshpots, but in order to climb the Dent Gerard on the Trois Pucelles. We thought of starting up the Grange gully and then seeing if we could find a more interesting route. Now that I had become a climber of some experience the Grange gully seemed so easy that I couldn't understand how I had almost met my end there. By contrast, however, the difficult new variation that we put up that day on the wall between the Dalloz crack and the Sandwich chimney was a real initiation for me into certain forms of artificial climbing, which I had never tried till then.*

Gaston got a long way up by the use of a good many pitons, but was then stopped by an overhang. He tried several times to climb it free but without success. I then had a try at it and greatly to my surprise got up, despite an annoying trembling of the limbs. New horizons began to open up from that moment.

We got back to Beaufort forty-eight hours late, to be greeted by Testo Ferry, the commandant of the centre, in unexpected fashion. This still-young man, who had distinguished himself by his courage in aerial combat, had a taste for dash and achievement. It was obvious that we appealed to him. With a twinkling eye and a suspicion of a smile at the corners of his lips, he told us off approximately as follows:

'In the first place I have to congratulate you on your brilliant placings on the course you have just completed. It is thanks to men of your stamp that we are going to build a brave new France. As commandant of the Paturaud-Mirand Centre I am proud of you. But I regret that you have been awaited for two days now in Chamonix, where you are to join a climbing troop. Your late return has considerably hindered the proper functioning of the course, which is already in progress. In order not to prolong this situation you are to leave for Chamonix in a few minutes' time, but in view of the fact that it would be a deplorable example to leave unpunished the grave breach of discipline of which you have been guilty, I have no choice but to be strict with you. Your

* *Translator's note.* 'Artificial' climbing is when the climber progresses by hammering metal spikes, called pitons, into the rock. 'Free' climbing is when he climbs the rock by his own unaided forces.

penalty is to have your heads shaved—and I mean a complete tonsure. Given the urgency of the situation it will be impossible to inflict this punishment before your departure. I therefore order you to go to a barber's shop either on the way through Annecy or on your arrival at Chamonix. I need hardly add that if these orders are not carried out I shall be obliged to punish you more severely.'

Far from plunging me into consternation this speech, subtly larded with the formality of the time and with a certain humour, raised me to heights of joy. Nothing could have delighted me more at that moment than to set off for my beloved range of Mont Blanc. As for my hair, to have it cut off was more of an advantage than a punishment for me. Although I was just twenty it had already started to moult liberally, and someone had told me that shaving the head would put off the evil hour—but in this as in so many other things life lost no time in showing me the extent of my naïveté!

At Annecy we had two hours to wait for the Chamonix coach, so we went off to the nearest hairdresser's. At the time of our condemnation Gaston, as befitted an idealist above the opinions and flatteries of the world, had affected the noblest disinterest in his capillary system. Now, face-to-face with the secular arm, he suddenly lost his pride. At the idea of imminently seeing his thick, curly locks lying at his feet, he was thrown into confusion. Forcing a thin smile, he asked me shyly:

'Do you think the old man would be satisfied with a very short brush cut?'

But I replied:

'Aren't you ashamed of yourself at the idea of cheating like that? Orders are orders, and our duty is to carry them out to the bitter end. Boy! Bring the razor, and let it shine.'

So I sat there radiating pleasure and malice as I watched my head assuming the appearance of a billiard ball, while Gaston's naturally long face grew longer still as his head was turned into a sort of tubercle covered in bumps and hollows. But his good nature soon got the better of him, and during the next few days he got everyone to finger his bumps, averring that one was the bump of mathematics, another the bump of business acumen, and so on.

Next day André Tournier, the guide in command of the Montenvers camp, had a bad few minutes as he watched two men climbing towards him whose shaven scalps shone in the gay morning sunlight like those of German soldiers! At that time such visits were apt to be worrying.

Situated next to the old Montenvers Hotel, justly noted for its magnificent site above the Mer de Glace, the so-called camp was installed in some disused stables that had been roughly converted into dormitories. Each Sunday some thirty virtual beginners would arrive from Beaufort for a one-week course in mountain climbing. There were theoretically five of us to look after the whole lot, but one was old and often tired or ill, and another would only lead parties on the very easiest climbs. For practical purposes there were only the three of us: André Tournier our chief, Rébuffat and myself. Despite his small stature, Tournier had Herculean strength, and his chest was of the proportions of a wardrobe. Aquiline, sallow, dark-eyed, with thick black hair, he might have passed for an Oriental if his deeply chiselled features, stamped with decision, had not lent to his face rather the beauty of an ideal mediaeval knight. He was a man of exceptional character in the prime of life, and a truly fine guide into the bargain. Authoritative and violent, he was also upright and just, and by contrast with many guides he did not hold my urban origins against me. Having discerned my ability to outlast many born mountaineers, he treated me like a friend. It was the same with Rébuffat, under whose phlegmatic and almost smooth exterior he recognised the exceptional driving force.

As often happens in September, the weather remained immovably fine, and thanks to this we were able to take half our beginners every day onto some summit or other. In this way all of them were able to get in three climbs per course. The actual climbs were not very difficult but nonetheless called for a certain technique, and they were relatively long. As each of the instructors towed three or four beginners behind him, chiefly distinguished by a total lack of aptitude, it will be easy to imagine the slowness of our progress up routes like the Blaitière, and the patience required to get everyone to the top and back again in good order. We would set out at three or four in the morning and quite frequently not get back till seven or eight o'clock at night. It would have seemed a hellish life to a good many people, and it would have been natural if these daily repeated climbs, carried out at a snail's pace, had become excessively boring. On the contrary, however, I loved every minute of the time, which seemed to go by all too quickly. Doing these easy climbs in such conditions was, after all, a real adventure. Constant care was necessary, to say nothing of ingenuity. Getting a party safely up them bit by bit called for the concentration of all one's powers, and gave me the sort of pleasure a child gets from succeeding in a difficult game.

I suppose we really amounted to nothing more significant than a gang of overgrown children delighting in the conquest of altitude by the force of our own muscles. Yet to see a companion arrive for the first time on a sunlit crest, his eyes full of happiness, seemed in itself an adequate recompense. Tomorrow he might return to the valley and be swallowed up by all the mediocrity of life, but for one day at least he had looked full at the sky.

It was in helping these uninspired parties of beginners, under the direction of André Tournier, that I began to love the guiding profession, and to understand its peculiar problems. I learned to make the most of the lay of the land, to be ready for emergencies at any moment, to foresee events, to keep the ropes unentangled, and how to make a group of clumsy beginners advance at a relatively respectable pace.

After these harassing five- or six-day weeks, we had earned a rest by the time Sunday came round. Far from profiting by the opportunity, no sooner had Rébuffat and I returned the last novice to safety on a Saturday evening than we would be off up to some hut thanks to André Tournier, who took all the responsibility with his customary kindness and more than ordinary generosity. The following morning, caring nothing for the fatigue that weighed down our limbs, we would do a big climb as amateurs.

Despite our brilliant placings on the leaders' course, although we were good climbers, we were not yet really excellent ones. Both of us had some of the qualities necessary to do the *grandes courses*, but in each of us these were to some extent cancelled out by equivalent weaknesses. Gaston was remarkable for his self-confidence: no doubt he thought, like Nietzsche, that 'nothing succeeds without presumption.' Thanks to this optimism he faced his chosen mountain with extraordinary calmness and cold-bloodedness. Moreover, without being a genius, he was an extremely good rock climber. By contrast, however, he was deficient in some of the qualities which distinguish the mountaineer from the climber, such as a sense of direction and ease of movement on mixed ground and snow and ice. I was completely his opposite. I was rather nervous and lacking in confidence and, apart from occasional flashes, a very mediocre rock climber. But I had an unusual sense of direction and was completely at my ease on all types of high mountain terrain.

Thus our qualities complemented each other, but for all that we did not make up a really first-class team. The climbs we did together, such as the Mayer-Dibona on the Requin and the Mer de Glace face of the Grépon, were quite good for those days but not really exceptional. The proof of the pudding is that during these climbs all sorts of strange incidents occurred, and even taking into account poor conditions and equipment our times were quite slow. The speed with which a party does a climb is an almost exact gauge of its ability.

Rébuffat showed the greatest enthusiasm for these Sunday climbs, and seemed to enjoy them, but his ambition made him look on them a bit patronisingly: they were no more than something to be doing while preparing oneself for the really big stuff. For me the mountain world remained wonderful and terrible. Each of our climbs put me into a state of delicious anxiety, every enterprise was an adventure, and my mind was not at peace until the summit was finally under our feet. Our successes made me feel at least as happy and proud as I did later on reaching the most inaccessible summits in the world.

The Montenvers camp came to an end about the end of September. My eyes still full of the splendour of the high summits, I returned after three months' absence to the more modest hills of Beaufortain. As before, I was sent to Roseland; and as our two old troops had been merged, Rébuffat went with me. Our life during the latter months of 1941 may not have called for efforts quite as prolonged and spectacular as those we had left behind, but it was still very tough and a great deal less inspiring. There was no more daily adventure, no more unceasing comradeship or joy of victory. J.M. was building two big chalets at Roseland, each designed to hold thirty men. The work was being done throughout by the youth corps itself, under the direction of the usual leaders. There were one or two professional masons to plan the work and put on the finishing touches. Despite my rank as a climbing leader I only counted as a volunteer still because my eight months were not yet up and I was set to work as a labourer. Well-directed and organised the work could have gone ahead in a happy atmosphere of creativeness, but unfortunately the prevailing climate was as morose and degrading as that of a prison.

We were heaped together twelve to an ordinary-sized room, and to say nothing of the discomfort or the difficulty of breathing in an atmosphere like a rabbit hutch, any privacy was out of the question. The food was almost exclusively composed of bread and overripe boiled vegetables. On twenty-year-olds working eleven hours a day at nearly six thousand feet in temperatures often below zero, the effect of this diet was to induce a state of semicoma suitable neither to good feeling nor good workmanship. Worse still, the huge quantities of vegetable matter we absorbed had a highly irritant effect, so that it was usual to have to get up four, five, and even six times a night.

The dining room consisted of an old barn. Through the gaps in its walls the wind blew gaily, and during those autumn months it froze hard inside. The barn was in any case half a mile from where we slept and over a mile from where we worked, so that every day we were forced to walk six miles or more simply in order to eat and get to our work. Given the excellent spirit which prevailed in the J.M. we would no doubt have accepted this brute existence in good part if only the work had been productive and properly organised. But we were short of tools, and the actual materials arrived at irregular intervals and in no order of priority, so that we would often be kept waiting for hours in an icy wind, only to have to work subsequently at a positively Stakhanovite pace.

In such conditions the great goodwill which animated almost all of us quickly disappeared. Everyone tried to get away with the minimum amount of work, and the universal motto was 'get out quick'. As almost always happens among men when conditions get too close to the survival mark, selfishness became pronounced, and the fine ideal of fraternity gave place to the law of the jungle, in which intrigue and mutual accusation flourished. I suppose that the terrible conditions in which the whole country lived at that time excuse a good part of this muddle, but how in that case can it be accounted for that in other J.M. centres the morale remained high, the food adequate, and the work productive? The responsibility must rest above all with the commandant of works, an arrogant, selfish brute, unfit to command. He took his sadism to the length of getting us up before dawn to do P.T. in the snow, clad only in shorts, while he directed us from his window, warmly clad in a fur-lined anorak. I remember that one day he made us roll around in eight inches of fresh snow. My rage was such that for the only time in my life I felt the urge to kill.

After three more months of this kind of existence I came to the end of my statutory time in the J.M. Nobody will be surprised that I was completely disgusted with the organisation, or that my health left a good deal to be desired. Far from wishing to sign on as an instructor, as I had originally planned, I had no other thought but to get home as fast as I could, and I got back to Chamonix about the beginning of January. While looking around for the means to execute a new project I took up my ski training again. Once again I went in for competitions, but with far less satisfactory results than the previous year. After the ordeal I had been through I needed about two months to get back into good physical condition, and just as I felt my form coming back I badly injured my knee.

With the return of spring the problem of earning a living once again arose, this time in acuter form because I wanted to get married to a girl I had met in the skiing competitions. I therefore pressed on with the daring project I had formed during the foregoing months and, with the aid of a small sum of capital furnished by my mother, rented a farm at Les Houches, a village six miles or so down the valley from Chamonix. I bought a few animals and set up as a farmer. Despite the Utopian element in my choice of this hard but worthwhile life I did not give it up until the Liberation, in September 1944, and then only with regret.

Having always lived in the country I had some idea of things agricultural, but I was far from being a professional peasant, and, as might have been expected, the running-in period was fraught with difficulties. During the first year my inexperience and idealism almost led to complete failure. I only avoided it thanks to the help and advice of my neighbours, M. and Mme. Tairraz, and also I think to sheer hard work on a scale not often contemplated even by the tough peasants of the upper valleys. It is a well-known fact that hill farming is harder and less profitable than farming in the plains. This is the reason why the inhabitants of the high valleys are, in ever-increasing numbers, leaving the land either for the cities, or for commercial activities connected with the tourist industry. In the Chamonix valley, however, the conditions are better than elsewhere. The soil is fairly fertile, and if, on the one hand, the valley sides are so steep as to render any cultivation out of the question, the floor of the valley compensates by being almost flat, making it possible to work with animals and farm machinery.

Today some of the more skilful farmers with the bigger farms can make a good living, without having to drudge, thanks to modern methods. But in 1941 such conditions, the result of continuous depopulation, did not yet exist. Although the Chamonix area was more suited to cultivation than a good many others, the tiny size of the individual farms made things very difficult. This state of affairs had brought about an immemorial poverty which forced the inhabitants to work by primitive and extremely laborious means.

At that time of food shortages, far from being deserted, the farmlands of the upper Arve were being worked right up to their remotest corners. I had the greatest difficulty in renting enough for four or five cows and a few acres of potatoes and vegetables. The fields I did manage to obtain were very expensive, scattered over a wide area, and in the case of a good third of them, steep and semi-sterile. From the outset, therefore, I was placed at a disadvantage relative to the farmer who inherits his own land, generally grouped around his farmhouse, and the position was made worse still by my technical ignorance. Fortunately my energy and liking for hard work, combined with my training in sports and manual labour, enabled me to pick up fairly rapidly the majority of agricultural techniques in use in the valley. Only the arts of threshing, scything and sharpening the scythe gave me real difficulty.

By unending work and ability to adapt to new conditions I managed to make up to a large extent for my technical handicaps, and I would no doubt have done quite well in the circumstances had I been less simple-minded, less full of ideals which had nothing to do with common sense. Thus a horse jobber unloaded a donkey onto me for an exorbitant price, which turned out to be suffering from a disease of the hooves. I also engaged my friend Gaston Rébuffat as my farm labourer. Despite all the goodwill in the world, he turned out not to be gifted in farming matters, to the extent of being unable to shovel manure without being sick. Naturally his output was less than a third of that of an experienced man; and, as was entirely natural, he also had a propensity for disappearing into the mountains for two or three days at a time, which reduced the said output still further.

Getting in the hay was a particularly dramatic performance for us that year. I had to gather enough fodder for four cows and two or three goats. This may not sound much of a job to a mechanised farmer of the plains, but was a terrible business in the prevailing conditions. Almost a third of the hay consisted of short grass growing on abrupt slopes scattered with bushes and boulders, creating a lot of work for the amount of profit involved. The worst of it was that we had to cut, dry and gather the hay with no other tools than scythes and hand rakes. To stack the hay in the barns, which were sometimes hundreds of yards away, we had to carry it on our heads in heavy trusses, or else to drag it on sleds across the slopes before trussing. The work is extremely hard even for those brought up to it from childhood, and for us, despite our natural vigour, it was absolutely exhausting.

Our lack of technique was a great handicap, and we lost a lot of time. The cutting was particularly laborious, and took us about double the normal time. We had to get up at four and even three o'clock in the morning and work through until nightfall, with no more rest than was needed to eat; and what with the bad weather and Gaston's occasional escapades, it seemed as though we were never going to finish. When I finally lifted the last truss onto my head it was almost as dry as straw, but I was borne up with the pride of succeeding where everyone had told me I would fail.

My reasons for becoming a farmer were complex. My first idea was to find a way of living in the mountains so that I could continue climbing and skiing. I also had other, more materialistic reasons which were perhaps excusable given the historical moment: to get enough to eat to satisfy my enormous appetite, and to avoid compulsory service in Germany. But to these logical reasons was added another, less palpable one—the love of nature and of the earth which had been with me from childhood. This in itself would have been enough to account for my decision. Even at school, years before, I had never wished to become a doctor, manager or magistrate like the rest of my family. As my chances of getting to university lessened, I dreamed successively of becoming a forestry officer, an agricultural adviser, and a gentleman farmer. As all of these projects went up in smoke, I had thought I could find a life to suit my ideals in becoming a simple peasant, and now that I had become one in fact, I sincerely meant it to be for good. After the fiascos of the first year, having made rapid progress in the arts of growing crops and raising animals,

I acquired the necessary technique and practical acumen, and indeed became as hard and crafty as a born peasant.

By the time I was forced to leave my farm in 1944, I was perfectly adapted to the life. My only other means of support were my emoluments as director of the Les Houches ski school in winter. Jealousy was not entirely absent from the sarcasm provoked by some of my agricultural methods, which were less traditional than those of many of my neighbours. My yields were excellent and my animals in exemplary condition. One of my cows became champion milker of the Charamillon alp over a hundred others.

My existence as a mountain peasant suited me perfectly, and there is little doubt that, if it had equally well suited my wife, I would never have quitted it. I had met her at Saint-Gervais-les-Bains, where she was a teacher, some months before adopting this career. We were married in the late summer of 1942. Very blonde, with porcelain-blue eyes, she was young and pretty, and it was in no way surprising that she should have a taste for things elegant and intellectual. She was far from entranced with this hard country life, which she had already known from childhood. With the patient obstinacy that enables women to win all their battles she never tired of edging me towards other ways of earning a living. When the chance finally appeared my resistance was exhausted, and I gave in easily.

During my four summers at Les Houches I had not stopped climbing, despite the strenuousness of my work in the fields and the small amount of spare time it left me. It was in fact during this time that I progressed from the stage of doing the major classic ascents to doing exceptional ones. By contrast to my gradual evolution up to that time, this happened all of a sudden—or, to be more precise, in one climb. During April and May 1942 I had done two or three climbs, notably the first ascent of the short but difficult west face of the Aiguille Purtscheller. Throughout June and July my farm absorbed every minute of my time, but around mid-August I was at last able to take a day or two off. My desire for the big climbs, so long frustrated, had been exacerbated by the daily sight of the mountains to a point where I was ready for no matter what mad project.

Happy to find me at last in a fit state of mind to carry out one of his grandiose plans, Rébuffat involved me in one of the most chancy adventures of my career: the first ascent of the northeast face of the Col du Caïman, with a return via the Pointe de Lepiney and the south ridge of the Fou.

Our route to the Col du Caïman has never been repeated, so I cannot tell how far our inexperience contributed to the great difficulty we encountered. But even today, when one looks at the narrow, almost vertical ice gully we climbed, its appearance is so frightening that everything leads one to think that, in spite of the progress in technique and equipment, it would remain an extremely serious proposition. One thing is certain. Neither Gaston nor I had at that time sufficient climbing experience, especially on ice, to carry out such an ascent with satisfactory margins of safety. But 'he who survives is in the right',* and we lived to tell the tale.

In those days I used to jot down my memories and impressions, sometimes amounting almost to articles, and it is largely due to these that today I can remember not only my actions but the feelings they gave me at the time. I still possess my contemporary account of the first ascent of the Col du Caïman, and although its ornate style makes it rather heavy reading, its lyrical tone and the passion which can be felt behind the words seem to me to give a clear impression of the state of mind in which I undertook my first great climbs, which is why I now reproduce it virtually unchanged:

Where can these two strange-looking people be going? After hurriedly crossing the Pèlerins glacier and literally charging up the moraine, they took no more than a few steps up the path before turning suddenly off it, jumping from boulder to boulder in a direction which leads nowhere. The first, tall and broad, sways slightly under an enormous rucksack. His breeches are heavily patched, his sweater more ragged still, and he brandishes an extraordinarily short ice axe in one hand. His eyes are burning with a strange flame. His more carefully dressed companion, by contrast, has something noble and calm in his great strides: yet the same flame is in his glance. So where can they be going? Do they even know themselves? They are seeking adventure. They are looking for hours of intense suffering and happiness, for battle and conquest. Far from the refuges and the popular summits, they want to revive in themselves the doubts and excitements of the first mountain pioneers.

The Alps have been thoroughly explored and all their summits climbed. The adventurous spirit of man has even led him up the most inaccessible mountain walls. In our time there is little left to be done: only a few of the coldest and most hostile faces remain to be conquered. By a paradoxical trick of fate, far from being hidden away in the most secret and remote corners of the Alps, some of these last bastions can be seen from one of the most popular climbing centres.

* *Publisher's note.* Nietzsche

The ring of wild crags between the Peigne and the Fou contains a few
of them, and this was the destination of the two friends we saw just
now. They had in fact no clearly defined objective, but were simply
determined to have a try at something big. To this end they were
carrying food and climbing equipment for three days and felt ready
for anything.

The weather was fine and they felt in their bones that it was
going to last. It was a bit late to be setting out, perhaps, but they were
prepared for bivouacs, no matter how uncomfortable. They were ideally happy to be at last putting into action one of the fabulous pipe-
dreams elaborated during long evenings over the fire the previous
autumn. They wondered whether to attack the dark, imposing north
face of the Aiguille des Pèlerins which now rose in front of them, one
of the finest of the unclimbed faces. After a rapid colloquy, however,
they hurried on to the foot of the hanging Blaitière glacier, above
which remained other still inviolate crags. From the Col du Caïman,
in particular, a narrow gully of ice descended among walls of vertical
granite, throwing down a challenge to the most daring, and it was
there that they finally decided to attack. But I have forgotten to tell
you that the two companions were none other than Gaston Rébuffat
and your obedient servant.

We tied onto a doubled two-hundred-foot rope, obtained almost
miraculously in those days of shortages. Our rule was for Rébuffat to
lead on rock and myself on snow and ice, and as today it was a case of
the latter I led off at once. The first obstacle was the hanging glacier.
Very few people had ever been around here, and its reputation was as
terrifying as its appearance. There was of course no information on
the best route to follow, and our vague memories of the epics we had
read, far from helping us, weighed heavily on our minds. As we got
closer to it, however, the wall of ice framed in smooth granite began
to seem less redoubtable, and shortly we could see a solution in a line
of ledges on the Blaitière side of it, followed by a climb straight up
where the ice and rock met each other. Two vertical steps were going
to be a serious problem, but our optimism made little of them.

At the foot of the difficulties we stopped for a moment to look
at the imposing scenery. Never had I been in any place so utterly
inhuman: everything was terrible and beyond our scale. Swallowed up
in the icy shadow of those grey, cold walls, we felt ourselves tiny and
alone, and were recalled to a forgotten modesty.

But from the Blaitière suddenly came the friendly sound of the voices of another party breaking the harrowing silence. We turned to look at the valley. Down there everything was bathed in sunlight, and in a moment we were cheered up by these distant manifestations of life, and felt ready to go on.

We reached the foot of the first ice step without any great difficulty, and had a quick second breakfast while fastening on our crampons. The Aiguille du Peigne rose opposite us like an elegant dolomitic spire. After a rope's length on a slope of no more than average steepness, I came to a vertical section of perhaps twenty-five feet. A few stones whirred over our heads, no doubt to give us the authentic north-face atmosphere. The wall of ice above me was pocked with holes of all sizes like a huge piece of Gruyère. Cunningly but as it turned out wrongly, I reasoned that these holes would make good natural holds and spare me a lot of hard work with the axe. With a great deal of trouble I did in fact manage to get halfway up in this manner, but at that point the ice pocks, which were already very smooth, became outward-sloping. The verticality of the wall was pushing me backwards, and, beginning to feel rather ill at ease, I tried to get my ice axe out of my waist loop in order to improve the holds and cut a few extra ones. Clumsily I let it escape from my hand in the process, and it fell into the abyss with a sound like the ringing of sarcastic laughter. There was no alternative but to get down. With a good deal of difficulty I got back to Gaston, whose impassive features revealed nothing of what he must have been feeling during this pitiful exhibition.

So there we were, short of an ice axe, the lack of which could not fail to hold us up considerably and might even cost us the climb. Fortunately we also had a short piton-hammer-cum-ice-pick which would serve to take its place in an emergency. I finally got up the wall by traversing to the left with the aid of an ice piton, and then climbing an awkward corner between the ice and the rock. The second step looked as hard as the first, but a mysterious intuition led me to cross a steep slope to the right towards some reasonably safe-looking seracs, or ice towers. At the top of one of those I found to my joy that I was at the level of the flat-bottomed bowl formed by the upper part of the glacier, which we reached by jumping a few little crevasses.

The scene now before us was so grandiose as to give us rather a shock, and we gazed round entranced at the semicircle of rock walls and spires. The mineral chaos, a last relic of the youth of the earth, found a sort of harmony in the contrasts of its lights and shadows, the aesthetic balance of rock and snow. I had never seen anything to compare with it. It would have seemed the most beautiful place in the world if it had been more isolated from the sounds of the valley which rose up to us, recalling a world we had sought to leave behind for a few hours.

But we had to be getting on. This was easily said, but we were now on completely unknown ground. We hesitated between two possibilities: Gaston wanted to get straight into the ice gully descending from the Col du Caïman, whereas I thought it looked quicker and easier to start off in the direction of the Col de Blaitière and traverse back to the right a bit higher up. In the end I won the day by the weight of my longer experience. We started off up the edge of the Reynier Couloir or gully, but after a few reasonably easy pitches we were forced back towards the centre of the wall. And there the fight began in earnest!

Above us was a triangular slope of ice inserted like a giant wedge between walls of polished granite. Fortunately an inch or so of hard snow lay on top of the ice, which greatly speeded our progress. The angle was not great to begin with, but rapidly increased. In spite of this, in order to gain time, we climbed straight up one behind the other without taking any security measures or cutting any steps. In these conditions the least false move by either of us would have sent us both down, and it goes without saying that our smallest gestures were made with extreme care. As I still had our one remaining ice axe Gaston had to be content with the hammer, but seemed to make out perfectly.

Quite soon the slope became steeper than anything we had met with earlier. Our crampons gritted on the ice, and I felt my nerves becoming stretched to the maximum. We had gained a lot of height, and below us the glacier basin gleamed like a frozen lake. Between my feet I could see Gaston's severe features rendered almost pathetic by intense concentration. How strange it all seemed—there we were suspended between heaven and earth on two little crampon points. The least slip on the part of my companion and I should be dead . . . yet I was more worried about my own possible clumsiness than his. Confidence is a wonderful thing.

The angle was now so great that the pick of my ice axe did not give me sufficient purchase to move up, and it became necessary to cut some small holds for my left hand. From time to time the snow would give slightly under my crampon points, and a shiver of fear would go through me. My calves started to get cramp. The whole business was becoming frightful. At last I spotted a tiny eight-inch ledge above me, at the foot of a band of rock, that would do for a rest. It was high time. I was pretty well at the limit of balance. With an almost desperate heave up I got onto the ledge: what a relief! Gaston followed immediately, but the ledge was so small there was barely room for us both.

With the rope belayed over a small spike of rock, I began to traverse to the left. Some handholds on the rock and a detached spillikin enabled me to make some progress without having to cut steps, though at the cost of some acrobatic moves—but then what confidence even a mediocre belay can give. After a few yards I was able to get on to the rock entirely, but the holds were all iced up and had to be cleared with the axe. My fingers were absolutely freezing and my progress snail-like. At last I managed to wedge an ice piton in a horizontal fault in the rock, and I took advantage of this anchorage to bring up Gaston.

Our way now lay up a slope of bare ice interrupted by short rock steps. There was nowhere one could get a rest, and I was periodically forced to go in for a bout of step cutting. The ice was as hard as plate glass, so we got on terribly slowly. The slopes leading to the Col de Blaitière were now away on our left, and to the right we had a good view into the ice gully of the Col du Caïman, practically in profile, so that we were finally able to judge its exact angle. Without any exaggeration this varied from sixty-five degrees to the vertical, the whole effect being that of a frozen waterfall. Surely we must be possessed to put our heads voluntarily into such a trap . . . for a moment we seemed to hear the voice of caution in our ears: 'It is getting late. The couloir is appalling and you won't get up before nightfall. You are already frozen stiff, and after a bivouac spent hanging from pitons in such conditions, you will be too enfeebled to carry on. Tomorrow you will have to make a highly problematical retreat in all the bitterness of defeat. You must be mad to do such a thing when by traversing to the left you can soon be basking on the sunlit slabs of the Col de Blaitière.'

But opposite us the Lagarde-Ségogne couloir pitilessly recalled the example of our elders, who, armed with nothing but ice axes and their own courage, had dared to attack an objective scarcely less formidable than our own. We were filled with shame at our momentary weakness, and once more steeled our wills. Why shouldn't we do as well as our forefathers? Certainly the problem in front of us was more redoubtable, but then we had other arms. If necessary we would just have to climb the whole thing with pitons, and if this involved a bivouac we would carry on next day no matter how tired we were. We had come here for an adventure, after all, and now we had one we might as well make the most of it. The cards were down.

I began to hack my way forward again into the unknown, feeling refreshed. A few feet above there seemed to be a ledge where we could rest, but when I got to it, it turned out to be no more than a slight relenting of the angle shining with water-ice, and we had to go on again along the icy, outward-sloping shelves. My fingers were so cold I could no longer feel them, and I had to stop every six or eight feet to warm them up. I hacked and cut, I wriggled, I even crawled on all fours, taking advantage of the tiniest roughnesses. At the foot of a chimney we at last found a minute platform where, by means of some gymnastic contortions, we were able to take off our sacks and have a badly needed snack.

The chimney did not yield without a real battle. A bit farther on, a sloping gangway we were traversing altered gradually into a kind of steep diagonal ramp. Although the rock looked loose and plastered with snow and ice, it seemed to offer plenty of holds, and all in all it did not appear particularly fearsome. I went up a few feet, clearing off the holds with my axe. As I went on, it became more and more difficult to let go with one hand even for a moment, and the axe was getting in my way. Finally I managed to jam it behind a flake of rock. Now I tried to insert a piton, but found I had almost run out of them. To go right back down to Gaston for some more would have wasted too much time; I had to find my own salvation. Finally I managed to get in a rather dubious-looking ice peg. It would just have to do, and I went on again, greatly embarrassed by the ice on the holds. I was having to apply every ounce of technique I possessed. Inch by inch I was nearing a ledge: three feet more and I would be there, but there was ice all over everything. I tried everything I knew without success. I could feel that I was starting to tire, that I was trembling all over, that a few seconds more and I should be off. It was all or nothing. For lack of any better hold I lunged at a large icicle, and by a miracle it held! A few frantic movements and I was there.

A good sound piton as anchor enabled me to bring up Gaston in perfect safety. I watched him like a hawk, anxious to know if my difficulties were due to the actual terrain or to my own lack of technique. He came up slowly, frowning with the effort. As he fought his way up the crux I heard him mutter: 'What the hell did he do here?' But thanks to his longer reach he finally found a good hold. When he finally stood beside me he said with a beatific smile: 'That, my friend, was genuine VI.'* Shortly after this we reached a little snowy saddle where we were able to move around freely for the first time since leaving the hanging glacier.

No doubt a bivouac here would not have been too dramatic. We were now only a few yards from the coveted gully which it had given us so much trouble to reach. The great question now was whether we could get up it at all, or if we should be forced to try to climb down. I descended a few feet in order to turn a bulge of granite, and there I was at last. In front of me was a vertical frozen waterfall, and any idea of climbing it direct was out of the question except possibly at the cost of a whole day and innumerable pitons. But happily I saw at the first glance that on my side of the gully its confining wall was well equipped with holds and cracks, and I gave a shout of joy to let Gaston know that all was going well. Without more ado I banged in a piton and cut a large step in the ice as high up as I could reach. Pulling shamelessly on the peg, I got my feet up onto the hold and then, by leaning back against the gully wall, I was able to free my hands to cut another step at waist level and a little pocket for my right hand. By a sort of chimneying movement I was able to get my feet up again, after which the whole performance could be repeated; and so it went on, slowly but surely.** A piton here and there made the whole thing almost easy, and it was just a question of proceeding carefully and in the right order.

* *Publisher's note.* Rock pitches are graded from one to six in ascending order of difficulty.

** *Translator's note.* Chimneying, or back-and-footing, is when the climber moves up by pushing with his back and his feet on opposing walls of rock. It can only be done where the chimney is the right width and the walls are reasonably parallel.

After a while it began to get more complicated. The gully steepened up to the vertical, the left wall began to join it at a less acute angle and at the same time became smoother so that it no longer helped. Was I to be beaten so close to the end? Some fifteen feet away on the other side of the gully I could see new possibilities of progress, but the problem was how to get there. The crossing of the vertical ice in the back of the couloir looked extreme, but as there was no alternative I had to go for it. Planting a last piton in the rock, I started to cut both steps and handholds with the hammer axe, but I had only gone six feet when the rope jammed somewhere behind me, so I climbed back to the piton and shouted to Gaston to free it. It seemed as though he was never going to manage it. I began to freeze up through lack of exercise, and my teeth chattered as I contemplated the yawning gulf below my feet and mused on the pleasures of mountaineering. Finally Gaston's voice floated up to say that it was all right again, but the ice hadn't got any softer or less slippery in the meantime and its high angle made it very difficult to hold on, so I had to move with extreme delicacy. In order to get a proper grip on the handholds I had to take off my gloves, and my fingers were giving me hell. A few feet more and I began to feel most unsafe. I had never done such acrobatics on ice, and the piton was now a good six feet below and off to the side. I wouldn't have believed that an ice slope could be so difficult! I couldn't go on much longer like this: it was absolutely essential to get in an ice peg. My left hand, with which I was holding on, was rapidly weakening with the cold. At last the peg seemed to be going in all right . . . but no, damn it, the ice was too shallow and it had brought up short against the underlying rock. Never mind, no time to waste, my hands were giving out altogether: quick, a carabiner*. . . phew! Only just in time.

It took me more than a quarter of an hour to get the circulation going again in my poor hands, after which the rest of the traverse seemed mere child's play by comparison. Once again I jammed myself between the ice and the rock and hammered in a piton, hacking out a veritable platform to stand on. Then I hauled up the more enormous of our two rucksacks, and Gaston came up hand over hand on one of the ropes while I protected him with the other. Above us smooth

* *Translator's note.* A carabiner, or *mousqueton*, is a steel link with a spring-loaded gate in it which climbers use to clip onto the ring at the end of a piton. The rope is then run through it.

slabs of rock formed an open corner with the ice slope. It all looked very difficult. The struggle was far from over, particularly as the light was fading and darkness was not going to make things any easier, but not for a moment did we contemplate a bivouac. I felt a great surge of confidence at having overcome the main obstacle of the wall. Nothing could stop us now!

But we should have to be getting on with it if we were not to be overtaken by night. I chopped furiously at the ice to try and find holds underneath, and luck was with us. By taking a few risks I quickly got up twenty feet, and then a welcome crack enabled me to hammer in a peg. The angle, while still steep, began to lessen slightly, and the holds which I hacked clear were better. Night had now fallen, but the stars diffused a dim light, and I was able to move faster all the same. Sensing that the col was not far away now I threw all my forces into the battle. A rocky spike gave us a last good belay, and after thirty or forty feet more of strenuous climbing the slope gave back. I cut my way through the cornice* with a few blows of the axe, and with a last heave I mantelshelfed up onto a terrace so horizontal that I had forgotten that such things existed. Gaston was quickly at my side, and, flinging our arms round each other, we shouted our joy to the moon like a pair of madmen.

Philistines may think that we were madmen indeed to go through such suffering and danger to arrive at this lonely spot. What did you hope to find up there, they may ask. Glory? Nobody cares about young fools who waste their best years in meaningless combats far from the eyes of the world. Fortune? Our clothes were in rags, and next day we would go back down to a life of slaving for the barest essentials. What we sought was the unbounded and essential joy that boils in the heart and penetrates every fibre of our being when, after long hours skirting the borders of death, we can again hug life to us with all our strength. Nietzsche defined it thus: 'The secret of knowing the most fertile experiences and the greatest joys in life is to live dangerously.'

The conquest of the north face of the Col du Caïman was my first really great climb. Nothing that I had done up to then had called out every ounce of physical and moral force in my being, by which experience alone mountaineering

* *Translator's note.* A cornice is an overhang of snow, usually found at the top of gullies and along high ridges.

is raised above the level of mere sport and enables us to discover unguessed-of forces in ourselves. I had been up all sorts of mountains, big and small, easy and difficult, but I had never really tried to rationalise what it was that drew me towards them. Like Mallory, I climbed them 'because they are there.' When all was said and done I climbed as I skied, simply because I liked it, and the main difference between the two sports seemed to me to be that one was a question of going uphill and the other down. I am sure that the majority of climbers seek no further justification for their sport. Of course I had always known that mountaineering involved grave dangers, and on more than one occasion I had seen how thin was the borderline between life and death. But anyone who is prepared to ski straight down the steepest slopes at flat-out speed also runs grave risks, and several of my racing friends had flattened themselves against rocks and trees.

But on the icy flanks of the Caïman I had had to employ all my resources for hours on end, and had only just avoided disaster on at least two occasions. Never before had I given so much of myself or run such risks. Safely back in the valley I remained profoundly affected by the experience, which seemed of a different nature from all I had known up to then.

I began to question the unconscious motives which had impelled me to prefer certain books and certain courses of action. I began to realise that the mountain is no more than an indifferent wasteland of rock and ice with no other value than what we choose to give it, but that on this infinitely virgin material each man could mould, by the creative force of the spirit, the form of his own ideal. 'There is not just one but a hundred different kinds of mountaineering', said Guido Lammer. For some, as Henry de Ségogne has suggested, 'the flanks of the sterile peaks become the ideal of an aesthetic, even an embodiment of divinity.' For others they are 'simply the background of their favourite sport', for others still 'a gigantic opportunity to flatter their own vanity', and for yet others, like Maurice Herzog, 'a bit of all that and something more besides': one of the few doors the modern world has left open on adventure, one of the last ways out of the armour plating of humdrumness in which civilisation imprisons us, and for which we are not all very well adapted.

From that time on, my passion for the hills took a more precise direction, and bit by bit I worked out for myself an ethic and a philosophy of mountaineering. But, in practice, the risk and suffering involved in picking the roses that grow on the borders of the impossible call for exceptional moral strength. Doubtless, for some, it is always present; but for others it can only be summoned at rare intervals and in exceptional and perhaps fortuitous circumstances, and it is to this latter breed that I belong. In fact it was to be many years before I again committed myself to a fight as total as that which won the narrow ice gully of the Col du Caïman.

Despite the farmwork which took up far more of my time than I could have wished, I got in a number of technically difficult climbs during the course of the following seasons, both on rock and ice. Some of these, carried out with a variety of companions, were repetitions of routes which then had a big reputation, others were first ascents, though not of major importance.

After his short and unhappy try at farm labouring, Rébuffat had found a job better suited to his tastes and capacities. The Central School of the J.M., which had moved to Montroc, close to Chamonix, had taken him on as a civilian instructor. He enjoyed quite a lot of spare time, and occasionally we managed to do a big route together: among others, in 1944, the east-northeast buttress of the Pain de Sucre, now become a classic, and more especially the north face of the Aiguille des Pèlerins, one of the last big unclimbed faces in the district. Some of these ascents were really quite hard by the standards of the day. It must be remembered that equipment was still primitive by comparison with what is now normal—for example we used to climb everything up to grade V in enormous nailed boots which had to be taken off and stuffed in our rucksacks for the hardest pitches, for which we wore gym shoes scarcely any better suited to the job. Ropes were of hemp of such poor quality in those wartime days that even when doubled they would rarely stand up to falls of more than about twelve feet. Pitons were very limited in variety and the use of wooden wedges quite unknown, so that a good half of the cracks one came across were no use for artificial climbing. And all this to say nothing of the various lesser aids since developed, such as twelve-point crampons, duralumin carabiners, lightweight bivouac equipment, étriers,* head torches, and so on.

Taking everything into account, our tools and methods were much closer to those of the original alpine pioneers of the golden age than to those of the modern sixth-grade climber with his muscles full of vitamins and even dope, his feet encased in special boots designed to take advantage of the tiniest holds, tied on to a nylon rope able to withstand the most incredible loadings, not hesitating to drill the rock if necessary and even, thanks to ingenious pulley systems, to get his sack hoisted by groups of friends waiting at the foot of the face—because this is really what we have come to.

But in spite of their difficulties and their scale, none of the climbs I did between 1943 and 1945 gave me the same feeling of total commitment I had

* *Translator's note.* An étrier is a short, three-runged rope ladder used for artificial climbing. This and the following paragraph are very controversial.

known on the Col du Caïman. This may have been partly due to the gradual amassing of technique and experience which, by increasing my possibilities of success, made the uncertainty of adventure harder to recapture. But the real reason was probably that my morale was insufficient to impel me towards the most heroic exploits of all. It was not as though they did not exist, either in the form of the most daring ascents that had already been done, or in new types of problem. Several narrow and indeed almost miraculous escapes were certainly responsible for my relative lack of audacity during those seasons. They had the effect of shaking my nerve and reminding me of the need for caution, which my youth and natural impetuosity had tended to make me forget. The disappearance of some of my dearest friends also played its part in this semi-cautiousness. Human nature is full of contradictions. My spirit longed for dangers and 'the toil without which existence would be a dreary and boring thing, well-calculated to make you disgusted with life',* yet my animal instincts made me fight shy of them.

To the majority of laymen the ascent of a difficult mountain sounds like a series of acrobatic dramas, in which the heroes only escape death by means of superhuman energy and miraculous luck. In reality such odysseys only occur to a few foolhardy beginners looking for a place in the headlines, but never to real climbers. If mountaineering were really as dangerous as legend would have us believe, the law of probabilities would not have allowed men like Heckmair, Solda or Cassin to survive dozens and even hundreds of extremely difficult climbs. It seems to be unknown to the public that climbing, like cycling or athletics, includes numerous different specialities, varying widely in the degree of risk they involve, and each calling for a technique which is complex and slow to master.

Now it is true that every year, in France alone, mountain accidents cause the death of thirty to fifty people: though when one considers the fifteen thousand active mountaineers this does not seem a very high figure. But what seems to be less widely known is that nine-tenths of these accidents happen to foolhardy novices or to climbers who have wildly overestimated their technical abilities. It is as stupid to undertake a climb without first having acquired the necessary technique as to try and take off in an aeroplane without having learnt to fly. To pursue the analogy, if one is a climber of no more than average ability and experience, it is as silly to embark on some of the really big stuff as to try looping the loop when one has just learnt to take off.

This is not to say that the experts in climbing run no risk. Literature, and even the climbers themselves, may have exaggerated, but it remains none the

* *Publisher's note.* Guido Lammer

less true that high-standard climbing, like car racing or aerobatics, though far from being suicidal, does involve danger. Even the best can make mistakes, and nobody has a charm against bad luck. Like pilots and racing drivers, some great climbers die of old age and some get killed.

My alpine career has been a full one, and I have done hundreds of difficult climbs in all the various special departments of the sport, yet I could not say that I have had more than a score or so of close escapes; and although I have had several long falls I carry no scars of any serious injury. This is in no way exceptional: on the contrary, a number of famous climbers, through skill and good luck, have had the most sensational careers without a single accident.

The specialised departments of mountaineering range from the acrobatic scaling of vertical and even overhanging cliffs to the laborious conquest of giant mountains of over twenty-six thousand feet. Each implies danger to life and limb, but in degrees which range in their turn from the simple to the unlimited. However odd it may seem, the danger of a climb has no connection with its impressiveness. Thus much the most impressive kind of climbing to watch is gymnastic rock climbing, but given proper technique it is also by far the safest. By contrast the ascent of giant mountains, which has practically nothing spectacular about it at all, is extremely dangerous.

It is often imagined that falling off is the greatest danger, but this is a complete mistake. The majority of accidents to experienced mountaineers are in fact caused by rocks and ice falling on them from above. As long as the climbing is easy there is in fact almost no likelihood of falling off. When the difficulty is increased by the holds getting smaller and farther apart, or by the angle becoming vertical or overhanging, the climber hammers pitons into the ice or (more often) the rock, onto which he clips the rope by means of strong carabiners so that if he falls he will be stopped by his companion holding the rope passed through them. In practice it is comparatively rare to go more than thirty feet without finding a crack that will take a piton, so that falls rarely exceed twenty or thirty feet. Very exceptionally they may attain sixty feet; that is to say thirty feet above the piton and the thirty feet below before the rope comes taut.

It may seem astonishing that it should be possible to drop sixty feet without killing or injuring oneself, and it does happen that even falls arrested by the rope have fatal consequences when the climber, in falling, hits ledges or protuberances. But when the climbing is really difficult the face is usually ipso facto vertical or overhanging, so that the body drops clear and strikes nothing on the way down. The moment of greatest danger is when the second man succeeds in arresting the fall. A shock loading ensues which, despite the stretch of the rope, is capable of breaking it or the victim's back. This risk has however been considerably lessened of recent years by the introduction of nylon rope, which is both stronger and more elastic than hemp; and there have been many cases of men falling sixty, a hundred and twenty, and even getting on for two hundred feet without serious injury. Some unusually daring climbers have even jumped for it deliberately in certain circumstances. I know a famous Belgian climber who has had more than forty falls in his still short career, and a well-known Englishman who has fallen more than sixty feet (sometimes over a hundred) on some fifteen occasions without hurting himself. For all that, falls are still to be avoided like the plague, because even the best ropes can get cut over a flake of rock, and even the most solid looking pitons can perfectly well be pulled out.

Personally, in about twenty years of really intensive climbing, I have had eleven or so 'peels' ranging from twelve to sixty feet, which is a fairly high number: but only one of them was nearly fatal. This happened in 1942, shortly after the ascent of the Col du Caïman. Having harvested all the potatoes and stacked the firewood, I had a few days to spare before the arrival of winter. Leaving my wife in charge of the farm, I went off with Gaston to the only training crags normally in good condition at this time of year, the Calanques, close to Marseilles. As I have already had occasion to mention, this is Rébuffat's hometown, and we were able to stay with his mother. We set out every morning to climb one or another of the imposing sea cliffs, with their elegant white ridges, which rise close to the town and offer short but extremely difficult ascents. This had been going on for three days when we decided to try a route called the *Boufigue*. I was leading nearly two hundred feet up on the vertical face when the piton I was holding onto came out, and I found myself headfirst in space before I knew what was happening. A second piton fifteen feet below was torn out without even slowing me down. As the earth continued to rush towards me, I came to the conclusion that both my ropes had broken and that I would be killed at the foot of the face. My mind worked at fantastic speed, and in a few fractions of a second I had time to think of my mother, my wife, and a great many other things. There was no sensation of fear whatever. The idea that I was going to die a moment later did not worry me, and my personality was involved in the fall more as a spectator than as an actor. But suddenly I felt a violent shock around my ribs. I could scarcely believe the evidence of my senses: I was not dead but dangling in space below an overhang.

The return to living seemed a trying business. There was a violent pain in the small of my back, and the rope was strangling me. The whole weight of existence descended on me at once, with all its problems, even the most banal. How was I going to get myself out of this? Was I badly hurt? Would I be able to ski that winter? And would I ever hear the end of it from my wife? It was only later I realised I had no right to be alive. One of my two hemp ropes had broken, and the carabiner had almost opened out completely. If the intact rope had not caught in the carabiner's gate catch I would have been dead.

Although I have only once come so close to death in falling off myself, I have almost been killed by falling stones or ice on at least nine occasions. These, together with snow avalanches and falling cornices, are in fact the greatest dangers of the high mountain climbing which has been my speciality. In the Alps stone falls are very frequent, especially during dry summers. They may be caused by climbers who knock them off by accident in the course of climbing, to the risk of those below, or, more often, by the action of frost eroding the mountain. In certain types of climbing such as the ascent of vertical rock needles the risk of falling stones is negligible, but it may be very high in mixed climbing where bands of snow and rock succeed each other. An experienced mountaineer can reduce the danger by crossing exposed places at a time of day when the stones are frozen in place, or by making long detours to avoid them, but he can never escape them completely. Speaking for myself, I owe my escape from pulverisation on several occasions to some stroke of luck.

The first of these terrifying experiences happened in June 1943. I had gone to spend a few days at Grenoble, seeing family and friends, and took advantage of my proximity to the Oisans to do a climb there. I set out with three companions, my late and regretted friend Pierre Brun, my cousin Michel Chevalier, and a Parisian climber called Roger Endewell with whom I had already climbed, and who because of his size is best known by his nickname of 'Micro'.

It was early in the season, so there was still a lot of snow around. It seemed that rock climbing might be awkward for this reason, and that it would be wiser to try an ice climb—I have always had a certain leaning towards this laborious, and nowadays not too popular, branch of mountaineering. As all three of my companions were hardened all-round mountaineers we chose the northern gully of the Col du Diable, a long, sustained and steep ice route, but without any exceptional difficulties.

The delicate tints of dawn were in the sky by the time we crossed the *rimaye*.* The sky was clear, but the night had been so warm that nothing had frozen. Strictly according to the rules we should therefore have abandoned

---

* *Translator's note.* The *rimaye*, or bergschrund, is the master crevasse separating a glacier from its surrounding mountains.

our project, owing to the risk of falling stones . . . but who takes any notice of the rules at the age of twenty? Anyway there seemed to be so much snow in the gully that the danger of stones didn't appear too great. Retreat was not considered for a single moment. After a few hundred feet up easy slopes the angle steepened to around forty-five degrees and our crampons began to grit on hard ice under a thin layer of soft snow.

Now in those far-off days practically no one practised the delicate art of walking up ice slopes in balance on their crampons. The rule was to start cutting steps as soon as the slope reached about thirty-five degrees, a harrowing and painfully slow proceeding. Personally, I did crampon up reasonably steep angles, but without using my ice axe in the 'anchor' position which I later learnt from my master, Armand Charlet. My poor axe position did not allow me to realise the full possibilities of my crampons, and on hard ice forty-five degrees was almost my maximum, so that it was rather precariously that I began to stamp my way up the couloir. My companions, who were less accustomed to this form of exercise, were ready to applaud but not to imitate, so that I had to resign myself to cutting steps for at least half of the time. Our advance was slow, and we had done no more than a quarter of the gully when the rays of the sun reached it.

It was not long before a few isolated stones began to bound down the gully in gracious parabolas. We knew that with a bit of care and a cool head it is usually possible to dodge a stone, and that anyway a human body does not take up much room on a slope two hundred yards wide. It would be rank bad luck if one of these damned projectiles actually hit any of us. We carried on, though a bit disturbed. But very soon the stones began to multiply, and some of them came straight at us. Transformed into alpine toreadors, we dodged them with quick twists of our bodies, but this rather too-frequently repeated exercise began to get on our nerves: acrobatics like this in such a place could not go on indefinitely without leading to disaster, but what were we to do? Go down? In order to gain time we had cut out steps very far apart, and even dispensed with them in places. Cramponning downhill is much more delicate than up, so that we should have to cut for hours, and our chances of getting down in one piece would be slim indeed.

Rather than have recourse to such a desperate solution, I decided to try and gain the shelter of a nearby rock buttress. We were traversing towards it as fast as we could go when from the rocky wall above us came a crash like thunder. We watched, our eyes wide with terror, as three or four boulders the size of wardrobes, surrounded by a hail of smaller shot, descended straight towards us in a series of fantastic bounds. There seemed no chance whatever but that we should be swept away like wisps of straw by the enormous avalanche. Perfectly conscious of the fate which awaited us, we flattened ourselves against the slope and waited for the torrent of stone to strike us. At the very last moment, when only about a hundred feet away, it divided into two for no apparent reason. Some of the big rocks rumbled past forty feet to our left, others passed to our right, and only a few pebbles actually hit us without doing any harm.

It was by an almost equally miraculous chance that I was spared a second time, a few months later, in the company of René Ferlet. In order to avoid any danger of stone fall, we had attacked the north buttress of the Aiguille du Midi a good two hours before dawn. It was a dark and rather warm night. After some weeks among the boring and sometimes ignoble struggles of earning a living, I was overjoyed at the prospect of a good honest fight among the splendour of the mountains.

Climbing in the dark is unpleasant, even on easy ground, and in order to avoid more of it we hurriedly traversed into the snow couloir on our right. True, it was a channel for falling stones and ice, but it did seem a quick and easy way of getting up the next hundred feet. We had not got half this distance when we heard the sound of a great rock avalanche above our heads. No sooner had I realised what was happening than I felt a blow on the shin and found that I was rolling at ever-increasing speed down the slope. As during the fall in the Calanques, my mind began to work with incredible rapidity and I remembered in a moment all the accidents from which the protagonists had emerged unscathed: Gréloz and Valluet on the Couturier Couloir, Boulza and Lambert on the Whymper Couloir, Belin and Rouillon on the Rouies, and others. Recalling that we had not climbed more than three hundred feet above the base of this couloir, I felt quite optimistic about the outcome. There was a more brutal shock ('the *rimaye*!' I thought in a flash) and, after rolling another fifty or sixty feet, I fetched up on the avalanche cone. I had lost most of the skin off my hands, but had no serious injuries. Ferlet was staggering to his feet beside me no worse off.

Whatever his skill and natural aptitude, the climber who abandons the beaten track for the profounder and more austere joys of the great alpine walls, or the highest summits in the world, will always have to undergo serious risks. The mineral world into which he forces his way was not made for man, and all its forces seem to unite to reject him. Anyone who dares seek the beauty and sublime grandeur of such places must accept the gage. But as far as the man himself is concerned, careful physical and technical training in the complex arts of surmounting rock and ice can eliminate almost all subjective risk.

However odd it may seem, master rock climbers rarely come to any harm, even among the most extreme difficulties, and this accounts for the way in which a few virtuosos can climb solo for years with complete impunity. Dangers stemming from the forces of nature, called objective dangers, are very much harder to avoid. In doing big climbs on high mountains it is impossible never to pass under a tottering serac, never to go in places where a stone could fall, or never to set out in any but perfect conditions. He who respects all the wise rules found in the climbing manuals virtually condemns himself to inaction.

Running risks is not the object of the game, but it is part of it. Only a lengthy experience, enabling observations to be stored up both in the memory and the subconscious, endows a few climbers with a sort of instinct not only for detecting danger, but for estimating its seriousness.

Weighing nearly 175 pounds, with abnormally short arms and heavy muscles, I am ill designed by nature for extreme rock climbing, and in fact I have never been brilliant at this branch of the sport. Despite all this I have quite often led rock faces of great difficulty, led on by my natural impetuosity and perfectionism—but only at the price of taking occasional risks, whence my relatively numerous falls, distributed throughout my career.

By contrast, the majority of nearly fatal incidents from objective causes, which I have been lucky enough to survive, occurred during my early years of mountaineering, and this although the actual climbing concerned was both easier and less in amount. It is possible that a chain of coincidences was responsible for the accumulation of dramatic moments, but it seems more likely that inexperience was to blame. Nowadays I would not be surprised if I peeled off a rock climb as a result of pure difficulty, but it seems most unlikely that I should again be involved in misadventures like those of the Col du Diable and the north face of the Aiguille du Midi. As I have already remarked, it is possible to climb hard for twenty or thirty years and still die of old age. The hardest part is to survive the first four or five years.

I learnt a great deal from the various adventures of 1942 and 1943, of which I have only related the most remarkable. During the seasons which followed I showed a lot more care, even to the extent of slightly limiting the technical level of my attempts. Rébuffat, on the contrary, still animated by the wonderful self-confidence which he had shown from the very beginning, seemed to have no fear of finding any climb beyond his resources. Training to perfection by his job as a mountaineering instructor and benefiting from abundant spare time, he succeeded in doing a large number of high-class ascents. Simple, quiet and reserved in his daily life, he showed no backwardness at all when it came to mountains. He reckoned that all he had done up to now was no more than training for bigger things, and that the only thing lacking was a companion able to follow him. Judging me worthy of this role, he literally pestered me to go with him to repeat the exploit of the Italians, who, led by Riccardo Cassin, had in 1938 climbed the north face of the Grandes Jorasses by the Walker* Spur.

This extraordinary face, consisting equally of rock and ice, is without any doubt the queen of the Mont Blanc massif. Visible from far around, it seems by its inaccessible appearance to throw scorn on climbers and to dwarf otherwise proud mountain walls. No mountaineer worthy of the name could fail to want to climb it. Like Rébuffat, 'the Walker' was my greatest dream. It was to me the most grandiose, the purest and most desirable of faces. But I certainly did not think of it as other than a dream. It seemed too formidable, too far above the rest, and I did not believe myself to possess the necessary class. Only supermen like Cassin and Heckmair were able to do this kind of thing, and I was sure that neither Gaston nor I were of this order. I therefore left him to his grandiose projects and followed my more modest path.

Rébuffat, however, succeeded in interesting one of the best mountaineers of the preceding generation, Édouard Frendo. It would seem that they were not yet ready for such an undertaking, because the time they took to climb the first quarter of the wall, at which point they were turned back by bad weather, showed clearly that they did not dominate the situation in the necessary way. But Rébuffat was in no way downhearted. With his invariable tenacity he determined to try again at the first opportunity. Two years later he and Frendo succeeded in doing the second ascent of the Walker after three days of hard climbing and two bivouacs, thus accomplishing the first really great exploit of post-war French mountaineering.

* *Translator's note.* The Pointe Walker, summit of the Grandes Jorasses, is named after an English mountaineer who, led by his guides, was the first to climb it in 1868 (from the south). By 'the Walker' climbers nowadays mean the buttress descending from this summit on the north face, led by the Italian Cassin in 1938.

| 3 |

WAR IN THE ALPS

DURING THESE TWO YEARS the course of my life was completely changed by the liberation of France and the end of the war. From 1942 onwards the region around Chamonix had been an important centre of resistance. The hills harboured bands of Maquis, and many of the local people belonged to various secret societies. For my own part I contributed to the feeding of these bands, among whose leaders I had a number of friends. Thus I lived in permanent contact with the resistance, and knew what was going on, without actually belonging to any organisation.

Nowadays I wonder why I did not take a more active part in the first phase of the liberation. I can think of lots of reasons, none of them really very good. In the first place I had no need to go underground. As a farmer in charge of a productive unit I was excused compulsory labour service in Germany, and with the exception of an occasional checkup I was never placed under any restriction. Then I had never taken much interest in politics, so that I had no axe of that sort to grind that would have led me to join the Maquis. The plain fact remains that the resistance sought to hinder and eliminate the German invader, and as a Frenchman I ought to have played a more active role in it.

During their early stages, the underground movements existed mainly to help political refugees or young men called up for service in Germany to escape their unenviable fate. At this time I felt that I was doing my duty to the full in revictualling the Maquis and in sheltering various 'wanted men' at my house. By the time the military side of the resistance became more prominent I must confess I was put off by the cloak-and-dagger atmosphere, and also by the petty rivalries between the various personalities and parties. No doubt I would have joined enthusiastically in any open rebellion, as I subsequently showed, but as there was nothing to impel me towards underground activity I never went in for it. I had, however, assured a number of the leaders that on the day when the fighting came out into the open they could count on me. I must admit, finally, that I was so taken up with the work on my farm and with my climbing, that I completely failed to realise that the resistance could play an important part in the liberation of France. I went blindly on my way without troubling myself too much with national affairs.

After the sixth of June 1944 the resistance got tougher and things began to happen more quickly. In Haute-Savoie the Germans remained in control only of the main towns. They were firmly in possession of Chamonix, where most of the big hotels had been turned into hospitals for the wounded, but the other villages in the upper Arve valley were virtually in the hands of the Maquis. It was obvious that open revolt was about to break out, and I asked one of my friends, Captain Brissot-Perrin, a regular officer in command of part of the local resistance, to let me know when I should be needed to take part in the fighting. It was not long before he sent word, and I went at once to his headquarters in the hamlet of Chavands. They were short of weapons for newcomers, so I became a dispatch carrier maintaining lines of communication with another group posted above the village of Servoz. The situation was confused; the heads of the different factions of the resistance seemed unable to agree, and my friend's authority was not recognised in all quarters. Two days after I had joined up I was standing in the sun waiting for orders in front of the old farm which served as headquarters, when a group of armed men suddenly appeared. They asked me excitedly if the captain was there, and when I replied in the affirmative they pushed me aside and rushed in. There followed the sound of a violent discussion and then they came out again. Soon afterwards Brissot-Perrin told me that he had been forced to resign. He advised me to go home, which I did at once. The Maquis now proceeded to surround Chamonix. In the face of this threat the Germans dug themselves in around the Majestic Hotel, and after much parleying surrendered without firing a shot.

France was now practically freed, but the Germans drew back to the Italian frontier which they held in strength, and from which they launched dangerous raids on the higher French valleys. The resistance was over but the war went on. The ex-Maquis were turned into military units, more or less directly linked with the First Army which had disembarked from Africa. In the Chamonix region the period of transition was highly confused, and the rivalry between various personalities and parties gave rise to positively music-hall incidents.

Like most of the Parisian climbers, among them Pierre Allain and René Ferlet, Maurice Herzog had gone to ground in the upper Arve valley and had requested a command appropriate to his rank as a lieutenant in the Reserve. As a newcomer he was not treated with any great respect by the leaders of the Armée Secrète.* He was so annoyed by this that, although he had no affiliations with the Communist Party, he turned, on the rebound, to the Francs Tireurs et Partisans. They were short of men, and Herzog was received with open arms and made a captain. Almost all the non-Chamonix climbers joined Herzog's company except Rébuffat, who after a few days in its ranks went back to the A.S., judging it more politic not to compromise himself with any group bearing the least taint of communism. Herzog was one of my climbing friends, and only a few days before the liberation of Chamonix we had been the first to climb the Peuterey ridge of Mont Blanc via the north face of the Col de Peuterey. He therefore asked me to join his troop, but I was not very impressed by all the muddles and internecine quarrels of the new army. I shut myself up in my farm and got on with the potato harvest, encouraged by my wife in no uncertain terms.

Around the beginning of October I had a visit from an old J.M. friend called Beaumont. He was in a Maquis group in Val d'Isère which had become famous for its exploits under the name of Compagnie Stéphane, this being the pseudonym of its commander, the regular Captain Étienne Poiteau. Stéphane had a lot of ex-J.M. mountain instructors in his troop, as well as amateur skiers and climbers from the Dauphiné. He now proposed to form a company able to take on the Germans on the high alpine ridges, and perhaps to dislodge them. In order to get more trained mountaineers he had sent Beaumont off to Chamonix with the mission of recruiting local professionals.

Beaumont had a smooth tongue—he has since done brilliantly as a representative. Using every trick of argument he sang the praises of the Compagnie Stéphane, its glorious past, its sound military organisation, its terrific spirit, and the key post I would find waiting for me. His masterstroke was to assure me that all my oldest mountain friends such as Michel Chevalier, Pierre Brun, Robert Albouy and J.-C. Laurenceau were already in the troop and asking for me to join them.

* *Translator's note.* Armée Secrète was a right-wing resistance organisation, and Francs Tireurs et Partisans, left-wing.

Captain Stéphane's fine reputation and the fact that his unit was a serious military organisation, containing many of my best friends, combined with my old love of adventure to tear me away from my wife's affection and the farm life that so much absorbed me. When I think about it today, I am lost in admiration for Sergeant Beaumont's recruiting talents. Not only did he succeed in getting me into the army at a time when I had a horror of all things military, but he lured back to Grenoble three other Chamoniards, notably my friend the guide Laurent Cretton who was not only married but the father of three children.

It is one of my principles never to regret anything I have done: but if there is one act of madness on which I have never ceased to congratulate myself, it is having joined the Compagnie Stéphane. The eight months I spent in it were among the most wonderful in my whole life. Naturally it wasn't as perfect as Beaumont had painted it. It was a human institution, and as such had many minor faults. But it was a most extraordinary troop, and above all its leader was an exceptional man who could communicate his enthusiasm and his belief in the cause to a degree I have never known in another human being. At the outset the company had been a simple Maquis with headquarters at Prabert, in the heart of the Belledonne range. Instead of letting his men go to pieces in the comparative idleness which was the besetting vice of so many of the Maquis, Stéphane put them through an intensive military training. They became a veritable commando with a special ability to melt away into the landscape and move from place to place under the most difficult conditions.

After the sixth of June, his team being in a state of perfect readiness, Stéphane went over to the offensive, putting into practice his personal theories about guerrilla warfare. Divided into 'sticks' of six or a dozen, each with a high firepower, his men moved virtually only at night and had no contact with the local populace under any pretext whatever. In this way they were for practical purposes invisible. Thanks to this method and great physical fitness, these sticks were able to carry out quick raids sometimes as far as sixty miles from base. Their objective might be to ambush a German supply column or attack a strongpoint. This done they would disappear, only to deal another blow five or ten miles farther on. The system rendered them almost uncatchable, so that they harassed the enemy to the maximum with minute loss to themselves. By their speed of movement and the number of their attacks they seemed to the enemy to be everywhere and nowhere, giving the impression of a small army.

At the time I joined the Compagnie Stéphane it was fresh from several months of intense activity and little diluted by the new elements which had come to it after the liberation. It was trained to perfection and animated by a tremendous esprit de corps. The prevailing atmosphere was one of enthusiasm, comradeship and human warmth, recalling the best days of the J.M. I need hardly add that I found these psychological conditions ideal, and from the outset I took to them like a duck to water.

For all that, my first few days were a bit disappointing. The Compagnie was in the process of being incorporated into the 15th Battalion of Chasseurs Alpins, then being formed, and as a result it had to be enlarged and reorganised along more conventional military lines. A certain amount of confusion ensued; discipline was relaxed, and apart from a few hours of military instruction per day, I spent the best part of my time listening to the heroes of the Maquis relating their adventures. Luckily this did not go on for long. We were posted to quarters a few miles above a small spa called Uriage for intensive training before going into the front line. The 'taming' of the company turned out to have been no more than superficial. In the event this rather special unit remained very largely independent, and the traditions of the Maquis were maintained.

Stéphane was fair-haired and very tall, with a school-girl complexion. Candid grey eyes lit up his slightly plump face. Under the exterior of a shy, clumsy young man, he hid the energy and courage of a condottiere, together with an abundance of intelligence, psychological insight and humanity. He now sought to preserve in his company the virtues which had made it famous: iron morale, toughness and mobility. To this end he led us a hard life. We slept in bivouac tents whatever the weather, and quite often on manoeuvres we would simply lie down fully dressed under a tree. We had no transport and no cookhouse. Each section of a dozen men was an independent unit which did its own cooking over an open fire.

Apart from firing practice, map reading and Morse code, the training mainly consisted of incessant manoeuvres among the mountains and forests of the Belledonne massif. Exercises of varying size and complexity succeeded each other uninterruptedly. One time it might be a section attack on a given map reference, another time it might be on company or even battalion scale against a supposed enemy unit of comparable magnitude. The main principle behind it all seemed to be to get us used to living in a state of perpetual readiness for action, whether by day or night.

The manoeuvres were often carried out with live ammunition and hand grenades. Naturally we were told to aim well over the heads of our 'enemies', and not to throw grenades actually among them. Nevertheless some of our old guerrillas took a malicious pleasure in sending bullets whistling about our ears or, worse still, letting off grenades only a few yards away; all of which was quite impressive to a raw recruit like myself. I particularly remember how, one day while crossing a glade, I was caught in the fire of a light machine gun hidden somewhere above. A first burst tore up the turf a few paces in front of me. I sprinted to the left, but the whizzing of bullets forestalled me at once; and when I fled back to the right I was quickly brought up short by other bursts in that direction. Finally, in despair, I threw myself to the ground and lay still until my tormentors should see fit to leave me in peace. All this playing around with real bullets may seem rather stupid, but in fact there were no serious accidents, and there is no doubt that it quickly hardened us to war. If we had had to go straight from our training into heavy fighting, many lives would have been spared simply because we were relatively used to being under fire.

During the whole of that month of October 1944 the weather throughout the Alps was truly frightful. It rained nonstop and snowed down to 5,500 feet, a height we sometimes passed in the course of manoeuvres. We were continuously soaked and it was almost impossible ever to get our clothes dry. In such conditions our existence, which was already hard enough, what with forced marches, heavy loads, night watches and insufficient rations, became trying in the extreme. This was particularly so for the new recruits, who had never known anything like it. But in spite of everything our hardened veterans gave such an example of infectious enthusiasm that the troop's morale remained high and we played soldiers with unabated zest. Everyone took these operations as seriously as if they had been real warfare. Personally, although I found it quite hard going, this fraternal life of intensive action in contact with nature suited me perfectly, and I gave myself up to it unreservedly.

About the middle of November, the 6th, 11th and 15th Battalions of Chasseurs Alpins went forward to take the place of the somewhat diverse units which had been holding the line for more than two months in the Maurienne sector, from Mont Tabor to the Col du Mont Cenis. The mountains were white with snow, the thickness of which made any military activity difficult, so that not much was going on. The greater part of our battalion was detailed off to guard villages and works of art, while the specialised skiing sections held the advanced outposts. Captain Stéphane instituted a series of raids of varying size, acting on the theory that attack is the best method of defence. His idea was to give the Germans a healthy respect for our fighting abilities. Together with several of my friends I was given the responsibility, in my capacity as a mountain specialist, of helping the officers to plan and carry out these attacks.

I rather doubt if Stéphane had any great faith in the strictly military value of these commando raids. No doubt he rightly sought to avoid any tendency to sink into apathy, and reckoned that these small exchanges would keep us on our toes and maintain our confidence. By the same token it should be mentioned that, apart from the occasional bombardment or burst of machine gun fire, the Teutons who faced us showed so little spirit of aggression that there was a real risk of boredom. It seems likely that if we had been content to leave them alone the whole winter would have passed by without a drop of blood being spilt, but this sort of passivity was in no way to the liking of our braves, who were on the lookout for scalps. Since the Germans would not come to us, Stéphane had no alternative but to seek them out in order to appease our thirst for action. This he proceeded to do with the greatest of intelligence and humanity, only involving us in affairs which were really more sporting than dangerous.

My first operation was a good example. I was detailed to assist the 'Ops' group, under Captain Bouteret, to study the possibility of harassing the Germans on their Col de la Roue flank. For a normal sort of unit this narrow saddle, situated between two very steep summits, would have been quite out of the question as an objective, but it was obvious that if a group of mountaineers could succeed in climbing the Grande Bagne (a summit of some 10,500 feet which overlooked the col) by a face hidden from the enemy's view, they would be able to fire on him. He could hardly fail to be surprised and shaken by such an attack, coming from a quarter which would normally be judged inaccessible at this time of year.

From a purely mountaineering point of view the plan was not lacking in daring. It was now winter, the cold was severe, and the steep face which would have to be climbed was plastered with snow. But fortunately my section included a number of guides and skilled climbers, and I knew that with men like this it was possible to do things that would otherwise be out of the question. I assured the captain that we could get to the summit of the Grande Bagne and fire on the Germans from a range of about 750 yards, and although our chances of actually hitting anyone were pretty slim in the circumstances he gave the order to proceed. The climb went more easily than we had expected, thanks to a steep gully of hard-frozen snow and a slightly dicey corniced ridge. The most difficult part in the event was to persuade Bouteret to come with us along this last bit, which was admittedly very exposed.* He was a jovial, likeable southerner, fonder of hunting skirts than climbing mountains.

---

* *Translator's note.* Climbers use the word 'exposed' to mean vertiginous, exposed to the void, unless otherwise qualified.

In his inimitable Bordeaux accent he called out to us: 'You'll do me in with all this bloody climbing. You can shoot Huns just as well without my help—I don't wish the poor bastards any harm.' Our brave adjutant was cut short by several disrespectful pulls on the rope which soon brought him up to us, and eight or ten of us reassembled on the narrow summit.

The Germans were clearly visible almost directly below us. They seemed without a care in the world. Some were sunbathing, others practising their skiing. At a range of 750 yards, and downhill at that, a light machine gun is of very limited efficiency. We had little real chance of hitting anybody, but Bouteret, once more conscious of his position as our commander, ordered us to fire a few bursts. The effect was spectacular. The enemy had no idea where the fire was coming from, and was thrown into complete disorder. Men ran in every direction in the snow, but no one seemed to be hurt. After a few minutes of this cruel game we grew weary of shooting at men who were unable to defend themselves and withdrew, satisfied at having carried out our mission.

During the course of the winter I took part in a number of other operations of the same kind, some of which were, however, rather more dangerous. One of these has been described by the writer-mountaineer Jacques Boell in his excellent book *A Ski-scout at War*.* Boell was at this time attached to our brigade staff, and his account is evidently based on conversations with a number of those who took part. It is largely accurate as to fact, but interprets the tactical and psychological motivations behind our actions in rather a personal way. In effect he has made a serious military enterprise, intended to crack the enemy's will to attack, out of an escapade more sporting than warlike, mainly designed to relieve the boredom of life in the advanced outposts. To each his own version. From the headquarters in Modane it probably did look like that. To us who lived the adventure it seemed quite otherwise.

Towards the end of December 1944 it was my section's turn to relieve the advanced post of Challe-Chalet, about seven thousand feet up on a north-facing ridge. It was difficult to hold and to supply, and could hardly have been more uncomfortable. Jacques Boell has described it thus: 'It was by far the most rudimentary I have ever seen. It consisted of two trenches in the snow linked by a filthy little hovel, inside which it rained and snowed just as much as if one had been outside. The lads who occupied it had given it the picturesque name of "Tin-can Palace". Less than two kilometres away across a small valley the Germans were installed on the Col de l'Arondaz, which commanded our position. I am sure that the enemy could have made life

* *Publisher's note.* Published by Arthaud as *Eclaireur skieur au combat.*

there impossible, whenever he wished, by means of mortars, heavy machine guns and night patrols. In point of fact practically nothing happened at all. Although it was in a most vulnerable position the post was never attacked; only, no doubt to keep his eye in, Jerry would occasionally send over a few mortar bombs or bursts of machine-gun fire. It can't have been too bad, anyway, because in several months there were no deaths and very few wounded.'

Without wishing to put on heroic airs, life at Challe-Chalet was distinctly unpleasant. Day and night it froze hard enough to do mortal harm to a brass monkey, and on some nights the thermometer fell as low as minus thirty-three degrees Centigrade. We had only one stove to warm thirty men, and the draughts were such that six feet from the stove wine froze in the bottle. As we had little equipment of the right kind it goes without saying that this permanent frost made us suffer considerably. Apart from a bit of skiing on the one unsuitable slope sheltered from German fire, and the hour-long lugging of food, wood and ammunition on our own backs, we had absolutely nothing to do. After a few days of this sort of existence we became profoundly bored, and a mixture of boredom and cold is very hard to bear.

To the right of the Col de l'Arondaz rose two small rocky peaks marked on the map as points 8020' and 7986'. On 8020, which was the closer to the col, the Germans had installed an observation post from which they could not only see all that went on at Challe-Chalet, but could also direct the heavy artillery which from time to time they turned on Battalion H.Q. in the village of Charmaix, or the mortar fire with which they sprinkled the supply columns going to the Lavoir fort. There was no doubt that Point 8020 was a serious asset to the enemy, but it had to be admitted that he used it with moderation. All in all the post didn't really matter to us too terribly, and anyway there seemed to be no way of stopping him using it.

One morning when, for something to do, we had spent an hour or two banging off our mortars at the Col de l'Arondaz and Point 8020, the exasperated Germans replied by firing a few rounds at Tin-can Palace. My cousin Michel Chevalier called out:

'If only we could get at them up there, the Jerries wouldn't look so bloody clever.'

I replied jokingly, 'Well, why shouldn't we?'

'What the hell are you going to do about it?' replied my cousin. 'They're in an absolutely impregnable position.'

Carried away by the spirit of the argument, I said:

'I don't know so much, it's not as bad as all that. The face of Point 7986 is out of sight of the Boches, so we could probably get up there. From there to the other top is easy enough to do by night if necessary. You'd only have to climb 7986 in the afternoon and attack the observation post just after night-fall, before they could get help from the Col de l'Arondaz. If you left fixed ropes on the face there'd be ample time to retreat, and it would really put the wind up them.'

Chevalier's rather wan grey eyes began to shine. Frowning with interest, he said:

'It would be terrific if one could do it, but do you really think we could get up the face? It looks pretty hard to me, and when it's as cold as this you can't do much.'

But I replied imperturbably:

'As far as climbing the face is concerned, leave it to me and we'll get there. I made a recce over there the other day, and there's a gully you can't see from here which makes the first two-thirds easy. Given enough time we can always get up the last bit. It would be more fun than dying of cold here, and anyway think of the look on the faces of the Boches!'

And so it began. Starting with a frustrated argument between a couple of climbers, the idea grew and grew. The next time Captain Stéphane came to see us, Chevalier, who was a sergeant major, told him of our project. Stéphane, who knew nothing about climbing, was rather sceptical at first about our chances of climbing Point 7986, but after we had assured him that this was the least of our problems he grew very keen on the idea and promised to discuss it with Lieutenant-Colonel Le Ray. The colonel was an experienced mountaineer and an old climbing friend of Michel Chevalier's, and after having thoroughly investigated the whole matter he gave his permission.

The plan we finally decided on was no longer to storm Point 8020, but simply to fire at the lookout from Point 7986, which was some 150 yards away. There were to be only three men in the team: Chevalier, the Chamonix guide Laurent Cretton, and myself. Nothing was left to chance. Cretton and Chevalier, who were both excellent shots, spent several days down at the range practising with a target at 150 yards, while I selected the necessary ropes, hammers, pitons and ice axes.

The day came. After three hours of difficult going on skis we reached the foot of a forty-five-degree couloir. Skiing was out of the question on a slope of this angle, so we continued on foot, sinking up to the waist in light pow-dery snow which would certainly have avalanched but for the bitter cold that bound the crystals together. After a while we came to rock, where the plaster of ice and snow made climbing a delicate matter. The last pitch of all was really dangerous, consisting of a smooth slab topped by a cornice that was ready to come down at any minute. On my first attempt I fell about ten feet, but was able to stop myself before I came on the rope. It was only towards noon that we emerged from the face, which had been rendered much more serious than usual by the snow on the rock and the absolutely arctic cold.

Only a light depression in the ridge now separated us from the enemy post 150 yards away on Point 8020, and we could see it very clearly. To begin with we took great pains not to be seen, but some time passed and there still seemed to be no signs of life. We hung on thinking that the garrison must be comfortably warming themselves inside, but, despite the bright sunlight that sparkled off the snow, the icy wind made our position almost intolerable. The chill went right through us and our feet began to lose all feeling. Soon we could stand it no longer. It seemed obvious that the Germans had temporarily gone down, probably for Christmas Eve festivities. We were just about to clear out when a sentry appeared, not on Point 8020 but on the Col de l'Arondaz. He was over three hundred yards away, and our chances of hitting him were pretty poor. Chevalier nevertheless decided to let him have a burst; but, when he pulled the trigger, the hammer would not come down sharply enough to fire the round. Although we had taken the greatest care of it, the gun was jammed by the temperature of minus thirty degrees Centigrade. In spite of numb fingers and the problems presented by stripping down a light machine gun on a ridge where a strong wind was continually whipping up the snow, Chevalier and Cretton toiled for over an hour to clear their weapon. It was no use. We could stick it out no longer, and there was nothing for it but to get down.

Jacques Boell depicts Chevalier as having been in despair over the frustration of our mission, but I can say that this is a great exaggeration. Neither he nor I had any real desire to kill the German sentry pacing up and down on the col, all unconscious of the danger that menaced him. We had long realised the slight military value of all this fighting in the Alps. Life in the front line had ceased to be a patriotic mission so much as a big game of cowboys and Indians, made all the better by the fact that it was played out among our beloved mountains. On the patrols and raids for which we always volunteered we did not really set out to slaughter Germans or anything of that sort. What we enjoyed in this pointless and obsolete form of war was its resemblance to mountaineering. We sought adventures where courage, intelligence and strength might enable us to overcome apparently impossible obstacles; action in a world of grandeur and light which appeared different from that of grubs crawling around in the mud.

These actions seemed no more serious to us than trying to climb mountains by their most difficult faces. But if, therefore, it was no more than sport, we carried it to the limit in just the same way. Reaching the summit is not the point of a climb, only the whistle for end of play. Very often the last few feet of climbing are not very exciting or difficult, but, for all that, real climbers go on to the top. In the same way, the actual game is not the underlying motive of hunting yet no hunter likes to return empty-handed. Thus shooting at the enemy was not for us the sole purpose of our operations so much as a simple rule of the game we played. And so, in the coppery light of that radiant evening, we arranged the ropes for the first rappel with quiet minds, conscious of having done all that was humanly possible towards the accomplishment of our task, and happy in the experience of a splendid adventure.

At the very end of his tale, Boell seems to have divined our true attitude. He quotes my actual words when I realised that our ascent of Point 7986 was not in fact destined to frighten a single German: 'When all's said and done it's a piece of luck that the L.M.G. isn't working. Nobody will know we've been here, and we can do it all again.' Perhaps he was right in concluding: 'Terray, a genuine sportsman and silent man of action, is of the breed who do not need hope in order to set out, or success in order to carry on.'

After three months or so of defending the mountain ranges separating Modana from Bardonnèche, the Compagnie Stéphane was posted to another part of the front where more serious and difficult assignments awaited it. At the end of the Arc valley the two villages of Bonneval and Bessans were cut off from the rest of Maurienne by a no man's land of eighteen kilometres. The reason for this was that the Germans were strongly fortified on the Col du Mont Cenis and the old Tura fort, so that it was impossible to defend the area open to their artillery fire at any acceptable cost. This area amounted to the districts of Lanslebourg and Lans-le-Villard. The people and livestock of Bonneval and Bessans had remained where they were, and it was necessary to protect them from the looting raids which the enemy could hardly fail to make sooner or later. The defence and supply of this enclave was a complex problem. Theoretically they could have been supplied by portages across the Col de l'Iseran, which was between us and the troops stationed in Val d'Isère, but such a long route would have been dangerous owing to avalanches, and would also have called for a large force of men.

Headquarters preferred to supply us by parachute, a system which was very popular at the time but not very practical. For technical reasons which I cannot now remember the aeroplanes were afraid to fly low over the valley, and dropped their loads from such a height that the least puff of wind dispersed them over a wide area. The containers came down all over the hillsides. Many were lost, and the recovery of the remainder was a tiresome job. The whole business was so slow and inefficient that it was decided to try the riskier method of bringing supplies through the no-man's-land at night. Thanks to the darkness there was no great fear of German shells, but the valley was narrow and ideally suited to ambush. In the event the enemy turned out to be not much more aggressive than in the Modane sector, so that there were no more than two or three clashes even though dozens of men passed in both directions every night.

Throughout the early winter the sector had been defended by a company of the 7th B.C.A. After three months virtually cut off from their own side they needed a relief, and Compagnie Stéphane was given the job. We were to see a lot more action on this front than on the one we were leaving, some of which was to prove really thrilling.

After helping to install a telephone line between Val d'Isère and Bonneval, I and some other N.C.O.s were detailed to take charge of the supply columns through the no-man's-land. I did this journey five or six times in both directions. In spite of our fitness those eleven miles of stumbling through the darkness under loads of up to ninety pounds always seemed extremely hard, but the physical effort was nothing in comparison with the nervous tension. Virtually the whole of our route lay open to attack by the enemy, and although we tried to reassure ourselves that such attacks were in fact rare, this knowledge created a very unpleasant anxiety neurosis. The worst part was going through Lanslebourg. There was absolutely no way of avoiding this village, placed in a narrowing of the valley. It had been evacuated and partly destroyed, so that the least breath of wind would rattle the half torn-off sheets of corrugated iron, or slam doors and windows. These sounds seemed incredibly sinister at dead of night as one passed through the ruins in the knowledge that a machine gun might be hidden behind every wall, and as they broke the oppressive silence even the bravest of us could hardly help jumping.

Around the beginning of March there was a patch of fine weather, which made possible a series of high-altitude operations in which my climbing and skiing abilities were again put to the test. The mountains of high Maurienne are over eleven thousand feet in places, and the cols which link them are high and steep. The weak forces of Germans and Italians which opposed us on this front had seen fit not to occupy the actual line of crests, which they doubtless judged to be militarily inaccessible at this time of year. These units, mainly made up of Italians who had been pressed forcibly into service, had been content to dig in around the highest villages of the three Stura valleys. Faced with this weak point in the enemy line of defence, the high command, probably encouraged by Stéphane, decided we should occupy not only the cols but some strategic points on the Italian side.

This move seemed to me to have a double purpose. In the first place it would enable us to make contact with the Italian Maquis operating behind the enemy lines because, starting from such high bases, we would be able to infiltrate between his strongpoints. In the second, we could take the enemy in the rear when the time came for a major attack on the Col du Mont Cenis, which I had little doubt was in the offing. To do all this with a single company called for an intense effort on the part of every single man, but more especially from the mountaineering specialists. As there were not enough of these to go round, they had practically no rest.

Captain Stéphane seemed to have great faith in my experience and judgement of mountain conditions, as he put me in charge of the technical planning for most of the difficult operations. It was indeed flattering to be so trusted, but it meant that in order to live up to it I had to make enormous efforts—not that I found this in the least bit displeasing. The most remarkable of the missions I took part in at this time was a four-day patrol. By going a very long way round, which involved a bivouac on the way, we were able to link up with a band of Italian partisans hiding close to the small village of Suse, twelve miles behind the lines at Mont Cenis. These men were able to give us the exact positions of several batteries of heavy artillery. The patrol was daring from an alpine as well as from a military point of view, inasmuch as we had to go along craggy ridges and cut across slopes which would have avalanched at the least fall of snow.

There were moments of drama during the four days. Suse was occupied by over eight hundred Germans, and while we were hiding out with the partisans, only about a mile from the village, someone must have given the game away. All the houses were being searched, but we were woken up by the Maquisards and got away under cover of darkness. A couple of hours later we were just coming out of the woods into the higher pastures when we saw two large columns making a pincer movement to cut us off. Fortunately the Germans did not see us, and we escaped by hiding in the branches of high trees. It is probable that if, as often happened, the Jerries had had dogs with them, the adventure would have had a less happy ending.

The following evening, half-starved and worn out by a long forced march carrying arms and ammunition, we were approaching the old generating station by the Lac de la Rousse when we heard the noise of firing. The post had been attacked, several men wounded and my friend Robert Buchet killed. Instead of finding the rest and nourishment we had been expecting, we had to participate at once in a counterattack and then fall back on the Col de l'Arnès, situated more than an hour's march above. As if my pack wasn't heavy enough in its own right I had to carry a wounded man's as well. By the time we reached the little hamlet of Avérole on the other side of the col it was the middle of the night, and I understood what it meant to go beyond one's normal limit of endurance. That day, marching virtually without food and with fifty-pound rucksacks, we had climbed and descended a total of over seventeen thousand feet, of which some nine thousand had been uphill.

I shared another interesting experience with Michel Chevalier three hundred feet or so below the summit of the Pointe de Charbonnel. With its 12,310 feet, this peak is the highest in the range. Without being exactly what one would call difficult it is quite steep on all sides, and it can only be climbed in winter when the snow is in safe condition. On one of those sublime days when the mountains glitter like jewels in the sunlight we had climbed a steep gully of hard snow, and there, three hundred feet below the top, had hollowed out of the slope a cave big enough to shelter us comfortably. From this igloo-like base we expected to be able to spend two whole days observing the new German installations on the Col de Ronsse, over the other side of the Ribon valley, on which an attack was being considered. The Pointe de Charbonnel was practically the only place from which such observations could be made discreetly. Our particular job was to get some idea of the size of the enemy forces, the siting of any minefields, and the outposts of the sentries.

Faure and Laurenceau, who had come along to help with the digging, spent the first night in the ice cave with us, then went down, leaving us alone on the mountain. There was not a cloud in the sky and the air was almost utterly still. Despite the cold we spent the day glued to our telescope. At nightfall we returned to our comfortable cave, got out our air mattresses and slept well after an ample meal. At seven o'clock in the morning I pushed aside the canvas sheet which served us for a door and got a lump of snow in the face for my pains. The weather had changed in the night and there was eight inches of new snow on the ground.

The snow was still falling in thick, wet flakes. In such conditions it would have been impossible to go back down the couloir without starting an avalanche. We were virtually cut off in our cave. This might not have been too serious if we had had plenty of food, but our reconnaissance was supposed to finish that day and we had practically nothing left. The weather didn't seem to be getting any better, and as the layer of new snow grew thicker it became increasingly likely that an avalanche would occur spontaneously. Although our position was not yet desperate it was becoming increasingly worrying. By noon it had stopped snowing and was getting warmer, thus reducing the stability of the slope still further. The boredom and hunger began to pall, and eventually I decided to try a rather risky way out which, however, I had already used successfully elsewhere.

Putting on my skis, I went a few yards easily to the right. Here I was on the edge of a couloir which went straight down into the little valley of Vincendière. On the other side of the couloir, only about fifty feet away, was a well-defined rib on which one would be safe from avalanches, and I skied straight for it as fast as I could go. As I had intended, the tracks of my skies undercut the slope and started the avalanche, but my passage was so quick that I was in safety before it had really begun to move. We were now free to swoop down the hard, smooth slope in a series of graceful curves. I have used this stratagem two or three times during my career, but obviously it cannot be recommended in just any snow conditions or, particularly, on just any kind of ground. It is absolutely essential to be moving at a certain speed when the unstable mass of snow ruptures, and to have a sheltered spot to aim for not very far away. But contrary to appearances, given a good skier and the right conditions, the exercise is more sensational than really dangerous.

I spent the whole of that winter and spring on mountain assignments at altitudes ranging from five to ten thousand feet and even higher. Military considerations often forced us out in weather and snow conditions which we would normally have thought out of the question. It would have been quite easy to pretend that certain operations were impossible for technical reasons, and our officers would have been in no position to contradict us, but we always played the game and frequently undertook to cross dangerous slopes. I was twice caught in large avalanches. The first time I was carried down for over a thousand feet, and only escaped by a double stroke of luck in losing my skis and in being on top of the avalanche when it came to rest. The second time I got away by going all out for a bunch of trees where I was able to find shelter. One of my comrades who could not ski so well was killed.

Very few people go out on the mountains in the heart of winter. At that time of year they ski on relatively low runs, and only with the return of spring, when the snow improves, do a few specialists venture on to the heights. Most of our officers knew little about the problems of winter mountaineering, and some of them had no idea at all. The majority of the missions they ordered, and which my section and I sometimes managed to carry out at considerable risk, were not likely to have any great effect on the course of the war. But for all that, as long as the odds were reasonable, I always volunteered. Most of my companions had no more illusions than I about the usefulness of these actions, but did the same. The war in the mountains was only a game to me, but like other parts of the climbing game I played it to the limits of my strength and courage. The very frequency with which I thus went to the extreme margin between safety and danger, a margin which most people keep comfortably wide, ended by giving me a knowledge of snow and avalanche conditions which few mountaineers normally have the chance to acquire.

This practical science of snow is made up partly of information which can be culled from books, and partly of a kind of intuition based on a natural flair and a mass of accumulated observations, more often than not subconscious. I learnt more about this field that winter than in the whole of the rest of my life put together, despite the fact that goodness knows I had often enough taken unwise chances on the condition of slopes. Many years later, on the occasion of a mountain tragedy so painful that I will not enlarge upon it here although it caused me to revise all my ideas about the brotherhood of mountaineers and even of men as a whole, it was with the confidence borne of this experience that I raised my voice against the timidity and incompetence of certain folk in spite of the troubles my action brought down on my own head. Despite all the silly capital made out of it by the press during those unfortunate days of January 1957, I will say once more that, as was witnessed in writing by the famous Swiss climbers who accompanied me, the mountain was in good condition and two lives could have been saved.* When my friends and I finally got tired of being messed about by 'the authorities' and set out, unhappily one day too late, we had no difficulty with three-quarters of the so-called impossible slopes and couloirs. Later we even returned down them despite the thick layer of new snow from the storm which halted our advance. It should not be forgotten that at the same time the Italian guides successfully rescued their countrymen Bonatti and Gheser from the Gonella hut, the approach to which is quite well known for its exposure to avalanches. Why was a thing possible on one side of Mont Blanc and not on the other?

In order to fire a few shots at the rearguard of an army worn out by five years of war, our officers on the Alpine Front did not hesitate frequently to expose their men to dangers far greater than those of Mont Blanc at the beginning of 1957. Early in April the Compagnie Stéphane was withdrawn

---

* *Translator's note.* The author is referring to the deaths of the young climbers Vincedon and Henry, who were lost in a storm while traversing Mont Blanc at New Year 1957.

from the Bonneval-Bessan sector in order to take up positions in Lansle-bourg and in the woods below the Col du Mont Cenis and the Tura fort. This pressure on a sensitive spot caused the Germans to react with artillery fire and with commando raids which were sometimes very daring. I found this campaign of cannons, booby traps and ambushes among the woods rather depressing, but I little guessed that I was about to see another and more horrible aspect of war.

Down in the Italian peninsula the allied armies were now striking giant blows at the Wehrmacht in order to effect a breakthrough if they could, or at least to divert the maximum possible number of German troops from farther north. Our high command ordered a strong general offensive. The First Army detached us considerable artillery support, while farther to the south bodies of infantry were sent to reinforce the alpine units. The first objective in the Maurienne area was to be the Col de Sollières and the rocky pinnacles that commanded it, Mont Froid and the Pointes de Bellecombe and de Clairy. If we could occupy these positions we would thereby render the plateau and Col du Mont Cenis indefensible.

On the night of the fifth of April scouts of the 11th Chasseurs Alpins surprised and captured the positions on the Pointe de Bellecombe and Mont Froid, but on the Pointe de Clairy a company of the 15th Battalion got involved in difficult ground and had no success. Ill-supported, outnumbered and untrained in the right sort of techniques, the conquerors of Bellecombe and Mont Froid finally gave way to German counterattacks after a heroic defence. The Germans now threw off their previous sloth and gave proof of all the warlike qualities for which their race is famous, together with all the cunning acquired in five years of unremitting warfare. Only the most perfectly organised of defences would have stood any chance of holding them, instead of which the inexperienced troops who were supposed to be supplying and relieving the scouts got bogged down in the deep snow on the lower slopes, or slipped and fell in the gullies higher up, which had been turned into veritable ice chutes by the cold at that altitude. Either these columns never arrived at their destinations or, when they did make it, they were so exhausted that they could not fight properly. Lacking any worthwhile support, the courageous scouts were forced to give way, and Bellecombe was retaken by the enemy only the day after its original capture. On the 11th a new attempt to seize the Pointe de Clairy was beaten back after heavy fighting. Finally, on the 12th, Mont Froid was also lost to the enemy. This last was a real tragedy. The ridge, which was about half a mile long, was defended by three pillboxes at the east and west ends and in the centre. On the 6th and 7th of April the eastern pillbox had already been the scene of some bloody fighting. Captured on the 6th after a fierce hand-to-hand combat, it had been lost on the 7th but recaptured by our side the same day.

All this fighting at close quarters had cost a great deal of blood, but that was only the beginning. On the 12th the Germans launched a heavy attack on the two ends of the ridge, which fell with the loss of almost all their defenders. The central pillbox finally surrendered after a desperate resistance.

As the 15th Battalion did not take part in this affair, I was lucky enough to be spared the butchery on Mont Froid; but to make up for this I was involved, albeit from some way off, in the second attack on the Pointe de Clairy, which was also exceedingly hard fought. The Pointe throws down a long, spiky, but not particularly steep ridge to the Col de Sollières. The Germans were firmly installed at several places along this ridge, so that to become fully master of the situation it was necessary to deal with all these as well as the summit itself. The attack was commanded by Lieutenant Édouard Frendo, who a few months later made the second ascent of the Walker Spur on the Grandes Jorasses. His force consisted of three sections from the 11th Battalion the Chasseurs Alpins, the 3rd Scouting Section from the 15th, and also on the extreme left, a combat group from the 1st Company of the same battalion, under my command.

The lie of the land was against us. The three platoons from the 11th had to crampon up a steep open snow slope which led to the ridge, without any shelter until they reached it. Similarly the section from the 15th, which was to attack the summit, had to crampon up a steep couloir containing no cover at all. During the night these four sections, entirely made up of sure-footed mountaineers, climbed so silently that they were not noticed by the sentries until they had almost reached the crest, where they charged with such skill and dash that they won a foothold among the rocks.

Unhappily only one enemy pocket of resistance was overcome by this first assault, and all along the spine of the ridge the Germans remained in their chosen positions, protected by stone walls and well supplied with ammunition. The job of my own group, on the left, was simply to cover the ground over which the enemy might have effected a flanking movement and so taken our men from the rear. Thus we played only a small part in the proceedings, and I contented myself with keeping my men undercover of some rocks from which we were able to fire on a few German attempts to send reinforcements from the Tura fort.

From my position I had a ring-side view of the battlefield. Both sides were putting down a heavy barrage, and I would go so far as to say that the French were probably deploying up to eighty or so field guns of various calibres, and the Germans about the same. The reader can imagine the racket produced by some 150 cannon all trained on an area of a few hundred square yards. It was like hell on earth. Up till then I had not had much to do with artillery, and I don't mind admitting I was terrified. Without knowing a lot about these matters, it seemed to me that on both sides the object of the bombardment was to reduce points of resistance on the ridge and to make their reinforcement impossible; but, whatever its cause, the shooting was remarkably inaccurate, and I was unable to see that it had any effect at all on the course of the fighting. Shells landed all over the place, and some of the French ones, intended no doubt for the other side of the mountain or at least for the summit, went off only a few yards from where I was lying. The deafening sound of the explosions, and the disagreeable feeling of being at the mercy of blind forces, threw me into a state of confusion such as I had never known in my life.

During all this time the scouts of the 11th and the 15th were fighting heroically on the ridge, trying to dislodge the Germans from their strongpoints. Several were killed; others gravely wounded. Jacques Boell tells vividly of their plight: 'It was impossible to evacuate the wounded, so that they were forced to save themselves by sliding down the hard snow-slopes into the Combe de Mont Froid. By lying down in deep furrows in the snow they were able to get most of the way under cover from the enemy snipers, who, whether out of humanity or being too busy elsewhere, did not in fact pay them much attention. Their sufferings can be imagined as they slipped and sprawled in the snow, losing blood and in certain cases even limbs that had been half sliced off by machine-gun fire. At the bottom of this agonising descent the victims fortunately found stretcher-bearers, led up under enemy fire by the chaplains of the engaged battalions.'

But despite all the courage and sacrifice of our troops, the enemy remained in command of the Pointe de Clairy and the greater part of the Arête de Sollières. It was becoming obvious that we would not only fail to dislodge him, but that as our men ran short of ammunition there would be a serious risk of counter-attack, which might be fatal. Faced with this desperate situation Lt.-Col. Le Ray, who was in touch with Frendo by radio, gave the order to retire in spite of the obvious dangers attaching to the descent of a snow slope under enemy fire.

This Battle of the Pointe de Clairy, in which I took part more as a spectator than as a fighting man, made a profound impression on me, and I went back down to the valley through the peaceful forests full of disgust. Spring was beginning to burgeon. Creamy snowdrops speckled the ground, and the air was full of odours evoking peace and love. As I descended through this poetic landscape I realised that the hell I had just left, in which so many men had meaninglessly lost their lives, could never again have anything in common with the naively sporting game I had played through the winter months. The whole abomination of war was suddenly and overwhelmingly apparent to me.

Faced with the foolhardiness of some young (frequently German) climbers, quite a lot of French mountaineers are apt to say 'it's not playing the game: climbing isn't war.' Yet it must be admitted that for many people it *is* a way of satisfying the primaeval aggressive instincts which find so little outset in modern life. I am one of these myself. If I had been born in another age I would probably have been a soldier or a buccaneer, and it may be, therefore, that climbing has been for me a kind of fighting. For five months fighting had even seemed a new kind of mountain challenge; but all that had nothing in common with the sort of warfare I had just witnessed in which man, far from raising himself above the material by his physical and moral virtues, was reduced to the level of a beast hunted by blind forces of iron and fire. No, climbing is not war: because war is no longer anything but an immense murder.

Some people have vehemently criticised these attacks, so costly in human lives, launched at a time when they could no longer have any valuable effect on the inevitable outcome of the war. I do not wish to set myself up as a judge. If in some cases the ambition of high-ranking officers must surely have weighed in the balance, I am sure that the great majority of the generals who took the decisions to attack the Alpine Front and the Atlantic Wall did so for patriotic reasons. Only, on looking back, it seems that the sacrifices involved were out of all proportion to any results that could have been obtained. Jacques Boell, an officer of the Reserve and beyond any question a patriot, ends his book dedicated to the glory of those who fought in the Alps with words in which we feel the distress and disquietude: 'I must confess myself haunted by doubt. All those young lives cut down before their time, all those wounds and sufferings ... were they strictly necessary only one month before the end of the war, and for this heap of sterile schists?'

One can understand that, to those who carried the actual burden, the gains did not compensate for the sacrifice. But *some* action had to be taken, or at least attempted. For the sake of honour the country had to take a hand in liberating its own soil in Alsace, the Alps, and along the Atlantic. By holding down as many enemy units as possible in this way, we kept them from the Italian Front. And most important of all, it was vital that when the time came for the making of peace treaties our leaders should be able to say: 'France, as a peaceful nation, needs a protective wall along the Alps. You cannot refuse her this barren ground for which so many of her sons have given their lives. We must have a juster boundary line at Mont Cenis, Chaberton, the Saint Bernard, Vésubie, Tende and La Brigue.'

Even as I ponder these matters I seem to feel the friendly presence of the dead around me, and hear them murmuring: 'We have not died in vain if we have succeeded in winning a little safety for our country.' Yet this justification of so much bloodshed and pain, inspired as it is by the noblest feelings, seems to me to have lost most of its validity today. Let the reader judge for himself.

The Battle of the Pointe de Clairy was not the last of the fighting as far as I was concerned, and indeed I very nearly had to take part in another contest of the same kind. The Col du Mont Cenis is protected on the French side by the Fort de la Tura de Lanslebourg. This ancient and massive fortress dates from the time of Vauban.* Built like an Inca citadel from enormous and meticulously fitted blocks, it has withstood all the ravages of time and is still intact. In September 1944 the Germans were sitting comfortably behind its mighty walls and as long as they were there it was impossible to get possession of the Col du Mont Cenis. The high command decided that they must be winkled out.

The operation began with a heavy bombardment, and for over twenty-four hours a deluge of fire descended on the fort. After this it was considered that not a single occupant could survive, despite the fact that the walls themselves were virtually undamaged. It only remained to walk in and take over. Accordingly, a company of the 15th Chasseurs came out of their cover in the woods and advanced on the glacis, some of them getting blown up by mines in the process.

When the French were nice and close, the enemy, who was very far from being wiped out, opened up with machine-gun fire. In the ensuing rout a good many dead were left on the ground. After this mortifying reverse our brass hats decided to use more up-to-date methods. It now seemed to them that the only way of getting into the Tura was to blow off the heavily armoured doors with charges of plastic explosive and bazooka shells. The 1st Company of the 15th was entrusted with this difficult mission, and a number of us were withdrawn for special training behind the lines. But Stéphane, a fervent patriot and born fighting man, was also a most humane leader and a convinced Christian. He seemed in no way inclined to get his men minced up for the sake of a few old walls when it was obvious that the war might end

* *Translator's note.* Vauban was a famous military engineer and Marshal of France at the time of Louis XIV.

any day. He spoke of the mission without enthusiasm and openly criticised the way the spring offensive had been conducted. Our special training was dragged on as long as possible, and one fine morning the observation posts suddenly noticed that there were no signs of life in the fort.

Down on the plains of Italy the overwhelmed Wehrmacht was fleeing northwards, hoping to form new lines in the Austrian mountains or even to ask for asylum in Switzerland. The units on the Alpine Front, not wishing to be cut off from the main body of their forces, had suddenly abandoned their positions. Without waiting for any orders, Stéphane launched his company in pursuit. Marching far in advance of the rest of the French army and fighting side by side with the Italian partisans, we managed to keep contact with the enemy almost as far as the outskirts of Turin. The war ended for me a few kilometres outside it, or to be precise at the village of Robasomero.

When one of my companions brought me the news of the armistice I wandered off along the edge of a wood, sick at heart. Everywhere spring was coming to its full splendour, and the air was full of the slightly listless warmth of the Italian countryside. A thousand barely perceptible sounds peopled the night, and far above the infinite worlds of the stars twinkled softly. Through renewed contact with the vast peace of nature which had been the joy of my childhood I sought to recover my peace of mind, which had been profoundly troubled by the events of the day.

My group and I had gone to the help of a strong contingent of Garibaldini who had clashed with a company of S.S., but we had only arrived at the end of the battle, too late to affect the issue. The Germans had been wiped out to a man, either in the fighting or by being shot afterwards. Among the prisoners were two boys of twelve or fourteen, sons of a black-shirt officer who had sought refuge with the S.S. By the time I arrived these two wretched victims of a world gone mad had been delivered up to the tender mercies of the local women, who were pulling their hair, scratching their faces and booting them savagely, although the children's piteous looks were enough to have melted a heart of stone. Outraged by these brutalities, so unworthy of folk who were supposed to be fighting in the name of civilisation, I instantly protested, only to be cursed for my pains by several big strong men in red neckerchiefs, with enough grenades, pistols and daggers in their belts to frighten an army. By their threatening manner I gathered that they were telling me to mind my own business. They then went into a huddle for some time. Finally, taking no notice of my indignant protests, these comic-opera heroes kicked the two boys up against a wall and hosed them with sub-machine guns. The murder was so brutal and swift that I could not believe my eyes, but stood frozen with horror. To my dying day I shall remember the crazed glances of those innocent victims. That day it came home to me truly that the modern world, for all its luxuries and its machines, had not yet emerged from the state of barbarism.

Northern Italy greeted the French troops with wild enthusiasm, and for us who came first there was absolute delirium. We marched through villages on carpets of flowers. The end of the campaign was like a huge, continual fair. But our great allies did not seem to be particularly pleased by the presence of French forces in the Italian valleys, and our armies were progressively moved back until they stood behind our own frontiers. The Compagnie Stéphane was quartered at Ailefroide, in the heart of the Oisans massif.

I was finished with war. During these eight months in arms I had lived a life of absorbed action, dedication and sincere comradeship which had lifted me above the sordid considerations of everyday existence. Only the blood shed by my friends and the beastliness of some men had dimmed the brightness of those days, but the splendour of the mountains had purified such stains. We were all volunteers, joined up for the duration of hostilities only. Now that these were over we should have regained our normal rights, and our retention in the army was quite arbitrary. Despite our devotion to the company, which had become a sort of second family, most of us wanted to get home and take up our positions in society. But the high command, which needed soldiers to occupy the French zones of Germany and Austria and, even more, to fight in Indo-China, was unwilling to let us go.

Recruiting officers appeared on the scene, extolling the charms of the mysterious East; but, for all its promise of adventure, not many of us were tempted by the idea of a colonial war, in which the word *patriotism* took on a more equivocal note. It was only later, after the occupation of the defeated countries, that a few of us who had achieved more or less exalted rank chose a military career and went off to fight in Indo-China. Some of these were never to return, among them my childhood friend J. C. Laurenceau and Captain Stéphane himself.

It soon became obvious that we were not going to be demobilised for months, and that before long our battalion was likely to be posted to Austria. During a war there may be some largeness of purpose and nobility about an army, but in peacetime it easily sinks into stupidity and meanness. This is such a truism that garrison life has always been an easy subject for slapstick humour. Stéphane was perfectly well aware of all this. A great leader of men in war, he took the trouble to remain so in quieter times when the world was slowly sorting itself out, by keeping us busy in the least futile ways available:

singing, sport and climbing. Thus I found myself doing many of the classic Dauphine routes that June, despite the snow which still lay thickly on the summits. While other units grew rotten with boredom and debauchery, our company, thanks to its leader, continued to lead a full life made all the better by our warm camaraderie.

The shrewd and humane Stéphane had also taken note of the fact that many of us were wasting time in the forces which could be put to better use elsewhere, and he went out of his way to get the older ones demobilised first. Thus Laurent Cretton, a true patriot who, although he was over thirty years and had three children, had always volunteered for missions, was able to get back to his family and his work; and Michel Chevalier returned to the direction of his family business. As I was only twenty-four I had no hope of early demobilisation, but Stéphane, against his own wish to keep me for the mountain training of his company, got me posted as an instructor at the École Militaire de Haute Montagne, which was being formed again at Chamonix. In this way, he had worked it out, I would be able to satisfy my passion for the mountains while also being united with my wife, the real victim of this military interlude.

The E.H.M. was, and so far as I know still is, designed to teach the elements of mountaineering to officers and N.C.O.s of the Alpine units, and also to produce experienced mountain instructors for the Scout Sections. For rather less obvious reasons it also takes a modicum of students from various other branches of the services, even the navy and the air force. In 1945 the school had two types of instructor, civilian and military. Apart from the pay and the uniform there was nothing to distinguish one from the other. I am very ready to admit that the commanding officer did his best to spare us the multifarious vexations of garrison life, and that apart from our work we enjoyed almost complete freedom; but our position was scandalously unfair.

Even allowing for the 'hostilities only' volunteers who were forced to continue serving under the colours, the army was short of qualified instructors. It had therefore engaged, at a substantial salary, a number of professional civilian guides. Many of these were middle-aged men whose course in not volunteering for the last phase of the war was perfectly understandable; but others were youngsters who, perhaps rightly, had preferred to remain civilians rather than risk losing money and possibly their lives for the honour of France. Thus, by a distressing paradox, the army punished those who had served it faithfully by refusing them their freedom, while rewarding with comfortable salaries those who had refused to put themselves at its disposal. Sometimes truth really is stranger than fiction!

| 4 |

I Meet Lachenal

THAT SUMMER OF 1945 MARKED a turning point in my fortunes. Mountaineering, which had hitherto been my guiding passion as I sought for a way in the world, now became my whole life—job, passion and torment all in one.

The weather always seemed to be good. My fellow instructors and I would take groups of students over the summits every day during the week. Without being in the top class some of these climbs were quite long and difficult, and after four or five of them in succession I could justly have looked forward to some rest at the weekend. But not a bit of it: far from quenching my thirst for action these ascents inflamed it, and I longed for contests of more uncertain outcome. As soon as work was over I would be back off up the mountain with the first companion I could find, often without even going home first. By dawn on Sunday, as the sun came up through the blue haze of the distance and reddened the granite spires far above the world of men, we would already have been fighting upwards for hours in our pursuit of grandeur and beauty.

I collected climbs at fantastic speed, often managing five or six in succession. Sometimes, if we got back to the refuge before midday, I would even try to persuade a friend to make a good day of it by setting out at once for another mountain. Nothing else counted for me anymore: I was devoured by a frenzied passion. Living in the courts of the sky I forgot I was of the earth. My eyes seemed immense in a face emaciated by under-nourishment on army fare. My wife was tired of being neglected, and was threatening to leave me. But nothing had any effect, neither fatigue nor the troubles of the heart. When the summits shone in the sun their appeal was stronger than reason.

In those days nearly all the E.H.M. officers were climbers, and some of the courses were commanded by Édouard Frendo, one of the best mountaineers in the country. With one exception, they all showed the greatest sympathy with the position of the retained volunteers, so manifestly unjust by comparison with that of the salaried instructors. Apart from the matter of pay I lived virtually as a civilian. Nobody made any demands on me beyond the actual instructing, to which I gave myself enthusiastically. Life would have been marvellous but for a certain petty-minded captain, who, not content with lecturing us from one day's end to another, took it upon himself to teach me a bit more respect for military discipline. Perhaps he was jealous of my success in mountaineering, for he himself was unskilful and timorous. Whatever the cause, he began by pulling me up over tiny details. The first time he got me because I wasn't wearing any decorations or badges of rank, and as a result I lost my weekend's leave. Next he caught me twenty feet from the barracks without a hat on. This, it appeared, was a grave crime, difficult to overestimate, and I was informed that henceforth I was not to go climbing on Sundays without asking permission. Luckily the commandant always gave it.

The day finally came when my enemy triumphed. I had been in bed with a high temperature all week, but by the time Friday arrived I was full of renewed energy. The sky was blue as in a dream, the voice of the mountains was calling me from the heights. I could hold out no longer. I wandered into the town, still staggering slightly, to see if I could find a companion. Down in the Place de la Poste with its grey, shapeless buildings, a bedizened crowd, typical of Chamonix in the summer season, was coming and going. Pushing between the fat middle-aged women in shorts and the office managers in paper hats, I bumped by chance into a well-known Parisian climber called Dr Jacques Oudot. Oudot was later to be one of my companions on the Annapurna expedition, where his courage and conscientiousness were exemplary, but at that time I hardly knew him though he was already a famous surgeon. Short, thick-set, sallow, ugly and almost bald, he looked more of a city dweller sickly from the foul atmosphere of the laboratories than a noted rock climber. Only as one came closer did one sense the extraordinary energy in his small, deep-set eyes. In fact he was one of the most persevering mountaineers I have ever known, capable of amazing feats out of all proportion to his physique.

I liked him at once, and without more ado asked him if he would come with me to try the north face of the Dru. In spite of its great reputation he accepted immediately. At that time it had only been climbed on four occasions, all of which had included a bivouac, and its crux, the Fissure Allain, was supposed to be one of the most difficult pitches in the Alps. Reckoning therefore on a night out at the level of the small hanging glacier known as 'the Niche', about halfway up the face, we caught the first train up to Montenvers. Morning found us tramping slowly up through steep slopes of alpine rhododendrons under a pitiless sun. The air was full of the enfeebling softness of the south wind, and we halted frequently. Oudot was as happy as a sandboy, and seemed ten years younger. Whenever he smiled his rather awkward, even brutal features were illuminated with an astonishing sweetness.

Despite the punishing heat and the lingering vestiges of the strange illness that had put me out of action for several days, we got on to the climb early in the afternoon. As we made our way slowly up its strenuous cracks, salvoes of boulders shot over our heads to disappear a thousand feet below. It had been a dry summer, and on a warm evening like this nothing could have been more natural than a bit of stone fall. Just after climbing the 'Fissure Lambert', we came to an overhang which seemed to me rather too hard to do with a heavy sack on my back. I climbed down and handed it over to Jacques, thinking that I could always give him a pull from above if necessary. I then went at the overhang again, but some holds I had failed to notice before made it much easier than expected. I was just going to pull over into a smooth but easy-angled couloir when I looked up and saw a gigantic block, perhaps a hundred feet across, slowly beginning to slip from its place in the niche and roll straight towards me. I hurriedly slid back and ducked under the overhang, fully expecting it to collapse under the enormous weight of rock. There was a terrible rumbling crash as the block bounced, missing me by about three feet, then took off in one bound, thirty feet out from the face, and thundered into the moraine like a bomb. A cloud of dust rose into the air. Five mountaineers who were about to install a bivouac nearby told me later that the block made a crater in the ice six feet deep. Paralysed with fear, we stayed where we were until the evening chill should have frozen the mountain into inactivity. Only with the infinite silence of the stars did we start to move again.

Unfortunately the heat of the day had turned the gully below the niche into a waterfall, and the darkness made it impossible to climb the more deli-cate slabs on either side. Thus we had to climb in the very bed of the torrent and arrived at our bivouac place soaked to the skin. The wind had veered round to the north and was blowing hard and chill. There was no shelter on the face, and the cold went through us like a knife. At that time we did not yet have the bivouac equipment which nowadays enables climbers to sit out the coldest nights almost in comfort. Apart from the clothes I stood up in, I had only a quilted jacket so worn that it was little more use than a sweater, and an old waterproof cape all stuck together with tape. I had nothing at all to cover my legs, and my damp breeches were soon frozen.

The night was hard to bear. The sun does not get round onto north faces until late in the day, so there could be no question of waiting for it. It took us some time to thaw out our stiffened muscles and start climbing again. The rock was icy, but a few strenuous pitches soon warmed us, and we were already at grips with the famous Allain crack when seven other climbers caught us up. By a curious trick of fate there were more men on the face that day than there had been since time began. To judge from their accent the first five were from Nice, and I reckoned that they must be part of a well-known group who had been knocking off all the best climbs in the Dauphiné during the last few years. The other two were Chamonix guides, Félix Martinetti and Gilbert Ravanel, noted for their sporting spirit and disinterested love of the mountains. The whole lot of them had set out at dawn, shod in light espadrilles* and carrying no bivouac equipment, climbing at a rate that a little friendly competition had done nothing to diminish. Our presence in the crack was now holding them up, and all the more so because we were having a tough time with it. Tired of waiting, Martinetti went off along a ledge to have a view of the crags of the west face, which in those days were still unclimbed. When he got to the end of the ledge he suddenly noticed another crack which looked feasible. A few strenuous pulls, two pitons, and he stood on a ledge sixty feet above us, having discovered the real line of least resistance. His route has been taken by almost everybody since. He now leant out and yodelled down to encourage us, but we were still fighting it out in our crack, one of the rucksacks having jammed just to help matters. All seven of the others now got ahead of us, but later on we were able to catch them up again and we went down to the Charpoua refuge together.

While we were doing this I had my second narrow escape from death in twenty-four hours. I had gone first, down an almost vertical gully, and Jean Franco was about to join me on a small ledge when we heard the sound of stones above our heads. Large boulders were coming straight at us, ricocheting from one wall of the gully to the other in fantastic bounds. One of them, weighing at least twenty pounds, hit the ledge and exploded right between us. Night had fallen by the time we reached the Charpoua hut. The strenuous climbing and icy bivouac had been an odd sort of convalescence for the

---

* *Translator's note.* In this context espadrilles, *Kletterschühe*, or *scarpetti*, are light suede boots with moulded rubber soles, designed for rock climbing only. They are usually called 'klets' by English climbers, 'espas' by the French.

short but sharp illness which had laid me out earlier in the week, and I felt quite abnormally tired; but by nine o'clock the following morning I had to be instructing on the Gaillans, a small crag on the outskirts of Chamonix.

No sooner had we merrily downed the few crumbs which remained in the depths of our sacks than I set the alarm for six o'clock, stretched out on a bunk, and fell into a dreamless sleep. When I woke up it was already eight o'clock. I was extremely vexed. The world would of course continue to go round and nobody would eat me alive if I didn't get to the Gaillans on time, but my sense of duty revolted at the idea. There was now no hope of getting there by nine, but by running like a madman I might just make it by half past, before the lessons had properly begun. I grabbed my sack and set off downhill without wasting a moment. Rushing at breakneck speed down the slabs below the hut, I tore along the moraines like a chamois and was on the glacier in twenty minutes. Running as if my life depended on it I reached Montenvers in another half hour. A further twenty-five minutes of wild descent brought me to Chamonix, my feet raw and my clothes soaked in sweat, whence the Gaillans was only a short ride on my moped.

The first roped parties were only just beginning to move up to the rocks, and if I had been properly washed and shaved my arrival would have passed unnoticed. Unfortunately my chin was black with a three-day stubble and half the seat was out of my breeches: I must admit that I was not exactly a picture of the well-turned-out soldier. At this point I was spotted by our busybody captain, who flew into a frenzy of rage. Purple in the face, his eyes standing out on stalks, his long nose planted in my face like a pistol, he kept me standing at attention for more than ten minutes while he read me a lesson which would have sounded ridiculous enough if I had been his adopted child, let alone a sergeant of twenty-four who had been mentioned in dispatches. Fury and contempt glittered in my eyes as I held on to my trouser seams to stop myself from hitting him, but I held out. Finally the gold-braided moron sent me about my business, and with a smart about-turn I showed him my bare arse. He was so thick-skulled he didn't even get the point.

I spent the entire morning shepherding beginners up and down the rocks, tortured by thirst under a torrid sun. Lunchtime finally came, and I was just getting ready to descend when a new bunch of pupils rolled up. When I asked them what they thought they were doing, they informed me in no uncertain terms that the captain had ordered them to go and climb with me throughout the lunch hour. Really, the only thing that gives any idea of the infinite is the stupidity of some men.

During the summer of 1945 I did my first climbs with the future companion of my greatest alpine ascents, Louis Lachenal. We had met early the preceding spring, while I was changing trains at Annecy. I was wandering around the streets to fill in the time when a poorly dressed young man, pushing a bicycle with one hand and holding a can of milk in the other, came up and stared at me.

'Aren't you Lionel Terray?' he asked.

I had no recollection of this pale, thin face in which two very keen eyes were twinkling. The youth's rather pitiful condition made me wonder if he was out of work, and after replying in the affirmative I asked him his name. He said he was called Lachenal, and suddenly I remembered that we had been introduced in the street at Chamonix some three years before, when his J.M. uniform and big beret had made him a rather more dashing figure. I also remembered hearing a great deal about him from my friend Condevaux, with whom he had climbed. It seemed that he was an exceptionally gifted climber and had graduated first from the Leaders' Course in 1942, but that he had subsequently escaped to Switzerland to avoid compulsory labour service in Germany.

I invited him to join me for a beer in a little bistro close to the station. He turned out to be talkative, quick-witted and inquisitive, his repartee frequently tinged with irony. My train did not leave until quite a lot later, and we had plenty of time to talk. I extolled the thrilling life we were leading on the Alpine Front, but he vehemently proclaimed his horror of war and of the army in a voice coloured with a slight Vaudois accent, using a mixture of Savoyard patois and Lausanne slang. Apparently he was without a job and was living on a small legacy while looking around, but he seemed to take little account of his obviously trying material circumstances. 'Everything will come out all right in the end', he said, 'and in the meantime I've got time to go climbing. I've a friend with a jalopy and some dough, and we'll go off and do a climb at Chamonix every Sunday. If we could do the Aiguilles du Diable, that would really be something!'

The thing that embarrassed him most was lack of equipment. He had an old pair of nailed boots which he had repaired himself.

'You see, I've a buddy who's a cobbler. I just watched what he did, and now I can do it as well as he can.'

But the real problem was espadrilles: he only had one.

'Can't you find this guy a sister?' he asked with a joyous laugh, rummaging round in a bag of provisions and producing an ancient tennis shoe all patched with bits of leather. To tell the truth I was not violently impressed with Lachenal on this first meeting. I liked his uncomplicated passion for the mountains, but his way of talking and his anti-militarism rather irritated me.

The E.H.M. was installed in a hotel above Argentière, right up at the end of the valley. Our own home was in Chamonix itself, so that whenever I wasn't away in the mountains I would make this journey of six or seven miles a couple of times a day on my worn-out old moped. As I was going through Argentière one day I saw Lachenal among a group of climbers, and drew up to say hallo. He told me he had got a job as an instructor at the Union Nationale des Centres de Montagne, a large new organisation aimed at encouraging the public to ski and climb. They had just installed a camp at the village, and after that we began to meet frequently.

Each time I passed that way I paid a visit to the old farm where Lachenal had rented a room. He was living there with his wife Adèle, a jovial Lausannoise of distinguished family who had married for love outside her own circle, and their little boy Jean-Claude, a magnificently vital and exceptionally noisy child. I soon discovered that Lachenal hid remarkable qualities behind his mocking exterior, and we became firm friends. One Friday I told him I was off next day to do the north face of the Aiguille Verte with J.-P. Payot, and to try the second ascent of the east face of the Aiguille du Moine on the Sunday. His eyes lit up at once with his own inimitable enthusiasm, and he exclaimed:

'What a programme! Would you mind if Lenoir and I followed you? We've got the weekend free too, and I think we ought to be able to manage it.' Lenoir was also an instructor at the U.N.C.M. I had climbed with him some years previously, and now gladly agreed to a party of four.

Watching Lachenal go up the steep Couturier Couloir in unfavourable conditions, and still more on the descent of the Whymper Couloir where a thin layer of soft snow covered the bare ice, I began to admire his extraordinary ease of movement. Whether on ice or on snowed-up, loose rocks, he already gave proof of that disconcerting facility, that feline elegance which was to make him the greatest mountaineer of his generation. The following day Lenoir and Payot both had a touch of snow blindness: the former because he had dropped his snow goggles on the climb, the latter because he had broken one of the lenses. There could be no question of their coming with us to the Moine, and so, by a quirk of fate, I roped up with Lachenal for the first of many times. The east face of the Moine is now one of the classic grade-five climbs, but in 1945 it had not been repeated since its first ascent by the excellent climbers Aureille and Feutren, who had quite rightly called it severe.

I was not a very polished rock climber in those days. I tended to get up by main force, but what I lacked in style I made up in speed. I also belonged to the do-or-die brigade. In climbing terms this means that I stuck my neck out by not taking a lot of precautions. In particular I used very few pitons to hold me in case I fell off. That day I was on great form and climbed fast, but Lachenal seemed in no way put out by our pace and showed himself as brilliant on rock as on ice. Relaxed and supple as a cat, he climbed without any appearance of effort, and I could not help envying him. We got to the summit far earlier than we expected, and had a long rest. Lying there sunbathing, we had plenty of time to admire the magnificent peaks which encircled us. Opposite us the Grandes Jorasses rose like a gigantic fortress, out of all proportion to everything else. Our eyes were particularly drawn to the Walker Spur, whose smooth black walls rose four thousand feet in one titanic pillar against the sky. We knew that Rébuffat and Frendo were attacking it that very day. The crags still looked rather snowed-up, and we discussed their chances of success.

'Do you think they'll make it with all that snow around?'

'Snow or no snow, I don't think so. They're just not good enough. Cassin took three days in good conditions,* and he's in a different class altogether, one of the greatest climbers the Dolomites have ever known. Anyway, think of the time they took on their last attempt two years ago: a whole day for a quarter of the face, even though they took the Allain start. It would have been two days if they'd taken the Cassin start. At that rate it'll take them a week to finish, and they've had it if there's the smallest bit of bad weather.'

'Yes, I know, but all the same Cassin was a Dolomite climber pure and simple. He wasn't used to ice or even granite.'

'That's what you think. He'd done plenty of granite in the Bergell. What about the northeast face of the Badile? It may be a bit shorter than the Walker, but it's in the same class. As for snow and ice he'd done lots of winter ascents, and anyway there isn't much on the Walker when it's in good condition.'

'Well, all right, but Gaston must be darned good at artificial after all he's done in the Calanques.'

'He certainly is very good when it comes to banging in pegs, but he's no better than you when it comes to free climbing, and you'd hardly compare yourself with Cassin. Everyone says he's a superman. In the Dolomites they

---

* *Translator's note.* In fact the conditions were not good, and the party arrived on the summit in a storm. The northeast face of the Piz Badile, another Cassin climb, is today considered a good deal easier than the Walker. The second ascent of this was also done by Gaston Rébuffat, with Bernard Pierre.

do all sorts of things we'd think impossible. After all they can climb hard stuff for six months in the year. There's nothing but vertical faces down there, they climb grade six all day long. Just think how fit they must be. That sort of thing doesn't exist here. What do we do in the way of hard rock climbing? Twice nothing. Half the time we're on ice, and when we do get onto rock you've got to be a genius to find anything more than grade five. Look at today: we've put in about four pegs and haven't done a move harder than that. Do you call that sort of thing training for the Walker? No, believe me. Our icy old mountains may be twice as beautiful as the Dolomites, where it's as dry as I don't know what, but as far as rock climbing is concerned we're babes in arms compared with those boys.'

'You don't think they'll make it then?'

'One never knows. Gaston's a real trier, and if the weather holds out anything can happen. But in my view the Walker's a good three standards harder than anything else around here.'

'One never knows, as you say. All these stories about the Dolomite boys might just be a load of bull. Have you ever been to see for yourself?'

'No, and I don't reckon I ever will.'

'Not even if they get up?'

'Well, of course, that would put a different complexion on everything. But the great problem is to find someone to go with . . . would you be interested?'

'Are you kidding? The Walker's my dream. But do you think I'm up to it? I haven't done much yet.'

'You may not have done much, but I've been watching you these last two days. You're a natural; it's enough to make anybody jealous. Done. If they get up, we'll have a shot.'

And so, on this modest summit, we became a team that was to conquer the greatest faces in the Alps.

That September the army gave me leave to go on the five-week course for the National Professional Guide's Certificate, and I had no difficulty in qualifying. As often happens in the Alps, the weather was fine that autumn. Officially I was still in the army, but as the courses were over for the year I was almost completely free. I took advantage of these circumstances to climb as much as possible, in spite of the inevitable cold and snow due to the lateness of the season. Particularly I remember an ascent of the Mer de Glace face of the Grépon which new snow rendered so delicate that it took us over twelve hours, whereas in dry conditions I have done it in three and a half. It was dark when we got down, and there was plenty of bare ice on the steep slopes of the

Nantillons glacier. We had no torch and no crampons. My companion was at the end of his tether and kept falling off; several times only luck enabled me to hold him.

Finally the army decided to let me go. Immediately we came up against financial problems. We had been living for the last year on money realised by the sale of my livestock, and only the strictest economies had enabled us to spin it out so long. We had now come to the end of the reel. It was true that the E.H.M. had offered me a job as a civilian instructor, and this would certainly have been the easy way out: regular pay, easy work, plenty of skiing and climbing—not much future, if you like, but also no further material problems for several years, perhaps even for life. To live by skiing and climbing was, after all, my dream. It was really tempting—yet I turned it down without a moment's hesitation. To live in society at all means by implication a certain submission to the will of others, but my experiences in the J.M. and the army had taught me that in vast organisations this happens very much more often than elsewhere. Nothing inspired me less than the idea of being subject to men whose fitness to command was, to say the least of it, variable. As far as I was concerned independence was worth more than security, and I turned resolutely towards a future that was full of doubt.

When winter came I took up my old post as ski instructor at Les Houches. The end of the war had brought back plenty of clients, of which I got a generous share through being a better skier than most of the other instructors, but the fees were still too low and it was a poor living for all my hard work. I had had to return my farm at Les Houches to its owners and now lived in a poor flat in Chamonix. I was so hard up that I was unable to afford the ten francs to take the train from one village to the other—though of course ten francs was worth a good deal more in those days than it is now. Morning and evening I would do the five miles of icy road separating Chamonix from Les Houches on my moped. On days when the weather made this impossible I would catch the train. In order to avoid having to pay, especially on the return trip in the evening darkness, I would leap on the train as it rumbled by and then jump off into a snowbank when it slowed down at the other end.

The U.N.C.M., where Lachenal worked, had now moved to Les Bossons, a mile below Chamonix. I used to stop off each evening at the old hotel building it had taken over, spending hours discussing our summer projects in the little room where he and his family lived all heaped up on top of each other. We had definitely decided on the Walker, and much of our talk revolved around it. The success of Rébuffat and Frendo had reassured us as to the technical difficulty of the ascent. We now knew that it wasn't necessary to be a superman to get up it, but we were a good deal worried by the length of time taken. Three days and two bivouacs seemed terribly long to our way of thinking.

In the Alps, even when conditions are ideal, you can never be sure what the weather will do tomorrow, to say nothing of the day after. We were only too well aware that on a face of the height and difficulty of the Walker a storm was more to be feared than perhaps anywhere else in the range. If a party was overtaken by really bad weather high on the face there would be a strong likelihood of its not getting down alive.

Apart from the elegant Cassin route which goes direct to the highest of the mountain's several summits there is also another route on the north face,* but it is considerably easier and leads to a lower point on the ridge, the Pointe Michel Croz. During an attempt at the first ascent the German climbers Haringer and Peters were caught in a terrible storm. Haringer died in the course of the retreat, and Peters, the eventual conqueror, only got back to Chamonix, where he had long been given up for lost, after several days of desperate fighting for his life.

This example and that of many parties lost on the Eigerwand, the Walker's great rival, gave us a lot to think about. Naturally we were willing to take our chances, but we also wanted to keep the risks to the possible minimum. To cut a day off the length of time required seemed to us to halve the dangers, and we racked our brains for a method of doing so. We could count to some extent on the fact that we were both fast climbers, but sheer pace does not solve all the problems in mountaineering. Quite often a little craft will find a way where even the greatest virtuosity will fail.

From the very outset it was obvious to us that one of the biggest time-wasters was sack hauling: a party that could dispense with this would be able to cut its time by at least 20 percent. The problem was how to carry thirty pegs, adequate bivouac kit, and food and drink for three days, without making the sacks too heavy for climbing difficult rock. It seemed about as easy as squaring the circle to begin with, but after a while we began to see that careful planning could greatly reduce the weight to be carried. We weighed every single item, cutting out everything not absolutely vital, and to our surprise discovered that we had got the total load for the three days down to twenty-five pounds. Then we were able to knock off another five by deciding a priori that the climb would only take two days. Even on quite difficult rock

* *Translator's note.* There is now a third, climbed by Couzy and Desmaison, which leads to the Pointe Marguerite.

a second man can climb with a twenty-pound sack, because if necessary he can always be given a bit of help with the rope; but it is still a considerable burden. He might easily slow down under the strain. How could we lessen his load without running into danger? Whichever way we looked at it we could not get the total below twenty pounds if we were to have an adequate margin of food, clothing and equipment. There was only one solution. Climbing with a rucksack is a nuisance to the leader, but only if the sack is heavy. He would never notice a matter of five or six pounds which, however, would be a very real saving to the second, probably enough to enable him to climb normally.

To be so exercised over such simple problems may nowadays seem ridiculous, but one must remember the mental climate of the time. Both food and equipment were very much heavier than they are now, but above all we were weighed down by traditions as old as mountaineering itself. People always carried a little more food and gear than they really needed, 'just in case'. It was not unusual to take twenty-odd pounds on a classic route, and forty or more would have been normal enough for something like the Walker. No wonder sack haulage had become a matter of course at every difficult pitch.

Nor were the loads our only preoccupation. As I remarked earlier, people used to climb in nailed boots as clumsy as canal barges, carrying gym shoes with them to change into for the harder rock climbing. Quite apart from their weight, all this changing to and fro would have lost us a lot of time on the Walker, where the pitches of rock and ice alternate. We knew that even before the war the Italians had evolved climbing soles of hard moulded rubber to replace the traditional clinker and tricouni nails, and that these could be used on all types of going. We had also read that when these 'Vibrams' were fitted to light, carefully designed footwear, the most severe pitches could be done in them. But prewar prosperity had not yet returned to either Italy or France, and articles of secondary importance like this had to wait their turn to be manufactured. In any case neither of us was rich enough to cross the Alps in search of new boots.

A year or so before this, it had become fashionable in French mountaineering circles to screw bits of tyre to one's boot soles as a substitute for the unobtainable Vibrams. Although they were rather slippery on ice, these improvisations gave worthwhile results. I had tried them out myself, placed under loose-fitting clodhoppers, but I did not find them as good as my gym shoes. I had formed the impression, however, that the awkwardness came much more from the large volume of the upper than from the sole. The conviction grew on me that, placed under a light, closely fitting boot, they could be worn with satisfaction alike on snow, ice or difficult rock.

No satisfactory form of footwear could be found on the market. The existing models were all too roomy, too floppy or too fragile. At this precise moment Lachenal's cobbling talents came to our rescue. Starting with my idea of something halfway between an espadrille and a mountaineering clod-hopper, he deftly produced with his own hands two pairs of boots which were to all practical purposes the same as what every mountaineer wears today. As soon as spring came we began to experiment with them. They were everything we had hoped—better even than gym shoes, because the greater rigidity of the soles enabled one to stand on smaller holds. Thanks to the perfecting of our equipment and our tactics, we began to nurse a secret hope of doing the Walker with only one bivouac.

Winter over, I found myself without a penny to my name. Once again I was faced with the problem of what to do. My great ambition was to be an independent professional guide in the traditional style, which, since the golden age of mountaineering,* has meant accompanying climbers and tourists on holiday into the mountains. Shortly after qualifying for my Guide's Certificate I had been admitted, by an act of favour then very rarely accorded to those not born in the valley, to the Compagnie des Guides de Chamonix. Thanks to this kindness of my autochthonous colleagues there was some hope of succeeding in a profession which is almost automatically closed to natives of the plains; but I could hardly have chosen a more uncertain way of life.

In order to understand the difficulties I faced, one most know something about the profession as it then was, and in particular about the Compagnie des Guides de Chamonix. Literature and the press have had a lot to say about them both, but very few people have any real knowledge of the subject.

Founded in 1823, the Compagnie des Guides de Chamonix was born of the local peasants' need for an association to assure fair conditions of hire in the traditional occupation of leading tourists in the mountains. They rightly thought that such an association would improve rates of pay, and also attract more climbers to them through their guarantees of competence and good character. There was no National Guide's Certificate until about twenty-five years ago, and in those days nobody was admitted to the rank of guide until he had proved his competence through several years of mountain portering. Later on a badge was issued under the control of the police. Persons found guilty of dishonesty or immorality were excluded, and drunkenness and slovenliness were severely punished, sometimes by expulsion. A tariff was established for every climb in order to avoid cutthroat competition; a benevolent

---

* *Translator's note.* This 'golden age' is generally taken to be the fifties and sixties of the nineteenth century, when most of the great Alpine first ascents were made.

fund was set up to aid the families of guides lost in the course of their work; and finally a bureau was opened to enable new clients to find their guides without having recourse to the all-too-interested advice of hotel porters. This bureau was also very useful to the guides themselves, if at any time they were short of a known client, inasmuch as it made a twice-daily distribution of engagements on a 'first come first served' basis.

Such an organisation, at once social and commercial, was in advance of its time, and shows a remarkable degree of initiative and community feeling on the part of this rather remote society. It was subsequently imitated in most of the high alpine valleys. The grouping of guides in a regulated association proved beneficent in every respect. The professionals were able to earn a better living, and so develop a sense of pride in their profession. It avoided febrile competition and all the vices to which it can give rise, in particular the sort of public prostitution which grew up in certain Swiss valleys where guides accosted potential clients in the street, just like tarts in Montmartre. I have no wish to imitate some popular literature in suggesting that it was a band of saints, but it did give its members an esprit de corps and a belief in the nobility of their work which led to high technical and moral standards. Thanks to the development of these qualities the guides of Chamonix have often shown devotion and even heroism in the rescue of injured climbers. The Compagnie has also helped in the construction of huts like the Charpoua, the improvement of pathways and the installation of fixed cables on popular climbs which would be dangerous without them.

This century-old institution has stood up well to the test of time, and has adapted itself to the changing face of mountaineering both from a commercial and from a technical point of view. Admittedly all this has not happened without argument, and sometimes the Compagnie has dropped a bit behind the times: like any other human institution it falls short of perfection. But broadly speaking it has never ceased to do a good job, procuring enormous advantages for its members and rendering important services to the cause of alpine climbing. Any attempt to earn a living as a guide in the Chamonix valley without belonging to this society is almost certainly doomed to failure. A good many outsiders who, like myself, had become guides out of sheer enthusiasm have made the attempt. To the best of my knowledge only two have succeeded, and in any case they were admitted to the family circle after a time.

One of the society's oldest traditions used to be never to admit anyone not actually born in the valley, and up to the last war only two exceptions had ever been made to this rule. However, since 1945 the number of locals wishing to become guides has considerably diminished, and the habit has grown up of accepting young men of suitable quality provided they have connections with the valley such as, for example, having married into a local family, or having owned property in the area for a number of years. In this way some twenty or so 'foreigners' have become Chamonix guides since the war. I was one of the first, and I have no doubt at all that it was solely due to this privilege that I had any hope of earning a living as a professional in 1946 without being forced into the employ of the army, the U.N.C.M., or some such organisation.

My various first ascents and repetitions of famous climbs had made my name known among the climbing cognoscenti, but I was still unknown to the public at large. I had done plenty of big climbs as an amateur, and my experience as an instructor in several organisations had in fact given me a solid professional experience, but for all this I would never have succeeded in finding enough clients to earn a living without the 'first come first served' system of the Bureau des Guides. Even with the system an independent guide's life is uncertain and hard. Very often it is in fact only a supplementary, seasonal job to a man who, at other times of the year, may be a labourer or a peasant. Even when rounded off with ski teaching it is not the sort of occupation on which a man grows fat, and this was still truer in 1946 than it is today. Finally it is subject to all the whims of fate. To say nothing of serious accidents, it only needs a long stretch of bad weather or a sprained ankle to bring you to the verge of starvation.

To embrace such a career of one's own free will, unimpelled by any sort of family tradition, calls for a love of the mountains and of independence amounting almost to foolhardiness. Nevertheless I was about to take this hazardous step when René Beckert, Director of the École Nationale de Ski et d'Alpinisme, offered me a job in his establishment.

This school, which has since gone on from strength to strength, is chiefly intended by the state for the training of mountain guides and skiing instructors. It also aims to promote mountain sports in a number of ancillary ways such as giving courses to amateurs of a certain standard, holding conferences, publishing manuals, making films, and so on. The instructors at the school are recruited from among the best skiers and guides, and their work, without being invariably very difficult, does demand a constant output of energy and initiative. To anyone who believes in its aims and objects it offers a fascinating way of life.

At that time E.N.S.A. was still young, and had not yet had time to settle into rigid moulds. The courses were intensive, and whenever the weather permitted the climbing would go on day after day. Between courses, by contrast, the instructors had several days of complete liberty, which they could use either to climb for their own pleasure or to round out their incomes by guiding personal clients. Beckert's proposition was therefore extremely tempting, not only because it flattered the vanity from which I am no more exempt than anybody else but also because it offered a steady and interesting living while still leaving me the time for the routes of which I dreamed, notably the Walker. The concluding argument was that the chief instructor was none other than my friend André Tournier, whose qualities I had grown to respect so much in the J.M. With such a boss there would be no question of unreasonable treatment or incompetence. In the end I was overwhelmed by so many advantages and signed my name on the line. All my problems evaporated and life became one long enchantment.

Lachenal had also found an interesting position as an instructor in another state organisation, the Collège National de Ski et d'Alpinisme, more commonly known as the Collège des Praz from the name of the village near Chamonix where it was based. This institution had similar ends to the E.N.S.A., with which it was later amalgamated, but the instructors it trained were intended for the U.N.C.M. and other such bodies for the propagation of mountain sports which were formed after the war. The courses were longer than at the E.N.S.A., and the general education side was particularly stressed. Its chief was a man remarkable for his intelligence, energy, organising ability and climbing prowess. This was Jean Franco, the leader of the group of climbers from Nice who had overtaken me on the north face of the Dru. Subsequently he was to play an important part in the history of French mountaineering by a brilliant series of ascents in the Alps, and also by his leadership of the successful expedition to the twenty-seven-thousand-foot Makalu in 1955. The fine team of instructors he had chosen and his own strong personality got his Collège off to a flying start. It soon exceeded the somewhat restricted role for which it was originally destined, becoming a sort of postgraduate department of mountaineering which shed lustre on the years following the war.

At the Collège, Lachenal found ideal conditions for his development both as a climber and as a man. He made rapid progress, and his altogether exceptional class began literally to shine forth. Working in different establishments did not hinder our preparations for the Walker. During the week our professional climbing built up our fitness and stamina to a high level, and every Sunday we would set out hoping to do something really big and difficult. Unfortunately the weather was always against us, and invariably we would end up on some relatively minor route, or beating a retreat in a blizzard. July came, and we had still done nothing of note. It is difficult to drive two cars at the same time, to work as a guide and still climb as an amateur. That season of

1946 really brought the fact home to us, and we realised how much easier the accomplishment of a big ascent was to a party of amateurs who had nothing to do but wait for favourable conditions than to a pair of guides climbing constantly in different parts of the range. The problem was further complicated for us by working in different establishments, because our free days did not always coincide, and, when they did, the weather was wrong.

We made four more attempts to do a serious training climb, but were rained off on each occasion. August came and we had still had no practice in really difficult climbing, though our many classic routes had made us very fit. The Walker was out of condition, and as the bad weather seemed interminable we began to talk about other things. Suddenly, however, a warm wind sprang up and completely changed the picture. On the third of August four of the best Parisian climbers, with Pierre Allain as their moving spirit, went up to the Leschaux hut; but we were so depressed and tired from overmuch work that we did not even think of following them. Since we weren't in a fit psychological state to tackle the Walker, we decided that the north spur of Les Droites might be suitable. It was as long as the Walker and had only been done three times. Nobody had yet succeeded in climbing it in one day. Thanks to favourable conditions and our general fitness we reached the top only eight hours after the attack, and from there we were so transported by joy that we reached the Couvercle refuge in an hour.

However, even our brilliant success on the Droites did not cheer us up for long. We had lost faith, and decided to spend our few spare days earning a bit of extra money. But the account of the climb which the Parisians gave me on their return from their great exploit rather modified my ideas. I acquired the conviction that it might be possible to bivouac only a short way below the summit, and perhaps not at all. These prospects revived my flagging enthusiasm, and my wife's exhortations did the rest. She had such confidence in my climbing abilities that she fully expected us to walk up it. Far from trying to hold me back, therefore, as she was occasionally to do in later years, she almost nagged us to go!

I had a week's holiday ahead of me, so I telephoned Lachenal up at Montenvers. Unfortunately he could not get away until the Thursday lunchtime. Meanwhile I got everything carefully packed up in the way we had agreed, five or six pounds for the leader, fifteen or so for the second. But on Thursday I found an exhausted Lachenal. One certainly could not blame him: he had done the Charmoz-Grépon traverse that morning, and the Blaitière-Ciseaux-Fou the day before. For all my impatience he had to be allowed a day of rest, and as things turned out this was very nearly fatal. The weather that afternoon gave us something to worry about, but the sky was clear again by the following morning, Friday. The plod up to the Leschaux was carried out in an atmosphere of sunlight, confidence and noisy joking. We halted frequently to admire the face, which seemed more beautiful than ever in the limpid air. At long last we were about to make our dream come true and launch out on the great adventure, so religiously prepared for, so ardently desired. The wild, proud crags which had haunted us so long, defying us wherever we stood in the range, were about to become ours. It was good to be alive that morning with luck on our side and the mountains shining in the sun.

Later in the day the weather took a turn for the worse, but this had become so usual in the last few days that we went to bed in a state of modified optimism. For the first time in my life I slept badly before a climb. I was not afraid in the strict sense of the word; rather I felt in suspense like a gambler who has risked his whole fortune. I did not pass the night working things out, or thinking of the joys or the dangers that awaited us, but simply lay there watching the hours go by and wondering which way the dice would fall.

At one o'clock the auguries were bad: the sky was as black as ink. However, we had seen the wind change at the approach of dawn often enough not to give up all hope. By half past two there was no sign of a change, and we voiced our impatience in blasphemous fashion. We were finished with climbing as amateurs, and in the meantime we were going back to bed! We did nothing of the sort, however. It seemed impossible that so much meticulous planning, so many sacrifices, dreams and desires should come to nothing in this way. At a quarter past three our luck turned: the air was still heavy, but stars twinkled here and there in the sky. We set off at once, moving fast with no other thought but to make up lost time. When we reached the foot of the face it was already light, and the weather was not altogether reassuring. On our own side of the range the sky was still marvellously blue, but it was not as cold as it should have been for the time of day, and large, ominous-looking clouds were wreathing around our mountain. What should we do? Give up? But if the weather then held out we would be bitterly disappointed. Next week we had to start work again, and any hope of the Walker would be finished for this year, perhaps even for ever, since one could not know what the future might hold. Go on, then? But if the weather broke we would be caught in the storm, an act of rashness that could cost us dear on the Walker. In the end we decided to compromise by climbing as far as the famous 'Pendulum' pitch and waiting there, if necessary until the next day, for the weather to make up its mind.

I crossed the *rimaye* at exactly ten past five, three-quarters of an hour later than we had originally intended. Moving quickly on easy ground, we reached the foot of the 'Hundred Foot Corner' much sooner than we had expected. I was far from brilliant on this vertical wall with its few, awkwardly arranged holds. Lack of suitable training caused me to get cramps in the arms and calves, so that I had to spend a long time at each piton, resting. When I finally got up after an hour and a half of laborious progress I was completely demoralised and suggested retreat, adding that we had neither the class nor the training for a climb of this sort. The more optimistic Lachenal reasoned with me that I always took a long time to warm up, that we had now done the hardest pitch anyway and that this particular type of climbing on steep, open walls had never suited me. In the end he persuaded me to push on a bit farther.

The ground now became easier again, and despite a slight mistake in routefinding we soon came to the foot of the notorious 'Three Hundred Foot Corner', which looked almost friendly. It is a tall, right-angled groove, mostly less than vertical, and a thin crack running from bottom to top gives promise of certain progress. The first pitch confirmed my favourable impression. I reached the stance in a few minutes of delightful climbing, and Lachenal came up at once. This was much more my style of thing, and I tackled the second pitch with confidence. About halfway up it a small overhang forced me to hammer in a peg and use an étrier, but by now I was warmed up and it didn't take long. We fairly raced up the final third of the corner, which is its best and most sustained part, and found that we had done the whole thing in one hour. Entranced with the beauty of the ascent and the pleasure of our own success, we began to go at such a rate that we reached the 'Pendulum' by eleven o'clock.

I remember that as I installed the rope for the rappel I remarked to Lachenal that the weather, which hadn't changed much, would probably hold out for the day, but that it wouldn't do to count on it for tomorrow; and that we therefore ought to aim to reach Frendo and Rébuffat's second bivouac site that evening. Guy Poulet had told us that from there it should be possible to finish out even in the event of bad weather. Lachenal, always the optimist, replied that at the rate we were going the climb was in the bag, and that we were now so far ahead of our most sanguine time estimates that he had every hope of sleeping in the hut that evening!

We made a mess of the Pendulum. The ropes got so snarled up that it took us over half an hour to disentangle them. This operation, which was punctuated by words disapproved of by the clergy and by polite society, was conducted in a place so ill-adapted to the outward and visible signs of bad temper that we had to anchor ourselves to a piton. Finally, three-quarters of an hour later, nothing remained but to pull down the rope which still linked us to the world of men. Once this had been done retreat would be a grave and perhaps even an insoluble problem. There was still time to choose between sterile prudence and the daring which must lead either to success or disaster. My own choice was made, but, seized by a sudden scruple, I turned towards my companion and said significantly:

'Are you quite clear in your own mind?'

Despite his affirmative reply I hesitated a moment. Then, putting aside every softening thought, I burnt our bridges.

By noon we had reached the first Frendo-Rébuffat bivouac site, from which we could see no way forward. Neither of us was of an easily frightened disposition, but this was really a bit too much. There was nothing but an unbroken wall and, far above it, the sky. Some feet above us a piton, with a carabiner hanging from it, seemed to mark the limit of possibility. With a great deal of difficulty I climbed up to it, but at this point I found myself in an impasse. An attempt to traverse left came to nothing. Finally, by going right to the limit, I managed to get over the overhang above me, and mantelshelfed onto a narrow, outward-sloping ledge where another peg could be inserted. As far as I could judge I didn't seem to be any better off for my pains, because I still couldn't see any way on from there. As I scrutinised the gently overhanging wall above, however, I began to wonder if one couldn't, by sticking one's neck out a little, get up it after all. Allain had mentioned a difficult overhang somewhere about here—this must be it. I consequently brought Lachenal up to the peg and then launched out without hesitation, my body hanging back in space over the enormous drop. There was absolutely no feeling of fear, only a wonderful sensation of being freed from the laws of gravity. Completely relaxed, I pulled up on the tiniest holds with ease and confidence, and the emotional aspect of my situation did not occur to me. I simply thought: 'If I fell off here the rope would break, and I would fall over a thousand feet clear to the deck.' Somehow this did not seem to apply to me, but to some external object which did not concern me. It was as though I was no longer the same earthbound man who only surmounted his fear and fatigue by a constant effort of will, because I no longer felt either. My personality had dropped away, I was borne upward by the winds, I was invincible, nothing could stop me. I had in fact attained that state of rapture, that liberation from things material, sought by the skier on the snow, the aviator in the sky, the diver out on his high board. After fifty feet of this divine madness I stopped and put in a piton. Immediately it occurred to me that even an angel can't climb where there are no holds, such as now seemed to be the case . . . but no, over on the left, I spotted some tiny excrescences which would enable me to do a tension traverse worthy of Dülfer himself.* No sooner said than done. I gave a few quick directions to Lachenal, who was watching me from below my feet in a worried sort of way. Then, held against the rock only by the tension of the rope as it was slowly paid out, defying all the laws of balance, I traversed across the wall on minute flakes. Eventually I came to a jughandle.** Turning a small corner I came as if by a miracle to a platform about the size of a chair, with a piton just a few feet above it, into which I clipped the ropes. It was now up to Lachenal. He climbed quickly up to the traverse, hesitated a moment, then executed a daring pendulum across to my stance. Feeling more committed than ever, we had a look round at the sky. The northern side of the range was still clear, but the clouds which hooded our own mountain had grown and were now coming down lower. There was no time to be lost.

We continued along the system of slanting slabs, interrupted every so often by walls, which spiral up from left to right and make it possible to out-flank the otherwise unclimbable obstacle of the 'Grey Tower', a well-known feature of the climb. No more splendid climbing could be imagined. The rock is firm, the difficulty is sustained at a high level without ever becoming extreme. I was climbing as never before, quickly, unhesitatingly, without making any mistakes. My fingers seemed to divine the holds, and our progress was almost more like a well-drilled ballet than a difficult piece of mountaineering. At three o'clock we arrived at the Allain bivouac. Its six-foot width seemed like a boulevard by comparison with the rare and narrow ledges we had encountered hitherto.

We decided to make the most of this unwanted comfort by having a bite to eat and a council of war. A comparison of our time with that of the Parisian party showed that we ought logically to be able to get very high before dark, perhaps even to the summit. We had five hours of daylight ahead of us, and Allain, moving considerably more slowly than ourselves, had covered two-thirds of the distance to the top in that time. Unfortunately we were now

---

* *Translator's note.* A tension traverse (also called a Tyrolean traverse or horizontal rappel) is used to cross a blank wall between two lines of possibility. By leaning out on the tension of the rope paid out through a piton, the climber is able to pull himself across on holds which would be inadequate if he had to support his whole weight on them. Dülfer was a famous German climber who developed the technique before 1914. Gaps can also be crossed by swinging across on a rope fixed above and to one side. This is what is meant by 'a pendulum' in climbing.

** *Translator's note.* A 'jughandle', or just a 'jug', is a climbing term for the sort of ideal hold that the hand will go round completely. They are also called 'Thank God' holds if they come at the end of a difficult bit.

in thick cloud, which reduced the visibility to a few yards, and just to cap everything it began to hail. It now came home to us what a trap we had put our heads into. What was the best course? To go down? To retreat down those vast slabs up which we had climbed diagonally seemed almost impossible, and even if we managed that, how were we to get back up the Pendulum? There was nothing for it but to go on. We should get to the Frendo-Rébuffat bivouac before the weather got really bad, and once there we would win our way through sooner or later.

Our only guide was a sketch which Guy Poulet had given me. This showed a slight detour to the right, with the words 'shattered slabs'. So far as one could make out through the murk this description seemed to fit the slabs now on our right, and not for one moment did I think of climbing the overhang above our heads. Two delicate pitches brought us to a series of cracks cutting up through some vast dark-coloured slabs. Not so easy, these cracks, not easy at all; despite my excellent form they gave me a lot of trouble. As we made our way painfully upwards we kept looking for a way back to the left, but the lie of the land constantly forced us in the other direction. It was becoming rather worrying, especially as our sketch made no mention of such difficulties. A few pitches farther on we came up against a completely hold-less stretch of rock. The way ahead was blocked, and our position began to feel serious. The only thing was to go back down—but would we find the way? And what a waste of time it would be. Suddenly, through a gap in the clouds, I saw a way out of the impasse. On our right was a fairly easy-looking couloir. If we climbed some way up this we would be able to traverse back onto our buttress higher up, where some snow bands crossed the face. We placed the ropes for a rappel and swung across into the gully, which however turned out to be much less easy than it had looked. The angle was about sixty degrees, and the rock, some kind of schist with small, friable, outward-sloping holds, offered little or no opportunity to put in pitons. In spite of all that we had to get up, and get up quickly. Any idea of protection was illusory as we began our dangerous balancing act up the gully, and rapidly though we advanced, the night came down more rapidly still.

What with the dusk and the cloud, we were soon unable to see more than about six feet. Were we going to be caught out by darkness in this couloir, with the prospect of spending the night on holds less than a square inch across, and not even a piton to hold us? Well, we weren't finished yet. I still had plenty of energy left, and my blood was up. Putting all thought of security out of my mind I climbed at a crazy speed, and all the time my companion stuck to me like a shadow, splendid in his nearness and calm. At last the slope gave back a little, and we noticed a narrow snow ridge on our right. Evidently the couloir was double and the two branches joined here, forming this providential little ridge on which we could safely spend the night. However, the prospect of sitting all night in melting snow rather cooled our joy, the more so as we had both already tried this unpleasant experience elsewhere. On the right of the ridge a rock about the size of a man's head stuck out of the snow, which would do at a pinch for one of us to sit on. As we dug the snow away from around it we found first a crack which would take a good safe piton, then another stone which, cunningly arranged, would double the ground area of our little palace, bringing it up to some twelve inches by eighteen. The next thing was to don our bivouac gear, consisting of a quilted jacket and a waterproof cape. Lachenal also had a *pied d'éléphant**, for which I tried to compensate by pulling a pair of socks over my boots and putting my legs in the sack.

We had hardly sat down when a violent storm began. Hailstones like marbles forced us to protect our heads with our hands. After a bit the calibre fortunately diminished, and I took advantage of the lull to get going on the food, devouring bacon, butter, cheese, dried fruit and Ovomaltine. Lachenal was not hungry, and I had to force him to take something to keep his strength up. Torrents of hailstones were still breaking over our arête, and although we were out of the main stream we had to keep clearing them away as they piled up against our backs, pushing us outwards. But despite the fury of the elements, the continuing hail, the noise of thunder and falling stones, and despite our uncomfortable position on one buttock, squeezed up against each other with our feet swinging in the air, the night gradually crept by. We passed the time alternately singing anything that came into our heads and discussing our chances of getting through alive. I felt that the situation was not without hope, because a good storm often clears the air and it might be fine the next day. Lachenal thought that in any case we were near enough to the top to receive help if necessary. All this is not to say that we were not extremely worried, but somehow something told us that we would win through. We kept in quite good spirits, therefore, and my own love of adventure was so strong that in my deepest self I was not sorry to have lived through such an exceptional experience.

The storm died down towards morning, and in spite of the cold we dozed off. A dismal, freezing dawn revealed our situation for the first time as truly dramatic. It was impossible to gauge our position on the face because of the

---

* *Translator's note.* A *pied d'éléphant* is a wind- and waterproof bag of light material used for pulling up over the legs on bivouacs. Sometimes a waist-length quilted bag is worn underneath.

swirling clouds that cloaked and distorted everything. The next part of the couloir was just like what we had climbed the day before, but it had been covered in hail during the night and now the biting cold had transformed it into a sheet of black ice. From the very first move it became obvious that it would be impossible to climb in Vibrams, but, by a stroke of luck, I had brought along one pair of crampons on the advice of Pierre Allain. There was only one possible solution: to climb the slabs in crampons, trying to get over to the left onto the proper route as we went. Still wearing my cape and quilted jacket I set out to try my luck, filled with the energy of despair. It was delicate and dangerous work. The only points of contact for the feet were the two front spikes of the crampons, which frequently had to be placed on minuscule holds while my numbed hands painfully cleared the rock ahead. The pitons never went in more than half an inch, and were so loose that Lachenal was able to pick them out casually with his hands. Every movement was a feat in itself. I was continually at my limit, and the best I could do for my partner, whose rubber-shod feet kept skidding off, was to help him keep his balance by holding the rope as tight as I could. There would have been no question of holding a real fall, and we only got up this part of the climb alive thanks to his exceptional class.

For all my efforts I could not manage to traverse left, and in the end I was even forced in the opposite direction onto an ice slope, up which we notched little pockets. I was literally obsessed with the need to hurry, because if it once came on to snow that would be the end of us. This ruthless concentration enabled me to overcome obstacles that I would not even have considered in normal circumstances. In a sense it was rather like the time I had been caught in an avalanche and had been forced to swim desperately to get back to the surface; there was the same fantastic surge of unsuspected forces, the same cold-blooded summing up of the situation. So now I followed lines of least resistance almost more in a spirit of curiosity than of trepidation, though I was quite clear in my own mind that it would probably be impossible to reverse them.

Finally we came up against a vertical wall split by a huge chimney. The small part we could see looked climbable, so we proceeded to bury ourselves in its depths. The clouds thinned out for a few minutes, and we made the most of our relatively secure position to look down at where we had come from and where we had gone wrong, imprinting it on our memories. Then we climbed on again, finding it all as desperate as ever: a succession of overhanging chimneys choked with loose boulders, interspersed with short, deceptively easy-looking couloirs. The walls of the chimneys sloped away from each other unpleasantly, calling for great efforts, and sometimes for all-out artificial climbing. The rock was so rotten and the pitons gripped so badly that sometimes I took half an hour to gain only a few feet. At these times Lachenal was in the less enviable position, constantly running the risk of being brained by the stones I could not help knocking off, despite the greatest precautions. His prodigious agility enabled him to dodge most of them, but one block twice the size of a man's fist scored a direct hit on his head. Miraculously he was only knocked out for a couple of minutes. Sometimes he would have to spend a whole hour hanging from a peg by his waist loop, racked by cramps and deprived of the physical and mental heat which the leader generates in the battle. But he bore up wonderfully. Shivering with cold, dodging the stones, but still smiling and jovial, he never ceased to encourage me, referring frequently to a certain slap-up meal we were going to have before long.

Above each overhang I kept hoping to find easy ground at last, but I was constantly disappointed. Each time it would turn out to be a slab with small, friable holds, all covered in rime and verglas,* and each time I would have to do a dangerous balancing act in which I would succeed only at the price of running enormous risks. The climbing was physical torture, too. My hands were so cold that I constantly had to beat them raw to get any feeling back, and as for my feet it was so long since I had felt anything in them that I had given up bothering. Terrible cramps in my calves, thighs, neck and left arm added to the uncertainty of my progress. But worst of all was the unending fear (that at any moment we might come up against some unclimbable overhang, beneath which we would die slowly of cold and hunger). By this time I was climbing like an automaton, in a kind of trance. Every pitch provided some sort of peril from which we only escaped by a miracle. Once, a huge flake of rock slid off as I passed, almost touching Lachenal as it whizzed by. In another place I had just crossed a smooth slab, and shouted to him to pendulum across to me. As he did so the spike of rock round which he had placed the rope broke off. Luckily the rope flicked round my wrist as he fell. As the strain came on me I was pulled outwards inexorably . . . but managed to hold on. Farther on we came to an overhang capped with snow. I pushed the shaft of my ice axe into it and was pulling up when it gave way, and I landed on another lump of snow ten feet lower down. Fortunately this one held.

At last the cloud thinned for an instant, and a few feet above us I could see the vapour being blown by a strong south wind. The summit ridge must be just beyond this last overhang—another eighty or ninety feet and we should

---

* *Translator's note.* Verglas is hard, glassy ice formed by melting and freezing. It is different from névé, or ice formed by pressure.

be there. All at once my nerves, too long stretched to breaking point, seemed to go slack: I became aware of all the clangers that surrounded me and was almost paralysed with fear and fatigue. That last pitch seemed to me the hardest of the whole lot, though in fact it was relatively easy, and I only got up it thanks to a ridiculous number of pitons. Pulling out through strong gusts of wind onto the snowy ridge I felt no well-defined emotions, only the impression of having done with a repeating dream. Months of preparing and dedication thus found their consummation on this perfectly unremarkable patch of snow. Who can say that happiness lies not in desire but in possession? The adventure was finished, a page of my life had turned over, and already, staggering slightly, I was swallowed up by the mist.

Up to the time of our ascent of the Walker, Lachenal and I had always been rather modest in our mountain ambitions. The mightiest alpine walls attracted us by their grandiose wildness and the adventurous character of their ascents, but they still seemed a fearful world, hostile to the presence of man. Face-to-face with the last great problems of the Alps we were far from possessing the quiet confidence of a Rébuffat or the exuberant cocksureness of certain very gifted young climbers. On the contrary, we were timid and uncertain of ourselves. It certainly never occurred to us that we might be good enough to triumph over obstacles so far above the human scale. Our success on the Grandes Jorasses gave us a better idea of our possibilities. In spite of bad weather and of losing the way we had done the climb in a considerably shorter time than anybody else before us, and it is interesting to note that even today, with all the improvements in training methods and equipment, only five or six out of some twenty-five ascents of the Walker have been completed in a shorter time than ours.

From this time on we knew that, even if our lack of opportunity to practise prevented us from becoming virtuoso 'XS men',* the frequency and intensiveness of our high mountain climbing had given us an almost unrivalled rapidity on only slightly easier rock, as well as on ice or on mixed ground. Further, we climbed very much better together than either of us did apart. Our differing characters and physical aptitudes complemented each other, each of us making up for the other's weaknesses.

Lachenal was by far the fastest and most brilliant climber I have ever known on delicate or loose terrain. His dexterity was phenomenal, his vitality

* *Translator's note.* Specialist rock gymnasts are called '*sestogradists*' on the continent, from their system of grading difficulty from I to VI. The nearest English equivalent, used here, comes from our adjectival grading system, of which the hardest is 'Exceptionally Severe', or 'XS'.

like that of a wild beast and his bravery amounted almost to unawareness of danger. On his day he was capable of something very like genius, but strenuous pitches gave him trouble, and above all he was unpredictable. Perhaps because of his very impulsiveness and incredible optimism he lacked patience, perseverance and forethought. He also suffered from a bad sense of direction.

For myself, I was the less gifted partner on any kind of ground; but I had more stamina and was stronger, more obstinate and more reflective. I suppose I was the moderating element in the team, but it also seems to me that I gave it the stability and solidity necessary for the really major undertakings.

After the Walker we felt that our rope, united by a close bond of friendship, was ready to try anything the western Alps had to offer.

My feet had been mildly frostbitten on the Jorasses, and up to the end of September I had all I could do to carry on with my job. Gradually the swelling and the pain diminished, and by early October I was practically cured. Courses were over for the time being at both the E.N.S.A. and the Collège des Praz, and the weather was set fair. We were in no way satiated by our long months of intensive activity—rather the peaks seemed more wonderful to us than ever through the limpid air of those autumn days. Why suffocate among the fogs and clatter of the valley when a world of incorruptible purity was waiting for us up there? Having seen rather a lot of the Mont Blanc range in recent months we decided to make the most of this Indian summer by trying some of the great Swiss climbs.

After a visit to Lachenal's in-laws at Lausanne we set out for the Argentine to get a bit of practice at limestone climbing. While Louis took his father-in-law up one of the classic routes, the excellent Genevan climber Tomy Girard and I made the second ascent of the hardest climb on the crag, the Grand Dièdre. Next, we went up the Rhône valley to the south-east ridge of the Bietschhorn, a beautiful ascent of grade V standard that we had heard much about.

By this time we were so fit and acclimatised, both mentally and physically, to living in high mountains, that we had virtually overcome the normal human lack of adaptation to such surroundings. Our ease and rapidity of movement had become in a sense unnatural, and we had practically evolved into a new kind of alpine animal, halfway between the monkey and the mountain goat. We could run uphill for hours, climb faces as though they were stepladders, and rush down gullies in apparent defiance of the laws of gravity. The majority of climbs seemed child's play, which we could do without any particular effort in half or a third of the time taken by a good ordinary party. The Bietschhorn ridge gave a spectacular example of this 'over-mastery'. We set out shortly before dawn and reached the top in five hours of unhurried climbing. The sky was of that perfect blue which only comes in autumn, and all around us the mighty shapes of the Oberland and Valais peaks rose dazzlingly above the dreary plains. On our remote summit, life seemed so far away that it might never have existed. Nothing betrayed the presence of man; no barking, no tinkling of cowbells rose to us through the still air. The silence was so absolute that we might have been transported to another planet. We lay there for a long time despite the biting wind, letting the infinite peace sink into us, our muscles still tingling from our recent efforts.

The way down is via the north ridge. After a few minutes we found ourselves going along the top of a steep snow slope on the east face. Lachenal said:

'Let's go down there. I noticed it from the hut. It's good all the way, and there's hardly any *rimaye*.'

'Well, the snow's in perfect condition. If you're sure it runs out at the bottom, why not? It'll be something a bit more out of the ordinary than freezing solid on this confounded ridge', I replied without hesitation.

And so we turned at once down the fifty-degree slope. The snow was perfect, with the top four or five inches unfrozen but firm, and we went down together without taking any belays. After a few moments Lachenal called out:

'Why don't we glissade with our crampons on? It works very well on snow like this with a slope of about this angle. Armand Charlet told me he'd done it on the Whymper.'

But, more cautious by nature, I replied: 'Yes, and what happens if we come to a patch of ice? We'd go head over heels, and good-bye to the pair of us.'

'Sez you. I tell you I had a good look at it from the hut. There's not a patch of ice on it anywhere.'

And without waiting for my reply, Lachenal let himself go like a skier. I was completely taken by surprise. It was impossible to pull him up without running the risk of being jerked onto my back, in which case I would still have gone down, but not in such good control. There was nothing for it but to take off after him in his daring glissade. One minute later we had made a controlled swoop of a thousand feet. At 11.30 a.m. we were back in the charming Baltschieder hut, deserted as though it had been specially built for us, feeling as fresh as daisies.

I was later told that the famous Zermatt guide Alexander Graven had been up to the hut to do the Bietschhorn a few days later. Seeing the times we had entered in the hut book, he exclaimed:

'That's impossible. Those young men must be liars.'

But the next day he saw our tracks down the east face as he descended the ridge, and declared:

'Obviously, if they can do that, they can do anything.'

After the Bietschhorn we went up to Zermatt to try the Furggen ridge of the Matterhorn, together with our Genevan friends Tomy Girard and René Dittert. I had long desired to climb this elegant pyramid, the ideal of mountain form, perhaps the most beautiful and certainly the most famous peak in the Alps. How many evenings had I not spent as a small boy, dreaming over the books of Whymper and Mummery? And suddenly there it was, in the radiant October morning, as we rounded a corner, standing over the tawny pastures in all its sublime loneliness. I was slightly shocked at first: in that soft romantic landscape of autumn colours there was something brutal in the effect of its immense black horn reared against the sky. Never before had any mountain seemed so striking. I was captivated in a moment by the spell it has cast over men since mountaineering began.

I devoured the crags with my eyes, looking for the routes I had so often read about. In particular I sought the 'Furggen Nose' whose vast overhangs, profiled against the sky, had so long withstood even the boldest climbers until Louis Carrel, the famous Valtoumanche guide, had triumphed at last. Since then it had only been repeated once, by De Rham and Tissières, the 'climbing scientists'. I could hardly believe that tomorrow we would be suspended up there between earth and sky, such a tumult did fear and desire make in me.

In the end, however, the ascent turned out to be another parade for the mountain goats. Beautiful from a distance as a woman of classically unfading loveliness, the Matterhorn begins to lose its charm as one gets nearer, and from close up it turns out to be no more than an immense heap of schist wrinkled with innumerable gullies. Nothing remains of the stone flame that seemed to defy the laws of gravity. The dark, fractured rock constantly breaks off in dusty avalanches, and anyone who has known the sheer granite breast-plates of the Aiguilles of Mont Blanc, rising hundreds of feet without a fault or weakness, will find little charm in this ruined fortress.

We reached Carrel's overhangs in under two hours without even bothering to put on the rope. At this point the mountain recovers some power and dignity, but the rock is unbelievably fissile. I have never climbed anything at once so steep and so loose, and found it quite paralysing. But Lachenal, the acrobat of the abysses, was not in the least bit worried. Uttering cries of joy he clambered upwards with scarcely a piton, raining stones behind him. With a nice strong rope above us it did not take the Swiss and myself long to follow up this 250 feet of dangerous rather than really difficult rock.

Our autumn campaign ended with this ascent, and we went back to Chamonix full of boyish high spirits. Yet in spite of all our enthusiasm, something seemed to be missing. We had expected more from these climbs than they had been able to give us, for all their qualities. They didn't seem to be serious enough. We had never once felt (though of course we were mistaken) that anything could go wrong, or stop us reaching the summit. In a confused sort of way it seemed that we had had fine scenery and fine sport, but not *grand alpinisme*.

The fact was that perfect training and modern equipment had turned us into overdeveloped instruments for the job in hand. Since technique had thus blown away the scent of adventure we should have to seek it elsewhere. After the Walker, only one climb in the Alps could give us the same sort of emotions: the face of faces, the north face of the Eiger.

| 5 |

THE NORTH FACE OF THE EIGER

THE IMMENSE NORTH WALL of the Eiger, better known as the Eiger-wand, is the highest, most famous and most deadly mountain face in the whole of the Alps. Its black and slippery crags rise five thousand feet sheer out of the fertile pastures above Grindelwald, in the heart of the Bernese Oberland. Today it has been climbed some twenty or more times, at the cost of as many lives, but in 1946 it had still only been scaled once. Repeated attempts resulted in the deaths of eight men before an Austro-German party succeeded in climbing it in 1938, after a desperate three-day struggle. Their victory was probably the greatest feat in the history of the Alps.

Even the Eigerwand has now been to some extent surpassed in the continuing development of mountaineering. It has been climbed in one day by Waschak and Forstenlechner, and quite recently an Austro-German party of four performed the almost incredible feat of doing it in winter. Only on the highest summits in the world can modern tigers find adversaries worthy of their prowess. But neverthe-less this wall will always occupy so important a place in the annals of man's conquest of the mountains that it seems to me impossible to put the second ascent in its context without telling the epic story of the first.

The face is composed of a dark limestone, hardly relieved by its few bands of ice. It begins at around 7,500 feet in the pastures above Alpiglen and rises with scarcely a break in its appalling savagery to the summit of the Eiger, at 13,039 feet. The lower third consists of ledges and short walls of no especial difficulty, and near the top part of this zone are the two windows of the Jungfraujoch railway which spirals up inside the mountain. The more easterly of the windows is called the Eigerwand Station; the other, called the Stollenloch, is simply a chute for rubbish from the tunnel.

The first major obstacle is a very high cliff of smooth limestone, highest at the right-hand end where it is called the Rote Fluh. Immediately to the left of its lowest part is an ice slope of medium steepness, separated from a much larger and steeper ice slope above by a vertical wall. Running down the wall between the two is a narrow, icy gulley. Above the ice fields stands an enormous vertical cliff called the Gelbewand, and above this again, where the face becomes markedly concave, is another ice slope called the Spider. This is linked to the summit by a system of steep couloirs, the most noticeable of which comes up slightly to the left of the highest point.

It will be seen that the face presents uninterrupted difficulties, and that the Rote Fluh and the Gelbewand in particular are major obstacles. Yet, although these two sections are made severe by the quality of the rock, at once so loose and so compact that it is difficult to put in pitons, the Eigerwand would never have merited its reputation on these factors alone. First among several other hazards are the objective dangers, variable from day to day. Stones of all sizes fall from the moldering summit slopes down the great central hollow of the face, bounce over the Gelbewand, and sweep the ice fields and the lower crags. They are impossible to predict or avoid.

Less spectacular but also very important is the succession of cliffs and ice slopes the whole way up the face. These latter melt during the warm part of the day and gush over the rocks, turning the chimneys and gullies below into veritable waterfalls. This of itself would be no more than a minor inconvenience, but, as the wall is high and north-facing, the hours of warmth are short, and the rest of the time the water freezes into a real armour-plating of ice all over the rock. In such conditions even easy pitches can become extremely severe or even impossible, and only the finest climbers, accustomed to climbing in crampons, stand a chance of getting up them safely.

Finally, the fact that the difficulties are sustained over more than three thousand feet of rock and ice means that candidates have to load themselves down with bivouac and other equipment, thus tiring themselves out and slowing down their progress. This was another great obstacle to the original ascent. Allowing for the sake of argument that the climb was technically possible, it would still require several days, and to remain so long on such an inhuman wall involved immense risks. A rope caught by bad weather would have its work cut out to get off alive, because at the first fall of snow the avalanches sweep down across the entire face.

It will be seen that the north face of the Eiger is defended by an extraordinary accumulation of difficulties and dangers. Few will deny that its reputation for inaccessibility, which had grown over the years, was well merited. Yet these very barriers, by defending it successfully against all comers, grew into positive attractions for those who sought high adventure. From all over Europe the mountaineering elite gathered to lay siege.

A party from Munich made the first assault in 1929. In 1934 three Germans got as far as Eigerwand Station before the leader fell, and they were saved by ropes dropped to them from the window. The first serious attempt, and one of the most remarkable, was made by two daring Bavarian climbers, Karl Mehringer and Max Sedlmayer. They had done a number of the hardest climbs in the northern limestone Alps, but this was their first visit to the really big ranges. They launched their attack in perfect weather on Wednesday August the 11th, mounting quickly as far as the foot of the Rote Fluh, where they proceeded to force directly the enormous featureless wall below the first ice field. This prodigious exploit, which still earns the admiration of connoisseurs, took up a whole day of extremely difficult climbing. Although the difficulties were less after their first bivouac the two climbers must have been tired, moving so slowly that they did not reach the second ice field until Thursday afternoon. There the stone falls were so frequent that they had to stop and bivouac again. That night a violent storm broke over the mountain, followed by snow and heavy frost. By dawn the face was plastered with snow and black ice, rendering it completely out of condition, and it remained masked in cloud all day so that it was impossible to know what was happening. On Saturday the mists cleared for a moment around noon, when the two were spotted on the small spur which limits the left end of the large ice field, but soon their agonies were hidden again from the eyes of the world.

Their corpses were carried down by the winter avalanches and later found by parties searching for yet other victims. Two pitons now marked the new borders of the unknown. But the tragic ending of the story did not discourage others from trying their chances, and the early summer of 1936 found three more German ropes at Scheidegg. Weather and conditions were not at first conducive to an all-out attempt, so the six men set up camp and spent their time reconnoitring the face and getting fit on other mountains. In a sense the Eigerwand thus indirectly claimed a third victim when Teufel was killed on a training climb. Despite the almost incessant bad weather the four who remained made several reconnaissances, in the course of which they carried loads up to the foot of the Rote Fluh and in particular found an easier way up it. During one of these explorations a climber fell 120 feet, but landed on snow and did not hurt himself.

It may be as well to introduce these four young men, who were shortly to die in one of the most terrible of all mountain dramas. The first rope consisted of two young Bavarians. Toni Kurz was a professional guide who had done a number of first ascents in the eastern Alps, and Andreas Hinterstoisser had been his constant companion. Their biggest climb had been the north face of the Cima Grande. They formed a strong party in themselves, capable of confronting the most difficult rock climbs. Unfortunately the same could not be said about their two Austrian companions, Willy Angerer and Edi Rainer from Innsbruck. There is no doubt that they were competent climbers, but not yet having done any big ascents they were hardly qualified to tackle the Eigerwand.

The weather appeared to change at last, and both parties set out at two o'clock on July 18th under a sky full of stars. Moving quickly, they soon reached the foot of the Rote Fluh, where Hinterstoisser led them up the new and cunning route they had discovered. This involved a very difficult overhanging crack, followed by a daring tension traverse to the left. Having reached the first snowfield in good time they took five hours to climb the short wall separating it from the second, and installed their bivouac at seven o'clock in the evening. They had climbed a good half of the face that day. If the difficulties became no greater they had every chance of reaching the summit.

During the night the weather started to change, and heavy clouds began to trail across the face. No doubt because of this dubious outlook the party did not set out from the bivouac until 6:45 a.m., cutting steps slowly across the ice field towards the left. The fog grew thicker and thicker until the watchers on the Kleine Scheidegg lost sight of the climbers. Not until the following morning could the second bivouac site be seen: it was almost exactly the same as that used by Sedlmayer and Mehringer. Nobody could understand why progress had been so slow on the second day, and it was generally supposed that the party must be exhausted and would therefore retreat. At eight o clock in the morning, however, the men were observed advancing once more. After a few hours they turned back, and it could be seen that one of them had a wound on the head.* The first bivouac site had almost been reached when

---

* *Translator's note.* There are batteries of powerful telescopes at Kleine Scheidegg.

further clouds obscured it from view. A clearing at about five o'clock revealed the party descending the wall between the two ice fields. All due precautions were being taken, and two men were looking after the injured one, so that it was not until nine o'clock at night that they reached the lower ice field.

By the following morning the weather was definitely bad, and it rained and snowed abundantly. Voices could be heard on the face from dawn onwards, and at eleven o'clock the four men were seen at the foot of the first ice field. At noon the stationmaster climbed out of the Stollenloch and heard the party in action some six hundred feet above him. Thinking that they would be descending to the observation gallery, he went off and made tea. As they still did not arrive he went out again and managed to make contact with them by shouting. They said they were all safe and sound. Two hours later he tried again, but this time there was nothing to be heard but cries of distress. He therefore telephoned the Eigergletscher Station for a rescue party, where the guides Hans Schlunegger and Christian and Adolf Rubi happened to be on the spot and were quickly sent up on a special train. That day the three guides reached a point about three hundred feet below Toni Kurz, who was half hanging from a rope, half holding himself onto the vertical face by small holds. He called down that he was the sole survivor and that as he had no more pitons he could descend no further. In this terrible position he passed his fourth night on the wall. Next morning the rescue party set out again at four o'clock, augmented by the guide Arnold Glatthard, and reached the foot of the Rote Fluh. Kurz was tied on some 120 feet above them, and they had no trouble in speaking to him. He called out:

'I'm the only one left. Rainer died of cold higher up, Hinterstoisser fell off last night, and Angerer's hanging on the rope strangled.'

Kurz then carried out a series of tasks at the behest of his rescuers that gave proof of his exceptional toughness and courage. His only chance was to free the rope to which he was tied, so that he could then pull up pitons and a rope to rappel on. To this end he descended as far as Angerer, who was hanging some forty feet lower down, cut him clear, then climbed back up the rope to the tiny stance he had just left. Despite his frostbitten hands he spent several hours untangling the forty feet of rope he had thus recovered, joining it to the rest until it was long enough to lower for the equipment he needed. After six hours of perseverance he was finally able to start sliding down the rope, and it seemed that the incredible was about to come true. He had almost descended to the point where it would have been possible to reach him with an ice axe when all movement ceased, his arms opened, and his head fell back.

Toni Kurz was dead, after having fought for his life with almost superhuman energy.

Nobody will ever know what happened between the stationmaster's second and third tours of inspection. Probably the party tried and failed to get back across the Hinterstoisser traverse, and was attempting a direct descent when it was hit by falling stones. The climbers may have all been knocked off, but held by the pitons through which their ropes were passed.

After the dramatic endings of the early attempts it might have been believed that the Eigerwand was indeed unclimbable, yet the best climbers of the time were more or less unanimous in considering it possible. One thing, however, was certain: a successful party would need all-round technique, indomitable energy and plenty of luck.

The siege began again the following summer. Germans, Italians and Swiss contenders appeared, and it is no exaggeration to suggest that some ten ropes were seriously interested. In spite of the Federal Council's fatuous decision to make the climb illegal numerous climbers were prowling around the foot of the face, and a veritable competition began as in the case of the north face of the Grandes Jorasses not long before.

It has been said that the German, Italian and Austrian climbers were not motivated solely by sporting considerations. This will always remain a vexed subject, and there is no doubt that certain parties were subsidised. It is even probable that the eventual victors were rewarded. But everyone who actually knows the great German and Italian climbers is nowadays of the opinion that political and material considerations played no vital part in the affair, any more than they did in the ascents of the other last great problems. More than twenty years after the first ascent, when there is no longer any possibility of profit, glory or political prestige, young climbers continue to come from every country in search of pure adventure, whatever the risk. The true explanation of the swarms of candidates must be sought rather in the high level of technique already attained at that time in the eastern Alps, and in the warlike and adventurous instincts of the German race. This species of daring was very rare in those days among French mountaineers.

During the summer of 1937 the northeast face of the Eiger, as distinct from the north face proper, was the scene of various misadventures to ropes who were training on it for the Eigerwand. The Salzburg mountaineer Gollaker died of exhaustion, and his companion Primas had both feet frostbitten. But despite the number and ability of its assailants the mountain retained its mystery throughout the season, efficiently guarded by bad weather and conditions. Only Rebitsch and Vörg got far up it.

Having reconnoitred and equipped the face as far as the first ice field, they attacked on 11 August, reaching a point slightly higher than Sedlmayer and Mehringer's last bivouac. At this point they were surprised by bad weather, and only got down again after three days of struggle. Thanks to their all-round experience and exceptional class they were the first to reach the central part of the face and return alive.

With the summer of 1938 the attempts began again, still more numerous and more obstinate than before. On 22 June two excellent Italian climbers, Mario Menti and Bartolo Sandri, were killed by stone fall at about the level of the Eigerwand Station. Both of them were mountaineers of the first rank, as they had shown on the south face of the Torre Trieste, the south ridge of the Aiguille Noire de Peuterey and other grade VI climbs.

But at last human perseverance was rewarded. The Germans Andreas Heckmair and Ludwig Vörg and the Austrians Fritz Kasparek and Heinrich Harrer climbed the gigantic wall for the first time 21–24 July 1938. Perhaps these protagonists should be introduced before we proceed to the story of their ascent. All four were climbers and mountaineers of exceptional class, with experience in the Dolomites, the western Alps and the Caucasus, and were well known even before the Eigerwand.

Heckmair was a professional guide in the Bavarian Alps. As early as 1930 he had done, among others, two of the longest and most difficult climbs in the Dolomites at that time: the Solleder route on the Civetta and the east face of the Sass Maor. These were respectively the fifth and second ascents. The following year he had laid siege to the north face of the Grandes Jorasses, but all his attempts were foiled by weather and bad conditions. While in the area he also did the second direct ascent of the north face of the Grands Charmoz.

Ludwig Vörg, who came from Munich, was also a specialist of the eastern Alps, but in addition he had taken part in two expeditions to the central Caucasus, where he had done two climbs, among others, which were quite remarkable both for length and for difficulty. In 1934 he did the first south-north traverse of Ushba at the price of four bivouacs, and in 1936 he made the first ascent of the gigantic west face of the same mountain. The following year he and Matthias Rebitsch had made the third ascent of the north face of the Gross Fiescherhorm and also, as we have seen, an attempt on the Eigerwand which got farther than any others up to that time.

It will be seen that the Bavarian rope was one of the strongest that could have been imagined, particularly for the ascent of the Eigerwand. Its members were both rock climbers of the first order, and experienced mountaineers into the bargain. Above all, with Rebitsch away, Vörg was the only man who knew the lower part of the face.

The second rope was also composed of doughty men. Fritz Kasparek, from Vienna, was one of the finest climbers ever to come out of the eastern Alps, and the list of his amazing feats in pure rock climbing is so long that it would be boring to quote it. We need only mention the first ascent of the north face of the Dachl, the third of the north face of the Cima Ovest di Lavaredo, and in particular the first winter ascent of the Comici route on the Cima Grande, which he did as a training climb for the Eiger.

The youngest member of the party was the academic Heinrich Harrer, who has since become famous also for his adventures in Tibet and for his writings. He too had done numerous difficult ascents.

The Austrians formed a remarkable team of tough and daring climbers, but in my opinion they had far less chance of success on the Eigerwand than the Bavarians because, like the first eight victims of the face, they had too little experience on ice and in higher mountaineering. As will presently be seen, they would probably not in fact have got up without the assistance of the German pair.

Having heard that Vörg was off to the Himalayas, Heckmair had come to an agreement with Rebitsch to climb together. In the end Rebitsch was chosen for the Himalayan expedition rather than Vörg, and Heckmair and the latter only met and decided to form a team quite a short time before their ascent. They began training in the Kaiserge-birge on 20 June, planning to leave for Switzerland on 10 July, but they found it difficult to stick to this decision in view of the news from Grindelwald where Kasparek and others were already installed at the foot of the face. As soon as they seemed sufficiently fit they went straight to Munich to buy equipment. Thanks to the support of the Orgenburg-Sonthofen organisation they were able to get everything they needed, and they chose equipment suitable not only for rock but particularly for ice climbing, which Vörg reckoned to be the crux of the problem. Then they set out at last for Grindelwald and pitched their camp on the grassy slopes around Alpiglen.

After waiting several days for fine weather they attacked on 20 July, but they were so heavily laden that they had to bivouac in a hollow at the foot of the Rote Fluh. Next day the outlook was doubtful, and they were getting ready to descend when they saw Kasparek and Harrer climbing towards them, followed by the Viennese Fraisl and Brankowski. This unexpected development did not, however, cause them to change their minds. The weather was definitely dubious, and anyway they deemed it unwise to have six on the face at the same time. But in their own words:

'As we descended the weather got finer and finer, and our faces longer and longer.'

They reached the foot of the face at ten o'clock in a state of despair. From Alpiglen they could follow the slow progress of the four Viennese, and before long Brankowski's rope turned back after he had been injured by a stone. After telephoning to Berne for a weather forecast they decided to attack again, and spent the afternoon stuffing themselves with food. They were off by three in the morning, making ground at fantastic speed. They passed their previous bivouac at four, and by ten o'clock were across the Hinterstoisser traverse. An hour later they reached Kasparek's bivouac site in the eastern part of the second ice field, and thanks to the latter's freshly cut steps caught him up by 11:30 a.m.

A short discussion followed in which they decided to join forces. Then they went on steadily until they reached the ultimate point attained by the earlier attempts, a sort of rocky rib which divides the main ice field into two distinct parts. Thinking of Sedlmayer and Mehringer they kept on towards the eastern end of the Gelbewand, which they rightly believed to be its weak point. This section of the climb, which they called 'The Ramp', is a kind of slanting gangway, not very difficult at first. Subsequently it fades out in a step split by a vertical chimney which narrows to a crack. The right wall was yellow, loose and overhanging, and they considered it out of the question. The other side was vertical and smooth. Just to improve matters, a waterfall was coming down the chimney itself. As it was seven o'clock in the evening, too late to be tackling pitches of this kind, they decided to bivouac on the spot.

Twelve hours later they started up the chimney, in which the waterfall was now replaced by solid ice. They got up it at the cost of two falls and a desperate struggle only after bringing into play every resource of modern technique, including artificial climbing on ice pitons. Above the chimney the Ramp reappeared, this time in the guise of a steep slope of ice. As soon as they could they traversed off it in the direction of the Spider, along an outward-sloping ledge of extremely rotten rock. A delicate sixty-foot wall then led to another long, exposed ledge, which finally ended in the Spider* itself.

The weather, having held out so far, now began to change for the worse. Thunder could be heard, and Heckmair therefore decided to unrope temporarily from the Austrians, who were holding him up, in order to see as much

* *Translator's note.* This long traverse leading to the Spider is often called 'the Traverse of the Gods'.

of the upper part of the face as possible before the clouds got too thick. He cramponned straight up the Spider and had reached the central couloir when the storm broke in earnest. Not long afterwards an avalanche of hail swept the whole of the slope below. The Germans, who had escaped through being in a sheltered place, thought that their friends must have been carried away, but by a miracle the latter had only a moment before put in an ice piton which enabled them to hold on. The storm soon abated, and despite an injury to Kasparek's hand the two ropes were able to reunite. The whole caravan then continued on up the steep central couloir, which was heavily iced over.

At last they came to a miserable platform where there was sufficient cover to bivouac. That night was extremely trying. Half the party had now bivouacked twice already, and all of them were worn out from the enormous exertions of the climbing. Above all they were in the grip of anxiety. The snow fell all night in huge flakes, and it was a very real question whether they could hope to escape from the face alive in such conditions.

The last day was highly dramatic. Although the actual ground becomes less difficult at this point, it was in such terrible condition that Heckmair peeled off several times. His last fall in particular was very nearly fatal, as he sprained his ankle and spiked one of Vörg's hands with his crampons. The danger of avalanches increased the difficulties. Every so often they would sweep the entire gully, and the party was nearly carried away twice despite the fact that they had worked out the frequency of the falls and were protecting themselves with numerous pitons. At last the gully opened onto the summit slopes, the angle gave back, and they came to the final ridge. Thanks to the technique and bravery of four men the greatest problem in the Alps had been solved.

After our successes of 1946, Lachenal and I became aware of our possibilities. We felt morally and technically ready to repeat the exploit of the Austrians and Germans on the Eigerwand, and this now became a definite part of our programme for the following season. That November, however, all our projects were endangered owing to a trivial accident. I cut my right hand very deeply on a broken drinking glass, slicing the tendons of my index finger clean through, and as a result of subsequent infection I nearly lost the use of the hand altogether. After a month of intensive treatment in hospital the finger was still practically useless, and my ability to grip was seriously diminished. It might have been worse: I could still continue being a guide, but it seemed most unlikely that I would ever again be able to do the hardest rock climbs since, as can be imagined, they call for great strength in the fingers. Even if some years of patient adaptation should make such climbs possible for me again eventually, they seemed out of the question for the following season. I therefore decided to make the best of it, gave up all my plans and settled down to build myself a chalet.

After several years of somewhat chilly relations between my father and myself, due partly to the incompatibility of our characters and partly to the difference in age, we had now once again become firm friends. Despite his strict principles and obstinate ideas I had learned to recognise the man of real kindness behind the austere façade. For his part, having confidently expected me to go to the bad, he was most relieved to see me earning my living in a decent and honourable way. True, my profession was not what he would have chosen for me himself, but my brilliant success in it poured balm on his soul. My passion for climbing was as incomprehensible to him as ever, but the austerity of my way of life and the pains I had been to in order to follow it seemed to him worthy of respect and even of encouragement.

In the course of the last few years he had frequently offered to help me according to his means, but my excessive pride had always made me reject his proposals. Now, realising how important it was to have a home of my own, and being quite unable to provide one from my own resources, I decided to swallow my pride and rely on his generosity. With his aid I was able to take advantage of an unusual opportunity to acquire a site in full view of Mont Blanc at a very low price, and also a complete chalet that some rich owners were about to have demolished. By carefully numbering every plank as it was taken down so that it could be re-erected on my own land I made sure of a roomy and comfortable home. Naturally I had to do most of the work myself, but the gaps between my professional seasons were sufficiently long to make this possible, and many of my friends offered a helping hand.

I gave myself up to this labour so completely, and found it so all-absorbing, that I became quite resigned to living without *grand alpinisme*. A sudden access of respectability even made me feel that it was time I began to settle down. Lachenal, however, was far from any such thoughts. Aware of his capacities and bubbling over with vitality, he was dying to get at the Eiger. He was quite prepared to try leading the whole climb, and reckoned that I would be an acceptable second even with a disabled hand. He therefore began to work on me, finding a valuable ally in the shape of my wife, who was rather sad to see me giving up all my mountain ambitions and settling into the humdrum life of an ordinary guide at the age of twenty-five. She hoped that a success on the Eiger, which she never for one moment doubted, would give me back my enthusiasm. Never a day went by without either Lachenal or

Marianne—if not both together—getting at me to start training so as to be ready when the moment came. They even went so far as to place a photograph of the celebrated face opposite my bed.

In spite of remedial therapy my hand was still very weak, and my forefinger very sensitive to cold, by the time May came round. Far from feeling like a conquering hero, I toiled all the harder at the construction of my chalet. The weather got better and better, until conditions were just right for the big ice climbs. If I paused for a moment from my hard and tedious labours, I could not help but see the Aiguilles and hear their siren voices calling down to me. Bit by bit I succumbed to nostalgia, and by the time Lachenal came along at the end of the month and suggested doing the third ascent of the Nant Blanc face of the Aiguille Verte I could hold out no longer. To make up for this weakness I made him promise a day's work to compensate for the one I was losing, and refused to set out until I had finished my afternoon's labouring.

After a hurried supper and a short bicycle ride, we left the village of Tines at 7:30 p.m. An approach march of somewhat over three hours up steep, rhododendron-covered slopes brought us to a good bivouac site close to the face. Less than five hours later we had to be off. Conditions were ideal from the very beginning. The initial couloir, which is one of the steepest in the Alps, was covered in hard snow, making it possible to crampon up quickly and safely. Louis was climbing like an unleashed greyhound as usual, and we literally rushed upwards without taking any safety precautions. After we had done about a quarter of the face, a short pitch of iced-over rock slowed us down for a moment or two, but soon afterwards we came to a snow rib which enabled us to resume our mad career. It was now certain that we would be off the difficult part of the face before the sun softened the snow.

It was our first climb that year. I was in good physical shape thanks to skiing all winter and to the heavy work I had been putting in all spring, but naturally lack of acclimatisation to the altitude made it impossible to sustain efforts as easily as in mid-season. After a virtually sleepless night and two hours of climbing at racing speed my limbs began to feel like lead. There seemed no point any longer in climbing as though we were making a bid for freedom, and I suggested relenting a little. Despite the fact that it was his first climb too Lachenal remained insensible to fatigue, almost as though he were no longer made of mortal flesh and blood but had entered into a state of grace in which miracles might occur. Far from slowing down he accelerated his pace, cursing me into the bargain for my weakness. I was goaded by his will like a driven beast, and somehow or other managed to keep up with him.

In this way we reached the easy slopes of the summital cone in just over four hours, where a curious phenomenon took place.

Now that the nervous tension was all over, the effects of altitude struck down our untrained bodies like a bolt of lightning. I was invaded by an enormous weariness, and Lachenal's inhuman vitality went out like a match in the wind. He was in an even worse state than myself, and could hardly hold his head up. We collapsed in the snow, weak as puppies, every twenty steps. This last bit of the climb took us three times as long as normal, but in spite of that we finished the whole ascent in the altogether exceptional time of five and a half hours, a figure which gives some idea of our mastery as a team in those days.

This brilliant success on the Nant Blanc reanimated my enthusiasm and gave me back the confidence to attempt a little rock climbing. Although the rocky stretches on the climb had been very short, I had noticed that my hand bothered me much less than I had expected. Work started again at the École Nationale in June, and I was detailed to instruct the young candidates for the Guide's Diploma. The weather was constantly fine, and we did some classic ascent almost every day. Thus I was able to get the strength back into my hand gradually, while coming into good all-round form.

Vibram soles were still unobtainable in France, so we asked our friend the Italian guide Toni Gobbi to get us some. With his usual kindness he agreed at once, and after an exchange of letters a smugglers' rendezvous was arranged on the Col du Midi for a certain Sunday in June.

To plod all the way up the Vallée Blanche, or even up the shorter but equally uninteresting Glacier Rond, seemed a boring ordeal. In order to combine business with pleasure we decided to get to our assignation by the elegant and difficult north rib of the Aiguille du Midi, a somewhat more devious but also more interesting method of approach. The upper terminus of the old Téléphérique des Glaciers served us as quarters for the night. When the alarm went off it was still dark outside. Ominous clouds clung to the flanks of the mountains, and it was drizzling softly; there could be no question of attacking in such conditions, so we quickly returned to our bunks. At dawn patches of sky could be seen here and there, though it was very far from being good weather. But the rain had stopped, and that was all we needed. If we were to have any chance of keeping our appointment we should have to move very fast indeed. We were at the foot of the climb in half an hour. Five hours later, climbing as though pursued by the foul fiend, we stood on the summit, despite the fact that we had spent half an hour eating two-thirds of the way up!

As one climb succeeded another I began to get back my strength and my confidence; but, unfortunately, the ascending curve was broken towards the end of the month by a curious incident. While climbing the west face of the Peigne, a route that I had pioneered, the sling on which all my pegs and carabiners were hung came undone just as I was getting to the crux, and the whole lot shot into space. To improve matters, the previous party had taken out most of the pegs which were normally left in place.

I decided to carry on in spite of all these setbacks, but the weakness of my right hand turned out to be terribly embarrassing on such a difficult and exposed pitch. I successfully managed the traverse across to the final crack nevertheless. At this point I was clinging on, just in balance on tiny toeholds, above a yawning drop. I could neither go on nor get back. My right hand lacked the strength to grip the hold requisite to the next move, and as my left hand was rapidly tiring I felt my body beginning to tremble. Since I was about to fall in any case I decided to risk everything on the throw of the dice, and with a convulsive jerk upwards succeeded in getting a better hold for my left hand and a place to jam my left foot in the crack. After a moment's rest I was then able to finish the pitch properly.

This occurrence could hardly help but affect my morale, and I wondered how on earth I had ever been able to envisage calmly committing myself to the most redoubtable face in the Alps. Once the Guide's Diploma course was over I decided that the only thing was to take the bull by the horns and try a really big climb, thus proving whether I was fit for the Eiger. Lachenal had work to do, but my friend the guide Jo Marillac agreed to go with me to try the south ridge of the Aiguille Noire de Peuterey which, with its four thousand feet of climbing and pitches which were then considered grade VI, seemed the ideal test piece.

In order to train ourselves for a training climb in itself so renowned, we decided to attempt the first direct ascent of the big step in the southwest ridge of the Pèlerins, known as the Grutter ridge. With its reputedly impossible overhang this short climb seemed likely to be exceptionally difficult, and our expectations were in no way disappointed. Free climbing over the overhang proved to be a real problem, and so did several other pitches. The fact that I managed to lead them all despite my weak hand gave me back some of the confidence I needed.

The south ridge of the Aiguille Noire de Peuterey is one of the most beautiful rock climbs in the whole of the Alps, if not the most beautiful of all. Only a great author could worthily evoke the power of the titanic pillars which buttress it, the elegance of its pinnacles, the warm colour of its granite;

and at first view even the most hardened climber cannot help feeling a little intimidated.

Long and sustained though it may be, the south ridge is not quite a top-ranking climb from a technical point of view. Urged on by dubious weather, Marillac and I did the whole thing in nine hours despite a serious mistake in routefinding. Since then it has even been done in under seven by certain fabulously fast parties. I have repeated it five times as a professional guide, and can claim to know it fairly well. Most of my clients were climbers of quite modest ability, yet none of them found it totally beyond his own capabilities at any point, which would hardly have been the case if the pitches were genuine VI.

Although the test did not, then, turn out to be particularly searching, the ease with which I had performed gave me back sufficient confidence to agree to follow Lachenal on the Eiger. My friend's leave was drawing near. Properly speaking I should have been instructing a course of *aspirants guides* at this time, but the director of the École Nationale, René Beckert, very sportingly gave me leave of absence. I had unluckily sprained my ankle on the descent of the Aiguille Noire, and it was taking rather a long time to clear up. I was still limping, and should really have rested it for a few days; but I could hardly rest up during the first part of the course and then ask special permission to go off to the Eiger during the second. This would have been to risk hearing repeated the words of the captain who was so put out at my return from the north face of the Dru:

'Either one is ill or one isn't.'

His character was too vulgar to be capable of understanding that some men can transcend any circumstances in order to accomplish what is in their hearts. And so I continued to work in spite of the pain, limping along at the tail of the party. Heaven was on my side, however: the weather grew worse and we were reduced to climbing on little crags along the side of the valley. In these circumstances the ankle soon began to improve.

For his part, Lachenal had made the most of the fine weather at the beginning of the season, piling up big climbs and speed records, and even doing the fourth ascent of the Croz buttress on the north face of the Grandes Jorasses. He was in stupefying form, literally overflowing with life and high spirits. I can still see him arriving at huts with his feline stride, his thin, handsome face lit up by eyes sparkling with gaiety and intelligence. Joking with one, slanging another, constantly coming out with unexpected sallies and backchat, he would warm up the atmosphere in a moment with his torrential vitality.

The omens, then, seemed good for our attempt on the Eiger, and only the continuously bad weather put everything in doubt. The day before we were due to leave things began to look brighter, however. There was new snow high up, but lower down the mountains looked to be in good condition. There was nothing for it but to go.

Mountaineering is not always thought of as a sport; it seems an arguable point. However that may be, it differs from other sports in that there is in principle no contest for glory among men, only between man and the forces of nature, or man and his own weakness. With a few rare exceptions the climber has no renown to hope for, and no audience to encourage him apart from his companion on the rope. Alone among the silence and solitude of the mountains he fights for the joy of overcoming his chosen obstacle by his own unaided powers. In its simple, original form no other sport is so disinterested, so removed from human considerations, and it is precisely in this kind of purity that much of its grandeur and attraction lie.

But mountaineers are far from being angels, even if they do frequent a world of light and beauty. They remain men whose hearts are soiled by the world from which they came and to which they must presently return. Few of them indeed are able to look fame in the face and pass by, once they have come close. There is no getting away from the fact that there has always been competition between leading climbers, and the rivalry for certain summits and faces, even for their second or third ascents, has often been as feverish as anything known in the stadium. There have been many cases of grown-up men calling each other names and even coming to blows at the foot of a climb. Others have gone farther still, seeking to eliminate their rivals at any cost, giving them inaccurate information, stealing or hiding their equipment, or actually cutting their rope.

Lachenal and I had always found this sort of thing totally beneath contempt, and it has never failed to astonish me how men who have chosen a sport for its intrinsic grandeur could reveal such pettiness. I think I can honestly say that we were very little moved by the spirit of competition. For example we did comparatively few first ascents, though opportunities were certainly not lacking at that time. The repetition of the really great Alpine routes seemed to us much more interesting than discovering obscure little climbs in remote corners. Like ugly girls, many of the ridges and faces which preserved their virginity until comparatively recently did so more from lack of attraction than from intrinsic difficulty. As for the minute facets and riblets on which some climbers try to build a reputation today, they will never have more than the ephemeral interest given to them by a press ignorant of mountain values—but perhaps that is all such climbers require.

It might be brought in evidence against us that, having neglected first ascents, we made up for it by attempting record times, a still more sterile form of competition. Obviously it is impossible to disprove such a charge, and I can only say I am certain that Lachenal climbed so fast simply because he was boiling over with vitality, because perfect execution implies speed, and because he was like a dancer playing with gravity. Many of his fantastic times are unknown to the world, and many climbs begun at meteoric speed subsequently turned into quiet strolls for the sheer pleasure of admiring the scenery like any tourist. As for myself I was drawn along by my friend's magnetic power, sometimes willingly, sometimes protesting as hard as I could. No, I can sincerely say that competition never meant a great deal to us, though there were times when we were not completely exempt from it. The Eigerwand was one of these.

That July of 1947 we were aware that there were other parties in the running, and deep in our hearts we hoped that fate would allow us to be first to repeat the climb. Our main rivals seemed to be the Parisians who had done the Walker ahead of us the preceding summer. Their moving spirit was Pierre Allain, the leading French climber of prewar days. They were all virtuoso rock climbers in a high state of training, carrying the very latest equipment, and with plenty of time to spare. Their chances looked pretty good, and the only things they lacked were a greater experience on ice and a longer period of acclimatisation to altitude.

Since the year before a friendly rivalry had grown up between us, but it looked as though their long holidays would give them the edge on us once again. As things turned out, luck was with us. Three of them had been at Chamonix for several days already, but Allain, having heard of the long spell of bad weather, had put off his arrival. The weather actually began to improve on the very day we were free to go, and so we stole a march on our competitors.

We journeyed to the Oberland democratically by train. Our patience was rudely tested by the uneventful hours as we rolled through the Swiss countryside, and Lachenal in particular found them interminable. Having no taste for reading, unlike myself, he just sat there puffing away at innumerable cigarettes. Although we produced our guide's cards they refused to give us the normal discount on the Scheidegg rack railway, which was a black mark for the much-proclaimed Swiss hospitality. We finally got to Kleine Scheidegg at ten o'clock in the morning on 14 July, and there opposite us was the north wall of the Eiger, sombre and majestic.

After having pored over so many photographs I had expected the face to look quite familiar, but in practice it was so much more formidable than anything I had imagined that I hardly recognised it. A shiver passed through me. As we scrutinised its colossal walls we began to exchange impressions. I could only mutter stupidly:

'It looks impossible from here. We'll have to go and get a closer look.'

Lachenal, who had already seen the face in winter, seemed disagreeably impressed by its bare, dolomitic summer appearance. Scratching his chin in a way he had, he whimpered comically:

'Nasty! Nasty! It's as smooth as my arse! If only my mother could see that!'

After a while the first impression began to wear off, and our habit of weighing up the difficulties objectively reasserted itself. We noticed a swarm of details and had no trouble in tracing the line of the first ascent: the Hinterstoisser traverse, the first and second ice fields, the Ramp, the Spider. The sky was radiantly blue and only a few wisps of vapour clung to the sides of the mountain. Everything seemed set for a spell of fine weather. The face itself, however, did not look in such good condition. There was new snow higher up, and the walls were streaming with moisture. It would really have been prudent to wait a day or two so that the face could have the chance to dry out a bit in the heat, but we did not want to waste a moment of the perfect weather and decided to stick to our original plan by attacking the same day.

Our only guide was an account by Heckmair which had appeared in the magazine *Alpinisme*, plus a few contradictory snippets picked up here and there. We had not therefore been able to form any very precise idea of what awaited us, but for lack of anything better we had been forced to base our plans on what we had. It appeared that the lower part of the face was easy up to the Hinterstoisser traverse, after which the difficulties were mainly on ice as far as the pitches leading from the Ramp to the Spider, that these would be the crux of the climb, and that the final slopes ought once more to be relatively easy.

Supposing these details to be correct, we decided to start in the early afternoon and bivouac just after the Hinterstoisser traverse, leaving a rope fixed across it so that we could retreat in the event of a change in the weather. Because of our abilities on ice, we reckoned we could get from there to the top of the Ramp towards the end of the following morning, after which it should be possible to reach the summit the same day, climbing the last part in the dark if necessary. A timetable of a day and a half like this would be quite normal today, but in 1947 it was highly unconventional for a face still shrouded in mystery and legend which had killed its first eight suitors, and which had called for three days of desperate effort on the first ascent.

Having come to our decision, we got on the rack railway again to go up to Eigergletscher Station, the best point of departure for the Eigerwand. There we proceeded to put away a large picnic we had brought with us from France, partly for reasons of indigence, partly on account of language difficulties. We then deposited a sack containing dry clothes and food against our return, together with a letter of explanation which we asked the cloakroom attendant to open if we did not reclaim it in three days. This done, we resolutely turned our backs on the world of men.

After walking along the foot of the face on a disagreeable slope of small scree, we eventually found a good point to attack it. The climb began at five minutes past one. The difficulties were not of a very high order, and for the time being the rope could remain in the sack. Since we did not intend going very high the first day there seemed no point in tiring ourselves out with unnecessary haste.

The greatest alpine faces are not necessarily more difficult technically than any of the others—on the contrary, some shorter but steeper climbs may in fact call for more extreme gymnastics. What gives routes like the Walker and the Eigerwand their superior value is their great length and the time required to do them, placing the climber very much at the mercy of the weather. Once a certain point is passed retreat becomes highly problematical in the event of storm, to such an extent that most people prefer to forge on for the top whatever the cost. While experience has shown that men faced with the imminent prospect of death often save themselves by the calling out of hidden reserves due to the instinct of preservation, the risk of bad weather on the great walls remains a real one. This is why, at least until the science of meteorology is sufficiently developed to predict conditions reliably for a day or two ahead, only the hardiest spirits among technically proficient climbers will adventure themselves on ascents of this sort.

But that day it seemed set fair. The sky was blue, a light breeze was blowing from the north, and there seemed no reason to fear a change. This time, luck was on our side. And so we climbed light-heartedly upwards into the highest and most murderous face in the whole of the Alps.

We chatted away to each other as we climbed. From our position low on the cliff, due to foreshortening, the slopes ahead did not look particularly steep, and their relief was so much emphasised that they began to look almost easy. I remarked jokingly:

'It's all getting so reasonable that I'm a bit scared of reaching the top this evening.'

Despite our optimism, however, we were a little disturbed by the quality of the rock, and especially by the constant rattle of falling stones. The rock was a smooth, compact limestone, forming a succession of short walls and ledges. At present the lowness of the walls made the going quite easy, but it could be seen that higher up, where the ledges grew narrower and the walls longer, we should come up against some delicate ground quite different in style from our own Chamonix granite, and we wondered if we should find ourselves all at sixes and sevens on it.

The falling stones were much more worrying. For the moment they were no more than isolated pebbles, and it was; easy to protect ourselves by leaning against the rock whenever we heard them coming. Yet undeniably their presence began to build up a certain nervous tension, and their continual clacking reminded us that at any moment the face might be raked by an avalanche of boulders which it might not be so easy to dodge. As we got closer to the Rote Flüh we suddenly heard detonations above our heads and some large blocks thundered past, shattering themselves to smithereens fifty yards below us and covering us with dust. The acrid, powder-like smell was the scent of battle.

Presently we found the first signs of human passage in the form of a torn hat and some rags: Had they belonged to those who had given their lives for the conquest of this useless world of stone? The sadness that could be evoked by such castoffs was indescribable. Everything I had read about the early adventures on the face ran through my head, and I pictured the heroes with glowing eyes who had passed through their last agonies on this spot. Beside these traces of men who died reasserting their humanity in a world where the machine had become master it was ironical to find numerous bits of scrap-iron from the construction of the Jungfraujoch railway. We looked around for the Stollenloch from which they had been ejected, and from which the rescue party had later set out to try and save Kurz and his companions, but all we could see was two huge pitons cemented into the rock.

After a vertical section more prolonged than any that preceded it we came up against a real pitch, down which hung an ancient, blackened rope, swinging idly in the breeze. It was time for us to tie on. A few feet of delicate climbing brought Lachenal to an overhang, which looked as though it was going to be difficult. It was tempting to use the old fixed rope, but it was too dilapidated and he preferred to climb free. The smoothness of the limestone with its small, infrequent holds made it quite a problem, but happily three old pitons were already in place and made a lot of difference. With a heavy sack I found the overhang most awkward when my turn came.

Shortly afterwards we came to the Hinterstoisser traverse on our left. This pitch receives a lot of water from the slopes above, and the several old ropes we found dangling there were in such a state of decomposition that we didn't dare touch them for a moment. It looked delicate and exposed, and Lachenal decided to take off his sack. Once he had launched out, however, he found plenty of pitons in place, and moved quickly in spite of the waterfall that poured around him. Our rope annoyingly turned out to be too short, so that we had to take a stance part of the way across. I tied the end of the rope we had brought with us to leave here to a piton, and began to climb with both rucksacks on my back. The straps were too short and hurt abominably, cutting off the circulation in my arms. I had all the trouble in the world reaching my partner, but this was only the beginning. Next came a sort of vertical chimney in which I positively sweated blood, and it was a real relief to pull out onto the wide ledge where Lachenal, cigarette in lips, greeted me with a comic face and the words:

'Well, Mr Guide, what do you think of our bedroom?'

One could not have thought otherwise of it than well. It was large enough for us both to stretch out full length, its floor had been carefully smoothed out by previous occupants, and most important of all an overhang protected it from stones or rain. In such a situation nothing better could have been hoped for; our eagle's nest seemed a real little palace.

It was now six o'clock in the evening. Clouds had come up from the valley and enveloped us even while we were on the Hinterstoisser, but it was fine-weather cumulus and, far from disquieting us, it filled us with renewed optimism. In the cool of the evening these clouds were ravelling out into rosy wisps of vapour, and after a while they evaporated altogether. We prepared our bivouac without haste. First of all we had to tidy up the curious bric-a-brac that littered the ground: rotting garments, tins of sardines and meat, pitons of all shapes and sizes left here by those who had climbed up in the mad hope of forcing the bastion which towered above us. How many of them had crouched here soaked and shivering in the bitterness of defeat? How many had paid for their ambitions with their lives?

In one corner we found a carefully fastened metal box containing various inscriptions in German, and added to them a piece of paper mentioning our visit together with one or two rude messages to the Parisian climbers who would probably soon be following us. We had taken the trouble to carry up ample food and slid into our bivouac gear feeling quite replete. We had with us quilted jackets, waterproof capes and doubled potato sacks, a most unusual luxury to protect our legs. These new-style *pieds d'éléphants* were intended to ensure our comfort for the one night only, after which we would dump them and carry on as light as possible.

The mist had now cleared completely, and the night was marvellously clear. We leant back against the face with our feet dangling and savoured the strange poetry of the place, feeling as calm as though we were on an ordinary climb. The sky was full of stars, and I thought of the lonely shepherds all over the world who must also be looking at them at this moment. Had I not dreamed of becoming a shepherd and sleeping out under the stars? Other lights below us recalled the presence of men, so near and so remote, almost within earshot. The peasants would be ending a long day down there in their wooden chalets, dwellings out of the past. Some would still be milking cows whose bellies were distended with fresh grass; others would already be leaning over their own plates slowly munching a primitive meal. Farther down to the right in the bottom of the valley were the solemn, spacious hotels of Grindelwald in which tourists would be sitting in fashionable boredom, or giving themselves up to the hearty pleasures of taverns and nightspots. Occasionally we caught the sound of a horn, a dog barking or the shout of a herdsman.

But there were other noises to tear us back from these rural maunderings to the realisation of the hostile world around us. The mountain echoed with rumblings and crashings, and from somewhere to our right came the roar of a torrent. Salvoes of stones whirred and banged in the darkness. We sat without speaking, overawed by our surroundings. Even Lachenal had lost his normal exuberance and smoked silently, and for once in my life I also lit a cigarette. Before long we began to feel drowsy and slept like children, huddled up against each other.

Our cooker was alight by four o'clock. It was still dark and the mountain had grown silent. It occurred to me for a moment how our light must intrigue anyone down there who might chance to glance up at the Eiger, but I realised at once how unlikely it was that anybody should be looking towards us or thinking about us at such an hour. Suddenly I was oppressed by our utter loneliness. The hostility of our surroundings and the insanity of our actions appeared horrifyingly plain. Why go on with the whole crazy business? There was still time to express my horror of these frozen rocks, to recall Lachenal to reason, to flee towards human warmth and life. But in fact I said nothing. A mysterious force kept the words in, and I knew in my heart that it was too late for such thoughts. The die was cast; we must win through or die.

Light came back slowly into a radiant world, and we were soon ready. A few slabs thinly coated in black ice led across to the first ice field, which we mounted quickly until we came up against the cliff separating it from the second field above. The solution to this lay in a narrow ice gully over on our right which looked anything but tempting, and would certainly require a long bout of cutting steps. It seemed at first to be the only way, for the rocks above us were without a fault, but then we noticed a shallow corner on the left of the gully which might perhaps be hiding a possibility.

Lachenal decided to have a look, and soon beckoned me across to him. Although the corner was overhanging and contained nothing but a thin crack he reckoned it was possible. In a moment he had whipped off his crampons and started up on the left of the corner, then began a difficult traverse back into it. A first and rather shaky piton gave him enough support to tip off a large loose block which showed that nobody had tried this way before, then a second and still worse one gave him the confidence to try a long, risky stride. Since there was no crack to take third peg he placed the extreme toe of his boot on a tiny hold, held himself in balance by leaning sideways against the face with his left fingers around a minute flake, then gradually ran the fingers of his right hand across the rock like a spider, straddling with his legs until he reached a good hold. A couple of quick moves, and he was there! With the two sacks on my back I hauled myself up the rope shamelessly to join him.

Another hard pitch led to an old ring-peg on the right bank of the ice gully. Once again the obvious thing was to put on our crampons and climb the gully, but putting on crampons in our present position would have called for some real acrobatics, and anyway the gully still looked tediously steep. The slabs on our left were very smooth and disposed like the tiles of a roof, but they seemed to lead to a good ledge which in turn looked as though it offered comfortable egress onto the bottom of the ice field. Lachenal was now warmed up. He went for the slab without hesitation, and finding himself quite at ease on this sort of terrain, at which he was a past master, he soon reached the supposed ledge. He called down:

'It's no more a ledge than a piece of cheese. There's only two good holds and nowhere to put in a peg. Watch out you don't come off, I'm not sure I could hold you.'

I wasn't very thrilled with this piece of news, and called up:

'Listen, Lili, if it's as bad as that come down again. We'll go up the ice.'

But a furious voice shouted down:

'You cowardly bastard, there's no time to waste. It'll go from here on. Hurry up, for God's sake.'

When I got to him, I saw that the 'ledge' was no more than a shallow scoop where one could stand on one or two reasonable holds without getting tired, but also without any possibility of safeguarding whatever. What worried me a good deal more was that, far from growing easier, the slabs steepened up ahead of us and were largely covered in verglas. The growing exposure and the total lack of security made me feel quite sick, a sensation rather like that of a burglar caught on a too-steep roof, not able to move up or down.

Lachenal was off again without leaving me time to argue, dodging between the slabs of verglas with catlike neatness. He moved fast, but was soon held up by a steepening of the angle. He hesitated some little time, tense with concentration, then, placing his palms flat on the rock with the fingers pointing downwards, launched into a daring mantelshelf. Only too aware that the least false move on his part would take us both down to the first ice field in one bound, I crouched on my holds with nerves stretched to the limit. Only my confidence in his fabulous skill gave me any hope of a successful issue, but I knew now that if he met with an unclimbable obstacle higher up he would never manage to reverse what he had done. There would be no chance of getting a peg into this concrete-like limestone. Bit by bit he would grow exhausted until at last he slipped, and that would be the end. How much easier the lot of the leader, who, in the heat of action, has no time to reflect on the danger!

Now I could see Louis' foot being placed with infinite delicacy between two streaks of ice. He raised a hand and felt around over his head until he appeared to find a roughness, then began to straighten up gradually. But would his foot stick on? Instinctively I clutched at my holds. Very slowly he brought the other hand up to the level of the first, then stepped up quickly. He had done it! At last my tortured nerves could relax a little as I heard the sound of a peg going in. Then he called down:

'That's it. It looks as though it should go now. But this peg's not much use, so don't come off. I can probably help you a bit.'

Knowing how much worse I was than Louis at delicate climbing, and having to cope with the weight of the sack into the bargain, I embarked on the pitch feeling like a condemned man. At the crux it took me some time to work out the unusual move he had made. Balancing up on the palms alone seemed extremely precarious, and I called out:

'Hold it tight then.'

Immediately I felt the rope take part of my weight, and this made all the difference. He had not deceived me about the following slab. It was still steep, but much richer in holds—yet we still could not see the ice field, and the risk

of coming up against an unclimbable section remained. With a few movements like a wild beast Louis disappeared above my head. The rope continued
to run out steadily, then stopped. Every second seemed an age, and I was just
starting to get worried when he called out that he had found a good natural
belay. I found him in a high good humour sitting on a ledge, and collapsed
beside him. After such nervous tension we needed a few minutes' repose, and
passed the time discussing the situation.

Far from saving time by avoiding the gully we had undoubtedly wasted a
good deal, and only my friend's extraordinary talents had got us alive out of
the snare. This grave error of judgement was undoubtedly due to our lack of
experience on limestone faces. But in any case there was nothing dramatic
about the situation: we were now at the second ice field and there should
be no major difficulties until we reached the Ramp. On this 'high mountain'
terrain, which was our speciality, we ought to be able to make up all the lost
time. But not if we hung around talking all day.

We were on the ice field in a matter of minutes, disappointed that the
dryness of June had not caused the ice to shrink back and leave a ledge of bare
rock along its foot. In fact it ended in space. The slope was about fifty degrees
and quite bare of snow, but the ice, which was grey in colour, turned out to
be soft enough for us to crampon without cutting steps. We could also have
moved together without worrying about security measures, as we often used
to do, but there seemed no point in running unnecessary risks. The weather
was set fair and even if we had to bivouac again it wouldn't matter, so we put
in an ice peg at the end of each rope's length.

Our line went gently upwards and across to the left, and we made good
time. The sun was beginning to get round onto the face and warm things
up, and a few small stones whistled past, but we soon reached the top of the
ice field where we were sheltered by the wall above. We now went along the
wall until our way was barred by a small buttress. Rather than descend to go
round it we decided to climb it direct, but the rock was so rotten that we had
to move as softly as Indians on the warpath, which took us another half hour.
Presently we came to a piton. The old loop of abseil-cord that hung from it
showed that it had been put in for purposes of retreat, probably by Rebitsch
and Vörg.

The way still lay to the left, so we continued traversing towards the rocky
buttress which separated us from the third ice field. Somewhere along here
we had to find a way over this, but there seemed to be nothing above us but
smooth slabs plastered with ice. Suddenly the keen eye of Lachenal spotted
a peg: ice or no ice, that must be the route! Climbing in crampons on this

difficult ground he wrought miracles, but it called for every bit of technique he possessed as well as two more pitons to get to a stance. Soon afterwards we reached the crest of the buttress, where two rusty, twisted pegs were the sole remaining relics of Mehringer and Sedlmayer.

Instantly I remembered the photographs of their handsome faces, Mehringer's all lit up with childlike joy, Sedlmayer's more sombre, a sad smile at the corners of his lips. Half-exhausted from their heroic efforts they must have sat down here to wait for the weather to improve, fighting for many hours against the mortal cold until the snow gradually covered their bodies and they went out like a match in the rain. The seasons with their storms passed over, the ropes turned to straw, and one day the rock was bare again as in the beginning of the world. No token remained of their spirit but these pegs.

I quickly put away such thoughts. Our bodies were full of life; the warm sun bathed us in its rays until joy flowered in our minds. A few more hours of stirring combat and we should be standing above the abyss, ruffled by the breeze on the summit.

It was now one o'clock. The time had flown inexplicably, and we must be getting on. Caught up in the intensity of action I was for continuing at once, but Louis, who was being griped with hunger, insisted on stopping for some food. I had to give in, but after all, what did it matter? The sky was blue as in a dream, and there was no fear of bad weather. We flung down our sacks on an inviting little platform and argued as we gobbled down our food. From our position on the buttress, which stood out from the surrounding slopes, we commanded an excellent view of the face. The question was, would it be possible to find an alternative route to that of the first ascent? But wherever we looked our gaze was lost in the immense walls of the Gelbewand. The Ramp was now quite close also, and we examined it with distaste. It appeared to be a kind of outward-sloping gutter, and its lower part steepened into a vertical chimney between two smooth walls. From where we sat it looked absolutely frightful, but all our experience made us distrustful of first appearances and we decided to reserve judgement.

Although these immediate prospects naturally rather obsessed us, we could not help also seeing the peaceful countryside stretching away to the horizon. The tinkling of cowbells and an occasional hoarse shout floated up from the pastures, dotted here and there with brown chalets, which covered the rounded hills before us. Occasionally a more strident note would break in: the world of machines was also not far away, in all its ugliness and discordancy. There is something altogether singular about the Eigerwand, the most terrible of all mountain faces which is yet almost like a seat in the gods over the stage of life. On the Walker the climber is utterly alone in the heart of the mountains. Wherever he looks there is nothing but rock and ice and the thunder of avalanches, and never a trace of life. He feels as though he were on another planet, and nothing comes to untemper his determination. Here in this mineral world where only the ravens were at home, we were still accessible to all the contrast of civilisation. What mad pride forced us to abandon the sweetness of life for this vertical desert?

Just as on the previous day, a few clouds would form from time to time and drift up around us, then the wind would chase them away, showing the valley still bathed in sunlight. Suddenly a thunderous noise made us jump: over on our left an avalanche of boulders was bounding down the second ice field, exactly where we had been a short time before. We had been sitting idle for too long, it was time to get moving again. Lachenal suggested my taking the lead for a change. Still somewhat doubtful about my right hand, I was torn between the fear of letting him down and the desire to recover the old sensations of mastery over the forces of nature. In the end he persuaded me, and I set off first across the steep ice slope leading to the Ramp.

This part of the climb is continually peppered with small stones, some of which are as big as a tennis ball. It is a genuinely dangerous place, and I kept an eye peeled for the arrival of trouble as I cramponned delicately across. We reached shelter at the beginning of the Ramp with heartfelt relief; we were most surprised to find it completely different from what we had expected. Far from being a narrow, difficult gutter, it turned out to be a comfortable couloir. It was so easy we were almost disappointed and climbed up it together, eager to see what came next.

Presently the Ramp came to an end in a high narrow chimney splitting a wall that bristled with overhangs. There was no doubt that this was the route, but unfortunately a heavy waterfall was foaming down it. It was in fact so heavy that we seemed likely to get washed off it if we tried to climb it. We weren't expecting to be held up by a liquid obstacle, and felt rather stumped. Surely a thing like this wasn't going to stop us when the goal seemed so near! One thing was sure: we wouldn't get anywhere without trying, so I stoically began to pull on my waterproof cape. Suddenly Lachenal, who had been looking up at the wall, called out:

'Just a minute! It looks as though it might go up there on the right, where the crack goes through the overhang. It's just the thing for a thug like you, and it looks easier above. You could traverse back left between the other overhangs to the top of the chimney.'

I wasn't altogether convinced by this piece of reasoning, but even the over-hangs seemed preferable to the waterfall, so I decided to have a look. A few yards of easy traversing to the right brought me to a little grotto, in the roof of which was a crack some eight inches wide. This, it appeared, was the route Lachenal had in mind for me. After putting in a long piton for security I tried to climb up into the crack, but the only way lay up a fault of yellowy, rotten rock which came away in the fingers, and I didn't even manage to get up the seven or eight feet separating me from its base. After several attempts I got disgusted, and was preparing to return to my second when I suddenly noticed that the wall on my right, though very compact, was rippled with horizontal wrinkles. The idea came to me that by climbing up the wrinkles one might reach a sort of mantelpiece of rock twenty-five feet or so above, from which there seemed to be a line of weakness back towards the chimney.

I had now reached the condition of divine madness which makes a man oblivious of danger and renders all things possible. Normally I would have considered the wall quite beyond the pale, but now I felt a great upwelling of decision. I was just starting up the wall when I felt the rope dragging me back. The peg I had inserted in the grotto was turning it through too sharp an angle and so blocking it. I looked round for somewhere to plant an alternative piton but there was nowhere, not even the least suspicion of a crack. The rock was as solid as a concrete pillbox. Finally I found a hole about an inch deep, too thin for an ordinary peg, but I remembered that I had picked one up that morning on the bivouac ledge not much larger than the prong of a fork. Sure enough I found it among the jingling ironmongery round my shoulders, and it might have been made expressly for this cracklet. With such doubtful security I then went at the wall.

Leaning out from the rock, holding on with my fingertips and the very ends of my boot soles, I got up over halfway. At this point the wrinkles got farther apart, but by cramping my fingers onto the holds as hard as I could I managed another five feet or so. The ledge was now very close. When I stretched up I could almost touch it, but my holds were so small that I found I could not let go with one hand without starting to fall back. I could feel myself tiring, and had clearly reached the point of no return. Rather than drop off the wall like a ripe fruit I decided to gamble all. Remembering a technique used on the boulders at Fontainebleau I brought my feet as high up as possible, then bounded upwards, reaching out with my right hand as I did so. My fingers seized the edge of the ledge, and a moment later my left hand was there also. In a flash I realised that the hold was good enough, and a wave of euphoria passed over me. My feet hung clear for a second, then with a jerk and a twist I was up. Once again luck had been on my side.

Panting on all fours on the ledge I savoured the pleasures of security, where a moment before I had felt the abyss pulling me down by the heels. Then I came back to the present and began to examine my surroundings. Only then did I realise the full precariousness of my situation. I stood on a ledge perhaps three feet by three feet, but much good it did me when all around the rock was smooth and featureless.

To try this kind of thing one must at least have a good peg in for security, but I couldn't even find the smallest crack. Could I do it on sheer 'uplift' like the last bit? A few wrinkles made me wonder for a moment or two, but I was still tired from my previous efforts and anyway the divine madness had now worn off. I no longer felt the sensation of superhuman powers which enables one to confront such risks. There was nothing else for it but to go back down.

It was all very well to say turn back, but how was I going to do it? There were no spikes of rock or cracks in the vicinity where one could place a rappel. I was caught in a trap. Overcome with fear and anger I stamped up and down the ledge, but quickly returned to my senses. Perhaps I could hack out a little spike on the edge of the platform with my peg hammer? As I bent down to have a look I saw the solution: hidden by dust in the angle between the ledge and the face was a tiny crack which, with a bit of luck, would just take an 'extra-plat'.* The thinnest one I had went in about halfway, but by hammering it down against the floor of the ledge, it was possible to make it mechanically sound. It looked pretty depressing, but logically it ought to be all right. Anyway, since there was no alternative, it just had to be tried.

I quickly tied a loop of abseil-cord to the peg, then arranged a rappel with one half of the climbing rope. I remained tied on in the middle, and Louis assured me with the other end, if one could call such an arrangement assurance at all. Just as I was about to suspend myself from the contraption I felt my whole being revolt at the idea, but I pushed myself backwards with the whole force of my will . . . nothing happened. It really takes surprisingly little to hold the weight of a man! With beating heart I let myself slide down the rope, the face overhung to such an extent that I immediately swung clear into space. I was dangling like a spider: Where would I fetch up? After swinging to and fro a few times I managed to get back to the grotto.

* *Translator's note.* Pitons are classified by length and thickness: among them are 'ace of hearts', the tiniest of all; '*extra-plat*', the next category; normal blade pegs of various types; and U-pegs with a thick channel-sectioned blade. Ice pegs are much longer.

Time had flown in the heat of battle, and now I suddenly noticed that we were enveloped in thick fog. There was also a curious pattering sound like hail on rock, though none seemed to be falling until we looked away from the face. Then we realised that we were sheltered by the overhangs. Twenty feet out from where we stood the hail was coming down in sheets. Was this the advent of really bad weather or just a short evening shower? Surely it had been too fine to change as quickly as this.

I now had to decide whether to traverse back to Lachenal and attempt the waterfall after all. If I could surmount the overhang which had stopped me before it would certainly be a more comfortable way of doing things, and after so much time already wasted another minute or two would be neither here nor there. I decided to have another try. Steeling my will, I made a couple of swift moves up the loose blocks. They duly collapsed under my weight, but by then I had an arm jammed in the crack above. It was a fight to the death, and at the precise moment that I felt my weight dragging me back a flailing foot landed on a hold and pushed me up a few inches, just sufficient to enable me to grab a hold. My luck had turned, and with a tremendous heave I mantel-shelfed into a small cave.

Without wasting another moment I hauled up the sacks and then Lachenal, who was glad of some help with the rope. When he got to me he exclaimed:

'What a bastard of an overhang! You had a nerve to try it. I never thought you'd make it; you were fighting like hell and getting nowhere. A good thing you had a bit in reserve.'

There wasn't much room in the cave for two, and I made haste to get out of it. After some vacillating I succeeded in traversing to the left; the going then became much easier and I soon reached the top of the waterfall chimney. The sacks now jammed under an overhang, and at first it seemed as though nothing was going to get them clear. Finally I managed it and hauled them to me. Without even taking the time to put on my crampons I sprang at the next pitch, a thirty-foot wall covered in ice. Fortunately the ice was very porous, and it was not too difficult to hack holds in it with my piton hammer. This led to another waterfall chimney about twenty feet high. A huge mass of ice had formed around it, and the water ran down a sort of tunnel in the middle. In my attempt to make up time I once again neglected to don crampons. Huge holes in the ice served for holds, and it did not take long to reach the exit of the chimney, but at this point the ice became hard and slippery. The absence of crampons now really made itself felt, but I had to get up somehow. By nicking out pockets in the ice with the peg hammer I was able to make insecure progress, but several times it seemed as though I might come off. Providence was on my side that day.

Spouts from the waterfall kept breaking over me. Despite the waterproof cape I was blinded and half in the water, which came in through the seams, down my neck and along my sleeves. Eventually I climbed out into a wide ice gully, and there, just where I needed it, was an old piton to which I could tie myself while hauling the sacks and bringing up my partner. When he reached me we looked at the time: it was nearly six o'clock.

We both looked like drowned rats, but it was no time for mutual commiseration. The place where we stood was exposed to stone fall, and we were still far from easy ground. The next thing was to traverse across on little nicks to the rock spine which formed the true right bank of the gully. Here everything got easier again, and we pushed on as fast as possible. It was still hailing hard, and thunder could be heard in the distance. We hoped it was only a local storm, but it was certainly very worrying. Since our dramatic ascent of the Walker we were only too uncomfortably aware of how dangerous it was to be caught by storm on a high face. At all costs we must get the worst of the difficulties behind us that evening. This didn't seem an impossible task—we should reach the Spider in two hours, and another two hours from there ought to see us on the top.

After a while we found a ledge on our right which appeared to end in a vertical sixty-foot wall, and I immediately set off along it, moving delicately over rock like piled-up crockery. Louis, however, reckoned that the traverse must start higher up the couloir, and called me back. I retorted that this was exactly like the aerial photo we had seen of the four men traversing during the first ascent, but he argued that this ledge was so situated that it couldn't be photographed from the air at all. My dislike of argument made me give in as usual. Convinced that he was heading into a blind alley, I suggested that he climb up a bit and have a look. After forty feet he came across a duralumin piton. It seemed obvious to me that this had served to protect a retreat, but he heaped noisy sarcasms on my head at the very idea, particularly as there was a sort of uninviting traverse line at his own level.

He was off again, without leaving me time to argue, along a delicate ascending traverse on horribly loose rock. It was getting dark, and when my turn came I did not take out all the pitons in order to save time. Fifty feet higher there seemed to be a terrace of some kind which it looked as though we could reach. Excited at the prospect I led straight through, but after thirty feet came up against extreme difficulties. Lachenal then tried a bit farther to the left, climbing with his usual agility. Soon afterwards he called down:

'Another ten feet and I'm there.'

Almost at once, however, all movement ceased, and he started to curse.

'Just a little high voltage and I'd be there, but the pegs are all so loose it's too dangerous. It might go over on the left: I'll have a look.'

Through the murk and the gathering darkness I saw him descend a little, then disappear round a corner. We were in a sort of Scotch mist. Everything I had on was drenched, and I began to freeze with the inaction. The rope had stopped running out some time ago, and sounds of hammering and falling rocks showed that Louis was in trouble. The atmosphere was depressing in the extreme. Cramped to the face in the foggy dusk I felt utterly alone, and my determination began to melt like sugar in the rain. Suddenly I heard a strangled cry and a heavy sound of stones. Faster than thought I braced myself to take the strain of a fall, but nothing happened. I shouted up:

'Louis, what's going on?'

After a moment a panting voice replied:

'I pulled off a big piece of rock, but I just managed to grab something else in time. Don't worry, it'll go now.'

So our lives had been saved only by Lachenal's lightning-fast reaction! Suddenly the full seriousness of our position came home to me, and my whole being revolted against this mad nocturnal climbing. I called out pleadingly:

'For pity's sake, Lili, don't push it. If you go on like this we'll have an accident. We've got to get back into the couloir before there's no light left at all.'

Louis grumbled that the pitch would be easier now the loose rock was gone, and that there was a ledge above him, but the conviction had gone out of his voice and I sensed that he was half won round. This time I refused to give way, and shouted back:

'You silly bugger, if you won't come back I'm not going to give you an inch of slack. You can damn well bivouac where you are.'

This argument seemed to convince him, because he thereupon climbed back down to me. It was now ten o'clock at night, and the darkness was almost total. By feeling around I found a crack which might take a piton, and after several tries succeeded in hammering one home. We unroped and installed a rappel. Louis went down first, and I was just starting to follow him when at the precise moment my weight came on the rope the piton came out. I just managed to grab the rock in time. A shiver ran through me from head to foot, but after a few moments of confusion I managed to pull myself together. I forced myself to bang in another peg, but by now I was working in pitch darkness and the rock was so rotten that it just broke up under my blows. After several futile attempts I came back to the original crack and inserted a rather thicker peg than the previous one. It seemed all right, but all my confidence had drained away. Rigid with fear and not daring to trust all my weight to such a dubious point of support, I tried to climb down while still keeping the rope round me in a rappel position. This is in fact always a bad idea, and after only a few feet I slipped and came heavily on the rope. For a moment I thought the worst had happened, but in the event the peg stood up perfectly to the strain and I abseiled back to Lachenal in normal fashion.

We now had to abseil again, but this time on two really sound pegs. The situation remained serious for all that because we were above the wall which overhung the ramp, and we were painfully aware of the fact that our rope was too short to reach it. This meant that we had in effect to reverse the difficult ascending traverse, an operation which, between the darkness and the rotten rock, turned out to be delicate in the extreme. If either of us came off we would dangle under the overhangs, a position from which it would not be easy to get back.

Once again Lachenal went down first. Conscious of the danger he moved slowly, making the most of his dexterity. These moments were almost unbearable to me, alone and motionless in the dark. Finally there came a cry of joy: he had reached one of the pegs I had left in on the way up, and the click of a carabiner told me he had clipped one of the ropes into it. But he had to reach the second peg before he was out of the wood. Finally another click told me he was there, and shortly afterwards he called to me to follow. My own descent was easy due to being held through the pegs from below.

I had noticed certain rather indefinite balconies on the true right bank of the couloir on the way up, and I now suggested we try to regain them. We eventually found a place where we could sit down about midnight. Exhausted as we were, it took an enormous effort of will to arrange the necessary minimum of safety and comfort. We were soaked to the skin and shivering with cold, and the thought of pulling on a nice dry quilted jacket did one good. I stripped to the waist in the icy drizzle and drew mine on with a feeling of positive luxury. It had remained perfectly dry, rolled up in my rubberised elephant's foot.

Unfortunately Lili had not taken the same precautions, and his down-filled jacket turned out to be no better than a saturated sponge. Even after he had wrung it out it had lost all its warmth, and there was no doubt but that he would pass a chilly night. Eventually, by dint of throwing down some stones and building up others, we evolved tolerable positions some twenty feet apart from each other. I wasn't in the least bit hungry, but I forced myself to eat in order to conserve my strength. I recommended Louis to do the same, but he could hardly choke down more than a mouthful or two.

Our water bottles were still fairly full thanks to the various torrents we had crossed during the course of the day, but we simply lacked the willpower to make a hot drink on our little meta-cookers. I didn't take long to doze off, but soon woke up feeling strangled; I had slipped off the ledge in my sleep and was hanging on the rope. I clambered back to my resting place, but as this was no more than a notch in a little ridge on which I was straddled I slipped off to one side or the other every time I went to sleep. Despite my utter exhaustion I spent a wretched night. Lachenal was better placed, but he was so cold in his drenched clothes that his teeth never stopped chattering the whole night long.

Round about three o'clock in the morning we heard the rumble of a storm in the distance, but although the occasional flash of lightning lit up the clouds around us nothing happened on the Eiger. The drizzle had stopped and it was getting colder.

We were now seriously worried, and began to discuss our best course. On the Walker our retreat had been cut off in any case, so there had been no decision to make—it had just been a matter of getting up or getting killed. The situation here was more complex. We knew that the previous summer Krähenbühl and Schlünegger had got as far as this before being caught in a storm, and had managed to retreat to safety despite the snow, the avalanches and the shaky pitons. There was therefore an undeniable possibility of saving ourselves by going back, however dangerous the attempt might be. Although I was in despair at having to give up when the goal was so near this seemed to me the wisest course. Lachenal on the contrary calculated that we could be on the top in a few hours, and that it would be more dangerous to go down than to go on. If he told me once he told me twenty times that the well-known Grindelwald guide Adolph Rubi had personally assured him that the couloir from the Spider to the summit was just an easy scree slope, and I had to admit that Heckmair's account in *Alpinisme* seemed to confirm this theory. After all, his party had gone up it in spite of bad weather and frequent avalanches.

But in my heart I was only half-convinced. Without quite liking to say so, it seemed to me that Louis' judgement might be affected by the apparent proximity of success. He had dreamed yearningly of this climb for so long that he would go to any length for it. In the end, however, his enthusiasm and his will to win carried the day. In the bitter murk of dawn the way down looked anything but attractive. We had come here for an adventure, and now we had got it we might as well make the most of it.

By five o'clock we were already at work on the tottering crockery of the traverse. The air was heavy, and all the indications were that it would snow before long. We could only go as fast as possible and hope that providence would grant us a few hours' respite. After two pitches on which I felt that the whole mountain might collapse around us at any moment, I came at last to a solid platform. An abandoned lantern and a piton with a loop through it showed that last year's attempt had ended here. A short traverse on ice now led to the foot of an uninviting-looking wall, the first few feet of which overhung. To begin with I couldn't find any cracks that would take a good firm piton, but eventually I succeeded in inserting an ice peg in a wide crack in the rock at arm's length, on which I then heaved up for all I was worth.

The morning frost had covered the damp rock with verglas, and the holds were all encrusted with old snow. I climbed in crampons with my sack on my back to save time, but in the circumstances I was far from happy on such a vertical face. Every hold had to be cleared individually, and progress was both slow and painful. After forty feet I was close to a ledge, but once again there was an overhang in the way and all the cracks were too wide to hold a peg. Well, I would simply have to do it without. I could just reach a small incut hold which might solve the problem . . . but no, I was too tired, and I could feel the weakened fingers of my right hand opening out under the strain. If I tried to force it I would peel off. Three times I tried, and three times I had to return hurriedly to my holds. The last peg was twenty feet below, too far to justify deliberately risking a fall, but at the same time I could hardly let six feet of rock stop me now. By feeling around with my left hand I discovered a better crack, and in a very awkward position managed to plant one of the specially thick pitons that Simond had kindly made for me. What would have happened if I hadn't talked him into doing it I don't know! With this security, anyway, I was able to go to the limit. I gathered myself for the effort, and a moment later I was on the ledge.

Most unfortunately my peg hammer had caught under the overhang as I moved up, and the violence of my effort had broken its leather sling. Its loss was a potential disaster. From now on it would be practically impossible to recover any pegs we put in, and I dreaded to think what would happen if anything went wrong with the other hammer.

The 'Traverse of the Gods' turned out much easier than I had expected. The rock was certainly loathsome enough for anybody, but there were several old pegs in situ which made it safe. We climbed the Spider as fast as we could go, not stopping to take any belays or cut any steps. Fortunately the ice was fairly soft, and broken bits of rock sticking out of the snow here and there also helped. Victory now felt quite close, and we rushed into the base of the couloir with shouts of enthusiasm. At first its easy angle seemed to confirm Adolph Rubi's predictions. We penetrated into a constricted gully, and an old piton showed that we were on the right road. Shortly, however, we came up against a thirty-foot step of compact, vertical rock covered in verglas an inch thick.

I got up six feet or so, placing the two front points of my crampons on tiny holds, then nearly came off. There seemed to be nowhere to put a peg, and I returned disconsolate. Louis then tried in his turn, and got a peg through the verglas half an inch into a superficial crack behind. By some miracle he then managed to move up on this precarious support and repeated the operation on four more equally doubtful pegs before he arrived at the top of the pitch. It was a real tour de force. I made vigorous use of the rope in climbing up to join him, and had no trouble in tweaking the pegs out with one hand.

The slope now gave back again, and we were able to move up steadily in spite of the verglas which covered everything. After a few more pitches we once again fetched up short against a step of light-coloured rock. The step was split by an overhanging crack which we could have laybacked quite quickly in normal conditions, but this technique was ruled out by the verglas. I thrutched* my way painfully up to the overhang, where I eventually succeeded in planting a long ice peg. By bridging until I was practically doing the splits I got another peg above the overhang, but it was hammered into a pile of slates that didn't inspire me with much confidence. There was literally nothing else to pull up on, so for lack of any alternative I grabbed the peg with both hands and tried to walk my feet up the wall. They kept skidding on the ice, but I had almost done it when there was a ping! and I found myself twenty feet lower down, behind Lachenal but still upright. The whole thing was so sudden that I hadn't even the time to be frightened, and the strain had been taken so gradually that I felt no shock whatever. Louis goggled at me clownishly:

'What's the idea—are we playing birdies?'

Then he added more seriously:

'Nothing broken? Do you want to have another go or shall I try?'

Furious at the incident and still hot with the effort, I replied:

'It's all right, I'll have another shot. Don't worry about it, it'll go this time.'

I went at it again without a moment's rest. This time I got the second peg in more reliably and mantelshelfed onto a good hold. Now I had to cross a slab to the left, an operation rendered delicate by the ice. The weather was

* *Translator's note.* 'Thrutch' is a climbing word denoting awkward progress.

more menacing than ever. Sullen clouds were sinking lower and lower, and sounds were becoming hushed. Everything pointed to a heavy snowfall before long. I looked desperately for ways of avoiding the icy slab, but there seemed no other way out. It just had to be done, and quickly: it was a matter of life and death.

Deliberately shutting off my imagination I pushed the points of my crampons into the black ice and set off across the slab. There was nothing for the hands and no opportunities for guile. By concentrating all my forces and accepting all the risks I got across, though more than once on the verge of falling. It did not take long to haul the sacks and bring up Lachenal, who took a pull on the rope to save time. Another overhang loomed above us: Would this diabolical couloir with its verglas and its overhangs never come to an end? This one looked really unclimbable, and we could not imagine how the Germans had dealt with it. Perhaps we could escape round the corner to the left into the next couloir? A few moves took me out onto a little shoulder which overlooked it, but it looked even worse than the last one. Suddenly I noticed a rope jammed in a crack, and at the same moment the solution became clear: the Germans had abseiled to a ledge below which led round to yet a third couloir.

I grabbed the rope, taking no notice of its decayed state, and a moment later I stood at the base of a wide, steep chimney. Naturally it was full of ice and looked far from prepossessing, but with some very wide bridging and plenty of optimism it ought to go. No sooner had Lachenal reached my side than I was off, bridging so wide that at times it seemed I might pull a muscle. The rock was extremely compact and practically impossible to peg, but just as I had almost run out of rope I found a place where I could get a piton in an inch or so, and with this pitiful belay Lachenal had to be content.

It began to hail heavily and a torrent of hailstones poured down the gully, but luckily a convenient overhang saved us from the full weight of it. The difficulties now seemed to be diminishing at last, and a tremendous feeling of joy began to seethe inside me. I knew now that we were saved. The main obstacles were all behind us and there was nothing more that could conceivably hold us up, even though the hail had turned into big, thick-falling snowflakes. But an hour more in reaching this point and our chances would have been halved.

Presently we came to a steep slope of broken-up rocks. Knowing the summit so near we were torn with impatience and had been climbing together as fast as we could, but I quickly realised the danger of such haste on ground as delicate as this. It seemed best to take no further chances, but to belay carefully pitch by pitch. Lachenal grumblingly agreed, and we went on at the steady pace of the traditional mountaineer.

But how long this pitch did seem? To be sure it was positively never-ending! Presumably impatience and fatigue made it seem so, and yet . . . surely there was something funny going on. Perhaps Lachenal, carried away by his wish to get off the climb, was following me after all? No, there he stood, quite motionless with a belay. I couldn't understand it at all, and decided to keep a very sharp eye out. Oh, the crafty devil! He was climbing up behind me, and every time I made to turn round he would stop and pretend to be belaying.

But all things come to an end, even slopes of loose rock. More snow showed that the summit could not be far away, but we were now so weary that we were incapable of increasing our pace. Suddenly we came out on the Mittelegigrat, and this time it was really true: we had vanquished the Eigerwand.

I felt no violent emotion, neither pride nor joy. Up in the cloud on this lonely ridge I was just a tired and hungry animal, and my only satisfaction was the animal one of having saved my skin. I badly wanted to rest, but Lachenal would not allow it. He was obsessed with the idea of getting back to the valley to reassure his wife at the earliest possible moment, and had worked himself into a sort of frenzy. But I could only prod heavily up the final ridge in spite of his invectives and we did not reach the summit proper until three o'clock.

The adventure was by no means over, and we now began the frightful ordeal of the descent. The layer of fresh snow was already more than four inches deep, and in order not to slip we were forced to keep on our crampons. By the same token, of course, we were constantly turning our ankles on hidden stones, and my bad ankle gave me hell. Lachenal, who seemed miraculously immune to fatigue, ran in front of me cursing his head off. Since we were still roped together I had no choice but to follow, but the pace exhausted me and in the depths of my heart I began to hate him for a hectoring tyrant.

We had made the mistake of not getting precise details of the way down. All we knew was that it was supposed to be easy and that it was on the west flank of the mountain. A quick glance at a postcard had shown us that the face was bordered at the south end by a snow couloir which didn't look particularly steep, and we had simply come to a snap decision that this must be the right way, and that the whole face looked a piece of cake in any event. Now we were searching for the couloir in the storm. An ill-defined track led off but soon disappeared and left us guessing, blinded by the wind and snow. There was a crash of thunder from somewhere close by, and our hair began to buzz disagreeably with electrical discharge.

Being caught on a mountain by an electric storm is a terrifying experience. The deafening peals, the sparks crackling on your scalp, the shocks which can sometimes even knock you down; all give a tangible quality to the danger that can strike fear into the boldest heart. Even more than an artillery barrage such a storm makes a man feel at the mercy of impersonal forces which might wipe him out at any moment. Reduced to the condition of a hunted beast, his weakness and loneliness become clear to him in all their totality. The danger is in no way illusory, and quite a large number of mountaineers have been thus electrocuted, badly burnt or thrown from their holds.

But I had gone beyond fear for that day, and even the storm failed to upset me. I advanced as in a dream, thinking only of a place where I could at least eat, drink and sleep. As for Louis, the storm only served to increase his excitement. Not for one moment did he think of taking shelter. His only remaining idea was to descend, and he ran here and there, shouting and gesticulating as though possessed by the devil.

We had been finding our way down between the limestone ledges and steps for quite a long time when suddenly we saw the white slopes of the couloir in front of us. Once again we were on easy ground, and we ran downhill shouting with joy at the prospect of an early end to our sufferings. All at once, however, the couloir ended in a cliff. It was too high to rappel down, and there seemed no way out either to left or to right. We appeared to have put our heads in a trap. Presumably the correct route was farther to the north, and we would have to climb back up some way to find it: the question was, would we find it before nightfall?

Once again all our cares returned. It was growing late, the storm was at its height, and in our present state a third bivouac would be dramatic. For a moment we recalled the tragic end of Molteni and Valsecchi, who died of exhaustion only three-quarters of an hour from the hut after conquering the north face of the Badile, and I could not prevent myself wondering gloomily if a similar fate awaited us. During a brief rent in the cloud I thought I saw a possibility of descent on the left bank of the couloir, but Louis was adamant for the right bank and luckily I was too tired to argue.

Painfully we trudged back up the couloir and took the first ledge leading back onto the west face. This turned out to be an almost impenetrable labyrinth of rocky bars and ledges of unequal extent. The rock was still very compact and we had practically run out of pitons, so that we couldn't have rappelled even if it would have done us any good. It was only the short chimneys and gullies, which every so often led from one ledge to the next, that made descent possible at all. It appeared that we might find ourselves blocked for good at any time by a higher, unbroken step, but the solution always turned up at the last moment.

Lachenal's vitality and concentration were still unimpaired. With incredible skill he ran this way and that across the snowed-up slabs, seeming to be everywhere at once. Thanks to him we continued to descend at a fair rate in spite of the complexity of the route. But always our minds were weighed down by a painful sense of drama. What was to become of us if we met with an unbroken piece of cliff? Would we have the strength to toil all the way up again, and would we survive another bivouac? And then, all of a sudden, our anxieties were dissolved. Everything was simple. Thirty feet below us the face died out in a gentle snowfield. Turning our backs on the world of rock and storm where we had experienced such unforgettable hours, we ran down the slope that led to the world of men.

Telephone calls asking for news of our progress had meanwhile robbed our attempt of its secrecy, and at Eigergletscher people were getting extremely worried. The German Swiss are a cold and not always very likeable race, but I must say that on this occasion we were treated with the greatest kindness by everybody at the station hotel. Crowds mainly pass through during the day, and that evening we were almost the only guests. The whole staff went out of its way to attend to our comfort and make us feel at home. We were literally ravenous, and for hours had thought of little else but the feast that awaited us. Perhaps it is one of the major virtues of climbing that it gives back their true value to simple actions like eating and drinking. But alas, now that we were actually seated in front of a sumptuous meal we were unable to do more than choke down a few mouthfuls.

We passed a wretched night, tortured by chronic thirst. We kept on having to get up and drink, but the liquid would only quench our thirst for a few moments. In such circumstances it was impossible to sleep. I have never understood why the Eiger should have affected us in this way. The Walker is a more strenuous climb and very little shorter, yet it didn't try us to anything like the same extent. Since then I have done still harder climbs, notably the final step on the FitzRoy peak, but have always been able to eat and sleep normally afterwards.

We were up early, and had hardly set a foot out of our room when a journalist was upon us. He had come up on foot during the night, hoping to scoop our account. Before long, telephone calls started coming in from all over the place, and the first train up that morning disgorged a dozen reporters and photographers. This sudden craze to hear about our adventures came as a surprise. It had not occurred to us that a mere second ascent would arouse such widespread interest, and the idea that our names would appear in the headlines all over Europe had never crossed our minds for an instant. Our new routes, our extraordinary performance on the Droites, even our dramatic ascent of the Walker, had never excited more than a few lines in the local papers.

In those days mountaineering was still something of a world on its own, in which the press had no interest apart from accidents. Blood and death are saleable commodities wherever they come from. The public reacts to tragedies even when it doesn't understand them, because they appeal to the most basic human instincts. Anyone can imagine himself in the same position. But the story of a climb, however remarkable it may be, can only be boring for those who do not understand the technicalities of the sport. To hope for any notoriety from mountaineering would have been a doomed pastime in 1947.

I would be lying if I suggested that we hoped no one would ever hear of our ascent of the Eigerwand: vanity is one of the prime movers of the world, and neither of us was a saint. But although it was one of the most redoubtable faces in the Alps it had already been climbed once, and this was bound to have dissipated much of its hitherto fabulous aura. The second ascent of the Walker, for example, had passed almost unnoticed, whereas its original conquest had been the object of tremendous publicity. We expected our Eigerwand climb to increase our reputations among the limited circle of the elect, but had absolutely no inkling of the ephemeral glory which became ours in the event. We were dumbfounded, and to this day I still wonder what served to focus the interest of the press on what might so easily have passed unnoticed.

There exists nothing more contrived than this kind of fame. Take the example of the event which caused more ink to flow than any other in the history of French climbing, the ascent of Annapurna. In the first instance it received no more than a couple of lines in two or three Paris dailies, and only on the following day was it generally decided to give it prominence.

Once the curiosity of the journalists had been satisfied we found ourselves again alone with our problems. It only remained to catch the train like any other tourists, of which we looked a particularly shabby version with our emaciated faces and damp, torn clothes. By the time we had paid the hotel bill we had practically nothing left to buy food, but fortunately we were treated to a meal by a second wave of reporters who were lying in wait for us at Berne. We were even recognised and stopped in the street by a passerby who offered us a drink. At Geneva we received a triumphal welcome from members of the famous Androsace climbing club with whom we passed an evening celebrating at my friend Pierre Bonnant's house. This display of genuine human warmth gave us more pleasure than all the blown-up headlines. The following day our friend Paul Payot, later mayor of Chamonix, drove over with our wives to fetch us home.

A day later I went up to a hut with members of the *aspirants-guides'* course. Everything was back to normal. Thenceforward I knew that fame consisted of no more than a few headlines, a few raised glasses and the pleasure of a few friends. As for the Eigerwand, it was no more than a great memory. Other adventures were waiting for us on other mountains.

In my view the Eigerwand is the greatest climb in the Alps. It does not call for extreme rock-gymnastics, but by reason of its peculiar character modern climbers get up it very little faster than their predecessors, despite all the advances in technique and equipment. This is by marked contrast with most other routes. If one compares it with the greatest feats that have been performed farther afield, such as the Cerro Torre, the south face of Aconcagua, the FitzRoy, the Muztagh Tower, Chacraju, and others, it is not, if you like, any longer an exceptional exploit. But this is less due to any diminution in its value by the progress of mountaineering than to the fact that present-day climbers are willing to make greater efforts and take greater risks than their forefathers.

However good he may be, and however favourable the conditions of his ascent, anyone who returns from the Eigerwand cannot but realise that he has done something more than a virtuoso climb; he has lived through a human experience to which he had committed not only all his skill, intelligence and strength, but his very existence.

These days the story of the Eigerwand is almost complete. Early in March 1961 four German climbers, Walter Almberger, Toni Hiebeler, Anton Kinshoffer and Anderl Mannhardt, made a winter ascent of the face after six bivouacs and seven days of climbing. This exploit, unequalled in the history of the Alps, was conceived and organised by Toni Hiebeler, who was also its real leader although he did not climb at the head of the party. The project was thought out with a care and ingenuity never before brought to bear on an alpine problem. Months were spent in the perfecting of every detail. The most modern equipment then in existence seemed inadequate to them, so they proceeded to develop their own boots and clothing.

Bad weather foiled the first attempt at the height of the Stollenloch, through which they escaped. A week later they returned to the face through the tunnel, then set off resolutely up the really difficult part. They carried so much food and equipment that they could have lived and climbed efficiently through ten days of bad weather. These loads gave them great security, and they climbed with a methodical care that reduced the risk of a fall to the minimum. This apparently prudent technique was not however without its disadvantages. The huge weight of the sacks and the strict adherence to the rules of safety in fact exposed them to the enormous danger of being on the face for a week.

It is permissible to wonder if somewhat lighter kit and less careful methods might not actually have reduced the danger by cutting two or three days off the time taken. They gained their victory thanks to their own courage and ability—and to an exceptionally long spell of fine weather. What would have happened if a long and violent storm had caught them in the middle of the face? The margin between victory and disaster is sometimes very fine. The hard law of the human tribe raises up victors as heroes; the vanquished are relegated to the ranks of weaklings, lunatics and fools. Hiebeler and his party have become heroes.

The hours I passed on the Eigerwand are among the most thrilling I have known, yet of all my ascents I number it with Annapurna and the FitzRoy as one I would not willingly repeat. The falling stones, the loose rock, the almost perpetual verglas and the difficulty of retreat raise the level of risk beyond what is normally reasonable; after all, the number of people killed on the face is nearly equal to the number who have climbed it. One may tempt the devil for a good enough reason and get away with it once, but one cannot make a habit of it and last long.

After our ascent, therefore, it seemed most unlikely to me that I would ever revisit the mountain. Of the other ways up it only the Lauper route is of much technical interest, and the Oberland seems rather remote when there are so many other good climbs all over the place. But one should never be too sure. Ten years later I had another exciting experience on the Eiger, which I will now relate.

In 1957 I numbered two excellent Dutch climbers among my clients. Since they had begun climbing seven years earlier I had taught them practically all they knew, and their natural abilities had made them into accomplished mountaineers. Somewhat unusually, their tastes and talents lay particularly in the direction of ice climbing. Together we had done some of the hardest north faces in the Mont Blanc range. On two occasions they had even taken me with them to Peru, where we had done some difficult first ascents. These shared adventures had made us into close friends.

That season, knowing how many good ice climbs there were in the Oberland, we decided to go there. The weather was ideal, and we had already done the northwest face of the Wetterhorn and returned to our base in the Grindelwald valley when the excitement began.

'Look, I can see them! There, on the big snowfield, by that angle of rock.'

'Oh yes! Now I can see them too. But there's three of them—can't you see the third?'

Rather irritated at being woken up by these excited Belgian voices just outside my tent at eight o'clock in the morning, I rolled over and curled up again in my sleeping bag without paying much attention. As I dozed off again their meaning gradually began to penetrate the layers of my subconscious, and before long I was wide awake. I remembered a local guide telling me the day before that there was a party on the Eigerwand—no doubt this was the sight that was setting everybody chattering. I shook Tom and Kees and rolled out of the tent, a pair of binoculars in my hand.

Everybody on the campsite was staring up at the sinister, five-thousand-foot wall, with towers so close above the valley that parties can sometimes be seen on it with the naked eye. People were gabbling away in twenty different languages, and I heard a prodigious number of fatuities and much wrong information being exchanged. Some said that thirty men had died on the face; others that it had never been repeated. The babel was liberally interspersed with remarks like: 'You must have to be off your head', and 'Only a madman would try such a thing.'

Propping myself against a car wheel I examined the face minutely and had no difficulty in seeing not three, but four climbers. They were on the upper part of the second ice field, keeping close to the rock, heading for Sedlmayer and Mehringer's death-bivouac on the buttress. It looked as though they were all roped together in one party, and their progress was incredibly slow. I knew from experience that the slope was not more than forty-five degrees. There was no sign of bare ice, and although the snow had probably not frozen hard in the mild conditions you could see that it was good enough to move quite fast on. Ten years earlier Lachenal and I had gone at least twice as fast across these slopes in spite of bare ice. I was unable to think of any good reason why these men should be moving so slowly.

What seemed even more inexplicable than their slowness was the fact that they should be persevering at all when a storm was obviously brewing up rapidly. The blue sky of the previous few days had given place to heavy clouds of ill omen which, as the morning went on, became increasingly menacing. I could perhaps just have understood an extremely fast and daring party pressing on, if the mountain were in perfect condition, in the wild hope of reaching the summit that evening. Lachenal and I had done something of the sort on the Walker eleven years before, but with the difference that the weather then was infinitely less threatening than on that Tuesday, the sixth of August 1957.

I simply failed to comprehend. What was going on before my eyes was a hundred times more stupid than the normal run of heroic follies which the nature of the sport sometimes entails. The mountain was obviously in bad condition, and the four men had taken a day and a half to climb the easiest part of the face, usually done in a morning. (Only later did I learn that the Italians had attacked on Saturday and the Germans on Sunday, which makes the whole thing madder still.) Now, on a simple snow slope, they were advancing at a snail's pace, despite every sign of imminent bad weather. It would still have been possible to retreat without too much difficulty, instead of which they just trailed on at the same tedious pace as though they were not mortal and reasonable beings, but robots insensible to pain and death.

Sitting helplessly on the grass, I saw at once that these men were heading for certain disaster. I couldn't understand what motivation could drive them thus to continue a doomed ascent. No ideal, no technical gifts could serve to explain it. The time was long past when, as some say, an exaggerated patriotism caused certain climbers to run mortal risks for the prestige of their country. In attempting the twelfth ascent of the Eigerwand these men could hope for neither gain nor glory. The least glimmer of common sense must have shown them that they were already at the limit of their capacities, and that bad weather would render them helpless however stout their morale. It was no longer a question of adventure, of pushing back the frontiers of the impossible, or any of the other motive forces of high-standard mountaineering; it was high time for an honourable and sensible retreat. Only a monstrous vainglory stronger than instinct could lead them on like this to certain death.

But still they pushed slowly on, reaching the foot of the Sedlmayer-Mehringer buttress at midday. At 2:30 p.m., by which time they should have attained the ice field beyond, there was no sign of them on it when the clouds parted for a moment. There seemed nothing to be done, and we left Grindelwald until the Thursday evening. The weather seemed quite good on the Wednesday morning, rather as though fate was giving them a last chance, but later it broke up. A terrible storm was followed by an absolute deluge all day Thursday. On Friday morning a clearing enabled me to get another look at the face, and tracks could be seen leading from the buttress to the Ramp. Some campers told me that they had seen the party two days before trying to escape onto the Lauper route on the northeast face. My Dutch friends, less accustomed than myself to goings on of this kind, were very harrowed by the whole business. Tom, whose excitable and generous nature comes from an

Irish grandmother, was pacing up and down in despair at not being able to do anything. He suddenly burst out:

'For heaven's sake, Lionel, can't we do *something* for those poor devils?'

'In weather and conditions like this it'd be madness to try. There wouldn't be a hope of succeeding, and every chance of getting chopped ourselves in the process. There's nobody more willing than I to try and save people when there's the remotest chance, but I'm all against turning one accident into two for no good purpose. Believe me, I know the face—they're still too low on it. You couldn't do much until they'd got to the level of the Spider, or at a pinch the Lauper route, and even then you'd have your work cut out.'

'Well, anyway, if they get that far, will you try and get up a rescue party? It would be terrific if we could save them.'

'Listen, Tom. You know what happened last winter. I got called every name under the sun because instead of standing around talking I tried to help two poor lads who could have been saved without any bother if people had got on the job a little earlier. People who behave badly don't like having it pointed out. If the Eiger were in France I might have a shot at it even so—I know enough people to call on there who might come with us. But what can I do here? I don't know anyone, I don't even speak a word of German. The local people have made their position perfectly clear, in any case. They've even put it down in black and white that the Eigerwand is strictly for nutcases, and anybody who goes on it does so at his own risk. What do you expect me to do about it after that? Anyway, after the Mont Blanc business, I don't feel like rearing my ugly head again; everyone will just say I'm looking for publicity and write me off.'

'But if someone else got up the rescue, wouldn't you take part? If we went along as a party of three nobody could say anything against you.'

'In the first place, who do you think is going to bother to get a party up? Nobody cares two hoots about those poor bastards up there. Anyway, I wouldn't go even if they did. Somebody would find a way of twisting my motives, and they can manage quite well without me—one person's as good as another. There's plenty of climbers around in Switzerland who know how to run a rescue party.'

'Lionel, you disappoint me! You've no right to put personal feelings before duty. There's no doubt at all that you could help, and if so then you damn well ought to.'

'No, to hell with it. I'm browned off with the whole business. On Mont Blanc it was a question of some good kids who'd had a bit of bad luck, but these characters are just idiots. I've no wish to get chopped for a bunch of cretins like that.'

'You mean you wouldn't go, even if you were asked?'

'Ah, that would be another matter. If I were formally asked I'd go for the sake of solidarity. But since only Rubi knows I'm in the vicinity it's not very likely.'

And so the morning went by. The Eigerwand was still cloaked in cloud, but overhead a number of blue patches showed that the weather was improving. Having nothing to do around Grindelwald we decided to go and do a climb, and in view of the poor conditions we settled for the relatively modest Nollen ridge on the Mönch. About mid-afternoon we took the train up to Kleine Scheidegg, intending to stroll on up to the Guggi hut. In the train no one could talk about anything but the Eigerwand, and one passenger told us that Seiler, a climber who had taken part in the fourth ascent, was organising a rescue party.

It was raining so hard at Eigergletscher that we decided to sleep there and set out at one o'clock in the morning if things improved. Nobody said much over the evening meal. My friends could see that I was preoccupied, and they too were unable to forget that four men were in mortal agony a few hundred yards away. Kees suddenly broke the silence:

'Lionel's got to go up and join the rescuers. That's where he belongs.'

I answered:

'Maybe so, but I'm not going unless the leader of the party actually asks me.'

Tom got up without a word, walked to the telephone and called Jungfraujoch. He got through to Seiler and began talking to him in German. I could make out the words 'Bergfuhrer', 'Terray', and 'Chamonix', then he held out the receiver towards me:

'Seiler wants to speak to you.'

Conversation was easy, as Seiler spoke excellent French. He asked me to come up at once. He had plenty of helpers, but most of them were not particularly strong from a technical point of view and he desperately needed guides and experienced amateurs. It was by now nine o'clock, and there were no more trains that evening. We decided to go up on foot through the tunnel, but the railway employees placed an absolute embargo on the project. Tom got through on the telephone to one of the directors without any better success. The rules were the rules, and no rescue party was going to change them!

Faced with the insurmountable stupidity and ill will of the railway staff, we came to the conclusion that our only course was to set out at four o'clock via the west face of the mountain in order to meet the others on the top. When the alarm went off Kees was feeling ill and stayed behind, fearing to delay us. The weather seemed a bit clearer as we walked out of the station, but a violent wind had set in from the north which could hardly fail to complicate the rescue. We decided to go up in any case and see. We were very fit by this time, and climbed fast. We reached a point on the northwest ridge only about a thousand feet below the summit by 7:30 in spite of finding the rocks plastered with verglas. In good conditions this point commands a fine view of the north face, due to its general concavity, but now the clouds allowed only a few glimpses of ice-armoured crag.

It seemed patently absurd that anyone could have stood up to a week of bad weather in such an inhuman place, and if I had agreed to take part in the operation it was more from approval of the generous and humane action of the Swiss rescuers than from any real hope of hauling the victims from this apocalyptic gulf. It was therefore without much conviction that I leant over the crest of the ridge and shouted, during one of the rare lulls. As I expected, there was no response but the roaring of the wind. We were getting ready to start again when to our extreme surprise we distinctly heard a voice. At first we wondered if our excited imaginations were deceiving us, but other cries soon proved that there were indeed human beings still alive and calling from the depths. We therefore hurried on at once, buoyed up by new hopes of actually doing something useful if only the weather would improve, as now seemed possible.

Soon afterwards we saw parties of climbers on the Eigerjoch ridge battling against the wind. Convinced that there would already be a large group on the summit we forced the pace, only to find it deserted when we arrived at 8:45. I felt a medley of emotions to be standing once again on this crest, where, ten years earlier almost to the day, I had emerged into the storm exhausted from two days of concentrated struggle. The feelings of that ardent moment returned to me with the utmost intensity.

The freezing wind cut us to the bone, and in order to get warm in a useful sort of way we started hacking platforms out of the ice. We had been at the job for nearly two hours before the climbers eventually arrived. Decisive-looking, craggy-featured and sparing of word and gesture, they greeted us briefly, then sat down and made tea. Tom, who could speak not only German but even Swiss German, began to question them at once, and we learnt that the rescue party had started out at one o'clock in the morning, but had been terribly impeded by the gale on the narrow ridge of the Mönch. They had been forced to fix ropes and goodness knows what else, but their arrival would not be much longer delayed. We also learnt that the larger of the two men was none other than Eric Friedli, inventor of the rescue equipment adopted as standard by the Swiss Alpine Club.

I realised at once our luck in having this specialist in difficult rescue operations with us. After a quick snack the German Swiss began working on a platform where cables could be anchored. The rock was so broken that they had to put in numerous pitons and even wind their cables round a large block. I took the liberty of suggesting to them that the final couloir was in fact somewhat farther to the east, but they took no notice and carried on working where they were. The other parties started arriving about two o'clock, and before long the summit got positively crowded. All these good folk were members of the Swiss Alpine Club, mostly from Thun and Berne, but also a few Biennois who spoke French. They told me that a dozen German climbers had arrived from Munich the previous evening and were coming up the northwest face. The famous pilot Geiger came and made signals to us that the victims were still alive, and quite soon there were two or three aeroplanes circling the summit and diving spectacularly but uselessly down the face. Their noise and aerobatics created a fairground atmosphere rather unexpected in a place of this sort.

The cables were all in place by three o'clock, and Friedli asked for volunteers to make a reconnaissance descent. Seiler, the excellent Biennois climber Perrenoud, and myself stepped forward. Friedli chose Seiler, who after descending only two hundred feet was able to shout up that the couloir was farther to the east. This meant that everything had to be moved and all the installations remade on the new site. While the experts from Thun were getting on with this task, we set about preparing places to bivouac. Part of the team was to descend to Eigergletscher for the night and come up again next day with food and more equipment, but more and more people kept on turning up.

First came the Germans led by Gramminger, a man who had himself accomplished some of the most difficult rescues ever made. Later we got a welcome surprise at the arrival of the famous Italian climbers Cassin and Mauri, who had hurried from Lecco to help their compatriots. Just before nightfall eight more stout-looking fellows emerged onto the summit, bowed under heavy loads. They turned out to be a group of Poles who were in the area to climb some of the great north faces and had come up to join us as a spontaneous fraternal gesture. The mountain had turned into a veritable Tower of Babel, and Tom's multilingual capacities were invaluable. Apart from Dutch he can talk equally well in four languages. His eyes sparkling with intelligence and good humour, he was here, there and everywhere among the various groups, gesturing and explaining until they all understood each other.

Over thirty men were now digging and hacking along the summit ridge, clearing platforms to sleep on and even caves to shelter them from the still violent wind. Having the Latin tongues in common, the two Italians, the Lucernois Eiselin and Tom and I all settled down together in a friendly group. It would be exaggerating to say we weren't cold, but we had all been in much worse situations in our time, and despite our lack of equipment it was just an ordinary bivouac.

At dawn, while we were making tea, the Germans sent a man down on reconnaissance, and soon afterwards the news spread along the ridge that he had made contact with the survivors. It seemed they were at the top of the Spider, and an attempt was to be made to hoist them up without further delay. It looked as though providence was about to recompense the generosity which had assembled so many men here on an apparently hopeless mission by seeing that their efforts were not in vain. But although there was now a hope of saving some of the party we were still very far from the actual realisation. Many problems remained to be overcome, and the key factor was the weather. In mountains anything is possible while this is in your favour, but once it turns against you everything becomes a hundred times more difficult. In fact the prevailing signs gave cause for both hope and fear. The previous day's icy gale had dropped, and it had even become quite warm, but by contrast the blue sky had given way to a heavy ceiling of cloud. At present it was well above us, but it looked so black and menacing that we could hardly doubt it would snow eventually. Our success or failure depended mainly on the respite it allowed us.

Eventually Friedli sent down the young German climber Hellepart, chosen for his herculean physique and strength. He was armed with a walkie-talkie so that he could keep in touch with those at the winch about things as they happened. After the steep summital snow slopes he continued without incident down the gullies and chimneys above the Spider, only the occasional vertical step slowing up his progress. The cable was wound round a wooden drum which made it easy to regulate his speed at will. Every three hundred feet he had to be stopped so that another length of cable could be bolted on.

After about a thousand feet Hellepart announced that he was getting close to one of the survivors who seemed to have climbed much higher than the others, whom he could hear but not see. Two hundred feet lower down he reached the man, who turned out to be the Italian Corti. Incredibly enough he was still fairly fit. Hellepart gave him various injections, then loaded him on his back in a special 'litter' harness.

Theoretically we now only had to turn our windlass to get the two men up again, but Friedli was not sure whether it would be highly geared enough to overcome the friction of the cable against the wall, and made us prepare a haulage track along the two hundred feet of crest. He was soon justified. A few fruitless efforts showed that the windlass was not powerful enough to do the job on its own. Without any signs of emotion he made us lay the cable along the prepared track, then attached haulage loops to it every twenty feet by means of ingenious couplings which could be taken off and put on again in a moment. Each loop was long enough for four or five men, so that in the end more than thirty of us could pull on the cable at once. But despite the enormous force thus deployed we did not succeed in budging it an inch at the first trial. Presumably one of the bolts linking the sections of cable had got jammed in a crack, which made the situation rather serious. Our fine optimism began to give way to a slight panic. If we couldn't hoist the two men on the cable we should be forced to abandon Corti, and would probably have great difficulty in getting Hellepart back up with ropes tied end to end.

Reinforcements were called up, and one of the Bernese with a stentorian voice directed our efforts. The better coordination of effort thus achieved finally did the trick, and after stretching alarmingly the cable began to come in. Each time we hauled in twenty feet or so Friedli would hold the cable on the winch while we moved our couplings forward, then the manoeuvre would be repeated again. One thousand two hundred feet of cable at twenty feet a time represents a long job, particularly as Hellepart's enormous muscular efforts obliged him to rest quite often. It took more than an hour and a half to get the two men to the base of the final slopes, but thenceforward we knew that nothing could stop us recovering them. A life was to be saved against all reason by the generous impulses which still survive in the hearts of men in this age of steel.

Quite soon after, the weary Hellepart was able to set down his burden on the arête. Corti had stood up to his eight-day ordeal in the most extraordinary way, though at first his emaciated face and contracted pupils were rather horrifying. He was nowhere seriously frostbitten, and could not only stand up on his own but also chatter and gesticulate excitedly. Unfortunately it was impossible to extract any clear picture of the situation from him, and in fact he seemed more interested in whether this would be counted as the first Italian ascent of the Eigerwand than in the fate of his companions. He incessantly contradicted himself, but it did appear that the Italian Longhi was still alive somewhere on the Traverse of the Gods. This tallied with the information given us by Cassin and Mauri, who had been able to exchange a few words with him from the northwest ridge the previous evening. The fate of the two Germans remained a mystery. So far as one could make out Corti had climbed with them as far as the top of the Spider, at which point he had fallen off and had been left by the others with some bivouac kit pretty well at the place where Hellepart had found him.

Since Hellepart had seen no trace of any other party, it seemed that the Germans must have fallen off. Whatever had occurred, somebody else now had to go down as far as the foot of the Spider to look for them and to help Longhi. Friedli and Gramminger asked me if I was still willing to do this, and I accepted at once.

The cloud ceiling, which had stayed high all morning, was now descending, and I put on all my clothes in case of bad weather. Somebody wedged a crash helmet on my head to protect me from falling stones, and the walkie-talkie was strapped on my chest. Then the indefatigable Friedli gave me a bit of advice on the gentle art of giving injections and I was off down the snow slope, accompanied by the encouragements of my friends. At the point where the angle changed to the vertical I could see grooves worn nearly an inch deep in the bare limestone by the action of the cable. Here there was a halt of several minutes while a new length of cable was bolted on, then the descent started again, down the same gullies and chimneys I had climbed with the energy of desperation ten years before.

I had never expected to see the place again, but nothing seemed to have changed. Snow and verglas coated the outward-sloping holds in just the same sort of way, and menacing clouds were shrouding the summit. As snowflakes began to drift past I relived those moments with amazing intensity. Even Lachenal's chaff came back to me, and I could see him emerging from a chimney, supple as a cat, his eyes shining with malicious pleasure as he called out:

'Well, Mr Guide, did you find it an interesting climb?'

All of a sudden the cable stopped. I called the summit to find out what was happening but got no reply—instead, there was a conversation in German between the summit and Kleine Scheidegg. Finally the summit called me:

'Hallo Terray, hallo Terray. Are you receiving me? Over.'

I replied:

'Hallo, summit. Receiving you loud and clear. Why have you stopped me here? Are you receiving me? Over.'

They didn't seem to be able to hear me. There were calls in German and in French, with long silences in between. The thing seemed to be going on indefinitely. In my bosun's chair I yo-yoed quite comfortably at the end of the line, but time began to weigh rather heavily. For something to do I pendulumed to the left in order to have a look at the chimney where I had got cramp bridging in 1947, and even succeeded in spotting the crack where the final piton was hammered in. After a few swings back and forth, however, I noticed that the cable was grinding heavily against the rock, and suddenly its quarter-inch diameter began to seem rather thin.

Snowflakes continued to waver past, and occasionally a small slide from the slopes above would envelope me in its cloud. Finally I heard a voice:

'Hallo Terray, hallo Terray. This is Scheidegg. Are you receiving me? Over.'

In the course of the long conversation which followed I gathered that the radio on the summit was still transmitting perfectly but that it could no longer receive. Occasionally vibrations came down the cable, or I would be lowered or hoisted a few inches. To pass the time away I shouted to a party which could be seen on the northwest arête, but in reply came cries from the depths below me. It was Longhi, still hoping against hope.

The chances of saving him were getting less and less with every minute that went by. Soon it would be four o'clock, and the weather had now definitely broken. It was impracticable to do anything more that afternoon, in any case. If conditions got really bad it would be not only unreasonable but humanly impossible to put enough men on the Spider to carry Longhi across the thousand feet from his present ledge to a point below the winch, and then get them all up again. Even in fine weather such an operation would take a whole day at least. We had enough good climbers to make the thing possible, and I felt sure that, given a sporting chance with the weather, several of us would be willing to spend several days on the face to save Longhi from the death he had so courageously resisted. But in a storm it would be another matter; with the best will in the world we should be powerless. Presently the cable tightened and I began to walk back up the face. Friedli had decided that to descend farther without either visibility or radio contact would be too dangerous, and was hauling me back again. Soon Tom was greeting me on the ridge.

It was now after four o'clock, and I was surprised to see that Corti was still there. Despite the care he had received he seemed much more subdued than at the moment of his arrival, and it was obvious that if possible he should be spared the ordeal of a ninth bivouac. Still excited from my abortive adventure and somewhat exasperated at this display of Germanic ponderousness, I proceeded to shake everybody up in no uncertain terms. Gramminger, Friedli and I drew up a plan of campaign. Friedli's Swiss team was to remain where it was, ready to start operations very early if conditions justified the attempt. The rest of the party was to get Corti down the same evening and come back up at dawn, weather permitting.

A few minutes later Corti was strapped on my back. At the top of the northwest arête we rolled him in sleeping bags, then lashed him to a special stretcher. The first part of the descent was awkward. The cables had remained on the summit, and the stretcher had to be lowered on a couple of two-hundred-foot ropes. Each time they ran out we planted new pitons and started again. Unfortunately the going consisted of outward-sloping ledges of rotten limestone plastered with ice, on which lay a blanket of crumbly snow. Worse still, the lie of the land forced us to traverse diagonally rightwards rather than go straight down. It didn't look in the least spectacular, but in fact it was really delicate and called for great experience in the art of rope management. In order to make any speed on such ground every member of the party would have had to be completely at ease, which was far from being the case. Most of them were all gripped up and could only move with extreme care for all their goodwill. Some of them were in fact more of a hindrance than a help, and I half dreaded another accident. One Polish party did in fact slip, and were only saved thanks to Tom's quick reactions.

After a few pitches the five or six best climbers took charge of the whole operation, and from then on we did succeed in establishing a certain method. As we got lower the falling snow became mixed with rain, so that before long we were all soaked to the skin. Just before nightfall Friedli's team caught up with us. After helping for a short time they carried on down. They had rightly thought that after another bivouac in such conditions they would not be in a fit state to do anything very effective the next morning, so they had left their gear in position and gone down to sleep at Eigergletscher. If the weather changed during the night the idea was to go up early with fresh reinforcements. It grew darker and darker. The wind blew with increasing violence, whirling the snow up into our faces and blinding us. To have gone on any longer would have been to run the risk of an almost certain accident.

Gramminger and I, who had directed the whole descent between us, decided to stop at the first half-reasonable site. We were all worn-out from two days and a night of hard work, low temperatures and high wind, and this second bivouac was extremely trying. None of us had eaten much for a long time, and all were sodden. The majority were short of bivouac kit into the bargain. After we had anchored Corti to a vaguely level section of ridge I found myself all alone beside him, exposed to the full force of the gale. All the others, of whom Tom had been the last to leave, had taken shelter where they could find it. After an hour or so Corti dozed off and I crept away to look for some shelter of my own, but after less than half an hour curled up in a little hollow I heard him cry out heartrendingly. Waking alone on the ridge amid the hurly-burly of the storm, no doubt he thought himself abandoned. I went back and gave him something to drink, then, frozen to the marrow, returned to my wretched shelter. No sooner had I got there than more cries called me back to the stretcher, and so it continued.

At daybreak several more parties were seen climbing towards us. By the time they reached us we were ready to start, and the lowering began again at once. The newcomers were mostly elderly guides. Unfortunately none of them had any crampons and consequently they were not really much use, with the exception of one whose amazing agility made up for his lack of equipment and even for his grumpy nature. The snowed-up ledges began to give place to a series of vertical and overhanging walls, a formation which could hardly have been more awkward for the diagonal lowering of a loaded stretcher. It was particularly tough on the rescuer harnessed to the stretcher as its guide, but fortunately the excellent guide Hans Schlunegger soon arrived and performed this task to perfection. Next we met a likeable party from Château d'Oex, one of whom was the well-known climber Betty Favre. They had brought thermos flasks of hot drinks with them which gave us renewed strength. Soon we were literally surrounded with helpers from all over the place, and at last Friedli and his group arrived and took turns on the rope, thereby speeding our progress considerably. In spite of this it was three o'clock in the afternoon before we finally got to Eigergletscher.

A hysterical crowd of onlookers, reporters and photographers was waiting at the foot of the glacier and around the station, a portent of less disinterested struggles to come. The whole affair provoked violent polemics in Switzerland, Germany and Italy. Some folk who had taken good care to keep away from the action indulged in criticism of the rescue's organisation, and even of its having taken place at all. Of course no hurriedly improvised action can ever be perfect. The fact remained that mountaineers of many nations had combined together in a wave of spontaneous human feeling to save the life of a particularly foolish colleague, in spite of hopeless-looking conditions. It had been a magnificent example of what can be accomplished by courage, enthusiasm and willpower, and if only for this reason it was a great achievement. The rest is nothing but dirty gossip.

| 6 |

GUIDE ON THE GREAT CLIMBS

THE SECOND ASCENT OF THE north face of the Eiger was the apogee of my Alpine career. Subsequently I gave less time to my own amateur climbing and devoted myself to professional activities which I sought to practise in as many ranges and on the most difficult climbs possible. It was not until later that I was lucky enough to become active as an amateur once more, but this time it was in the course of eight* expeditions to the Andes and Himalayas. In a lesser degree Lachenal followed the same course.

There is perhaps something a bit larger than life about mountaineering at times, a quality engendered by its dangerous and sometimes heroic character, but for all that it in no way escapes from the laws of sport or of nature. A naturally gifted man who frequents mountains from boyhood on, overcoming innumerable obstacles and doing hundreds of climbs, gradually becomes surer-footed and acquires stronger fingers, steadier nerves, more stamina and a more refined technique. Thus he may eventually reach such a degree of mastery that even on ascents of extreme difficulty he has plenty in reserve and runs no great risks. The mountains, once so full of mystery and traps for the unwary, become friendly and familiar, and faces which once demanded every ounce of coinage and energy he possessed seem no more than healthy exercise. I ran more risks and had more trouble in climbing the Aiguille Verte for the first time by the ordinary way than I did later on its Nant Blanc face. In between I had been up the mountain nine times

* *Translator's note.* The number is now eleven.

(among innumerable ascents of other peaks) by six different routes. In climbing, as in any other sport, miracles are rare. Talent, experience, technique and training are the keys to success.

Once a skier has achieved mastery of technique he no longer sticks to nursery slopes; he would soon get bored if he did. In the same way, each advance in a climber's ability leads him to try a more difficult ascent, and so he progresses. To keep up his enthusiasm he must seek new problems, and there's the rub. A skier can always find steeper and rougher slopes, an athlete can always try to run faster or jump higher, but a mountaineer can only climb the peaks and faces which exist.

After the Walker we had begun to wonder if we had not attained a level of fitness, morale and technique such that the Alps no longer afforded us the opportunities we sought for self-surpassment. The Eigerwand, done in bad weather and bad conditions, more or less clinched the matter.

Now that we had climbed the highest and hardest faces in the Alps we had nothing left to hope for. I remember writing somewhere or other: 'In order to renew the adventure the mountain must rise to the measure of its adversaries.' Thenceforward the mountains of Europe could only provide us with a sporting form of tourism or with simple trials of technical virtuosity. For those of us whose ambitions went beyond aesthetic appreciation or mere gymnastics, the only way out of this impasse seemed to be to change the rules of the game, either by climbing the hardest faces solo or by doing them in winter. Obviously we would rather have measured ourselves against the highest mountains in the world, which will always provide game even for the hardiest, but how were we to get to them without money?

Some readers may be provoked to remark that, although we had repeated the hardest climbs done up till then in the high western Alps, a number of big routes such as the west face and southwest pillar of the Dru were still awaiting their first ascents, and that moreover we hadn't climbed a single one of the great Dolomite faces. As everyone knows, the last-named range contains the longest and hardest crags ever scaled by man. Contrary to what I have said, then, these readers may conclude that even after the Walker and the Eiger there remained plenty in the Alps to keep us busy, and up to a point they would be right. But, as I have already had occasion to remark, mountaineering includes a number of different specialities. Greater mountaineering is one of these, extreme rock climbing is another. Very few people feel an equal enthusiasm for them, and fewer still manage to shine at both, since their techniques differ widely.

I remember two very famous Dolomite specialists being so ill at ease on the way down the Eiger after the rescue that my friend Tom could literally run circles round them. I could also cite the instance of two other *sestogradists* who achieved the almost incredible distinction, after a slightly late start, of bivouacking on the easy Dent du Géant. Again, there was the case of an illustrious party from the eastern Alps who took three days to do the Walker in normal conditions; to say nothing of the unbelievable slowness of the German-Italian party on the Eiger, who were all, be it noted, first-rate rock climbers. One of them was indeed considered to be rather a phenomenon, and held speed records for a number of rock climbs. But if it is true that the majority of climbers from the Dolomites are not at home on the ice, mixed ground, or even the rock of the high western Alps, the same applies equally to the 'greater mountaineers' when they get onto the loose, overhanging limestone of the eastern Alps.

Lachenal and I were determined 'occidentalists'. Climbing to us meant summits and faces where there was snow and ice as well as rock. For us this fairyland of silver glaciers and shining snow had incomparable charms, and by comparison faces of pure rock seemed painfully monotonous both aesthetically and technically. Neither of us had ever been much attracted by the lower ranges, and we didn't really think of them as proper mountains. 'Dolomitism' seemed different in nature to mountaineering. It wasn't that we were unable to climb rocks, as we had shown on the Walker—Lachenal was in fact quite exceptional on delicate ground—so much as that mixed or even pure ice climbs inspired us more, particularly in cases where rock climbing meant a lot of artificial work, which we detested.

Now a good many laymen and even climbers may imagine that this technique in which, as everybody knows, one progresses by pulling up from one piton to the next, is really not very difficult. I have quite often heard it said:

'There's not really much to it. It's just a question of banging in the pegs and then stepping up on little ladders.'

This, however, is a gross over-simplification. Except on some all too rare occasions, artificial climbing calls for considerable strength, intelligence and courage. It is extremely strenuous to spend hours and even days on an overhanging face, swinging around on stirrups, and constantly hammering, in the most uncomfortable positions. Getting the pegs to hold in all sorts of inconvenient cracklets and arranging the ropes and carabiners so that they don't jam is a work of art in itself, and to climb faces of over two thousand feet in this way, at a speed of a hundred or even sometimes 120 feet an hour, demands more than ordinary willpower and perseverance. In positions where the rock is friable and the exposure very great only the most genuine courage enables men to trust themselves to a long series of insecure metal spikes which might 'unzip' at any moment. I know of nothing which gives a greater sensation of insecurity.

Neither Lachenal nor I would ever have suggested that artificial climbing was not difficult, or that it did not demand remarkable qualities; we just didn't care for it. The thing we loved about climbing was the sensation of escaping from the laws of gravity, of dancing on space, which comes with technical virtuosity. Like the pilot or the skier, a man then feels freed from the condition of a crawling bug and becomes a chamois, a squirrel, almost a bird.

Far from evoking this feeling of mastery and ease, artificial climbing gives the reverse impression. Progress is slow, laborious and due solely to mechanical subterfuges. Fettered to the rock, the climber feels thoroughly clumsy and fragile. Art, strokes of genius, have no place in his success, which is due only to hard labour. Nearly all the big Dolomite climbs involve long sessions of more or less artificial climbing, and quite apart from the fact that their scenery did not attract us, this alone would have been enough to put us off.

For precisely the same reason we never dreamt of trying the three or four then unclimbed faces of any amplitude in the western Alps. I would also add that in 1947 the all-out use of wooden wedges in cracks too wide for ordinary pitons was definitely 'out'. At that time nobody dared to have recourse to such methods, but it was only due to their use that the west face and southwest pillar of the Petit Dru were eventually climbed.

Only two faces then still virgin could have provided us with adventures comparable in kind to the Eigerwand and the Walker, to wit, the northeast face of the Grand Dru and the north face direct of the Droites. If we had had a little more spare time during the summer season we would certainly have made all-out attempts on these. We did in fact bivouac at the foot of the Grand Dru twice, and I also made an attempt on the Droites with Tom de Booy, but on all these occasions we had no luck with the weather.

As for solo climbing, much practised by German climbers and certain Italian *sestogradists*, it makes certain techniques so difficult as to bring even the greatest aces down to the level where they are once again forced to fight hard and run major risks. This branch of the sport not only calls for absolute mastery but also an altogether unusual force of character, if not an actual kink. Lachenal and I never went in for it, for reasons less technical than moral. We frequently did not bother to rope up on difficult ground, and still more often climbed simultaneously, roped but not belayed. Theoretically, therefore, we should have been capable of doing difficult ascents solo. But Louis was an

186 ~ CONQUISTADORS OF THE USELESS

extremely sociable man, who hated being alone. Personally I often enjoy it, but in the mountains it makes me acutely conscious of nature's threats, and I become quite incapable of getting up pitches which I would easily do unroped if I had some company.

In my view mountaineering is an essentially individual experience, and I have always considered absurd the opinion, voiced by some authors, that the forging of bonds of friendship is its primary motivation. If this were really so, why would anybody risk his life or exhaust himself on the most fearsome climbs? If friendship really needed any such catalyst the ascent of easy summits would serve as well. True, we encounter every summer, bands of happy warriors singing, guzzling and drinking their way up and down the ordinary routes, finding in the fresh air and exercise an incitement to 'good fellowship', but this temporary glow is no more real friendship than the same thing generated at a banquet or a party. It may indeed be that these feelings are genuinely the purpose of such outings, but in any case they are only a very minor form of mountaineering.

It is equally true that dangers and labours shared, as in war or on difficult climbs, may link men in a mutual esteem that over the years may deepen into genuine friendship. But friendships born of a particular situation have a way of fading once it is over, effaced by all the petty circumstance of life. Whatever the legends so carefully maintained by some, the mountaineering game is far from a garden of universal fraternity. It is simply that the dangers of the sport, together with the fact that it is carried on in little groups of two or three, create an environment favourable to human warmth, which therefore happens to be commoner, or perhaps I should say less rare, among climbers than among most other communities.

The majority of climbers are complete individualists. Dislikes and rivalries are common among them, and comparatively few go on climbing together year after year. Odder still, it is not unknown for two who positively dislike each other to climb together because the arrangement enables them to do the climbs they want.

Personally I hold friendship one of the most precious things in life, but like everything of real value it is rare. We do not become friends with just anybody simply because we happen to have shared danger or for that matter pleasure with him. It is a powerful emotion, like love, which has to be cultivated; and in the same way it becomes devitalised if given too often or too easily. I have felt a deep and enduring friendship for some of my mountain friends, especially Lachenal, and there is no doubt that climbing is a finer experience when done with such a person, but it would be stupid to pretend that it cannot be done otherwise. If so, it would soon become a rare activity. Anyone who hopes to do a lot of climbing cannot always pick and choose too carefully. It is interesting to reflect that the man who has become the great evangelist of climbing for friendship's sake was at one time in the habit of climbing with the first comer.

I have always refused to go out with people I disliked, but circumstances have often forced me to do so with those who were indifferent to me. Their presence added nothing to my pleasure, and I would have enjoyed myself as much climbing on my own had I been capable of it. But some moral weakness which I have never properly understood has always made me incapable of climbing difficult rock on my own, and even unroped I need the presence of another human being.

In winter all climbs become much more difficult owing to the presence of snow, cold, wind and the shortness of the hours of daylight. Anybody who wishes to do big ascents at this time of the year, without turning them into expeditions, runs even greater risks than on the most formidable walls in summer, but some climbers have thus found a way of satisfying their lust for battle. In many ways I share their enthusiasm, and yet, perhaps paradoxically, I would reproach them with carrying heroism too far. When wind and cold render conditions too inhuman as, for example, on Himalayan summits where the lack of oxygen enfeebles him, the climber's technical capabilities are greatly reduced. The climbing therefore becomes extremely slow and he is robbed of that feeling of lightness and mastery which should be one of his main joys. But for all that I wish I had had the opportunity to do more winter mountaineering.

However great our passion for the mountains we cannot spend our entire lives climbing. I am so designed by nature that I have to train hard to keep up my standard, and in winter I have always been too taken up with racing and my work as a skiing instructor to spare the time for serious mountaineering. Lachenal, by contrast, had such natural gifts that he needed almost no practice to keep on form, and in consequence pulled a number of big winter ascents as it were out of a top hat.

As I remarked above, during the years which followed my ascent of the Eigerwand I devoted myself more completely to my profession. No doubt this was partly due to a material need, but also I think because my guiding was sufficiently enterprising to absorb a lot of my energy and courage, leaving little hunger for further adventure. The virtues of the profession have been much inflated in books and the press, and it has become almost a cliché to call it 'the most dedicated job in the world', an empty phrase which I have also heard applied to medicine, aviation, seafaring and even bicycle racing. In this women's magazine story type of literature the guide is always endowed with the most remarkable qualities: not only is his mountain skill positively super-human, but he is brave, strong, good, honest and generous—a proper little plaster saint. Nothing could be more naive. By the mere fact of being a man no guide could possibly be such a paragon of the virtues. Alpine literature as a whole is, of course, astonishingly conventional, but on the subject of guides it really surpasses itself. If an author isn't lost in a rosy haze of folklore, he usually gets completely carried away by his hero's legendary reputation.

Personally I do not know of a single book which treats the subject in objective or even remotely credible fashion. It is quite true that the work calls for genuine physical and mental qualities, and that in order to succeed in it one must be reasonably tough, skilful, bold and capable of devotion to duty. But whatever the old wives' tales may say, it is by no means necessary to be either a saint or a champion.

Professional climbing has virtually nothing to do with what I call *grand alpinisme*; that is to say the passion, crazy or otherwise, for climbing the most improbable crags and peaks. Comparatively few guides go in for this kind of thing. Their work almost invariably involves them the whole time in much easier types of ascent, and it is in fact very difficult to combine the two because, since they both take place during the same short season, they cancel each other out. Guiding is poor practice for the extreme climbs, which demand a specialised and lengthy form of training, and in any case their moti-vation is so different that they require quite other qualities. Only a fortunate few, usually amateurs turned guide in order to live among the hills, manage to practise both arts satisfactorily, and even then one or the other usually becomes predominant after a few years.

The guide's job is to teach people how to climb, or to lead those who, for one reason or another, cannot or do not wish to confront the dangers of the mountains without a mentor. Thus most of his clients are beginners, weak climbers, or persons whose age or occupation does not permit them to become really fit, but who nevertheless long for adventure among the splen-dours of the high hills. By definition such persons are incapable of doing the hardest climbs, even behind the most brilliant of guides.

In the majority of cases, therefore, the professional must resign himself to relatively simple ascents. His function is not to break records but to teach a skill, to enable tourists to do climbs which would otherwise be out of the question for them. It is no more relevant to expect a guide to be a virtuoso mountaineer than to expect a physical-training instructor to be a decathlon champion.

These facts are so basic that they are implied in the very regulations governing the profession. There is no need to have done a lot of hard climbs to obtain your diploma. The candidate simply has to have a good all-round experience of the mountains, and to be able to lead the classic routes quickly and safely. As for pure rock climbing, it is sufficient to be able to lead grade IV pitches without any trouble, a level attained by a great many amateurs. The only difficult part to master is necessary facility on mixed ground, snow and ice.

It will be obvious from all this that to become a guide does not call for any really exceptional qualities, and that it requires less tenacity and toughness than *grand alpinisme*. But this is far from saying that it is just another job, even in its more humdrum aspects on the ordinary routes. For those who practise it from conviction and love of the game it is still a genuinely noble profession.

Up on the mountain, at the head of his party, the guide is still sole captain under God. He may be poor and in some sense a manual worker, but in his hands he holds the lives and trust of men. To be master of life and death is the privilege of kings, and few influential men dispose of such power. It is the same responsibility that surrounds pilots and ships' captains with their especial glamour. The guide lives in an environment of majesty and splendour where the pettiness and malice of society have no meaning, and it is rare to find one who has failed to absorb something of the largeness of his surroundings. The plaster saint of legend is of course equally rare, but at least you will practically never find a guide with the mentality of a lackey, a tendency which circumstances might well have encouraged.

Like any other human activity, professional mountaineering attracts all sorts: there are good guides and bad guides. The most brilliant technically are by no means always the best at their job. For its proper conduct the work calls more for moral qualities than physical dexterity, and this primacy of mind over matter is one of its main claims to dignity. One of its most attractive sides is, after all, the giving of happiness. A good guide must possess the considerateness to create an atmosphere in which his client can savour his pleasures to the full. Dedication is required not only to aid other mountaineers in distress, but more immediately to help a client to surmount his own weakness. Patience is a necessity, to put up with moving all day at a snail's pace without irritation. Psychological insight plays its part in bringing the tired and discouraged client safely to the journey's end. And only a steady courage can face up day after day to the risks which even the simplest climbs involve in such circumstances.

This does not exhaust the list of necessary qualities. To become and remain a guide, one must have a quite exceptional taste for physical effort, without which no man would be able to continue doing climbs of ten, twelve, fourteen hours, or even more every day in the season. Considerable ingenuity is required to devise ways of avoiding wasted time and effort, and also to make the best profit out of a season replete with activity but terribly restricted in time.

The ordinary routes will always be the daily bread of guiding, but a man with the right qualities has a chance of raising the standard of his work, and a few may even get the opportunity to do some of the great climbs in a professional capacity.

Comparatively few mountaineers have the ability to do the big climbs, even as seconds, and those who do are mostly gifted youngsters either living close to the hills or, as in the case of undergraduates, disposing of ample holidays. Climbing is their major passion and they give all their spare time to it. By intensive practice they quickly acquire considerable technique and experience, and the best among them are then able to undertake the great routes. These young enthusiasts rarely have enough money to consider engaging a guide, or, if they do, they generally prefer to climb with other amateurs. Many feel that the presence of a guide, whose technical mastery is a foregone conclusion and who knows every inch of the mountain, robs the sport of precisely that spice of adventure which is its main motivation. A good many also find such efficient help mortifying to their pride.

Mountaineering is a young man's pastime. Marriage, careers and growing responsibilities account for the gradual retirement of a good three-quarters of those who take it up. A few, however, are so possessed by it that they continue throughout their prime and even their entire lives. Desk jobs, age and lack of training soon reduce the abilities even of the best, but simultaneously, by the same token, their financial means tend to increase. Some climbers, in growing older, find all the happiness they need in simple contact with the hills, and are quite content to do progressively easier climbs. After all, if growing skill makes adventure harder to come by, the reverse must also hold good. But others are so taken with the majesty of the greatest routes and summits that they want to keep on frequenting them, and such men, when they have the means, do not hesitate to hire the services of a good guide.

A professional lucky enough to cross the path of such a client thus gets the chance to raise the level and interest of his work; occasionally he may even find a phenomenon with whom the greatest climbs can be attempted. But these are few and far between: in France for example, there are no more than a few dozen for the big climbs, and hardly any for the greatest. In fact very few of the really top-class ascents have been done by guided parties—the Walker once, the Eigerwand twice, the right-hand Pillar of Fresnay once, the northeast face of the Badile two or three times, the east face of the Capucin three or four, the north face of the Triolet twice. Up to the present none of the three severe routes on the Drus and practically none on the *sesto-superiore* climbs in the eastern Alps have been done by professionals climbing as such.*

Fortunately there is also another category of capable clients, namely that of naturally gifted persons who begin their climbing days with a guide and remain faithful to him as their own powers increase, whether out of habit, prudence or friendship. I have had several such, notably my Dutch friends and clients De Booy and Egeler, who I think constitute a unique case in modern mountaineering. They first obtained my services by the 'first come, first served' system of the Chamonix Bureau des Guides, at a time when they were still more or less beginners. By gradual progress we reached the point of doing several of the hardest ice climbs in the Alps together. Still more extraordinary (and only known once before in the annals of French guiding) they took me with them overseas, where we conquered some of the last unclimbed summits in the Andes.**

In recent years the opening up of practice crags close to the big centres of population has considerably improved the normal rock climbing standard of clients, but in spite of that all guides lumped together probably do not carry out above a dozen unusual climbs in any given season—and the majority of those will be done by two or three specialists. The restriction is imposed quite as much by economic as by technical considerations. A guide is working for his living, and even if he has other sources of income at other seasons he has a right to expect a just remuneration for his toil and danger. The shortness of the season, the instability of the weather, and above all the fact that his money has to come from quite a small number of people make his remuneration precarious and slight, relative to his perils, qualifications and responsibilities. Taking all these factors into account, the earnings of a guide on the great climbs are derisory compared with, for example, those of an airline pilot.

Still, the price of guided climbing may seem high when it is considered that it must be borne by one or two people at a time. Quite a lot of people can afford the tariffs for the simpler, classic ascents—among my clients I have had a carpenter, a garage mechanic and a number of school teachers—but for the bigger climbs the cost is too high for most, so that even those who would like

* *Translator's note.* Though often by professionals climbing as amateurs.

** *Translator's note.* And now also in the Himalayas.

to do them and have the ability must give up hope of realising their dreams. And yet the guides do not make much out of it. A big climb takes two or three days instead of one, and the effort they call for makes it essential to have a rest in between. Unlike ordinary routes, they can only be embarked on in perfectly settled conditions, which may entail further loss of time. Financially speaking, it is better to do a climb every day at a fee of a hundred new francs than to make a killing of three or four hundred every now and again. For this reason alone, then, a great many guides do not particularly push their clients into attempting anything very outstanding.

In 1947, as an instructor at the E.N.S.A., I was paid by the month, and this particular problem was no headache to me. But we were far from over-paid, and most of us tried to increase our earnings by finding clients to guide at weekends and between courses. In those days these interim periods were quite long, and with the weather on our side we could often make respectable sums in this way. Personally I used my spare time mainly for my own amateur climbing, but after the Eigerwand I felt satisfied for the time being, and what was more I badly needed money to finish off my chalet. I therefore decided to devote the rest of my free days that season to climbing with clients.

That summer was uninterruptedly fine, and it was possible to climb almost every day. Between my work at the École and my private clients I accumu-lated climbs galore, a process which led me to considerable feats of endurance. Thus, straight after the Eiger, I did eleven ascents in twelve days, seven of them one after the other. The easiest was the ordinary route on the Peigne, and the others included Mont Blanc, the traverse of the Aiguilles du Diable, the Ryan-Lochmatter on the Plan, and the Jardin arête of the Aiguille Verte. Add to the climbs themselves the time required to get from hut to hut, and you have a daily timetable which sometimes exceeded eighteen hours of hard labour.

To carry out a programme like this calls not only for physical stamina but also a continual effort of will. During this time I learned that doing the great climbs is not the only way of going beyond one's normal limits. This equally severe and less spectacular way gave its own kind of joy.

Luck, and perhaps also my growing reputation, brought me a few good clients, with whom I found it pleasant to be doing interesting climbs. I began to enjoy the climbing for its closer human contacts. At the École Nationale the instructor is given different students every day, and except on the moun-tain he does not share their way of life at all, so that he hardly gets to know them. Most are already mountaineers of some ability. The instructor watches and advises them, judging, and dropping a word of advice here and there;

but they don't actually need him in a direct sort of way. Most of them are not there simply to enjoy themselves, but to get a diploma. Rather as though they were back at school, taking their *baccalauréate*, the teacher seems a threatening figure, seeking to catch them out, and they rarely relax in his presence.

With clients it is all very different. They are there for their own pleasure and seek in many little ways to share it with you. They have chosen you because they like you, and there is a real feeling of human warmth. The client knows quite well that he depends utterly on his leader and would be lost without him, that he must trust himself without reserve to the guide's skill and devotion to duty. In such circumstances feelings of friendship and team spirit grow quickly, and the amateur usually remains faithful to his original choice. Quite a lot of my clients have developed into real friends, and I am still guiding some whom I first met in 1947.

The following season was detestable. It never seemed to stop raining, and the quantity of snow which fell on the mountains made difficult climbing out of the question. Lachenal and I did not succeed in carrying out a single one of our projects. But even in the most treacherous weather a guide who really knows his area backwards can snatch smaller brands from burning. He will seize a chance between two bad spells, set out in doubtful conditions and get back down in the rain. Since the big stuff was ruled out I devoted my time to doing small routes with my clients. After a terrible summer, October was fine enough to continue climbing, and despite the shortness of the days and the increasing cold I did the south ridge of the Aiguille Noire with a Dutch lady. By the end of the season I realised clearly that I preferred guiding to instructing. I already had the nucleus of a clientèle, and taking into account the number of people I had been forced to turn down it appeared that I could launch out on a guiding career with reasonable certainty of success.

I now began to think seriously about leaving the École Nationale, where the work had become a good deal less thrilling. It had recently merged with the old Collège d'Alpinisme, thereby becoming an institution of some size, and due to this enlargement and a natural process of aging the healthy empiricism of its early years had given place to rigid organisation. Routine had taken the place of enthusiasm and faith in the future, and dignity the ideal of duty. On each course the number of days spent on more or less useless activities had increased considerably, and by the same token the actual climbs had diminished both in number and standard. The instructors carried less responsibility and the old friendliness had given way to a more official atmosphere. I therefore began to lose interest in the work, and it seemed probable that matters would only get worse. Furthermore there were no hopes of promotion unless I adopted the drastic method of murdering the chief instructor and two or three of my colleagues.

To talk about leaving the École Nationale was, however, a good deal easier than to do so in earnest. The regular salary gave a stability to my way of life which I particularly appreciated after the difficult times at Les Houches, a feeling fully shared by my wife. My winter work at the École was also much more interesting than any I could hope for as an ordinary skiing instructor, which was all I could expect to become if I plumped for independence. At the École I taught nobody but future instructors and young racing skiers who wanted to polish their technique, and this was infinitely more fun than the sort of thing one normally does with clients, who are usually either beginners or mediocre performers.

All this instructing had brought me back to my old form, and as my weekends were always free I had taken up competition work again. Without being a great maestro, I became a reserve for the national team, and pulled off successes in regional and even national events. Among these I came in first by a long way in the slalom in the Mont Blanc area championships, always a very difficult race. I also did quite well at international trials such as the Kandahar, the most important after the world championships, where I gained eleventh place in the slalom. After these successes the director of the École, by agreement with the governing authorities of French skiing, entrusted me with the instruction of all the courses in racing skiing, including those for the reserves of the national team. The whole business was enthralling, and I was extremely loth to risk losing it; yet it seemed difficult, if not impossible, to resign from E.N.S.A. in summer but not in winter.

I was still hesitating when an unforeseen occurrence changed everything. One evening I received a telephone call from Gaston Cathiard, president of the Syndicat National des Moniteurs de Ski. He had just had a letter from Canada asking him to recommend a coach-instructor to succeed Émile Allais. It was a most interesting proposition, involving the direction of a ski school and the training of a strong competitive team. All expenses were to be paid and the salary, while not princely, was at any rate double what I earned in France. All my problems seemed to be solved, and the gates opened on a prospect of freedom, travel and adventure. Images from Jack London and Fenimore Cooper flashed before my eyes, and already I could sense the romance of the great plains with their herds of caribou and famished wolf packs. I could almost see the tall forests where the snowshoed trappers plodded from snare to snare.

And then there were the Indians, the Eskimos, the huskies, the saloons . . . even Maria Chapdelaine!* I took the decision without a second thought.

I embarked early in November at Liverpool. My excitement at this first voyage overseas was quickly quelled by chronic seasickness, and after six stormy days I tottered off the ship at Halifax more dead than alive. My ideas about Canada were of the haziest and most romantic kind. I knew that part of the population spoke a kind of old-fangled but just about intelligible French, so I wasn't expecting any language problem. But no sooner had I disembarked than I came up against the manifold difficulties which confront any poor and lonely traveller in a foreign land. The language barrier cuts him off from his fellow men. Surrounded by an ocean of indifference and even hostility, he feels tiny and utterly helpless.

It seemed as though there wasn't a single man in the whole of Halifax who understood a word of French, and the few phrases I tried to concoct out of memories of schoolboy English did not get me any further. Everyone appeared impatient and in a hurry, with a kind of brutality I had never encountered in Europe. The simplest actions became problems; I could not even find out the time and place to catch my train. The customs wanted me to pay fantastic duties on my four pair of skis. I argued and shouted, demanding the presence of an interpreter, but the customs officers were as indifferent to my plight as to the raw November fog.

I was so determined and vehement in my protests that eventually a French Canadian docker was sent for. I more than half expected him to address me in some ancient dialect, and mentally congratulated myself on having spent so many hours in my youth poring over the works of Rabelais, Montaigne, Ronsard and others. It came as a considerable surprise to find that, apart from a strong rustic accent and a few odd expressions, he spoke exactly the same language as myself.

Actually French is spoken as their normal and sometimes only language by some 30 percent of Canada's eighteen million inhabitants. These are not scattered evenly among the others, but are concentrated almost entirely in the Province of Quebec, where they constitute over three-quarters of the population. In Montreal, for example, the proportion is around 60 percent of a million and a half: in Quebec, the ancient capital of Nouvelle-France, 90 percent of two hundred thousand.

Anyway, thanks to the timely arrival of this docker, my difficulties with the customs were soon solved, and by eleven o'clock I was on the Montreal

* *Translator's note.* The heroine of a romantic novel about French Canada.

train. A glance at the map had given me the impression that it was not all that far from Halifax, and after a complicated discussion in English one of the stewards succeeded in explaining that we were due in around five o'clock. The train now entered a scattered forest of small deciduous trees. At 4:45 I began to collect my things, though outside in the forest there were still no signs of the outskirts of a big city. A quarter of an hour later nothing had changed and I sat down again, presuming we were running late. By six o'clock there was still nothing to be seen but trees rushing past, and I got up to ask the steward if I hadn't misunderstood him. Either my English was too poor or his skull too thick for us to communicate, but he kindly went to look for a French-speaking colleague in the next wagon. This worthy seemed rather astonished by my question, and replied:

'*Oui*, Monsieur, you are quite right. We are due at Montreal at five o'clock— but tomorrow evening.'

I was beginning to discover the true scale of the world: that France is a mere dot on the surface of the globe, that Canada alone is as big as Europe including Russia, and that four days and five nights are required to get from Halifax to Vancouver.

My ultimate destination was Quebec, where I was to be put up in the Château Frontenac, a vast pseudo-mediaeval hotel in the heart of town, boasting seven hundred rooms and almost as many employees. I had two distinct jobs: to run the hotel's ski school on the one hand, and on the other to train the city's racing team.

Quebec is one of the most European towns in North America. Built on a hill with ancient ramparts and narrow, twisting streets, it has an old-world picturesqueness rare in a continent where most towns are built on flat ground and planned in rectangles. During the summer tens of thousands of tourists flock to it from the United States, but in winter, when snow covers the country from coast to coast and temperatures sink to minus thirty and even minus forty Centigrade, the Château is three-quarters empty. In order to attract more clientèle the management of the hotel had conceived the idea of starting a ski school, and this had already been in some sort of action for several years.

Now at this time the French national team had been carrying off most of the glory in the international skiing competitions, and as a result the 'French style' was all the fashion. In order to promote his ski school the manager of the Château had even gone so far as to employ the actual inventor of the style, Emile Allais; but apparently the results, while appreciable, did not quite match up to the champion's financial terms, and the arrangement only lasted one year. However, the movement was under way, and I had been engaged as Emile's successor.

My work was to teach the French style not to the public, but to the instructors; to supervise their teaching; and also to give displays and demonstrations. As this did not occupy all my time I was also given the job of coaching the city's racing team, which involved accompanying them at weekends. At first sight it all seemed too good to be true, but after a while, mainly for topographical reasons, I began to find it a little disappointing.

Every morning a group of students with three or four instructors would set out by coach for Lac Beauport or Valcartier, where they would spend the day. These were small resorts, mainly deserted except at weekends, each consisting of one fair-sized hotel and a few ski lifts. Unfortunately the slopes were easy-angled and no more than six or seven hundred feet high, good enough for beginners but rather boring even for an average skier.

To make matters worse my instructors were a crude lot who took little pride in their work, and the clients were not very exciting either. The latter consisted mainly of extremely rich men with whom I had nothing whatever in common. However, I was forced to learn English in order to converse with them, and this was to be very useful to me later both in my work as a guide and on Himalayan expeditions.

But if my work for the Château Frontenac Ski School was uninspiring, it was fully compensated by the racing team. Despite the lack of really good training grounds several of its members, students for the most part, were excellent skiers with a particular talent for the slalom. They were a likeable and enthusiastic crowd, and it was a pleasure to work with them. In spite of the lack of adequately steep or long slopes we managed to carry our training to an advanced level, especially in the acrobatic technique of the slalom, and some of the boys made considerable progress. One of them ended by surpassing me, and I had the pleasure of helping him to carry off first prize in the Canadian International Championships against the competition not only of his compatriots but also a number of well-known Austrians including the famous Egon Schöpp.

A noisy bunch of us would set off almost every weekend to take part in competitions here or there, sometimes even hundreds of miles away. Apart from the fact that they were interesting for their own sake, these trips would often take us to resorts where there were better skiing conditions, so that from time to time I could once again savour the thrills of a great descent taken at high speed. Before long I was allowed to take part in competitions myself, which put me in my seventh heaven, and I was thus enabled to carry off several prizes and a Canadian championship.

My transatlantic journey was less wonderful than I had imagined it, but by and large I had an excellent time, so much so, in fact, that I went back the following year with my wife and another French instructor. After two winters in the country, amounting to a total of some nine months, I had grown quite used to the way of life, and if the mountaineering possibilities had been better I might well have stayed for good. The advantages seemed to me to outweigh the drawbacks.

Canada, especially French Canada, is a country where most French people seem to have trouble in settling down. A good many emigrants come home in disgust after only a few months. All this is quite understandable, but in my view the fault is far more on our side than on that of the Canadians. Paradoxical as it may seem, I find the common tongue more of a hindrance than a help. French Canadian, especially in the big cities, is not so very different from the language as we speak it. Books from France are used at all stages of education, so that the divergence could hardly become very wide. Certainly there is no more difference than between English and American, or Portuguese and Brazilian.

One often hears that Canadian resembles old French. In fact this is far from the truth, archaisms being on the whole rare. One of the most frequently heard is the use of the word *'malin'* in its original sense. For example, people will say *'un malin temps'* instead of *'un mauvais temps'* for bad weather. The main difference between the two dialects is really one of accent. The Canadians speak the language with something like a Norman accent, only stronger. It sounds ugly, and does take a little getting used to. The next most important difference is the number of Gallicised English words. It is quite usual to say *'crosser la rue'* for *'traverser la rue'*. Often the English word will be unchanged, so I once heard someone ask:

'Avez vous eu un beau "show" au Mont Tremblant?'

Sometimes an English turn of phrase is adapted. One says *'on va se faire poser'* for *'on va se faire photographier'*. There are also some purely French-Canadian expressions, such as *'c'est bien de malheur'* instead of *'c'est bien malheureux'*, and *'c'est pas pire'* for *'ce n'est pas mal'*.* Odder still, they translate into French English expressions which have passed intact into our language. They always say *'la balle au pied'*, *'la balle au panier'*, *'la fin de la semaine'*, *'le*

---

* *Translator's note. 'C'est bien malheureux'* = 'How unfortunate' or 'bad luck'. *'Ce n'est pas mal'* = 'not bad' or 'not bad at all'.

chandail', '*le vivoir*'; instead of 'football', 'basketball', 'weekend', 'pullover' and 'living room'.

Only the lower classes speak anything resembling a patois, and even that is quite simple. I could communicate perfectly with peasants and lumberjacks in under a month; so much so, in fact, that after a few minutes conversation in a train one day with two lumberjacks, one of them asked me:

'You've got a hell of a funny accent. Where do you come from, anyway—out west?'

There is really no difficulty in making oneself understood, then, with anybody the least bit civilised, but that does not mean there is no language problem. The rustic accent and peculiar expressions undoubtedly make French Canadian sound rather comic to us, and it is difficult sometimes not to show it. During my second winter, my French friend and assistant Francis Aubert, who was extremely handsome, had enormous success with the girls. Before long, however, I noticed that he only went out with English-speaking women, in spite of the fact that the Québécoises were most attractive. When I asked him the reason for this, he replied:

'As soon as they open their mouths I start laughing, and that ruins everything!'

Having no problems of communication, French immigrants do not have to go through the normal process of adaptation to a foreign country. But it is precisely this difficulty which normally makes new arrivals humble and polite, thus creating a favourable impression on the part of the regular inhabitants. But in this case the newcomer speaks the language more elegantly than the native, so that the effect is reversed. The immigrants tend to be condescending towards their hosts. Priding themselves on coming from the wittiest nation in the world, many of them have the unfortunate habit of exercising their wit on the Canadians, teasing them about their manners and their rustic speech. This sort of humour is quite common at home, and no doubt they do it without meaning any harm, but the Canadians, who rightly consider themselves our equals or superiors in a good many fields, do not appreciate it. They have something of an inferiority complex about the whole thing which makes them very prickly to native Frenchmen. Thus the language they have in common, far from bringing the two sister races together, tends to cause friction between them. In support of my theory I would quote the odd fact that Frenchmen often get on better in the English-speaking part of the country.

Quite apart from the language question, the Canadians' way of looking at life is very different from our own. This is so to such an extent that the French often feel more at home in Brazil, Chile or the Argentine than in 'Nouvelle France'. The French Canadians, after all, have been cut off from the mother country for two hundred years. They live in a vast, bleak continent among extremes of climate, and they are deeply influenced by American civilisation. These circumstances have given them a character all their own, equally different from the metropolitan French and from the Americans. Two apparently contradictory influences have contributed to creating a mentality which others are apt to find disconcerting: religion and materialism. In the Province of Quebec where even apart from the huge French majority there are a lot of Irish people, Roman Catholicism is the dominant religion, by contrast with the rest of the country where Protestantism and even Puritanism are the norm. The people's devotion to their faith is fanatical, rather as in Spain, but with a character all its own, and manifestations of its influence on social life can be surprising to a Frenchman, even if he is a practising Catholic. One can go so far as to say that life is completely controlled and dominated by the church. Avowed atheism is practically nonexistent, and cannot fail to have serious consequences for anyone rash enough to profess it. Daily church-going is normal, and not to go to mass on Sundays is a sort of crime. A great many people go twice a day.

The clergy is prosperous and extremely numerous. In the town of Quebec it is difficult to walk a hundred yards without encountering a soutane or a biretta, and few families lack a member in holy orders. The church's temporal power is still considerable, its word virtually law. In 1948, for example, the bishop of Quebec forbade dancing in public places. The same gentleman also prohibited the Roland Petit ballet, in which one would be hard put to it to find any erotic suggestion.

The reader will easily see that so much piety and clerical power rob life of many of its graces, and can be very disconcerting to a newcomer. The most disappointing aspect of the business is that the effects are mostly external. One might imagine that such pious folk would be exemplary in their conduct, but one cannot in honesty state that people in Quebec are any saintlier than elsewhere. Quite objectively, I think that French Canadians are neither better nor worse than other races I have known. Only the Sherpas have seemed less evil than the others.

Sexual promiscuity is less openly displayed in Quebec than in France, but perhaps no less widespread. Drunkenness is frequent. People are more honest than in a good many other countries, but naturally there are those who will make the sign of the cross before playing a dirty trick. The manners of the working classes are brutal, and Christian charity is by no means always to be found.

Ice hockey is the main sport. It attracts enormous crowds, and I must admit I know of no other game so fascinating to watch. But it is impossible for anyone who has not seen it with his own eyes to imagine the brutality and violence with which it is played in Canada. Only bullfighting compares with it for the passion which it arouses in the spectators. Wrestling and boxing are also very popular. This taste for violence also finds outlets in daily life, so that to tread on someone's toe in a tram or bump into a passerby can easily become the pretext for a fight. This crude behaviour is, after all, understandable in a population which less than a hundred years ago lived almost entirely in small, isolated settlements in the depths of the illimitable and hostile forest.

But if religion is a determining influence on French Canadian life, by a curious paradox materialism is no less so. Here, perhaps even more than in the United States, the dollar is king. Economic life in this vast country, with its less than twenty million inhabitants, is entirely based on the most naked kind of capitalism, in which free enterprise implies pitiless competition.

Well-governed and efficiently administered as it certainly is, Canada is still in essence a nation of pioneers. Immeasurable resources remain to be exploited. Everything is susceptible of development, thousands of things still to be begun. The general level of prosperity is spectacular, and the whole life of the nation is geared to a gigantic effort of expansion. In such an atmosphere anything which does not contribute to wealth is discounted. Money is all-powerful, and the measure of a man's value is the size of his bank account. The first thing anybody asks about a man is 'How much is he worth?', an expression which I have always found shocking.

It goes without saying that in these circumstances conspicuous consumption becomes the first rule of life, and the net result is an excessive dependence on luxuries. This ostentation can prove trying to the few Frenchmen who still accord priority to artistic, intellectual and moral values, but it has to be recognised that such persons are becoming increasingly unusual. Since the war 'the American way of life' has spread alarmingly in our own country, and nowadays we have little to learn when it comes to materialism from our overseas cousins. The Canadians have their faults, certainly—who hasn't?—but they also have many fine qualities.

Once one has overcome their barrier of suspicion against French immigrants these qualities become evident. Thanks to my work I came into contact with a wide cross-section of the population and was invited into homes of every social stratum, so that I can fairly claim to have some knowledge of the subject. I learnt to appreciate their hospitality, their high spirits, their industriousness, their faithfulness in friendship and above all a certain steadfastness of purpose lacking in the French proper, whose sparkle and frivolity can become so trying in the end. I cannot go along with those who find life impossible among the French Canadians, since in a few months I was able, if not to assimilate their ways completely, at least to learn to suffer them gladly. I made several good friends in Quebec with whom I still correspond.

The main drawback of Canada is in my view the climate rather than the human factor. The six-month winter is altogether too long, windy and dark. Spending half the year in conditions like this is bound to be rather a gloomy affair, and the excessive heat of summer is hardly more agreeable.

The French always make the mistake of presuming themselves the salt of the earth, and their civilisation intrinsically superior to all others. If they could learn to accept Canada as it is instead of seeing it solely in terms of France, many of them could find there a field of action far wider than our overcrowded old world, and a second home which, though less smiling than the first, has more to offer than most other countries. Personally I owe a lot to those early overseas adventures. Nothing very exciting happened, but the encounter with new lands and men widened my horizons and showed me that there were other things in life than skiing and mountains. The human experience was to be very valuable to me later.

I had saved hard while I was away, and on getting back to France found myself with twice as much money as ever before. This relative affluence gave me just the cushion I needed for the change to independent guiding. Luckily the summer of 1949 was almost as fine as that of 1947, and my step in the dark turned out to have been a masterstroke. I accumulated clients and climbs at such a rate that by the end of the season I was declared '*le plus fort en masse*', in other words the guide who had earned most. According to the rules of the Compagnie each guide must pay 5 percent of his earnings into the '*masse*', or kitty; 3 percent goes to the running expenses of the Bureau, and the rest to a kind of insurance and benevolent fund.

I had in fact done over fifty respectable climbs during the season, and had also had the luck to be engaged by several excellent mountaineers, with whom I had done things like the first direct ascent of the Tronchey arête on the Grandes Jorasses, the Route Major and Sentinelle Rouge on Mont Blanc, the Aiguilles du Diable, and the Aiguille Verte by the Arête Sans Nom twice. This last seems to have become one of my specialities, since I have done it seven times up to the present moment. But more than ever it was brought home to me how difficult it would be to specialise in guiding on the great routes.

Taking into account how few mountaineers engage guides to do big climbs, I had already had fantastic luck, yet advanced climbing had taken up less than half of my time. In order to earn a decent living without wasting any part of that perfect but all too brief season I had been obliged to do numerous classics, and even a good deal of very small fry indeed, such as the Petits Charmoz or the Clochetons de Planpraz.

I remarked above that guiding called for psychological insight. To be quite honest, this statement applies not only on the mountain but also in persuading the client to choose a financially interesting climb. To succeed in the profession one must be something of a salesman! A number of my colleagues are by no means to be underrated in this department, and one of them has become a veritable past master. His powers of advocacy have always been at once my admiration and my envy. To take one example: he is a fine climber, and he has discovered that the south face of the Dent du Géant is an excellent commercial proposition. It combines the virtues of brevity and quick accessibility, yet it is an undeniably impressive-looking peak, and as the actual climbing is quite difficult it commands a high tariff.

When a new client approaches him you may rest assured that, whatever the former's desires or ability, they will end up by setting out for the south face of the Géant. Sometimes all goes well; sometimes the climb turns out to be too hard. But no matter: one of the first skills one learns as a guide is how to hoist an exhausted man, and up goes the client like a rucksack. The extraordinary thing is that the client is almost always delighted. He may not have enjoyed the climbing as such, but to have done such a climb cannot help but flatter his vanity.

The great weak point of my career has been my almost total inability to persuade clients to do ascents which suited me rather than them. I have hardly ever managed to undertake a succession of engagements from one base, so that to fulfil my commitments I have had to make hurried and tiring journeys from one refuge to another. Sometimes I have thus even got myself into stupid situations, such as on one occasion when I had to do the Grépon twice and the Jardin ridge of the Verte twice in four days. The starting points of these two ascents are two hours' rapid march apart. Instead of doing the thing logically, that is to say the Verte twice in succession and then the Grépon, I did them alternately, thus giving myself ten hours of hut bashing instead of four.

The most exhausting combination of starting points I can remember occurred during that summer of 1949. The cable car being broken down, I plodded up to Plan de l'Aiguille the first evening in a couple of hours. The following morning we left the hut at 4:30, traversed the Peigne and the Aiguille des Pèlerins (by the *voie* Carmichael) and got back down by two o'clock in the afternoon. After a short rest I left my client and rushed round to the Requin hut via Montenvers in three hours, where a client from Zurich was waiting for me. We then toiled for another three hours through the soft evening snow to the hut on the Col du Géant, which we reached about ten o'clock. At three o'clock we were off again for the traverse of the Aiguilles du Diable, and as my client was off form this took us fifteen hours. A day and a half later we went up to the Aiguille Noire hut, did the south ridge and bivouacked on the descent.

But for all the energy and passion I put into my work, I did not give up amateur climbing. Lachenal and I were determined to do at least one really big climb that summer. As Louis was still an instructor at the École Nationale we could only get away during his two or three short leaves. The first was spoiled by bad weather, and the second, unhappily, came right in the middle of my guiding season; but I kept the time free, thereby deliberately sacrificing a considerable sum of money.

We had been wanting for several years to repeat the famous north face of the Piz Badile, a mountain on the border between Switzerland and Italy in the distant Bregaglia group. In those days this 2,500-foot wall still had an imposing reputation. Cassin and four companions had made the first ascent in three terrible days of climbing in a storm, and two of the party had died of exhaustion on the descent. Rébuffat and Bernard Pierre had taken almost as long over the second ascent. Since then the face had been done four or five times, but never without a bivouac; the fastest ascent having taken nineteen hours of actual climbing. Cassin had gone on record as saying that while the face was a bit shorter and less sustained than the Walker, certain parts of it were harder. Everyone was in agreement that it was one of the finest routes in the Alps.

Though certainly inferior to the Walker and the Eiger, the north face of the Badile seemed to be the sort of thing we were looking for. There was no doubt that we should have a long, hard fight on our hands to climb such a redoubtable wall, and one which fitted our definition of a true adventure: one in which a man could only win through by throwing every atom of his physical and moral strength into the struggle. True, it was a rock climb pure and simple, and so not strictly our line of country; but we knew that the climbing was mostly 'free' and that we should feel at home on its sound, rough granite, which resembled our own Chamonix rock.

When Lachenal's leave came round the weather seemed fine enough to justify even the day and a half's journey across Switzerland by train and coach. We arrived at Promontogno so late that it would be dark before we could get up to the Sciora hut. This was annoying, because it meant that we should have to set out without a proper rest first. After an hour's rapid march we came out of a narrow gorge and saw the face above us in the last gleams of day. It was proud and high, and looked appallingly smooth. Our morale sank a few degrees at the mere sight of it. All of a sudden we had the idea of bivouacking where we were, and then going straight up to the foot of the face, rather than flogging on up to the hut, which is a long way off to one side of the mountain. By saving a couple of hours walking these tactics would gain us an equivalent amount of sleep. The eaves of a chalet offered some shelter, and as the night was almost warm we passed it comfortably enough rolled up in our bivouac equipment.

At daybreak we were put out to see the sky half-overcast with clouds of ill omen. The air felt heavy, and all the signs were for an imminent break in the weather. After a long journey and so many willing sacrifices it was heart-breaking, but we had learnt our lesson on the Walker. We were all for battle, but not for sudden death. Life is never so sweet as when one stands in danger of losing it, and if one takes imponderable risks too often one is not likely to last long. Our motto was to take risks, but only calculated ones. The charms of nature were spread out around us as we lay on the pleasant greensward listening to the chuckling of a brook, and we felt no inclination to attack such a serious-looking face in threatening weather.

About seven o'clock the sky seemed to clear up a little, and we decided to go up and spend the night at Cassin's first bivouac site. There would be no trouble in getting back if the weather broke, and if by chance it was fine we could hope to reach the summit the following day. In fact these were more or less the same tactics we had planned for the Walker—and then not used!

There was no hurry, and we stopped frequently to admire the wild spires of granite which rose almost directly out of the pastures and romantic pine forests. The climbing proper began at 9:30, and without a care in the world we scrambled on upwards, laughing and joking, savouring to the full the elegant nature of the climbing. The slabs were steep and the holds small, but they were sound and relatively numerous. One overhang proved really quite difficult, and not long afterwards we came to a spacious ledge. It was not obvious where to go next, so we took out the technical description. There could be no further question about it; we had already reached the first Cassin bivouac, and this in spite of the fact that we had only been going for two and a half extremely leisurely hours. It seemed quite incomprehensible, but there was no getting around the fact that we had reached the place where Cassin and his party had spent the night after a whole day's climbing. At this revelation

Louis' eyes began to flame with that passion I have never seen anywhere else, and he cried out:

'Then they're just a lot of goons! A day to climb that? They must have been playing cards on every ledge! If it's like that all the way we'll be up in four hours! The weather'll hold out that long—don't argue, let's get going!'

And he was off like an arrow. The wild beast had slipped its bonds, and I had no choice but to follow. Once again it was devil take the hindmost.

Contrary to what some people later suggested, we did not climb continuously without belaying, but we were so used to each other's ways that it saved us a lot of time. Thus, for example, as soon as the leader could see that only easy ground lay between him and the next stance, he would call down 'it's easy', and the second would start climbing right away. Over a long series of pitches this amounted to a considerable saving. Needless to say, if the second could not see how to do a move immediately, he wasted no time over it but pulled up on the rope at once. Naturally we used as few pitons as possible; with the exception of the first overhang we did virtually no artificial climbing at all. In half an hour's sprint we reached the first real terrace on the face. Ahead of us lay the series of long grooves which constitute the crux of the climb.

'Go on', said Louis. 'Time you did some leading, or you'll be getting rusty next.'

All keyed up, I rushed at the first groove. My rigid boot-soles held to perfection on the small holds, and I went up like a monkey. Two pitons and a few minutes later I stood at the top of the pitch, and a moment afterwards Louis was beside me. The groove continued above, but after climbing it for thirty feet I was held up by an overhang. One peg went in, but I then spent a long time looking for somewhere to put another. It was most surprising—there was no trace of any previous passage, and I began to wonder if I had got off route. Meanwhile Louis had a glance round the corner and shouted up that the route lay to the right, so I got him to lower me with the rope through a carabiner. To do all this, untie and pull down the rope cost valuable minutes: my mistake had in fact wasted a total of half an hour.

I led three more pitches for appearances' sake, then, since Louis was after all the faster climber, I yielded up the 'sharp end' of the rope to him again. It was becoming obvious that we would reach the top long before night, so I now abandoned some of the food which loaded the rucksack and slowed me down. It was cloudier than ever, but it looked as though the weather would hold out for a few hours more. Far from slowing down, however, we climbed faster and faster, under a sort of spell which made all things seem possible.

The upper traverses were disposed of with the briskness of a trapeze act, and so we came to the final slopes, which were easy enough to allow us to climb together.

Lachenal, fresh as a daisy, scuttled off like a squirrel, but try as I might I could not keep up. Finally there remained nothing above us but sky; it had taken us seven and a half hours for the 2,500 feet of face. Spurred on by the threat of bad weather we had thus accomplished a feat which was considered stupefying at the time, yet without my mistake in routefinding, and if we had forced the pace from the very beginning, we could easily have knocked over an hour off this 'record'.

Certain people subsequently took it upon themselves to doubt the veracity of our timing, nearly three times as fast as the best hitherto, but history has shown that we did not exaggerate. A rope of three Germans did the climb in eight and a half hours a few years later, which for a party of that size is relatively quite a lot faster. The famous Austrian guide Hermann Buhl, climbing alone, put up a time of four and a half hours; and the German Nothdurft, later one of the victims of the big Eiger tragedy, three and a half.

In fact we did nothing that smacked of the superhuman. It was merely that our physical and psychological fitness enabled us to discover that the face was, in terms of strict technical standard, easier than had hitherto been thought. Our constantly accumulating experience and Lachenal's fabulous gifts had put us somewhat in advance of our generation. Nowadays the northeast face of the Piz Badile is no longer considered one of the most difficult in the Alps. Occasionally someone still bivouacs on it, but it is normal to do it in nine or ten hours.

This 'downgrading' phenomenon is in no way unique. Among others, it has happened to many of the great Dolomite faces, once considered of extreme difficulty. The improvement in modern methods of training and the spirit of competition between 'tigers' are quite sufficient to explain it. Mountaineering is at least partly a competitive sport. Man has never stopped trying to run faster, jump higher, throw farther: Why then should he not also try to climb faster?

Since my ascent in 1949 I have done the northeast face of the Badile with a client, the excellent climber Suzanne Velentini. We took a little under twelve hours, but if we had not been held up by a German party who would not let us overtake we could have done it in three hours less. Taking into account the fact that however good a young girl might be she could hardly approach the virtuosity of a super-climber like Lachenal, and that at the age of thirty-seven I could certainly not have had the same 'punch' as ten years earlier, it will be seen that our performance in 1949 was respectable without being phenomenal.

It was five o'clock when we reached the top, which gave us plenty of time to descend to the hut on the Italian side of the mountain. The prospect of food, hot tea and rest only an hour away was extremely tempting; but if we did this we should have to cross the Passo di Bondo the following day in order to get back to Switzerland, thereby losing a day. A quicker but infinitely harder way back was to descend the classic but difficult north ridge.

Still on the boil and rendered even more optimistic than usual by our amazing success, Lachenal was for the north ridge at all costs. With a bit of luck we should reach the pastures before it got completely dark, Promontogno in the small hours and Chamonix the day after. We knew that the descent had already been done in three and a half hours, and given our usual speed at this kind of thing we ought to be able to knock thirty minutes off that, so that technically, at least, the thing was possible. In the end I let myself be persuaded.

The memory of that descent is blurred. I remember that we heard thunder a quarter of an hour after leaving the summit, which added still further to our haste. Lachenal himself was literally overcharged, and drove us at almost nightmare speed. We didn't stop to place any rappels in the difficult places. I would more or less slide down on the rope, held by Louis, then he would swarm down with preternatural agility. Whenever the slabs were not too steep he would let himself slide too, braking with his rubber soles and leather seat.

At one point we went too far down the west face. Lachenal reckoned that we would find ledges below to lead us back onto the ridge, and wanted to continue, but I was convinced that we would end up among overhangs and refused to follow him. We thereupon had our biggest row, and finally Louis unroped in a rage and went on alone. I climbed back to the ridge and carried on calmly with the job of getting down. After half an hour, while I was installing the only rappel of the whole descent, Louis appeared, looking rather contrite!

We reached the last slabs just at nightfall. As we came tearing down them, two climbers who had just preceded us, and who had observed us on the face during the day, looked as thunderstruck as if they had just seen a pair of ghosts. We bivouacked in the pastures, having been unable to find so much as a drop of water. My throat was intolerably inflamed and I could only doze off occasionally.

Back at Chamonix I took up my guiding again at once. The weather was set fair and the clients too numerous to satisfy. One day it would be the Petits

Charmoz, the next the Verte, the day after that the Aiguilles du Diable, and so it went on. When the end of the season came I was exhausted but happier than I had ever been. I had reached my goal: henceforward, like Michel Croz, Lochmatter, Knubel and Armand Charlet, I was truly a guide, one of the leading ones in the valley. Was I not *'le plus fort en masse'*? Had I not, that season, done more great climbs than any other guide? And yet, to tell the truth, I had hoped for greater things. I had still only about ten climbs to my credit rarely done by guides and clients, and none of these was really an exploit apart from the Arête de Tronchey.

Subsequently I was luckier in this respect. Gaston Rébuffat and I did more and greater climbs in a professional capacity than any other guide of the postwar generation. Only, I had hoped to do better still; and this remains the one small disappointment my way of life has ever brought me. All my willing sacrifices and risks devoted to this end have brought a relatively small return.

Apart from the five great Andean peaks climbed with my Dutch friends and clients,* which have given me some of the most enduring satisfactions of my career, I have only done one really outstanding climb in the Alps as a professional, and that was the third ascent of the right-hand Pillar of Fresnay on Mont Blanc. This is a very long and sustained ascent on mixed terrain, providing several high-standard pitches at great altitude, and in those days was the hardest route to the highest summit in Europe.** I have also guided a number of routes only slightly lower in standard, among others the northeast face of the Badile, the east face of the Grand Capucin, and the north face of the Triolet.

Just as luck always seemed to be with me in my amateur career, so it always seemed against me in my guiding. Bad weather prevented the realisation of so many glorious projects, and every time I seemed to have a client capable of the really big stuff he would infallibly fall ill the following season, or die, or get married.

At a slightly lower level the record is more satisfying. In sixteen years I have guided some sixty routes not often done professionally, such as the south ridge of the Aiguille Noire, the Sans Nom ridge of the Verte, the Route Major on Mont Blanc, the north face of the Como Stella, the north face of the Piz Roseg, the north face of the Obergabelhorn. Gaston Rébuffat has a definite lead over me when it comes to guided ascents of the absolute top rank, but

* *Translator's note.* This list now includes Nilgiri in the Himalayas.

** *Translator's note.* The palm has now passed to the central Pillar, climbed in 1961 by Whillans, Bonington, Clough and Djuglosz.

I think I can claim that none of my colleagues have amassed quite such a collection at this sort of level.

Still, compared with the six or seven hundred ascents I have made as a guide or instructor, I cannot help but find this a disappointing proportion, particularly if one reflects that the grand total includes many repetitions: the Grépon by its various routes fifty times, the Aiguille des Pèlerins forty, the traverse of the Petits Charmoz twenty, and some easier still like the ordinary routes of the Aiguilles du Plan and de Tour. But I repeat that the job of a guide is not to do great feats, except on rare occasions, but to carry out classic ascents, and I would be quite wrong to bemoan it.

In fact I have never ceased to find pleasure even on the easiest climbs. A sort of symbiotic relationship almost always grows up between the guide and his client which makes human contacts in this profession pleasanter than in any other. Surely it partakes of the nature of a creative act to give a man the pleasure of an experience he could not attain on his own? To me, at any rate, it gives a craftsman's and even an artist's satisfaction. At whatever level you like to take it, it is much more difficult than it would appear at first sight. Although the majority of clients naturally choose climbs corresponding in some degree to their abilities, they are still not able to cope with them without assistance, and few of them ever manage to be fully in command of the situation. Thus the guide has to be constantly on the alert for trouble and ready to help a man who is out of his depth.

Sometimes, at the end of the season, it has been my lot to lead large parties of tourists up to one or other of the high huts. You could hardly call it mountaineering, but there are problems even at this sort of level. Such people know nothing about mountains. They have to be helped over the tiniest crevasses, and quickly become tired. Ice and scree are hostile elements to them, and they can slip at any moment without reason or warning. I have often had to catch them as they slid. The higher the standard of the climb, the greater the problem; and the wider, too, the gap between the client's skill and the technicalities of the climb. On ascents of any real difficulty the guide's life is a perpetual adventure, as is shown by the relatively large number who have been killed at their work. With a client thus more or less at the mercy of events, the leader's concentration must not lapse for a second. I couldn't count the number of times I have seen my second 'peel' at the very moment when he looked perfectly at ease.

I remember an occasion when I had got slightly off route on the south ridge of the Aiguille du Moine. To regain the right line I made an exposed but quite easy traverse which led to a narrow ledge without any belay. Lower down the ridge my client had romped up considerably harder pitches. It would have been a reasonable risk to bring him across without any assurance—I had often done so before in similar situations, because it is impossible to safeguard every step on a long climb. I had no hammer on me as it was only a classic climb, only a few pegs which I always carry in my pocket just in case. At the very last moment a sort of premonition made me decide to look for a crack where I could wedge one of them without needing to hammer it in. Having found somewhere suitable, I called to my second to come on. He advanced six feet, then, for no reason at all, let go and swung twenty feet through the air on the rope. I was able to hold him thanks to the piton, though I had some trouble getting him up to me again, but without it my name would certainly now be on the obituary list.

This is just one typical example among a great many others. Three-quarters of one's clients can be expected to peel at any moment without warning, particularly on snow and ice. Woe to the guide who lets his attention be distracted even for a second, and gets caught off balance: how many have gone this way!

Even concentration is not the whole story. One must have storehouses of cunning and patience to get clients up pitches—without too obviously hauling them—which they would never be able to manage without explanations, exhortations and perhaps a little discreet tension on the rope.

In the event of bad weather the difficulties can be multiplied in a matter of moments. Classics turn into major undertakings, and the client, weakened by the cold and terrified by the lightning, becomes virtually helpless. In such circumstances no one can really guarantee a happy outcome. Doing biggish climbs as a guide often calls for more worry and effort than doing the most extreme ones with a 'tiger'. I could cover many pages with descriptions of the harrowing positions I have been in with vacillating clients.

On one of my six ascents of the south ridge of the Noire I had just finished the delicate and exposed traverse which constitutes the escape from the big groove on the fifth tower. My client had done brilliantly as far as there, and although the traverse was long thought to be grade VI, I was pretty sure he would be able to do it without the complicated rope tactics (called by guides a *téléphérique*) necessary to protect him simultaneously from before and behind. I called out to him to start across. He was so impressed with the smoothness and exposure of the pitch, however, that he hesitated, fearing to fall into an irretrievable position under an overhang if he slipped. Each time he made a few tentative inches he would shrink back quickly to his starting point.

Knowing that he could do it quite well if only he could overcome his fear, I tried every trick I knew: technical explanation, coaxing, raillery, finally even curses, but all to no avail. He just stood there, hanging on to his belay piton, his eyes full of mute supplication. This performance went on for more than half an hour. The sky was clouding over and I wanted to avoid a bivouac. Reversing the pitch to install the '*téléphérique*' struck me as both a long and a delicate process, but I was just about getting resigned to it when in a thought-less moment of inspiration I shouted out:

'If you don't hurry up and do it we won't be friends anymore. I'll never speak to you again.'

The result could not have been more miraculous if I had played the magic flute to him! I had no sooner finished speaking than, to my immense surprise and pleasure, he launched out on the traverse with the energy of despair, and in a few moments stood at my side.

On the first direct ascent of the Arête du Tronchey I was held up for some time by an enormous overhang. Finally, by turning on the high voltage for a few feet and also applying every bit of technique I possessed, I got over it. The difficulties now decreased, the summit was not far distant, and success seemed within our grasp. Unfortunately, although my client M. Gourdain was an excellent climber, he had never done anything as extreme as this. Despite valiant efforts he was unable to get any higher, and the friction of the rope through the numerous carabiners was so great that I could not hoist him. It looked as though we were beaten within sight of victory, and would have to make our way painfully back down the ridge, which had cost us more than a day to climb.

It all seemed too futile, and I desperately sought a solution. By scouting along a ledge to my right I discovered that the overhang gave out into a smooth but not quite vertical slab. If I could just get my client across to there it seemed probable that I could then haul him up the fifty feet or so that separated us. After all kinds of strange manoeuvres I succeeded in getting the rope clear of the carabiners, which I deliberately abandoned, and threw it back down to Gourdain. Unfortunately he was unable to reach the slab, but, noticing a little ledge directly below me, I called down to him to pendulum across to it on the rope. This meant a twenty-five-foot swing in midair, and not many people would have faced up to it. However, he courageously let himself go, and a moment later he was on the ledge. This manoeuvre was irreversible, the ledge being lower than the point of departure. Gourdain's bridges were now burnt, and he had to be got up to me at all costs.

The slab turned out to be extremely severe, and after his efforts to climb the overhang Gourdain's arms gave out completely. I was in an awkward position on a narrow ledge, ill-placed for haulage, and could not bring my force to bear properly. Neither could I see any way of getting down from where I was. Unless I could find some rapid solution, the outlook was tragic indeed. At this precise moment a technique for rescuing wounded men from crevasses came into my head, and with the aid of a few pitons and carabiners I rigged up a sort of pulley. Thanks to the mechanical advantage thus obtained Gourdain was soon at my side.

On another occasion I was doing the southeast ridge of Mont Maudit with one of my oldest clients, then about fifty-eight. The mountain was in poor condition and our progress had been proportionately slow. In the early afternoon, as we approached the neighbourhood of the summit, the storm broke. Needles of flame stood on the pom-poms of our woollen hats, and I felt the old familiar panic which the presence of lightning always inspires in me. After a few minutes the storm passed over, but the mountain remained enveloped in cloud. Before long a violent wind sprang up, whipping the snow into our faces and plastering our goggles. We started down in an absolute blizzard.

Now the ordinary route, which we were descending, consists of huge, steep snow slopes, interrupted here and there by ice walls and bars of seracs. Even in fine weather the route is hard to pick out on such featureless ground. This state of affairs being exacerbated by the cloud and the driving snow, it taxed all my local knowledge to find the way. Unfortunately my companion had bad eyesight, and with his goggles all plastered up he was practically blind. As is proper in descent he was going down first, but I soon realised that even when I shouted instructions to him he had lost the power to move steadily in a given direction; instead, he was zigzagging all over the place.

However, we had to get moving if we were not to be frozen to death. The only solution seemed to be for me to go first, keeping my client on a short rope. By a cruel stroke of fate the slope, which was quite steep, was packed hard with the ice bulging through in places. The cramponning was delicate in such conditions, and an exhausted and half-blinded client seemed likely to slip at any moment. The reader can imagine my state of mind throughout this descent, peering through the thick cloud to seek the way and at the same time trying to keep an eye on my second lest he should suddenly shoot into me from behind and knock me over with the twenty spikes of his crampons.

In point of fact I have only had about a score of clients in my whole career who were really competent, and no more than three or four who could follow anywhere I could lead. One of these, a German Swiss, gave me an unusual and amusing experience. Normally he never climbed with a guide, but as his friend had been injured he engaged me in order not to waste the end of his holiday. We set out for the Mer de Glace face of the Grépon, a well-known classic which is, in fact, quite long and difficult. Going up to the little Tour Rouge hut the evening before, already about a quarter of the way up the face, I had quickly noticed his astonishing facility.

In the morning I set a brisk pace from the outset, and since my client appeared to have no difficulty in keeping up I soon pulled out all the stops. Every so often I would turn round to see how he was getting on, and always he would be just behind me, smiling and not even out of breath. Once or twice, for form's sake, I asked:

'All right? Not too fast?'

And each time he replied:

'No, no. It's going fine.'

Now and again he would pause for a moment to take a quick photograph, manipulating the camera with extraordinary dexterity. As the going got harder and we had to climb pitch by pitch the pace hardly slowed up at all. By the time I had turned round at the top of the pitch he would already be some way up it, climbing like a squirrel, and a few seconds later he would rejoin me. We reached the summit three and a half hours after leaving the hut, an hour and a half sooner than my fondest hopes, including halts for some twenty-odd photographs.

It was 8:30 a.m. I felt on tremendous form, my client was climbing like an aeroplane, and we had plenty of time to do another ascent. I suggested traversing the west face of the Blaitière to the foot of the south ridge of the Fou, then rounding off the day by doing the ridge. It was an unconventional and even rather far-fetched idea, but it struck me as amusing and it would make a wonderful gallop. To my vast disappointment, my Switzer replied mildly:

'Oh! No, Monsieur Terray, I'm not at all interested in ideas of that sort. I've never climbed as fast as that before, and I found it great fun, but that's enough for one day. What I like about mountaineering is being in touch with nature and looking at the scenery. Anyway, the weather's perfect, and since you're engaged for the day we'll just stay here until noon.'

If guiding an ascent is always more or less of an adventure, the organisation of a professional season is equally fascinating. During a prolonged fine spell the effort required is often just as great as on the hardest climbs. There is of course no actual obligation to accept every engagement or to tire oneself out, and some people may suppose that the sole motivation for doing such things is financial, yet I think I can honestly say that this has not been the case. It has been more like a sort of game in which the only rule was to do all that was humanly possible. In point of fact I have hardly ever voluntarily taken a rest day during the season; on the contrary, I have sometimes got so close to the end of my tether that I have only been saved by bad weather, as a boxer by the gong.

One day after a prolonged series of ascents I did the south ridge of the Fou, a sustained and strenuous expedition. My ageing client was rather slow, and we did not get back to Montenvers until late afternoon. Tired as I was, I had to go on up to the Requin hut the same evening to meet two Canadian clients. By the time I had finished eating it was nine o'clock. Our climb was to be the ordinary route on the Dent du Requin, a classic which does not command a very high price. The Canadians were extremely nice people who would have understood perfectly if I had cried off due to utter fatigue. To put it bluntly, it would have cost me little to miss the climb altogether. But I set out all the same. My head torch broke down on the glacier, and as it was a dark, cloudy night, I got lost in a maze of crevasses. I wandered around for some time before finding the way out, and by the time I reached the hut shortly after midnight I was ready to drop.

I rose again at three o'clock, light-headed and heavy-limbed. Ten times the tariff of the climb would have been a small price to pay for the privilege of staying in bed, but there stood my clients, all unconscious of my inner struggles, happy and excited at the prospect of a fine day on the mountain. There could be no evasion: like a soldier charged with a mission, I simply had to act without knowing why. The ritual words and gestures were gone through, and presently I found myself outside in the dawn wind, plodding painfully up the track. At this point I blacked out for a moment and almost fell full length—but the clients had noticed nothing, and I managed to pull myself together. As we climbed I lost some of my stiffness and felt better, and presently we reached the top. That evening when I delivered my clients back to Montenvers, delighted with their ascent, it was drizzling steadily, and I thanked my lucky stars for the chance of a good sleep. My two Canadians had not the faintest idea that the day had cost me a more heroic effort than our escape from the Walker!

On yet another occasion after a long, hard series of climbs, I felt my forces beginning to fail me on the ordinary route of the Petit Dru to such an extent that I seriously began to wonder if I could reach the summit. My client was on bad form that day, and had been climbing very slowly and laboriously from the beginning. Preoccupied with my own troubles, I had not noticed at first what a state he was in. Suddenly I noticed the mortal pallor of his cheek, his dazed eye and distended nostril: obviously he couldn't go on like this much longer, and to preserve my honour all I had to do was outlast him! Pitch after pitch went by and the wretched man looked more and more piteous, but he would not give in.

My secret match with him, not to reach the summit, but to avoid the shame of being the first to suggest giving up, was reaching the desperate stage when at long last the poor fellow sank down on a ledge. Sadly and politely he informed me that he could go no farther. He was terribly sorry from my point of view, but he had tried his best and it just hadn't worked. Now he couldn't climb another foot . . . I did my best to look concerned and put out, but could hardly restrain the animal joy that ran through me at the prospect of being able to lie down and sleep. Honour was saved!

| 7 |

ANNAPURNA

TOWARDS THE END OF THE 1949 season word began to go round about a possible French expedition to the Himalayas. According to the rumour Lucien Devies, the great power behind the scenes of French mountaineering, was determined that France should begin to play a worthy part in the conquest of the world's highest and most difficult mountains. Up to this time her role had been negligible— there had only been one French expedition (to Hidden Peak in 1936) as against thirty-odd from England, nearly as many from Germany, four or five from Italy, and even three from the USA despite the relatively recent growth of the sport there. The conquest of the first eight-thousand-metre peak* would make up for this neglect and give us the place we deserved in people's estimation. It would also give our best mountaineers, for whom the Alps were becoming too small, an adversary worthy of their ideals and skill.

The rumour turned out to be well-founded, as I learnt in a conversation with Lucien Devies that October. Devies had been one of the best and most enterprising French mountaineers in the years before the war. Climbing sometimes with the great French ice-specialist Jacques Lagarde, sometimes with the celebrated Italian climber Giusto Gervasutti, he had many remarkable achievements to his credit, among them the first ascents of the northeast face of the Punta Gnifetti, the northwest face of the Olan, and the northwest face of the Ailefroide. Only bad luck had prevented him from making serious attempts on the Eiger and the Walker. He is still climbing actively, though illness

---

* *Translator's note.* Equivalent to 26,247 feet.

and advancing years have forced him to give up the more grandiose ascents. Unable to realise all the dreams and projects of his youth, he has altruistically made them possible for others. All his formidable energy and enthusiasm have been devoted to the general expansion of mountaineering in France, and in particular he has aided and encouraged the leading climbers to attack the exceptional climbs of their day. Lachenal and I already owed him a great deal.

In 1949 Devies simultaneously held the three most important offices in French mountaineering, being president of the Club Alpin Français, the Fédération Française de la Montagne and the Groupe de Haute Montagne. His combination of enthusiasm and power made our Himalayan enterprise possible; indeed I partly suspect that this had been one of his aims all along in the immense efforts he had furnished to bring about unity and efficiency at a national level among our various mountain organisations. Our conversation revealed that he judged the moment ripe to follow the trail blazed in 1936 by Jean Escarra and Henry de Ségogne.

Whatever way you looked at them, the auspices were favourable. French climbing had gone ahead by leaps and bounds since the war both in terms of quantity and quality. Nearly all the first repetitions of the great prewar routes, put up originally by the Germans, Austrians and Italians, had been made by French parties. Thus we could hope to field a very powerful team which ought to be technically capable of conquering an eight-thousand-metre mountain, a feat which had been attempted over thirty times by parties of various nationalities, but so far without success. The highest peak then climbed was Nanda Devi, at 7,816 metres.*

Furthermore, political conditions had improved a good deal since before the war, when they had rendered attempts on the eight-thousanders mainly impossible. These mountains all stand within the borders of three countries: Tibet, Pakistan and Nepal. Prior to 1940 Tibet, traditionally closed to western civilisation, had opened its doors only to the British Everest expeditions, but with the subsequent waning of British influence in the east the country had become impenetrable to foreigners.

The northwestern portion of India containing the northern Himalaya and Karakorum ranges, where most of the attempts on eight-thousanders had been made up to that time, had recently become part of the new state of Pakistan. Political and religious disorders were still common, and the government's control of the remoter valleys was not yet fully assured. In such

* *Translator's note.* Nanda Devi was climbed in 1938 by Tilman and Odell. The author omits to mention that heights greater than the summit of Annapurna were reached by members of Everest expeditions in the 1920s.

circumstances a party of Europeans might easily find themselves in a delicate position. Finally, the Pakistan government had greatly complicated the technical problems by forbidding the entry of Sherpa porters.

By contrast with these two nations the small independent kingdom of Nepal, hitherto closed to Europeans, seemed to have changed its policy completely. During the previous summer two expeditions, one of American ornithologists, the other of Swiss mountaineers, had been the first to receive permission to enter the country. The outlook for 1950 was therefore quite hopeful, and the Fédération Française de la Montagne had begun negotiations with the Nepalese government for a French expedition. If this were granted, the next job would be to choose a mountain offering some chances of success from among the eight-thousanders, the majority of which were in Nepal.

Then would come the task of choosing a team and getting down to details of equipment, organisation and transport, all much more complicated than one might imagine. On Devies' recommendation Maurice Herzog, general secretary of the Groupe de Haute Montagne, had been appointed putative leader. Devies also mentioned that I had been thought of as a possible member of the party, and asked if I would be willing to go. It seemed like the fulfilment of all my dreams. A man's dearest wishes rarely bear any relation to mundane reality, and the Himalayas had always seemed so impossibly remote that I had never dared to imagine climbing there in very deed. In those days conditions in France were so unfavourable to enterprises of this order that any such thoughts, soberly considered, seemed doomed to disappointment.

And now at last I was going to see those fabulous giant summits, for me a paradise where all was great, and beautiful, and pure. The Himalayas represented the total adventure, the gift of self to an ideal so often sought, so rarely found. Of course they also meant the mysteries and charms of the Orient, new kinds of men, new and prodigious forms of nature. Visions thronged my imagination, avid for experience.

But first I returned in November to Canada with my wife and one of my most promising climbing friends, Francis Aubert. Letters arrived at intervals through the winter from France, keeping me in touch with developments. The Nepalese government was slow in coming to a decision, and by the time our permission finally came through there was less than two months before the date of departure. The result was a terrific flap and also a great deal of hard work. Despite their busy professional lives, Lucien Devies, Maurice Herzog and Henry de Ségogne, to say nothing of many others I lack space to name individually, threw themselves into the labour with a sort of holy passion which in the end accomplished the desired miracle.

The first major obstacle was to find enough money. The state, which often lavishes funds on much more dubious enterprises, was not excessively generous, but made a grant of six million francs,* barely half the necessary minimum. A public appeal was launched, bringing in gifts from all over the country. Thousands of mountaineers made small or large contributions according to their means. A small group of eminent men, all enthusiastic climbers in the twilight of their careers, worked ceaselessly to get us the substantial donations without which our plans would be impossible. Among these were the late Louis Wibratte, president of the Bank of Paris and the Low Countries; the late Jean Escarra, professor at the Paris Faculty of Law; and, among the living, Henry de Ségogne and Lucien Devies.

These important businessmen and administrators did not hesitate to go round knocking on the doors of the influential, and thanks to their position they were able to convince bankers and industrialists of the worthiness of our cause and of the prestige that would accrue to France if we succeeded. All the camping and mountain sports equipment manufacturers agreed to support us, and the majority not only fitted us out for little or nothing but, in many cases, developed special kit into the bargain.

Thanks to their efforts we were able to make considerable progress in the design of Himalayan equipment. Reading the story of Himalayan mountaineering between the two wars, one is equally struck by the heroism and tenacity displayed by men of all nations and by their lack of imagination when it came to developing suitable gear for the job. One can virtually say that no progress was made in twenty years. I think we can claim to have cleared our minds of a dead weight of tradition, and although we certainly made mistakes it is not too much to say that our expedition marked a major step forward in Himalayan technique, and that all subsequent successes have owed something to our discoveries.

Far away in Canada, I had comparatively little idea of the scale and difficulty of these preparations. Herzog and Lachenal wrote only that the trip was definitely on, and that was enough for me. For the first time in my life I was scared stiff of breaking a leg or hurting myself in some way. I took part in no further competitions and only skied at a reduced pace, which is rather awkward for an instructor. By the terms of my contract I could not get back to France until a few days before we were all due to embark, and on arriving in Paris I was somewhat taken aback by the scene of frantic activity at F.F.M. headquarters in the Rue de la Boétie.

---

* *Translator's note.* Equivalent in those days to very roughly six thousand pounds sterling.

Lachenal was responsible for the crating and packing, which was being earned out at the warehouses of a company which specialised in the work, and I was detailed off to help him. I found myself confronted with a small mountain of tinned foods, crampons, ice axes, cookers, tents and sleeping bags, all mixed up together. After my lofty ideas of an organisation worked out to the last detail and the last ounce, this was coming to earth with a bump! Horror-stricken, I raised my arms in despair and cried:

'Do you really think we're going to make any impression on all that swag?'

But Lachenal, always the optimist, quietly replied:

'We've got several days yet, and everything we really need into the bargain. We'll manage somehow without the nonessentials. The main thing is to get away on time.'

And as usual he was right. The necessities of a Himalayan expedition are completely different from those of even the biggest Alpine ascents. Whereas in the Alps one is only away from civilisation for three or four days at most, in the Himalayas it may be as many months, and part of this time will be spent in an area of complete sterility. A big Alpine route is really a series of individual exploits carried out by the members of the party in turn, but the ascent of an eight-thousander is purely and simply a matter of teamwork. On the highest mountains the individual is powerless. His willingness to pull his weight with the team is far more important than his technical skill or even his physical capacities.

It will be seen that in such conditions human qualities are of prime importance. In the rarefied air of great altitudes, where fatigue, danger, wind and cold push men to the utter limits of endurance, even the best become irritable. Driven in upon themselves, they reveal their profoundest nature, and faults become magnified to alarming proportions. Selfishness and irritability cause inefficiency to such an extent that whole expeditions have been paralysed by dissensions among their members.

Organisers of expeditions therefore try so far as possible to choose compatible parties, and sometimes deliberately exclude tigers on grounds of excessive individuality. The committee set up by the F.F.M. under the presidency of Lucien Devies to decide on a team for the 1950 expedition looked both for technical excellence and for the sort of character that could be integrated successfully in a group. The choices were made with great broad-mindedness and impartiality. Naturally all the major sections of the French Alpine Club had their particular favourites, whom they did not hesitate to push hard. It was therefore particularly meritorious of the committee to resist all local pressures and overlook regional or personal rivalries.

Maurice Herzog was chosen leader. This appointment, which caused a good deal of argument both then and later, was in my view fully justified. The objections were mostly on the grounds that he had done none of the greatest ascents of his day, and could therefore not be considered one of its leading climbers. What he did have, however, was an all-round experience of the mountains rivalled by few other French mountaineers. He had come to the sport in childhood and had done most of the classics at an early age, subsequently making a large number of important ascents. Without any particular natural gift he had made himself into a good rock climber; and above all he was a complete mountaineer with all the right qualities for the Himalayas, including excellent ice technique and exceptional physical stamina.

If Herzog's selection was justified on technical grounds, it was even more so on intellectual and human ones. Quite objectively, he was the best qualified among the two or three French climbers who could have been considered for the post at that time. A graduate of the H.E.C.,* an officer in the reserve, a businessman of standing, he was thoroughly accustomed to organisation and command. His flexible and friendly nature enabled him to get his way with individualists who would only have rowed with an overt authoritarian, and the fact that he had climbed with almost everybody in the team could not fail to facilitate his task. In one way and another, then, Herzog perfectly fitted the committee's conception of a leader who would be capable not only of organising the various camps from base but also of assuming personal responsibility for the final assault. Over and above all his other qualities, finally, he possessed the virtue indispensable to any good head of an expedition: faith. He had been one of the project's initiators, and he brought to it the faith that could move mountains. Without this quality of Herzog's, Himalayan mountaineering would have followed a different course.

In order to assure as tightly knit a party as possible, the committee selected by 'ropes', that is by pairs who normally climbed together. Thus they hoped to eliminate many causes of friction at the outset. The selection of Couzy and Schatz was no doubt partly due to this motive.

Couzy was the youngest member of the expedition. Highly intelligent, he was an engineering graduate of the Polytechnique. Later he was to become one of my most valued friends and a companion on Chomolonzo and Makalu. Eventually he became one of the greatest mountaineers of all time, with a list of climbs to his credit hardly ever equalled for difficulty and variety—but at the time we are now speaking of he was still little more than a youth. He had

* *Translator's note.* Hautes Etudes Commerciales—a business school located in Paris.

already done some very big rock climbs, particularly in the Dolomites, but his high mountain experience was definitely limited.

Schatz was also an intellectual, with a degree in science, but for family reasons he had become director of a big clothing store. Powerful and athletic, he was, like his great friend Couzy, a first-rate rock climber, but with limited experience in the field of ice climbing and all-round mountaineering. Their selection for a Himalayan expedition was, therefore, open to dispute on technical grounds.

Virtuosity on rock is practically irrelevant to the ascent of eight-thousanders, where the climbing is mainly on ice and snow. The highest summit in the world, Mount Everest, was after all conquered by a party neither of whose members had much experience of rock climbing. Hillary, the New Zealander, had done virtually all his mountaineering on the exclusively icy summits of his own country and the Himalayas, and the Sherpa Tensing, for all his justly famed toughness and daring, was in much the same case.

At first sight, then, it would seem that it might have been more judicious to have selected two less brilliant rock climbers but more experienced mountaineers than Couzy and Schatz. In choosing them the committee must have taken their characters into account, and also the advantages of having such a well-tried team at their disposal. I think, too, that Lucien Devies wanted to try out one of his pet theories, namely that the conquest of an eight-thousander required less technical skill, even on snow and ice, than willpower, courage and endurance: all qualities developed by high-standard rock climbing. In its favour he could quote the example of several German expeditions, composed mainly of rock climbers, which had nevertheless been very successful in the Himalayas.*

Since then history has proved him right. None of the eight-thousanders has turned out to be technically difficult, even as regards ice climbing. The main obstacles have been those of remoteness, length, routefinding, weather and the effects of altitude. The rarefaction of the air reduces the physical and mental abilities even of the most gifted to an enormous extent. In tough but not particularly acrobatic situations moral qualities, when allied to good form and physique, are the determining factors. Rock climbers, provided they are sure-footed on snow, can therefore be valuable members of a team as long as it also contains some experienced mountaineers. The story of Himalayan mountaineering is full of examples, one of the most remarkable being that of

---

* *Translator's note.* It may be that the author underestimates the value of training on the relatively short but extremely difficult ice climbs of the Eastern Alps and Scotland.

the British expedition to Kangchenjunga, the third highest mountain in the world, which was mainly made up of pure rock climbers.*

The second rope chosen by the committee consisted of Lachenal and myself. Our general experience and our ascents of the greatest climbs in the Western Alps were our qualifications.

The sixth member of the assault party was Gaston Rébuffat. He too was primarily a rock climber, but his wide mountain experience and great achievements made his selection a foregone conclusion.

The party comprised two other members, my friend Dr Oudot and the well-known film photographer Marcel Ichac. Oudot, who had an international reputation for his cardiovascular surgery, was to be our doctor. As a first-class climber in his own right he would be able to play a part in the ascent, and even to replace a member of the assault party if one should fall out. Ichac, who specialised in mountain photography, was to make a film of the expedition and to write dispatches for newspapers which had supported it. He too was a fine climber, and had taken part in the 1936 expedition to Hidden Peak. He was the only person with any previous experience of the Himalayas, and his advice was to be useful on more than one occasion.

Finally there was François de Noyelle, a young diplomatist attached to the French Embassy in New Delhi. He was to be our interpreter and transport officer, thanks to his knowledge of the local dialects.

The world of greater mountaineering is quite a small one, so that with the exception of François de Noyelle the whole team knew each other despite their diverse origins. Personally I was already firm friends with most of them, and only Couzy and Schatz were less familiar. Thus our assembly was more like a reunion of friends than anything else and there was no 'running-in' period.

The late arrival of our permit to travel in Nepal, combined with the fund-raising difficulties, had left us all too little time for our preparations. The work went on in an atmosphere of feverish haste, and even up to a few hours before we were due to leave it was by no means certain that things would be ready in time. Everyone toiled as for a sacred cause, however, and in the end all the obstacles were overcome and the last crate nailed down precisely on D-Day, less than two months after the decision to go had been taken. Just as Lachenal had predicted we had all the essentials, even if some of the details didn't bear too much looking into.

* *Translator's note.* All members of the party were experienced mountaineers, more than half of whom had been to the Himalayas before.

Owing to the impossibility of sending our food and equipment in advance by sea, a freighter aeroplane now had to be chartered, so that the team and its gear ended up travelling together. The plane was a DC-4 which could only transport us by short stages, landing at Rome, Cairo—where we saw the Pyramids by moonlight—Bahrein and Delhi, thus sparing us too sudden a transition from one civilisation to another.

Nature has endowed me with an unusual capacity for remembering the details of events, and after ten years I can still recall almost every moment of that journey, even down to our excited conversations. Most of the time I spent glued to the porthole, avid for new sights. The weather was perfect and we flew relatively low so that even the caravans of the Bedouin could be clearly seen on the vast tawny levels of Arabia, from which occasionally rose spikes of jet-black rock. The human figures looked like ants in the immensity of the sands, evoking images from my boyhood reading, like a mad pageant against the yellow screen of the desert: Mahomet, Lawrence of Arabia, Monfreid the smuggler of the Red Sea, and Ibn Saud, the last conqueror.

Flying over the north of India brought astonishment. With a mind full of Kipling I had imagined the luxurious verdure of vast tropical forests, but for hours on end we passed over a baked yellow soil finely divided into squares, where the only trace of greenery was the occasional isolated tree. It took me some time to realise we were not flying over a desert, but an overpopulated country. The great grill of tiny squares that stretched to the horizon was composed of millions of fields burnt by the pre-monsoon heat. At irregular intervals the monotony of the land would be broken up by clusters of small domes, looking rather like bunches of fruit. These were the villages near which men toiled, stunned by the heat and crushed by poverty, to wrest their living from the exhausted earth.

At Delhi we were received with the greatest kindness by the whole staff of the French embassy, including the ambassador himself, M. Daniel Levi, and his first secretary, M. Christian Bayle. In our hurry to embark we had rather neglected the Chinese torture of the customs regulations. Herzog's chronic optimism had led him to overlook many details on the theory that everything would work out somehow, but as soon as we got off the plane it became obvious that the officials of the young Republic of India, glorying in their newfound powers, were burning with zeal. It was almost as though they wished to illustrate Napoleon's dictum: 'Put gold braid on a fool and you have a tyrant.' Every little functionary had become a despot eager to exercise his arbitrary authority.

There was no need for anything more to be done to our baggage than to seal it and send it on to the Nepalese frontier. Unfortunately our case was virtually without precedent, so that no regulations had been drawn up to cover it. But customs men, like adjutants, live by the book, and they wanted to examine and levy duty on every separate item. This would have been fatal: apart from the enormous expense, every day before the monsoon counted, and a week wasted in this way on top of all our other delays would have greatly reduced our chances of success. Were we to be kept from our mountain by a mere mountain of paper? Were all our efforts and our enthusiasm to come to nothing in such a way as this?

Happily for us our ambassador threw himself into the struggle with the big guns of diplomacy. He went straight for the seat of authority without a moment's hesitation, and all the obstacles began to dissolve.

While Herzog, Noyelle, Ichac and Oudot were battling with these unforeseen difficulties the rest of us, all unsuspecting, were making our first contacts with life in India. It was different from anything I had ever imagined. Behind the immediate attraction of the picturesque, or the monuments of a refined and splendid past, I felt the profound gulf separating us from these men whose very processes of thought were so different from our own. Quite soon the superficial charm of the exotic began to fade before the obvious and heartrending poverty of the people.

Misery and famine have been part of the fabric of Indian life for thousands of years, and at this time the country had just emerged from what, by any reckoning, had been the greatest upheaval in its history. No sooner was it freed from the colonial yoke of England than the northwestern and eastern portions, thousands of miles apart and with nothing in common but their faith, had seceded in order to create that economic absurdity, the nation of Pakistan. This new state had driven the majority of Hindus over its borders into India, and India had acted in the same way to tens of millions of Muhammedans. Whole populations had been deported. Over a million people were murdered during the months of anarchy that followed, and no one will ever know how many died of starvation.

At the time of our visit the slums of Old Delhi and the refugee camps on its outskirts presented a spectacle to melt the hardest heart. It was as though a whole nation had just emerged from Buchenwald and Auschwitz, covered in nothing but vermin and foul rags. At every step one encountered living corpses, their eyes, full of utter misery, looming huge over their hollow cheeks. Many of them had legs so thin that there seemed nothing but skin drawn tightly over the bone. It appeared impossible that anyone could actually walk on such sticks, and one expected to see them snap off at any moment. The sick lay moaning in every patch of shade, stretching out their hands as they dragged themselves towards us, their eyes full of unfathomable distress. Sometimes a heap of rags would not move. At first I thought them asleep, but the swarms of flies soon disillusioned me. These were the dead. No one but the roadsweeper took any notice.

After a few more stifling days in New Delhi we finally made our escape. Public transport was still disorganised after the recent troubles, and it was decided that Rébuffat and I should accompany the baggage by rail while the others flew on to Lucknow. To make sure of its safe arrival we practically sat on it. Travelling in a goods wagon is not too comfortable at the best of times, and the heat and dust of this journey across the Ganges valley made it an ordeal. The train trundled slowly along, giving us plenty of time to admire the scenery, but unfortunately this was far from refreshing. It was, in fact, desperately monotonous. Such charm as the countryside could ever have possessed had

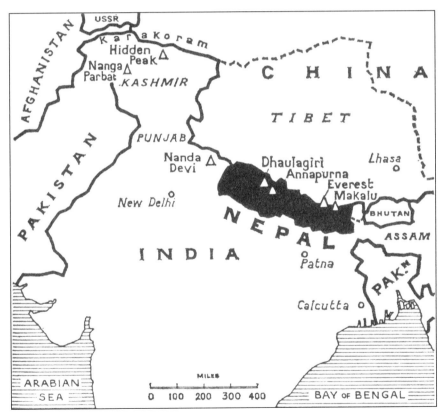

Map of India and Nepal

long since been scorched out of it, and our depression was only increased by the glum apathy of the wretched population. By the time we got to Lucknow we were dusty, tired and bored stiff.

Another train journey, this time with the others and on padded seats, took us close to the Nepalese border, whence there remained a twenty-five-mile trip across the execrable tracks of the marshy Terai plain in buses which could only have been designed by Heath Robinson. The next stage was jungle, genuine virgin forest inhabited by tigers and rhinoceros, and then, without any warning at all, high grassy hills rose before us like islands out of the sea or the first ripples of a storm of stone whose waves reached heaven. Our dream was coming true at last, and here, appropriately, the road came to an end. Henceforward our own feet were to be the only mode of transport, and men the only beasts of burden for our six tons of baggage.

The main body of the party now halted at the village of Butwal in order to recruit two hundred porters and to repack the loads for carrying. Lachenal and I were sent on ahead as scouts. The first afternoon lay through the thick belt of tropical forest which covers the western slopes of the Siwalik foothills like a layer of wadding between two different worlds. Night caught us still in the forest, but after marching on through the darkness for some time we came to a poor tea-merchant's shack where we were able to find shelter.

In order to avoid marching in the heat of the day we set off again at dawn. The light was as yet barely filtering through the underbrush and the great trees were dim, tormented shapes. The carefully flagged path was one of the five or six lines of communication between India and Nepal. The eight million or so men living behind the Siwaliks have virtually no other links with the modern world than these narrow serpentines of mud and stone. By the same token it was, of course, also the beginning of one of those astonishing Tibetan trade routes by which intrepid merchants traffic into China through narrow gorges and over cols nearly twenty thousand feet high.

During the dry season these tracks can be as crowded as the busiest Paris street. Gangs of porters bent under enormous loads are constantly coming and going, the half-naked men showing their bulging calf and thigh muscles, the women hiding their legs under long coloured skirts. Their merchandise includes bales of cloth, spices, sugar and knickknacks on the upward journey into Nepal, and on the return rice, corn, pottery, wool and hides.

There are also Gurkha mercenaries coming home on leave or setting out, like the Swiss mountaineers of mediaeval times, to sell their prodigious strength and courage to foreign armies. Some serve the British, others, more numerous, the Indians. Often their wives will be tramping along with them, carrying young children on their backs. During the last war many Gurkhas served in the Far East, North Africa and Italy, and it is by no means unusual to be greeted with a few words of French or Italian.

Every so often a merchant or a dignitary will come along, sheltered by an umbrella and dressed in a sort of black frock coat and tight white trousers, carrying his shoes in his hand, presumably so as not to wear them out. Again, they are sometimes followed by their wives, but these travel on litters like great ladies of the eighteenth century, richly ornamented and draped in bright saris.

More rarely one sees Tibetan caravenners, great raw-boned men whose long plaited hair and worn finery contrast strangely with the rest of the crowd.

At that hour of the morning the way was almost deserted, only a few isolated porters jogging down towards the plains under their fardels. We went on quickly towards the crest of the ridge which, as we left the trees behind, was touched by the first rays of early sunlight. Somewhere in the shadows arrowheads of gold were beginning to form, and I hurried still more not to miss the vision for which we had come so far. Then the miracle happened. Folded in light mist hill after hill rolled away into the distance from beneath my feet, and over this green ocean sparkled the vast icebergs of the Himalayas. Never in my remotest dreams had I imagined such beauty could exist on earth. Time effaces all our memories, but the feelings of that moment are branded in me while I live. Looking back today I see more, that it was not only the revelation of my dreams of youth, but the beginning of an experience which has influenced me more than almost any other—the discovery of Nepal, a world outside our time.

Since the day my dazzled eyes first saw that country I have had the fortune to visit it on four* distinct occasions, spending there almost a year of my life. About half this time was in the no-man's-land of the high peaks, but the rest was spent in the inhabited valleys. In 1950, by a happy conjunction of circumstances, Nepal was still almost untouched by Western influences, and even today it has hardly changed, apart from the capital, Kathmandu, and a few frontier towns. During my four visits I have covered over 1,200 miles of hill and valley on foot, coming into close contact with the people and sometimes sharing their daily life. The poetry of their simple ways and their calm and joyous philosophy have sunk deep into my mind, affecting my own attitudes.

* *Translator's note.* Now six.

I have loved nature and rural life from the first moment I can remember, to the extent that, as I have related above, I became a peasant myself and would have remained one but for circumstances I could not control. On reaching India, my head full of travellers' tales and avid for experience, I had expected new forms of beauty and poetry; but the drabness of the scenery, the filth and appalling misery of the people had turned out anything but exalting. But what I had missed in India I now found in Nepal. I was almost spellbound by this vast garden made by men out of nature in her most generous mood. There was enchantment in the clear colours of the fields and flowers, in the sounds of birds and streams, in the burgeoning of every form of life.

Evidence of human presence is everywhere, but here, for once, man has not destroyed the harmony of nature so much as completed and embellished it, as though it had first penetrated his own mind. The elegant yellow-thatched houses, shaded by banana trees, are scattered all over the hills, their bright ochre or white-washed walls emphasising the surrounding green.

The millions of peasants live a life of biblical charm. Their simple, almost puritanical manners lend them a calm dignity from which it is difficult to withhold the word *noble*. They all work tirelessly in the fields for their living, the men dressed in white loincloths, the women in gay robes, and the fertile soil often repays them with two abundant harvests a year. By contrast with India famines are rare and most people get plenty to eat.

The sugarloaf hills have been almost completely cleared, only a few clumps of trees remaining here and there. The steep slopes have been transformed by the ceaseless labour of generations into innumerable terraces where rice and maize grow abundantly, or barley in the higher places. The horizontal lines of these terraces winding along the hillsides, adding design to the green of the young shoots or the harvest gold, give a peculiar quality of elegance to the scenery. Even on my longest and most tiring marches I have never known the charm of this country and its inhabitants to grow stale. That I think with unabated enthusiasm of returning there in the near future is quite as much due to this atmosphere of a golden age as to the splendour of its great mountains.

When I saw Nepal for the first time that radiant morning, I knew practically nothing about it. Subsequently I learnt its geography by pacing out its ridges and valleys, or by chatting with the Sherpas in the evening, after a hard day, around the fire. It is quite impossible to understand a Himalayan expedition without some basic knowledge of these things, and yet the authors of expedition books never take the trouble to deal with them. A frequent fault is to quote names and facts at the reader as though he were already an expert.

But how many readers actually know anything about the Himalayas? How many, for example, know the background of the Sherpas?

It would seem that Nepal, like India, was originally inhabited by a negroid people called the Dravidians. Most of these were destroyed or absorbed by successive waves of conquerors, apart from a few pockets of which the most notable was in the Terai marshes on the southern border. Subsequently the country was invaded by tribes of Mongoloid stock whose descendants still occupy the larger part. Thus the Kathmandu valley, the richest and most populous of all, is inhabited by the Newars, a people remarkable for their manual dexterity, their artistic endowment and their commercial talents. In the south and east are the Raïs and the Limbus, a peaceful race of farmers. The Gurungs and the Magars, in the west and centre, probably arrived at a more recent date. These various Asiatic stocks form the majority of the caste on which the country's social structure is based. Castes in Nepal, however, are rather different from castes in India, whence they were imported. In the first place they are much more liberal, and in the second they tend to follow ethnic lines more closely. In many cases they are synonymous with tribes, retaining their own customs and even languages.

The historians tell us that the Indo-European minority did not settle in the valleys northwest of Kathmandu until around the year AD 1000. They were Rajputs from the Indian province of Rajastan, a traditionally warlike people. In Nepal they became known as the Khas caste, from which the present royal family is drawn. After the Muslim invasions of Rajastan around 1350 remnants of the Rajput armies settled in large numbers among the Nepalese hills, especially in the centre and west. Some authorities suggest that interbreeding between these newcomers (for the most part either of the Kshatriya warrior caste or Brahmins) and the local women gave rise to several of the Nepalese castes, notably the Chetris.

In my opinion this theory is to be treated with some reserve. It is more than possible that the Rajputs were not the only Indo-Europeans to settle in Nepal. During the first Makalu expedition, for example, we were surprised to meet a Chetri settlement in the upper Arun valley not twenty miles from Tibet. These aquiline six-footers with their ample beards, auburn hair and light brown eyes were of purely Aryan appearance, and contrasted almost comically with their Raïs neighbours, who were small and Mongoloid. The two communities had lived side by side for generations, spoke the same tongue, and their habits differed only in certain matters of religious observance. Yet the impalpable barriers of taboo had prevented any intermixture whatever, and each lived on their own territory.

I doubt whether these Chetris or a nearby community of Brahmins were in fact descended from the Rajputs. In any event their military and religious prerogatives had long since vanished, and they had become simple peasants farming even poorer and steeper land than the neighbouring Raïs. I have quite often encountered such Aryan outposts in various parts of eastern Nepal, calling themselves Chetri or Brahmin yet hardly differing at all from their neighbours in their customs. They have all seemed far more distinctively Aryan than the Khas or Chetri administrators and rulers one meets in Kathmandu. To sum up, Nepal is nowadays a patchwork of three different ethnic groups, sometimes in a pure state, sometimes mixed. These are divided into some thirty principal tribes and castes, themselves split up into innumerable subsections.

The history of such a country is necessarily complex. The ruggedness of both its terrain and its fighting men have kept it free of its powerful neighbours; Indian, Chinese and even British armies have made incursions, but none of them has been able to establish itself. Not until comparatively recently, however, has the kingdom been united within anything like its present boundaries. The number of principalities of which it was composed has varied widely across the centuries, the Kathmandu valley alone having contained no less than three. Their wars and intrigues and dynasties form an entanglement which even specialist historians have trouble in penetrating. Suffice it here to note that on several occasions enlightened rulers succeeded in imposing peace for considerable periods of time, during which civilisation went ahead by leaps and bounds. Literature and the visual arts attained a high degree of refinement, particularly in the area around Kathmandu, as many fine monuments remain to witness.

Around 1750 the country was split up into nearly fifty separate principalities. One of these was the small kingdom of Gorkha, eight days' march from the capital. Its inhabitants, the Gurkhas, were famous for their bravery in war, and thanks to this quality their ambitious King Prithivi Nakayan was able to conquer all the surrounding territories in turn. By a combination of unusual courage and running he eventually gained control of the Kathmandu valley in a series of bitterly contested wars, then went on to unite the country in approximately the form we know it today.

A century went by, and the royal family became decadent. The Prime Minister Jung Bahabur Rana took advantage of this state of affairs to seize power, giving himself the hereditary tide of Maharajah. The king was retained as the theoretical monarch on account of his religious influence, but Jung Bahabur was the real ruler, rather like the mayors of the palace in mediaeval France.

Historians agree that, by virtue of his courage, intelligence and energy, his government was beneficent. He brought a multitude of tribes to a sense of nationhood, and by a series of military and economic treaties with the British he went a long way towards remedying the country's traditional backwardness. His successors remained in power for a century, but shortly after our expedition in 1950 a revolution displaced the Maharajah and put the king at the head of a slightly more democratic government. In 1959 a still more democratic constitution was promulgated, though the king retains more power than in a western constitutional monarchy. These changes are undoubtedly responsible for Nepal's swift evolution towards a modern way of life.

Thanks to a well-maintained succession of enlightened and powerful leaders, Nepal has developed remarkably in the last two hundred years. The hill country has become populated to such an extent that today eight and a half million people live in a country roughly five hundred miles long by a hundred and twenty-five wide, of which almost half consists of high and sterile mountains.

Excellent cobbled ways resembling Roman roads have been laid between the more important towns, thanks to which places like Pokhra and Palpa-Tensing have become prosperous centres with well-built, meticulously clean and often artistic houses. Kathmandu is now a fine, spacious city, with getting on for two hundred thousand inhabitants. The varied architecture of its temples, differing widely according to date and going back in some cases over a thousand years, endow it with a strong aesthetic attraction.

The visitor who remains in Nepal for any length of time presently realises that in certain respects unity is still on the surface. The national language, Gurkhali or Nepali, which resembles Hindi, is learnt by the majority of the population, but five others are also current, to say nothing of dialects. Again, the Gurkhas have done their best to impose orthodox Hinduism, the faith of their Rajput ancestors, but this is far from being the only religion.

Buddha was the son of a petty king on the borders of India and Nepal, and it is known that 1,500 years ago most of the hill people were followers of his teaching. Nowadays Buddhism has virtually disappeared from India, but it is still very common in Nepal, though not in the pure form which has survived in Burma and Ceylon. Up in the valleys bordering on Tibet, where it is the sole form of religion, it has been strongly influenced by ancient animistic beliefs. In the rest of the country it is tinged with Hinduism in varying degrees—just as Nepalese Hinduism is tinged with Buddhism.

Tibor Sekelj writes: 'In most parts of the country the two religions are mixed. They coexist not only in the same town but in the same temple, and even in the minds and hearts of the people.' Later he goes on to add: 'It is often difficult to know which religion a man basically belongs to.' To understand such a state of affairs one must clear one's mind of all European preconceptions. To an Occidental religion is something defined and even codified, implying strict regulations, but to consider Oriental religion in this spirit can only lead to error.

Hinduism grew up bit by bit across the centuries, absorbing in its course legends, customs and gods from various other faiths. 'It is not a religion in the normal sense. Whereas most other sects have laid down certain dogmas and moral codes for their believers, Hinduism does more than this. It is the whole Indian tradition, literature and way of life as blessed and sanctioned by the Brahmin intelligentsia ... The simplest acts like washing, eating and dressing, as well as natural phenomena like rain, the phases of the moon and the flowering of trees, are all animated by religious belief.'

Thus Hinduism contains diverse and even contradictory elements, unity coming from a few general principles. One of these is polytheism, a belief in many gods, from whom each chooses a favourite to embody them all. Another is metempsychosis, the theory that the soul is not attached to any one body, but is successively reincarnated; though a very holy life may permit escape from this infernal cycle to the peace of Nirvana. Nirvana itself is not envisaged as any kind of a paradise on Muslim lines, but simply the eternal beatitude of loss of self in union with the universal spirit.

Buddhism is really an offshoot of Hinduism. One of the Hindu holy books says: 'To adore Buddha is to adore Shiva', and an ancient Buddhist work recommends the worship of Shiva. Buddha in fact figures in the Hindu pantheon as the eighth incarnation of Vishnu. In its original form his teaching is really a rule of life leading towards escape from the passions and the attainment of Nirvana. Only later, and only among the sect known as the Mahayana, or 'great vehicle', was Buddha deified and Nirvana transformed into the sort of pleasant paradise understandable by the masses.

In Nepal, apart from the interpenetration of Hinduism and Buddhism, both religions have been influenced by the ancient pagan customs of the first Asiatic settlers, and some of the Tantrist and Shaktist sects even give preponderance to these beliefs. And of course among the herd, as among equivalent Christian populations, religious spirituality often gives place to a sort of idolatry. Thus there is such a multiplicity of practices that one could almost say each caste is a faith in its own right. I have had much opportunity to note the extreme diversity of food taboos, for example. Some groups are so strictly vegetarian that they will not even take eggs; others will eat just a little goat or mutton; others again, such as the Tamangs, will go so far as to eat buffalo meat. Only the Sherpas and Bothias along the Tibetan border will kill and eat cattle, or rather yaks, and even then they do it clandestinely, such acts being crimes punishable by several years in prison.

In other respects, however, the Nepalese are more unified, and among these are agricultural methods and building styles. A notable characteristic is the complete absence of the wheel. Once beyond the Siwalik hills there is not so much as a wagon or even a cart. Everything is carried, and usually on human backs.

Being so overpopulated, Nepal has gradually become an extremely functionalised country. In some areas literally not a square yard of soil is wasted. Even the steepest slopes have been transformed into paddy fields, to the extent that a terrace three feet across may have a supporting wall eight or nine feet high. Paths are often no more than a foot or two across, so as not to waste growing space. Doubtless with the same object, animals for riding and beasts of burden have all been suppressed. To substitute human for animal labour in a country where the former is superabundant is no more than logical, especially since trained men can carry heavier weights than animals for a given number of calories. Only in the highest valleys are animals kept for transport; there they are pastured on slopes so steep and rocky as to be uncultivable.

With the single exception of a mule train across the Siwaliks I have never seen a loaded beast in the whole of the foothills, and the only riders have been officers or other high-ranking dignitaries. The transport of goods is of course a necessity in any but the most primitive societies, and Nepal is no exception to the rule. Since economic and topographical circumstances make animals and vehicles impossible, the inhabitants have literally taken the matter on their own shoulders, and human transport, laborious and wasteful as it is, has become one of the bases of the social structure.

The technique of carrying has been perfected in Nepal beyond anything known in Europe. From the moment they can stand children are taught to support loads by means of a strap passed across the forehead, from which is suspended a carrying basket. This apparently rudimentary method is very difficult to acquire unless one has been brought up to it, and I have never heard of any traveller mastering it fully. In order to support the weight without tiring the neck muscles, the force has to be kept exactly in line with the vertebral column, and only a lifelong familiarity enables this to be done over uneven ground. I have personally tried very hard to master the art, but my troubles were so obvious that the porters, with typical humour, nicknamed me 'the French Sherpa', a title always accompanied with roars of ironic laughter. In the end I adopted a compromise method utilising both shoulder straps and a headband.

Thanks to these headbands, then, the Nepalese carry unbelievable weights over great distances. By the age of eight or nine they can already transport more than their own weight for several kilometres. The strongest and fittest men are capable of unheard-of performances.

Fifteen years ago I worked as a porter on the construction of the Envers des Aiguilles cabin in the Mont Blanc range. Twice each day we would do a journey that takes a lightly laden man just under two hours, so that our total labour added up to the equivalent of over seven hours going in normal conditions, half of which was with very heavy loads that slowed us down considerably. Naturally, the days were hard and long. In such conditions I rarely managed to carry more than 120 pounds, and often a good deal less. All my mates were sturdy lads who had made a speciality of portering for the sake of the high wages, yet few could cope with more than 130 pounds. Only a gigantic Italian, six foot four and weighing over 220 pounds himself, would manage 145 pounds, and even 155 pounds on exceptional occasions. Yet in Nepal this phenomenal athlete, using the inefficient method of shoulder straps, would be made to look ridiculous by men a good sixty or seventy pounds lighter.

For the approach march to Annapurna a team of professional porters offered us its services. Some of them were quite big men, and all looked supremely fit. Their legs were particularly impressive, with tanned thighs as muscular as cart horses' emerging from the whiteness of their loincloths. There was not an ounce of fat on them anywhere, however, and the heaviest of them cannot have weighed more than 175 pounds. They sized up our loads, the average weight of which was 80 or 90 pounds, with an air of some disdain, then announced that they were not interested in the job. I was rather surprised at hearing this, and asked if the charges were too heavy. With a roar of laughter they replied that, on the contrary, they were so light that the wages would not be worth their while. Somewhat nettled, I declared that there could be no question of splitting up the loads and that we were not prepared to pay extra wages. To this I received the astonishing response that it would be a bit on the heavy side, but if we were willing to pay double the money they would carry double the load. They were as good as their word: transporting 170 pounds twelve or fifteen miles a day and laughing and talking as they went, they were never the last into camp.

Later, in exceptional circumstances, I was even to see Tibetan and Nepalese porters carrying 200 pounds over steep grass and scree at an altitude of twenty thousand feet, taking spells with the charge between two or three of them.

And these were not even professionals but local peasants, many of them rather skinny-looking and weighing no more than 130 pounds.

In 1950 Nepal had only just begun to open its gates to western influence, and the total number of European visitors had not exceeded a hundred, most of whom had gone no farther than the capital. To get there they had either had to ride on horseback or in a litter, or walk, there being no vehicular road linking it to India. Oddly enough, they found a few cars there before them. Had they been parachuted in, or transported in small parts? Nothing of the sort: they had been carried over the mountain trails complete, lashed to joists supported on the backs of hundreds of men, like the stones of the Pyramids. To anyone who knows the narrow staircases which pass for tracks over the Siwaliks and Mahabharats the idea of carrying a Rolls along them is almost inconceivable. Such examples help one to realise the amazing pitch of efficiency to which the Nepalese have raised the technique of human portaging, and, by the same token, how Nepal in 1950 was still living in another age.

Although, as I remarked earlier, the various peoples of Nepal are linked by a common culture and tradition, those who live along the frontiers of Tibet are an exception. By race, by religion and by culture they resemble the Tibetans far more closely than their compatriots, and despite the high ranges which fence them from each other they keep in close contact with their relations whenever the season permits. Dialects, clothes and manners are closely similar on either side of the border, and the form of religion, Lamaic or Tantric Buddhism, is identical.

The doctrines of the Buddha, in a sense more philosophical than religious, lost a good deal of their original definition in the process of being adopted by these primitive mountaineers, who mixed them up together with ancient beliefs of their own. Lamaism today is for the majority of believers a perfected form of paganism in which magic practices play an important role. The well-known prayer wheel is a mild form of it, but these are not in any case thought of as having the same type of significance as Christian prayers. Religious mottos engraved on walls or written on the inside of rolls of paper are not always intended to have any precise effect, and their symbolic meaning has often been lost, but their frequent movement in space is supposed to have a generally beneficent influence. This comes less from the meaning of the words than from the magic power of the movement.

Both in character and physique the Tibetans of Nepal differ considerably from the other inhabitants of the country. They vary a good deal in size, but as a rule they are small and quite frail-looking. Their rather unathletic appearance makes their stamina and load-carrying abilities all the more astonishing.

Living as they do at high altitude in an environment hostile to man, they only survive thanks to an extreme frugality. Apart from a few rare exceptions they never wash at all. Yet in spite of all their difficulties they are the jolliest people you could hope to meet, and any excuse will do for a drink and a dance. Intelligent, lively and full of initiative, there is a certain abandon about their attitude to life which is in contrast to the slightly heavy reserve and tidiness of their compatriots among the foothills.

The most numerous and interesting of these frontier tribes is undoubtedly the Sherpas, whose name is practically synonymous with Himalayan exploration. Literature, the press and the cinema have combined to make them famous, but few seem to have any real idea of what they are.

The Sherpas come from the Sola Khumbu valley, which drains the southwestern flank of the Everest range. A few of them also live in the upper reaches of neighbouring valleys. They are divided into two slightly differing castes, one living in the upper part of Sola Khumbu between eleven and fourteen thousand feet, the other, far more numerous, in its lower reaches. It is difficult to estimate their number even approximately, but it may be something between three and six thousand.

One thing is certain: there are too many of them to live off their few laboriously cultivated plots and their small herds of yaks. Quite a few live off the caravan trade over the twenty-thousand-foot Nangpa La, which leads from Sola Khumbu into Tibet. They are quite gifted commercially, and some of them become well-off merchants, but for the most part they turn into yak drivers or simple porters. Their profession takes them far afield into India and Tibet (the closing of the Tibetan frontier by the Chinese has badly upset their economy) and it would seem that this roving life has given the Sherpas their vivacity, adaptability and taste for adventure. Despite the important openings which the trade between India and Tibet has given them there is not enough to go round in their native valley, and a large proportion of them are forced to emigrate.

Towards the end of the last century the British built the little town of Darjeeling on a rather unusual site, a high hill dominating the plains of Bengal, close to the borders of Nepal and Sikkim. Situated at over eight thousand feet, it was designed to enable the families of British administrators to escape the furnace of the months preceding the monsoon in the fresh air of the mountains. For reasons hard to understand this region was relatively little inhabited, despite the overcrowding a few miles away in Nepal. The building of the town, and subsequently the clearing and working of vast tea plantations, provided an important source of employment in the area. Most of the labourers came from Nepal. Many of these were hardworking, disciplined Raïs and Thamans, but among them also were long-haired, turbulent little men all in rags, looking rather like the Bhotias of Tibet: these were the Sherpas. They had walked for three weeks to find this new land of promise.

At first, no doubt, the British did not make much distinction between them and their various cousins, but before long events were to display their special character. Even before the First World War English climbers had thought of attempting Mount Everest, but the time was not ripe. The idea continued to simmer during the war years, and in 1921 a reconnaissance party was organised. Permission was obtained from Tibet to cross its territory, and the expedition set out from Darjeeling, turning Nepal by the southeast, to explore the north side of the mountain.

Altogether six expeditions followed the same route between the two wars. Almost all of them got very high despite their archaic equipment, and some even exceeded twenty-eight thousand feet. They were astonishingly large-scale by modern standards, running in certain cases to nearly a thousand porters. Naturally a fair proportion of these were recruited at Darjeeling from among the Tibetan immigrant labourers and it was not long before the Sherpas came to the fore as high-altitude porters. Now there is no great difference between the various Himalayan races as regards their load-carrying powers or their resistance to the physical effects of high altitude, and it follows that the superiority of the Sherpas was really a moral one. They showed no fear of angering the gods of the high summits, like their Bhotia and Bouthanais cousins, but went enthusiastically with their European employers wherever they led. Their courage soon became legendary, and the British called them the 'tigers'.* They proved honest, straightforward and full of initiative, with an excellent sense of humour (not too easily found among Indians or other Nepalese); and rarer still, they had a real code of honour and devotion to duty. Whatever the dangers, they followed their sahibs to the end.

Himalayan history is full of examples of the heroic faithfulness of the Sherpas. Perhaps the most remarkable of all occurred during the 1934 Nanga Parbat expedition. Several German and Austrian climbers died of hunger, cold and exhaustion in the high camps. Their better-adapted Sherpas could no doubt have saved themselves by descending through the storm, but they stayed to look after their masters. Only when the last European succumbed did they try to escape from the trap, and only one succeeded. Notes found later on the remains of Welzenbach revealed the self-sacrifice of the others.

* *Translator's note.* The term was actually applied to the best among them. It is a normal British climbing expression for an outstanding climber.

Contact with civilisation has nowadays corrupted a few of the Sherpas, but the vast majority retain their ancestral virtues. The days I have spent in the company of these narrow-eyed little men with their huge grins have been among the happiest of my life. We have fought together for goals more symbolic than real, and it may be that the point of it all partly escaped them, but this in no way affected their enthusiasm and willingness. We faced the cold and storm, yet even when fear turned their tanned faces grey they remained capable of courage and altruism. Burdens were accepted and dirty jobs carried out with speed and good humour. Together, too, we trekked the pleasant pathways of Nepal in sympathy with nature. Many and many a time my Sherpa has turned to me with shining eyes, as we came over a crest upon some new harmony of earth and sky, with a cry of: 'Look, sahib, very nice!' Around campfires we have yarned for hours about our respective worlds, and in the coppery light cast by a giant brazier we have danced and sung our native songs under the stars. For me as for many others the contact with the Sherpa porters is one of the main charms of a Himalayan expedition. They have their faults, certainly, among them carelessness and lack of attention to detail, but their good-heartedness, gaiety, tact and sense of poetry give a renewed flavour to life, and after a spell in their company dreams of a better world have always seemed to me suddenly less foolish.

The conquest of the Himalayas had already begun in a small way before 1914, and with the first Everest expeditions it became a major undertaking. All the developed nations wanted to take part in the enterprise, and every year men came from all over the globe to join the assault on the abode of the gods. The British were the most active. Apart from strenuous efforts to climb Everest, they attempted and climbed numerous lower peaks while the Germans and Austrians, politically barred from attacking the highest mountain in the world, tried hard to be the first up an eight-thousander. Their assaults on Kangchenjunga and Nanga Parbat are among the bloodiest and most heroic stories in the epic of Himalayan mountaineering. The Americans, Italians, French and Japanese also played their part. Altogether, more than a hundred full-scale expeditions visited the Himalayas between the two wars.

All these parties required native porters to carry their impedimenta to the foot of the mountain, and also to establish camps on it. Nearly all the Himalayan races proved excellent carriers up to the point where the actual climbing began, but as soon as real hardship and danger came into the picture the superiority of the Sherpas was overwhelming. Before long their employment became automatic, and up to 1939 all the major expeditions had recourse to their help. At least a hundred of them, based on Darjeeling, became professionals, and some thus acquired sufficient experience and technique to be able to lead roped parties almost like a guide. In years when the demand for porters exceeded the supply at Darjeeling runners would set off, covering the 250 miles of switchback trails to Sola Khumbu in ten days, and returning at once with reinforcements of brothers and cousins.

The Himalayan Club, founded by British people living in India, presently drew up regulations for high-altitude portering. It fixed the fees, formulated the contracts and made lists of names. Each Sherpa received a number and a testimonial book, and at the end of every expedition the leader entered it up with details of the mountains climbed or attempted and the man's conduct. Once the British left India the club lost much of its authority, but after the ascent of Everest in 1953 the Sherpa Tenzing, a most intelligent man, had sufficient influence to set up the Sherpa Climber Association along the lines of the various Alpine companies of guides. In spite of initial scepticism in some quarters, this has turned out a reasonably efficient organisation.

For some time now this scheme of things has been a good deal upset because some expedition leaders believe that Sherpas arriving direct from Sola Khumbu are physically and morally superior to those recruited in Darjeeling. They assert that in learning to wash and cook and speak English, the city Sherpas have exchanged many of their ancestral virtues for European and Indian vices. Personally I find all this exaggerated. I have had occasion to employ both kinds without noting much difference. In my opinion Sherpas living in Darjeeling do not lose their qualities, even after a number of years, provided they were born and bred in Sola Khumbu. By contrast, however, those actually born at Darjeeling do not seem any better than the rest of the hill people, and have often acquired the vices of civilisation.

However that may be, there has recently been a growing tendency to engage Sherpas direct from Sola Khumbu, and despite a considerable demand for porters those living at Darjeeling have begun to find it difficult to get work. Some of them have even found it paid them to return to their native valley. Lately the situation has been further complicated by the Nepalese government, who, in an effort to profit from the touristic side of mountaineering, have tried to prohibit expeditions from recruiting any Sherpas not affiliated to an organisation it has set up in Kathmandu. Pakistan has forbidden the importation of Sherpa porters ever since independence, and Nepal is now by a long way their main field of action. From now on it seems clear that the best porters will have to leave Darjeeling and live in Nepalese territory.

But when I stood on the crest of the Siwaliks, that 7 April 1950, with the splendour of Nepal spread out before me, I knew nothing of all this. There was only the desire to learn every secret of this unknown land, and as we marched along day by day I tried to fulfil it. Maurice Herzog has already told the story of our approach march in his incisive, brilliant style, and anyone wishing to know all about it should read his book *Annapurna*. Personally I found nothing particularly exciting about these sixteen days. The route had only been followed once before by Westerners, a group of American ornithologists, but to recount all its details would be to copy Herzog with less talent. Only one thing still needs to be remembered: we were late in the field, and any waste of time would abbreviate still further the already short period available for our assault before the onset of the monsoon.

This absolute necessity not to lose any time lent a certain feverishness to our progress, and when our coolies came out on strike we went through agonies. Most of my companions, after the initial strangeness had worn off, became bored with the short but physically tiring days' marches in the tremendous heat. They had come to climb one of the highest mountains in the world and they could not wait to get to grips with it: these two weeks in its waiting room were a slow torture. I was as keen as the rest of them, but perhaps more attuned to nature. Every step of our slow advance brought some new discovery to be engraved in memory by surprise and delight.

Lachenal and I were the scout party. Each morning we would set out well in advance of the main body, accompanied by a few Sherpas. It would still be cool and for some time we could walk fast until the mid-morning heat became oppressive and the immense boughs of a banyan tree, growing on a shoulder above a curve of the river, would tempt us to rest in their shade. Then we would stretch out and gaze at the ribbon of water winding through the green paddies as they rose steplike towards the ridges above. Other travellers would also stop in the coolness of the shade, and with a Sherpa to interpret it was fun to gossip with them. The ones that intrigued me most were the coolies, loaded like mules and running with sweat. I used to ask them where they came from and where they were going. These unaccustomed questions would make their wide faces wrinkle up with astonishment until their eyes almost disappeared, but few of them could supply a coherent answer. For them, ceaselessly coming and going, life was just one immense journey from the cradle to the grave.

Sometimes we would bathe in one of the rivers, and the startled washerwomen would rush away giggling and screaming, much hampered by their skirts. Many of them were extremely pretty, somewhat in the Japanese style, despite the large gilded ornaments they wore on their pierced left nostrils.

But our preferred halting places were the villages, where we sometimes spent hours sitting in little tea shops watching the leisurely rhythm of life flowing round us. I loved haggling in the tiny stalls with their pigeonhole shelves stuffed with curious foods, wooden combs, jewellery, bright dyes and unappetising-looking spices. My Sherpa Aïla had been with Shipton and Tilman* and spoke passable English. I bombarded him with questions, and despite his natural good nature I think he found this abnormal curiosity rather trying at times. Lachenal was also very interested by all that went on around us, but patience was never one of his characteristics, and he found my halts too frequent. When he got tired of waiting he would lope off on his own, and I would find him asleep under a banyan a few hours later. Towards evening we would catch up with Panzy the cook, a veteran of many expeditions, whose job it was to choose the campsite for the night. He would start off with us each morning, but continue on his way when we halted. By the time we arrived his fire would be crackling under the fearful and invariable stew, a product of his own total lack of culinary talent, and of the habits acquired by long association with British masters. Shortly afterwards the rest of the sahibs would roll up, then the first of the coolies and Sherpas, the latter visibly lit up from the quantities of chang** they had imbibed in the villages along the way. Laughing and singing, they would pitch camp with the slickness of a conjuring trick, and in a few moments we could get into our tents and find our sacks unpacked, and everything laid out with the care of a perfect valet.

The bulk of the porters would drift in towards nightfall, in bands of ten or twelve. Still dripping with sweat they would set down their loads in the middle of camp, pick up the threadbare blanket and battered mug that constituted their total baggage, and trudge off to join their comrades. They cooked in little caste and tribal cliques, each with its own fire. Everyone had a job to do, the old men cooking vast quantities of the inevitable rice while the younger ones went off to chop wood and draw water. Meanwhile a few villagers draped in cheap cottons would gather in the shadows, silently contemplating these curious and fabled creatures which most of them had never seen before. I was invariably astonished by the philosophic way they accepted this new phenomenon—imagine the uproar and excitement if a Nepalese

* *Author's note.* Two famous British Himalayan explorers and climbers.

** *Author's note.* A kind of mild beer made from millet.

caravan camped on the outskirts of a French town! One could not help feeling that in learning to escape from passion and inquisitiveness these people had found wisdom, perhaps even happiness.

The children had of course not yet acquired the calm detachment of their elders. At first they would be timid, but before long they would invade the camp and start trying to get into the tents, causing our ordinarily gentle Sherpas to chase them like watchdogs. To see so many people ranked round the various fires was impressive, rather like a picture of an army bivouacking; and after all were not these muscular, flat-faced men, with enormous kukris* stuck through the tops of their loincloths, related to the Mongol hordes which had once devastated Asia and Europe? Were not their brothers in the British army the best soldiers in the world? They could have murdered us in a minute. To beings so deprived, our supplies must have seemed a treasure beyond price, and to escape from punishment would be no problem in such tortuous and sparsely policed country. Many more dangerous crimes have been committed for a great deal less, yet looking round their peaceful, laughing faces, one could see that for all their muscles and their kukris such an idea had never entered their minds for a moment. Personally I have never felt safer than I did then.

After a fortnight of this kind of thing we came to wilder country where the valleys narrowed to gorges looking as though sabred through the hills, each with its torrent. To negotiate these otherwise impossible obstacles, the track would turn into a veritable staircase among featureless walls of rock. I know of nothing which more spectacularly demonstrates the perfect adaptation of this mountain civilisation to its environment. Sometimes, as we crossed over a col, a glimpse of the great snow peaks would show us that we were approaching our goal.

We met with more and more Tibetan caravenners who, unlike those we had encountered among the foothills, were often driving flocks of sheep, goats and small donkeys loaded up with yak wool, sacks of salt and borax. Towards midday the animals would be unloaded and turned out to graze on the thin scrub and grass of the hillside until it should grow cooler. Then the long-haired drovers would gather them again with outlandish whistlings and plod on for a few hours more.

Finally the valley widened out and we came to a boulder-strewn plain, covered by the sediment of enormous floods. Above this stony desert Dhaulagiri rose into swirling clouds, vast and solitary. For twenty thousand feet there was nothing but the glint of riven glaciers, ridges that seemed like streamers

* *Translator's note.* Kukris—curved Gurkha knives.

in the wind, and sombre rock buttresses higher than the Walker. The sight was so overwhelming that we sat down by the side of the trail feeling slightly numbed. I could only think to myself: 'Well, there's your dream come true at last.' Then, as the first effect wore off, other thoughts came crowding: 'How can we climb a giant like that? Those glaciers look awful; the Alps are nothing by comparison. Will we find a way out of the labyrinth? Let's hope the other sides aren't quite so inhuman.'

Our base camp was pitched at the extreme point of the mountain's northeast ridge. The tents stood in neat rows on a wide terrace of scrubby yellow grass just above the village of Tukucha. It was quite different from the towns of lower Nepal, with its roomy, flat-roofed stone houses, able to serve both as stores and hostelries to the caravans that passed through several times a day during the season, coming and going between Nepal and Tibet. There the heavily laden men and women driving their pack beasts from dawn to dusk could buy the tea, sugar and rice which are the essentials of life to them, and the mules and yaks could find fodder to nourish them after the arid mountain pasture. All kinds of trade went on in the shade of those houses—including, it was rumoured, opium and guns. Despite the fact that the caravanserais were built in the traditional style of their own country there were relatively few Tibetans about, and most of these seemed to be servants of the Nepalese merchants.

In theory we had maps, made by Indian surveyors at the time of British rule, but although they were artistically executed they bore no relation whatever to the topography except in the immediate area of the valleys. The whole of this part of Nepal was in fact virtually unexplored in the modern scientific sense of the word, the only exception being the visit of the American ornithologists the year before. The one thing we were sure of was that there were two eight-thousanders in the vicinity, and we owed this certainty to the fact that in clear weather they were visible from the plains of India, whence they had been accurately triangulated by expert British surveyors.

For practical purposes mapless and without even photographs, we were feeling our way in the dark. This total ignorance of what to expect was the reason we had not decided in advance which of the two giants to attack: our plan was to reconnoitre them both, then to attempt the one that looked easier. Annapurna had always seemed rather the more probable, but Dhaulagiri was perhaps more desirable, being higher and very beautiful in its isolation. In the event we reconnoitred both summits simultaneously, and in order to cover the maximum ground with minimum loss of time we divided into four parties.

The only side of Dhaulagiri visible from the valley was the east face, so we decided to investigate it first. The lower part was really one great icefall, but we hoped that beginners' luck would enable us to find a way through it to the northeast ridge, which linked the summit with another, farther to the right, which we called Tukucha peak. The ridge rose at an almost uniform angle of forty-five degrees and gave every sign of being simple enough . . . if only we could get to it. We had begun to realise that the main problem on Dhaulagiri is to get started at all. Four separate parties tried to force the East Glacier in vain. Finally Oudot, Aïla and I got to within some six hundred feet of the crest, only to find the way barred by an impassable labyrinth of gigantic crevasses after all our risks. We retreated without any regrets, our route having been far too dangerous to justify any further attempts. Even if a few ropes might have got away with it, it was out of the question for the constant heavy traffic of an expedition.

We also tried twice to get onto the northeast ridge from its other, northerly, flank. A two-day march brought Oudot and myself to a col commanding a good view of the colossal north face, which seemed to consist of steep, overlapping bars of limestone like the tiles of a roof. It certainly did not look like a reasonable line of ascent, yet during the next few years five expeditions were to attempt Dhaulagiri by this route. The Argentine party of 1953 even reached the northwest ridge about a thousand feet below the summit, and some people have suggested that, given a little more luck with the weather, they would have climbed the mountain. Personally, I doubt it. By the time they got to the ridge they were exhausted, and their leader, my friend Ibañez, had such bad frostbite that he died of it later. At such an altitude a thousand feet of extremely jagged ridge would be a doubtful proposition for a fresh party, let alone one in their condition.

Nor did it look to us possible to attain the wide snow saddle between the northeast ridge and Tukucha peak. As far as we could see this sector of the mountain presented nothing but impossible bars of seracs, which appeared to go on round the corner. The whole cirque was so threatening that the idea of making a route up it anywhere never even occurred to us. Yet history was to prove us mistaken: nine years later the sixth expedition to Dhaulagiri reached the snow saddle by exactly this route, and the following year the seventh repeated it and went on to the summit.* They found a dangerous gangway through the ice farther to the north, almost on the Tukucha peak itself, but it must have been far from obvious if well-organised parties

* *Translator's note.* The sixth and seventh parties were Swiss.

of experienced mountaineers had succeeded in missing it for several years. It seems so extraordinary that I wonder if some major alteration to the glacier has not occurred.

Naturally I have sometimes regretted not pushing my reconnaissance a bit farther, but taking everything into account I do not think we would have got up Dhaulagiri even if we had succeeded in finding the way to the snow saddle. In 1950 the time was not yet ripe for such an exploit. We were short of time, experience and equipment; and above all we were short of Sherpas. Thus we had neither the strength nor the knowledge to exploit such a long, complex and difficult route. The English mountaineer Frank Smythe, one of the greatest of his generation, a member of five expeditions, the conqueror of Kamet and a man who had reached twenty-eight thousand feet on Everest without oxygen, had said flatly: 'Himalayan mountaineering offers such difficulties that it seems unlikely that any expedition will succeed on one of the dozen highest summits at the first attempt.' Smythe was a pioneer, and events have since proved him mistaken, but after all we were pioneering too, and Himalayan technique at that time had not progressed at all since his day.* The weapons which brought success on Dhaulagiri in 1960 had not yet been forged: the party used an aeroplane to land some of their men and supplies on the snow saddle.

Herzog quickly came to the conclusion that Dhaulagiri was too tough a nut for us to crack, and without waiting for any further confirmation he switched all our efforts towards Annapurna. This mountain was difficult even to find, and at first we didn't so much as succeed in getting a view of it. We almost began to wonder if it was another figment of our fairy-tale maps. In fact it was hidden from us by the Nilgiri range, and we had to get quite high up on the flanks of Dhaulagiri before we could see it. So far as we could make out there were steep crags on the south and east, but the northern side, which we commanded in profile, was a vast medium-angled snow slope, scarcely more than thirty-five degrees. There seemed no particular reason to suppose any major change of character lower down, and if we were right about this the ascent ought to be comparatively easy.

These favourable omens restored our morale. But in order to climb our easy snow slope we still had to find a way to the foot of it, and this was beginning to assume the proportions of a mystery. The Nilgiris, seen from a distance, gave the impression of an unbroken chain, and Annapurna therefore looked as though it began in another system of valleys beyond. Apparently we

---

* *Translator's note.* So far as I know Annapurna remains the sole exception to Smythe's dictum, much of Lhotse having been climbed in the course of Everest expeditions.

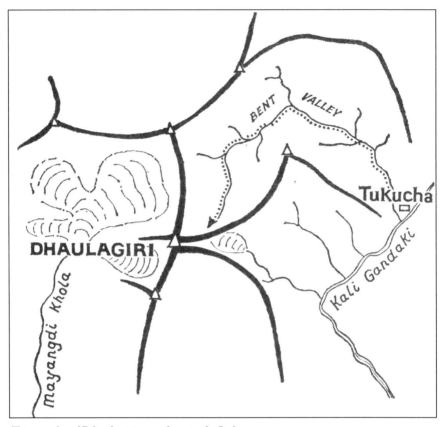

Topography of Dhaulagiri according to the Indian map

were either going to have to make an immense detour round the northwest of the range or cross it at some point of weakness, always supposing that one existed. We chose the latter solution as being the quicker, and the first recon-naissance attempted to cross the range by following the course of the Miristi Khola, which led to a deep breach in the mountain's defences.

To tell the truth we were rather intrigued by the amount of water that came down this defile: it seemed too abundant to be accounted for solely by the relatively minor glaciers of the Nilgiris. We had an inkling, despite all the evidence to the contrary, that it might drain the west face of Annapurna, or perhaps just possibly the north face; and the map, whose full inaccuracy we did not even yet suspect, appeared to bear this out. It showed the source of the river below the Tilicho col, and a straightforward path leading along it, over the col, and down to the Manangbhot valley on the other side. But it was too good to be true. Inquiries by the sirdar Angtharkay revealed that no one in the

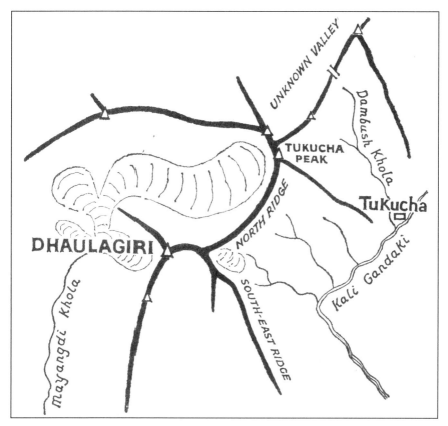

Actual topography of Dhaulagiri

area had ever heard of Tilicho col or of any path leading up the Miristi and over the range. It was certainly puzzling.

Our European minds could not adjust to the idea that any map could be so inaccurate, and after all it seemed as logical to trust it as the word of a bunch of villagers who had little interest in the remoter parts of the mountains. Wishful thinking led us to suppose that knowledge of the trail might have died out owing to trade changes. Such things had happened before, and only recently we had found the greatest difficulty in discovering a man who could guide us up the valley to the west of Dhaulagiri, though when we got there we found not only a path but signs of erstwhile inhabitation. In the end we decided to see for ourselves. If the river could penetrate the heart of the range, why shouldn't we?

Further inquiries by the Sherpas confirmed that the lower gorges of the Miristi were indeed impassable, but we had had certain views from Dhaulagiri which suggested the possibility of joining the river higher up. The obvious thing now was to put all this to the proof, and accordingly Oudot, Schatz and Couzy, accompanied by Angtharkay and some of the other Sherpas, set out to explore. They were able to get through the dense jungle of the lower slopes thanks to a tiny track placed by a beneficent providence precisely where it was most needed. This led them up to open country again, where they bore more to the right until they came to a shoulder on the southwest ridge of the Nilgiris. Thence a four-mile traverse along the sole ledge between a couple of three-thousand-foot precipices brought them back to the torrent just above the point where the gorges widened out into a valley again. By this time, unfortunately, they were exhausted from lack of food and could go no farther. Shortage of provisions forced them to turn back before they had explored the valley to its end.

The statements they made on their return did little to clear up the mystery that seemed to cloak the mountain. They were now quite convinced that the Miristi did drain at least the west face of Annapurna, and had also had a close look at a gigantic rock spur that appeared to lead to the northwest ridge. They had not found any obvious way of getting onto the glaciers of the north face, and the only possibility they could suggest seemed fantastic in its audacity: it consisted of climbing the spur and then the northwest ridge until the glacier could be gained from it. Presupposing that the hidden parts of the route did not reserve any nasty surprises, and given the fact that the main difficulties would come relatively low down, such a route was theoretically possible, but it was excessively complex and would raise technical problems so far never even considered in the history of Himalayan mountaineering.

None of this was exactly encouraging. Herzog, like the rest of us, felt that before committing ourselves to an enterprise of such uncertain issue we should find out definitely whether or not the North Glacier could be approached via the Manangbhot valley. While Oudot and I took a final look at the East Glacier of Dhaulagiri, therefore, Herzog, Ichac and Rébuffat would make a wide circuit of the range over the col separating the Nilgiris from the Muktinath massif. Though apparently unknown to the natives this pass offered no particular difficulties, but on the other side the party found themselves still cut off from Annapurna by an unknown chain of mountains which they dubbed 'the Great Barrier'. They got back to Tukucha on 13 May, and the topography of Annapurna remained as baffling as ever. Our minds, accustomed to the less complex formations of the Alps, had difficulty in formulating the idea that the mountain and its satellites might, like Nanda Devi, constitute a closed circle without other issue than one narrow defile.

Oudot and I had returned empty-handed on the 12th, and for the first time since our arrival the whole party was together. Two days later Herzog called a council of war in our big mess tent. The situation was getting desperate: it was time for vital decisions to be taken. We had now spent over a month wandering around the complex and unexplored Dhaulagiri and Annapurna massifs without finding a practicable route up either of them, and the monsoon could be barely more than three weeks away. Yet we could hardly give up so easily. Surely all those years of hope and dedication, those youthful dreams, those desperate fights on the hardest climbs in the Alps, could not lead to such a tame ending. It is said that faith can move mountains; well, we still had faith, in spite of all the wearisome disappointments. The enthusiasm which had overcome so many obstacles was still fresh, and now that we were on the field of battle the disappointment of those who had believed in us and toiled for us was not to be thought of. It was obvious that we had really undertaken too much, but for honour's sake we must see it through. The gleams of hope might have grown somewhat dim but they were not totally extinguished. The important thing now was to choose between these two eight-thousanders, and then do our best.

The mighty and isolated Dhaulagiri had yielded us all its secrets. We were well aware that it had only one weak point, the northeast ridge. If one could only get to its base by a very long and difficult traverse of the Tukucha peak, the ascent would be theoretically possible. With the time and equipment at our disposal an optimist might consider making the attempt, but it would be verging on suicide.

Annapurna, by contrast, remained a complete enigma. We had seen the mountain from afar off, lording it over groves of seven-thousanders, but the closer we got to it the hazier our ideas of its topography became, for all our painstaking reconnaissances. Three of our number, aided by luck and the wonderful flair of the Sherpas, had eventually accomplished the remarkable feat of penetrating to the heart of the sanctuary via the cyclopean six-mile gorge, but even then the best they could say was 'perhaps'. Now we had to choose between a most desperate enterprise and a complete gamble.

Maurice Herzog hesitated before the choice. Should he abandon a prize, however doubtful, in favour of a mystery so insubstantial? Could he expose men who had taken their oath to obey him to mortal danger? In full awareness of his terrible responsibility Maurice chose the more reasonable but uncertain course: we would attempt Annapurna.

Lachenal and I, guided by Schatz, were to set out at once. Maurice and Rébuffat would follow the next day, led by Couzy, then it would be the turn

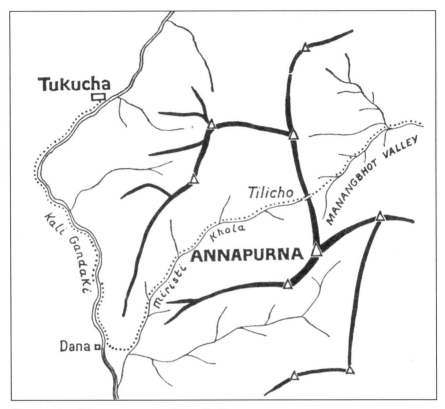

Topography of Annapurna according to Indian map

of Oudot and Ichac. Noyelle and Angtharkay would remain at Tukucha with the bulk of the supplies, making them up into loads and recruiting porters until the order was given for the assault. This amounted to a reconnaissance in force, able to be changed at a moment's notice into an all-out attack or into a swift withdrawal, according to circumstances, in which case we would console ourselves with trying one or two seven-thousanders.

We got our things together at top speed, overjoyed to be going into action at last. A few bare necessities were dumped into our sacks, then the loads for our four porters were hurriedly made up. Early in the afternoon I struck up a Chasseur song and led off, twirling my ice axe over my head like a drum major's mace. This time it was the big show. A rapid march across never-ending boulder flats, followed by poor tracks winding along the hillside, brought us shortly before nightfall to the village of Soya, at nearly eight thousand feet. We had done about twelve miles in one afternoon—obviously the porters were robust and morale high, and our three Sherpas, Dawatondu,

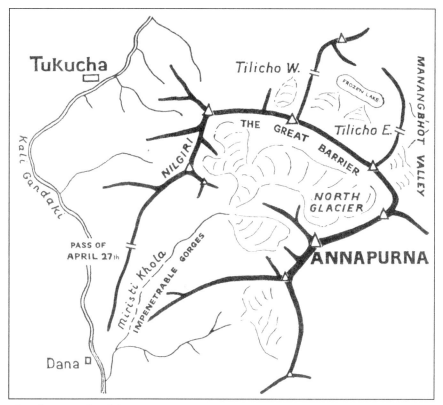

Actual topography of Annapurna

Angdawa and Adjiba, were doing everything they could to help. Camp was soon pitched on some comfortable flat grass and we enjoyed a meal of chicken before settling down for the night.

By daybreak I was already stirring the Sherpas into activity, and at seven o'clock we began the interminable grind up to the pass discovered by Couzy, Oudot and Schatz on 26 April. The weather was fine, as usual at that hour. I cast a last glance at Dhaulagiri. From this angle the north ridge looked almost easy, and for a moment I was seized with regret. But it was too late now, the chips were down, and it was better to go on without looking back.

We plodded slowly uphill past the terraces, observing with interest the highly adapted agricultural methods of this overpopulated country where every inch of ground is exploited even more meticulously than in the Alps. The cultivated area came to an end after about six hundred feet and we followed a remarkable path built out from the slope. Presently this descended steeply through a thick forest of bamboos until it reached the bottom of a gorge containing a clear stream, and started immediately up the other side. In places it was so steep that it virtually amounted to climbing through semi-vertical jungle. The trail was indistinct and hard to follow, but I blessed the luck which had put it where it was most needed, and also the Sherpas' flair in finding it.

After a time we came to a burnt-out stretch of forest, the gaunt remains of huge trees giving it an almost pathetic air. Here we made a halt and drank clear liquid which the Sherpas drew from a sort of birch. The uphill going was made pleasanter by the presence of magnificent shrubs, among which multicoloured rhododendrons contended with dog rose for the prize. As we approached the tree line it began to rain, making walking on the long, slippery grass tiresome and exasperating. We could now feel the effects of altitude, but on form and bursting with enthusiasm as we were, we wanted to get as far as possible that day. Despite their ponderous loads and the taxing pace the porters and Sherpas kept up valiantly. The path was ill-defined and sometimes disappeared completely, but led always to the left, so that we were following the line of a steep terrace between two enormous crags. Several times we had to cross snow gullies where I was worried by our porters' uncertain footing in their bare feet. A sort of gateway in the upper crag eventually opened onto easier slopes where we found the remains of many shepherds' camps, and at one of these the discovery of a pile of wood seemed to justify a slightly early halt. Our porters had, after all, climbed about six thousand feet with loads of nearly ninety pounds, and one could hardly expect more.

The day following another five- or six-thousand-foot drag brought us to a tiny notch on a secondary ridge of the Nilgiri massif. This pass, so insignificant seeming among the vastness of the mountains, proved to be one of the most important in the history of Himalayan mountaineering, for it was from here that on 26 April 1950, Couzy, Oudot and Schatz discovered the amazing traverse of the walls of the Miristi gorge, without which Annapurna would never have been climbed. After descending a short distance down a spur we were able to see the tumultuous rapids themselves, though not so much as a murmur rose to us through the nearly five thousand feet of intervening space. The hopelessness of trying to penetrate gorges of such inconceivable proportions, at least for anyone not knowing these mountains intimately, became quite plain to us.

Our ankles continually bent over until they ached, we now began the intricate six miles of interconnecting ledges across the high southwestern face of the southeast peak of Nilgiri. Sometimes the ledges were steep and narrow, sometimes broad and easy. Every so often one would come to an end, but by mounting or descending a gully, frequently with a torrent in its bed, we would come to the next, so that a tortuous switchback progress was always possible. The route constantly seemed to be barred, but at the very last moment an unforeseeable and generally easy way would open up ahead. A tiny cairned track made routefinding easier than it would otherwise have been in the afternoon rain and cloud, though conditions slowed us down all the same. Fortunately Schatz and the Sherpas guided us with great confidence and exactitude. A little cave with recent graffiti on its walls attracted our interest for a while, after which signs of passage became rarer. The cairns were getting farther and farther apart, until finally they gave out altogether. Fifty yards ahead, our ledge ended in a blank wall of rock.

I glanced at Schatz in anxiety, wondering what he would do now. Without batting an eyelid he marched confidently towards the edge of all things. Miracle of miracles! At the precise moment when all else failed a couloir opened at our feet, and a steep but relatively easy descent of somewhat over two thousand feet took us down to the Miristi Khola just a few hundred yards above the beginning of the gorges. Later I was to have the opportunity of observing that this was indeed the only possible way of getting from the ledges to the valley. Fortune had favoured us with such a fantastic stroke that it seemed impossible, henceforward, that she would abandon us again. An attempt to wade the torrent gave rise to some picturesque scenes, with a cowboy Lachenal lassoing porters as they were swept away. Eventually we solved the problem with an improvised bridge of branches.

Next day, 17 May, we carried on along widespread, seemingly endless moraines. Towards three o'clock in the afternoon we reached the farthest point of the previous reconnaissance. While Lachenal and the Sherpas looked around for a suitable campsite Schatz went on, hoping to see a practicable route. For a time I followed him, then, judging the visibility too poor to justify the effort, returned to camp. The low cloud ceiling hid all but the foot of the surrounding crags, but I could see enough to realise that all the routes so far suggested would be formidable in the extreme.

The end of our valley was occupied by an enormous glacier which descended in cascades of toppling seracs between titanic walls. Before turning back I scrutinised these through my binoculars in case they might offer a way past the icefall, but they looked so steep and featureless that I was put off entirely, though admittedly I was not well placed for a proper survey. The great northwest spur which rose above me into the clouds looked much more attractive. Those of the party who had seen it from some way off in clear weather reckoned that it linked up with the summital cone of Annapurna somewhere around the twenty-one-thousand-foot mark. It seemed a reasonable supposition that if we could climb the eight thousand feet or so to this key point, and rig them where necessary with fixed ropes, the rest would be comparatively easy. My now literally overflowing imagination went on at once to devise a plan of attack, and it did not take me long to convince myself that we would make short work of the spur.

Schatz got back shortly before nightfall, and we wasted no time in getting down to details. Lachenal and I wanted to investigate the whole valley to its end in order to be aware of all the possibilities and to get an unforeshortened view, but Schatz insisted he had been far enough to be certain that we would see nothing more. In his opinion we would be wasting a day that could be more profitably spent climbing Point 19,685 feet on the spur. This would give us a shrewd idea of the possibility of continuing, and also an excellent view of the range as a whole. Impatient to get to grips with the mountain, we let ourselves be persuaded too easily.

At 4:30 the following morning Lachenal and I once more formed the partnership which had so often brought us success, accompanied by Adjiba, who was to carry our sacks as far as the beginning of the real difficulties. It did not take long to cross the steep grassy slopes to the foot of the rocks at the pace we set, and when we got there we did not slow down for snow, verglas, difficulty or altitude. We were back on our old semidivine form, each reacting on the other so as to double his normal skill and strength almost in defiance of the laws of nature. In this supercharged state we literally played with the obstacles, running up them like cats, and by eleven o'clock we had reached the second point on the spur at an altitude of 18,553 feet, climbing in cloud and snow flurries. Strong gusts added to the difficulties, and in a brief clearing we saw a narrow ridge of snow leading to Point 19,685 feet. There was no reason to continue in such conditions, but in order not to lose a day I suggested bivouacking where we were. Lachenal did not agree, however, and soon talked me into a strategic retreat. We raced down the five thousand feet back to camp, including four rappels, by two o'clock.

At camp we found Herzog, Rébuffat and Couzy newly arrived. Discussion began at once, and we succeeded in convincing them that with the aid of eight or ten fixed ropes it would be perfectly possible to get Sherpas up to the point we had reached, and probably also to Point 19,685 feet, since the snow ridge did not look particularly difficult. What ignorance of Himalayan conditions! What an accumulation of errors of judgement! In the event it took Maurice and me three days of top-class climbing to reach even the first pinnacle of a fantastic ridge of purest snow lace, utterly invisible from below.

We were beaten again. Days of mortal combat had led us to no more than an unheard-of little summit.

For all that, however, this insignificant victory keeps pride of place in my heart. Nothing will ever surpass those desperate days when I gave myself up to the struggle with all the strength and courage at my command. The ascent of Point 19,685 feet on the northwest spur of Annapurna was probably the hardest piece of climbing done at such an altitude up to that time. It included four or five pitches of grade IV, some extremely difficult ice work, and a very exposed pitch of grade V plastered in snow and verglas which was twice led by Louis Lachenal.

Maurice and I got back to base on the evening of 21 May, after a hard day, to be greeted with good news. Lachenal and Rébuffat, who had been discouraged by the spur and had descended the previous day, had carried out a reconnaissance to the far end of the valley, whence they had seen the upper eight thousand feet of Annapurna. They had seen nothing to hold up a party in this section, but a wide shelf around the seventeen-thousand-foot level had remained invisible. They were emphatic that the shelf could be reached, however, by climbing the repellent-looking slabs which formed the right bank of the icefall. Now we had already seen the shelf from Point 19,685 feet, and it offered no obstacle whatever. It looked as though we were on the right line at last. Was it possible that our luck was about to turn and all our obstinacy and faith to be rewarded? We hardly dared to hope it.

Maurice quickly drew up a plan of campaign for next day. Lachenal and Rébuffat were to attack via the right bank of the seracs, sending back Adjiba when they had found a campsite. Schatz, together with Aïla and Panzy, was to try another line he had spotted on the left bank which he thought looked preferable. Herzog and I, worn out by a week of continuous action, would have half a day of rest, hoping to make a long stage in the afternoon with the aid of the energetic Sarki. Couzy would recover any kit left low down on the spur, then transport the lot to a new base camp at the end of the valley.

After a good sleep-in I started getting food and equipment together, impelled by a thirst for organisation which rarely comes over me in ordinary life. Sarki did the laundry, I repaired torn gaiters and even reached such a peak of form that I cooked lunch. Maurice, as befitted a big white chief, disdained such sordid details and just lay in the sun admiring the scenery. Early in the afternoon we shouldered our heavy packs and staggered away, cursing and blinding, up the interminable loose moraine. Presently we encountered Adjiba, who brought word that our friends had established Camp One after an easy climb up the right bank of the icefall.

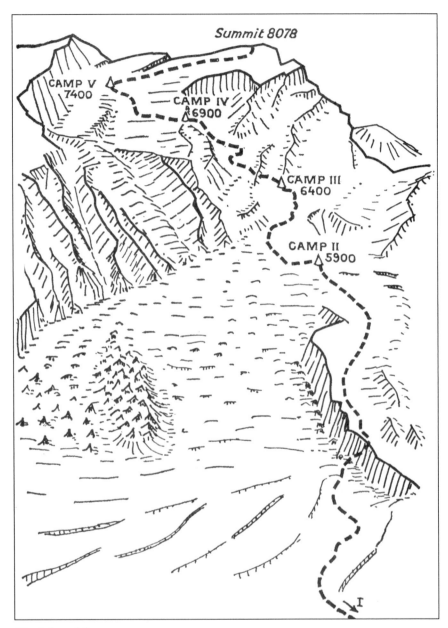

North face of Annapurna

The closer we got the more reasonable the slabs looked in contrast to their redoubtable appearance from a distance. Before long we even had the pleasant surprise of finding a continuous system of narrow zigzag ledges which made the ascent quick and convenient. The only drawback was the threat of ice falling from above. We could not help calling ourselves names for having listened to Schatz on the evening of our arrival in the valley. He had obviously been deceived by distance and the half-light of a misty evening which flattened out all relief and made the limestone crags seem more formidable than they really were. Seething after our long period of inaction, we had not even had the intelligence to spend a single day making certain of the matter, but had dashed ourselves against the spur like a flock of starlings.

Our lack of experience and our determination to get the better of an adverse fate had thus cost us five days of fine weather, perhaps even the ultimate victory. Narrow ledges and little couloirs seemed to have been waiting since the beginning of time for the exact purpose of conducting us without the smallest difficulty among these vast grey boilerplates. When we reached Camp One the sun was still on the north face. Decidedly the gods were with us—there hadn't been a clear afternoon for several weeks, and now, by a special dispensation, we could survey the mountain at our ease. After days of nothing but thousands of feet of verticality Annapurna's north face looked positively hospitable, and for a time we let our optimism run away with our judgement, but a closer examination quickly brought us back to reality.

To form a just opinion it was necessary to forget our Alpine methods of estimation. Only our recent experiences could help us to understand the colossal scale of the slopes before us. By this process of adaptation we finally came to realise that what appeared to be no more than an inclined snowfield was in fact a complicated face, bristling with monstrous seracs and interrupted by bands of rock three hundred feet high. The frequent rumblings of avalanches were a constant reminder of the objective dangers, but we thought we could make out two credible, if somewhat difficult and dangerous routes. After a certain amount of argument we agreed on the right-hand one as being the easier and less sustained.

Even the discomfort of being three in a two-man tent did not stop us getting a good night's sleep, and in the morning we felt ready for anything. Maurice gave Sarki a deliberately rhetorical message to carry back to Tukucha ordering the attack, and the devoted fellow ran day and night, showing phenomenal stamina, to cover in less than thirty-six hours a journey which had taken us over three days. We then struck camp completely, leaving only a sleeping bag and some food behind. Our loads were really much too heavy for seventeen thousand feet—some people's sacks weighing as much as sixty pounds—but we accepted the situation with good grace because it might save us a vital day or two. With less than two weeks to go before the monsoon it was no time for half measures. After a heavy drag across the plateau we clambered up a band of rock overhung by menacing seracs. The rucksack straps cut into my shoulders and I had to keep stopping to get my breath, but each time I looked up at those enormous tottering blocks of ice I was impelled forward. At last we came out onto long, safe snow slopes, only to be enveloped in cloud as the usual afternoon storm blew up. Maurice and I took turns with breaking the trail. Fortunately we only sank in a few inches, for by now I was trudging on like a sleepwalker, just as on those occasions when I had shot my bolt by doing too many climbs in succession as a guide. But for all that I was in no mood to give in, and could still find the energy to curse the others when they slumped down exhausted.

We had heard the yodels of Schatz and his party as they forced a difficult way up the left bank of the icefall, and now they joined us. Thus we were seven when we found a good shelf for a camp at around twenty thousand feet. We quickly decided that my four companions should stay there the night in order to take on a tent and some supplies as the nucleus of an upper camp, while the Sherpas were to go down to Base for more food and equipment. Since it seemed imprudent to let them climb down on their own I was to go with them as far as Camp One, where the sleeping bag we had left would enable me to bivouac. In this way I would avoid tiring myself pointlessly by a return trip to Base, and after a rest could rejoin the Sherpas on their way back up next day, provided always that their amazing stamina enabled them to do without a day off.

At Camp One, then, while the Sherpas carried on down towards the valley, I set about arranging a layer of flat pebbles to insulate me from the ice. By the time I had dressed up in every stitch of clothing I possessed and pulled the waterproof cape and elephant's foot over the sleeping bag I seemed all set for the most comfortable bivouac of my life. But before long a violent wind sprang up and it came on to snow, turning the night into a continual fight. If I opened my hood to breathe my face would be withered by the cold and snow; if I closed it to get warm I would start to suffocate. After several hours of this sort of thing sheer exhaustion made me drop off to sleep with my head jammed between two stones.

A clear dawn revealed me buried in new-fallen snow, shivering despite all my warm equipment. I curled up in a ball and waited for the sunlight to descend to my level. Interminable hours went by. For the first time in several days I had something to think about other than the next action, and my mind flew back to Europe, reviewing the whole of my past life. I felt no regrets. On the contrary, I blessed the providence which had vouchsafed me to experience this marvellous adventure. In my wildest dreams I have never imagined so much beauty and grandeur. My whole lifetime of platitudinous mediocrity seemed as nothing beside these hours of perfect happiness and total absorption in action.

At last the rays of the sun reached me, and before long it became unbearably hot. I tried fruitlessly to assuage my hunger by swallowing raw the little *tsampa** I had left. I felt utterly weak and exhausted. Finally I literally dragged myself over to a tiny patch of shade under a boulder, where I curled up again. From here I could make out the new base camp which Couzy had pitched near the end of the valley.

A scrunching of pebbles announced the arrival of the Sherpas. Adjiba, his balaclava all askew and his face running with sweat, rummaged in his sack for some food for me to be going on with. By the time I reached camp the tents were up and a meal ready. Bit by bit strength began to return, running through me like a warm current, and my anxiety abated. I was certain now that I would be all right tomorrow.

Shortly before dark Herzog, Lachenal, Rébuffat and Schatz passed through at whirlwind speed. They rapidly explained that after hours of ploughing waist-deep through the snow they had forced a difficult barrier of seracs, but that shortly afterwards Schatz had had a fall and this, combined with the arrival of bad weather, had led to their decision to beat a retreat after gaining only about 1,200 feet. A high-altitude kit** and some food had been left attached to an ice piton in an obvious place. They were now going down to Base Camp and would come back up as soon as they felt fit enough. The fantastic up-and-down ballet which leads load by load and camp by camp to the highest summits in the world had begun.

On 24 May I left with Panzy and Aïla, Adjiba being condemned on account of his herculean strength to carry the loads between Base and Camp One. His conscientiousness in carrying out this dull and obscure mission was admirable, and there is no doubt that the mountain would not have been climbed but for his efforts in transporting hundredweights of food and equipment, all in the space of a few days. Thanks to an early start we got to Camp Two just after ten o'clock despite our loads, which consisted of two high-altitude units and twenty-five pounds of food. I felt famished but still fit, so after a rest we decided to carry on, hoping to profit from the remains of yesterday's steps despite the snow which had fallen during the night. With the

* *Author's note.* Barley meal lightly roasted to arrest fermentation.

** *Author's note.* A kit including one tent, two sleeping bags and air mattresses, one spirit cooker and two billies.

intention of picking up the tent Herzog had left I only took one unit and a small amount of food.

There was no way of avoiding a seven-hundred-foot avalanche couloir. I tried in vain to hurry, but the steps had been filled in by the previous storm and were practically no use even when one could see them. We were up to the knees in snow rendered glutinous by the hot sun. At last we succeeded in getting out of danger. Avalanches came down the couloir every day, and in view of the fact that it was also used by several parties each day for a fortnight it was a miracle that there were no accidents.

We were able to get a short rest on a ledge among some seracs before struggling on. I had to sweep the powdery stuff away with my hands, then stamp it down with my feet. Digging out a veritable trench in this way we advanced at no more than three feet a minute. Labour of this sort is extremely exhausting at such an altitude, and despite the necessity for haste I kept on having to stop and pant.

A fixed rope helped me to scramble quickly up the difficult wall which had cost Herzog an hour's fight the previous day, but I reached the top in the state of semi-asphyxiation with which I was already familiar from the hard pitches on the spur, and which can scarcely be imagined by anyone who has not climbed at great heights. The Sherpas proved so clumsy at this gymnastic sort of exercise that I was forced to pull like a galley slave to get them up at all. The track now led to a steep traverse, then I lost it again. Once more I had to plough my own furrow. The high-altitude unit left by my friends seemed to have disappeared completely, but the daily afternoon blizzard was now upon us and there was no time to be lost in pitching the one small tent we had carried up. I found a little ridge of snow relatively sheltered from avalanches. It was not the moment to be choosy, and as we hacked out a platform and erected the tent we were already staggering in the force of the gusts.

Three men in a two-man tent is a hellish state of affairs. The smallest gestures have to be planned. Hungry as I was, I was too worn out to take the trouble to eat. We had only two sleeping bags, and it was Panzy who made the sacrifice of wrapping himself up as best he could in three down jackets, then snuggling down between us. We spent a night of terror listening to the avalanches that thundered down the couloir less than fifty feet from our tent, which shook with the wind of their passing. The Sherpas never closed an eye all night, but just sat there smoking cigarette after cigarette. As for myself, my teeth were chattering so much from fever and the lack of my down jacket that Panzy and I sounded like a pair of castanets, but eventually I doped myself so heavily with sleeping pills that I dozed off.

In the morning I climbed the wall of ice that had protected us even before the tent was packed away. Breaking the trail through fresh snow a yard deep was both slow and exhausting, and only a short sixty-degree ice slope interrupted the monotonous toil. Deep inside me, I was beginning to doubt. If it went on like this every day we should all be worn out long before reaching the summit, even if an avalanche didn't settle the matter before then. Only several days of unqualified fine weather could save the situation.

I forced the pace as much as I could across an ugly-looking couloir, but the effort used up my last remaining strength, and at the far side I slumped down in the snow. Panzy now took up the task for a while, but I was at my last gasp and the Sherpas seemed in little better case. Though we had gained barely six hundred feet there could be no question of going farther. I staggered across to a serac where I made fast all the kit and provisions we had brought up. The sunbeams were glittering like tinsel on the snow, so we stretched out luxuriously and devoured some food, making the most of the moment.

Far from getting better on the way down, I felt increasingly ill at ease. Not until Camp Two, where we ran into Maurice, Ang Dawa and Dawatondu, did I recover sufficiently to laugh and talk as we rested. The same evening I went on down to Camp One, hoping to recuperate by losing altitude. The bulk of the team were there, fully rested and ready to slay dragons. I was too done in to share their optimism and paid little attention to anything but culinary matters. We were in fact now beginning to get short of food, and I spent most of the next day sampling our high-altitude supplies, especially the fruit blocks, chocolate and biscuits. We seemed to have rather a surplus of these last. The Sherpas therefore devised a vast dish of crumbled biscuit and chocolate, and I confess I did my fair share towards demolishing it.

Plenty of food and rest soon revived me. On 27 May I fairly bounced up to Camp Two, arriving in time to follow Herzog and his Sherpas through the telescope as they descended from installing Camp Three the previous day a few yards above the highest point I had reached. It seemed probable that they must have also set up a Camp Four, but I was unable to make it out. I did notice, however, that they didn't seem to be following the easiest line, and later this piece of observation was to come in handy. As Camp Three was already occupied by Couzy, Lachenal, Rébuffat and Schatz, Herzog had to carry on down to Camp Two.

We spent the evening analysing the situation in extreme detail. Maurice was very put out by the poor physical and moral state in which he had found the others. Although he had spent no more than a few minutes in their company he considered them sick, discouraged and altogether incapable of effective action. His own form at around twenty-three thousand feet, by contrast, was very hopeful, and he still felt confident of victory as long as the daily snowfalls did not exceed six to eight inches. He also seemed satisfied with my own physical and mental state, and wanted me to husband my forces for the final assault. His plan was for me and the Sherpas to take a load up to Camp Three next day while he rested, and to rejoin him the same evening. Next day the four lightly loaded porters could clear the trail for us up to Camp Four, and we would take this on as high as possible in order to go for the summit on the following day.

Once again I spent a rotten night in order to be awake at the right time. The organisers of the expedition, needless to say, had failed to provide us with anything so simple as an alarm clock. The journey up to Camp Three was still tough, but not so bad as the first time. The snow was somewhat less thick and the tracks left by Couzy and Lachenal in their descent helped us considerably. We met them halfway. They explained that they felt too weak to carry any loads up to Camp Four, and were going down for a rest in the hope of recuperating. Shortly before arriving we encountered Schatz and Rébuffat coming down through the cloud, but they decided to go back up with us. No sooner had we reached camp than I fell on the provisions like a bird of prey, after which I felt ready to review the situation.

As a result of their lack of form my four companions had been unable to fulfil their mission of carrying a unit and more supplies up to Camp Four, and this threw the whole operation out of phase. A delicate question now arose: Was I to obey orders and go back down, or should I stay where I was with the Sherpas and carry out the uncompleted task? By doing this I would lose my chance of teaming up with Herzog, who at present was in the best condition and best placed for the summit dash, so that a bitter paradox would make a disinterested action the frustration of all my hopes. It would be so easy to obey orders and bow to a fate another had ordained. Nobody would ever hold it against me; after all, I was only a simple foot soldier who had taken an oath of obedience. And yet, and yet . . . it seemed to me that by going down at this juncture I would be letting down the side. The very idea gave me a pang such as one might feel at the suggestion of committing a crime. This internal struggle lasted no more than a few minutes. No doubt I was an ass imbued with mediaeval ideas, but I would take the finer and harder way by carrying on to Camp Four the following morning.

I told Rébuffat and Schatz what was in my mind, and Gaston, feeling somewhat better, decided to try and accompany me. Marcel was still too sick to be anything but a burden and resolved to descend alone in spite of the risk. Though it was little more than a vertical height of a thousand feet to Camp Four, it took us over seven dangerous hours to get there, due to the constant zigzagging and difficulty of the route. The deep snow and strong downhill wind made the going harder than ever before, and by the time we arrived a blizzard was in full swing. The tent had foundered under the mass of snow. We had all the trouble in the world to get it up again and also pitch the one we had carried. Gaston had felt nothing in his feet for some time and got in quickly to examine them, his thin features sharper than ever with anxiety. By means of rubbing and whipping I eventually got the circulation going again. Thanks to drugs we spent a reasonable night, but even if we still had some strength left we were nevertheless suffering badly from the effects of altitude.

By dawn the tents were half-buried in the snow. There was so little space left inside that one could hardly move. We had to dig them out with our mess tins and re-erect them as best we could, though they looked pretty sorry for themselves. The cold was positively arctic, and the strange downhill wind which had troubled us so much the day before was worse than ever. We were up against it already: How could we hope to climb another four thousand feet in such conditions? Victory seemed farther off than ever. However, we must just do our best to carry on.

It was a positive pleasure to leave this camp, installed as it was in the middle of an avalanche slope with no more protection than a moderate-sized serac. If this could not shelter the tents enough to stop them being half-buried in the night it seemed unlikely to keep off a really big slide. We made short work of the descent, and it was not until a long way down that we encountered Herzog, Lachenal, Angtharkay and Sarki. Louis seemed much fitter and said he was now back on perfect form. They explained that they were going to implement the plan that I was to have executed with Maurice, and that they had no intention of coming down before reaching the summit. I wished them luck without the smallest feeling of jealousy, for I was convinced by the previous day's experiences that the mountain was not yet adequately equipped. In my opinion they were simply deceiving themselves.

Next morning I scanned the mountain through powerful binoculars. The four men had already surmounted the very steep ice slope above Camp Four, and before they were hidden by clouds I could see them trying to find a way across the chaos of seracs to the left of the great arching wall of rock which divided the upper slopes. We called this wall 'the sickle'. Much lower down, I could see Couzy, Schatz and their Sherpas making slow progress in the direction of Camp Three.

Camp Two had by now practically turned into a village. Large, comfortable tents had been brought up from the valley, and Noyelle and Oudot were both installed there. They told us about all the difficulties they had had to keep us supplied. Only after innumerable complications both technical and diplomatic had they managed to get forty porters as far as Base Camp, and of these not much more than a dozen could be induced to do a few portages to Camp One. Two only would consent to help the indefatigable Adjiba in his ceaseless comings and goings from Camp One to Camp Two. It had in fact been touch-and-go whether our efforts on the mountain would be brought to nothing by a rupture of our lines of communication, and perhaps this dull and patient work in the rear was the finest example of team spirit shown on the whole expedition. Certainly we would have been able to do nothing without the devotion of our companions who, without hope of personal glory, performed the extraordinary feat of keeping us supplied across the five or six days of difficult ground that cut us off from the inhabited world.

One good day's rest sufficed to make Gaston and I fighting fit again, and we formulated a daring plan which would gain us a day. Light loads and an early start would enable us to reach Camp Three by ten or eleven o'clock in the morning where, with the help of Couzy and Schatz's freshly broken trail, we would carry everything on up to Camp Four. Oudot and two Sherpas would carry up a new Camp Three (which would be necessary for the retreat) the following day. For once everything worked out exactly as planned. We duly picked up our loads at eleven o'clock in the morning, and the ready-made track enabled us to reach Camp Four in an hour and a half instead of seven hours, despite the weight of two units and twenty-odd pounds of food. To climb getting on for three thousand feet with heavy loads in one day at well over twenty thousand feet is a sign of real form, which we felt augured well for the future.

On the way we met Angtharkay and Ang Dawa, forced to descend due to finding one tent fewer than expected at Camp Four. Faced as they had been with the prospect of humping double loads, therefore, Couzy and Schatz were naturally overjoyed at our unexpected arrival. I spent an excellent night, and in the morning started breaking the trail like a giant while the others struck camp. For the first few yards I was up to the chest in snow, but its depth gradually diminished until it was just a thin layer through which the ice penetrated here and there. The angle became as great as a difficult Alpine couloir. Cramponning is very exhausting at these altitudes and Sherpas do not seem very adept at it, so I nicked out well-spaced steps which Schatz enlarged and multiplied behind me.

After five hundred feet of this exhausting pastime we came out on the upper edge of 'the sickle', where we found a tent craftily pitched in the shelter of a serac. We immediately named this Camp Four B. In the tent were Antharkay and Sarki, who explained to us in their broken English that they had gone with Herzog and Lachenal to establish another camp quite a lot farther on, after which they had received the order to return and wait here. They had frostbitten feet and seemed in poor shape. Our own two Sherpas were also complaining about their feet and lost no time in scrambling into the tent to get warm.

Following Angtharkay's directions we now began a long traverse to the left, making use of a network of ledges which wound in and out of enormous seracs. Schatz ploughed relentlessly ahead through the deep snow. Rébuffat took over for a short time, but had to give up owing to loss of circulation in his feet. At the end of the traverse I went to the front again, zigzagging up through the icefall. To find the track in cloud would obviously be very difficult, and we did our best to pick out and memorise landmarks as we went along.

A breakable crust through which we plunged up to the calf had now taken the place of deep snow. Sometimes we had to crampon for a few yards where the crust had been particularly hardened by the wind. Despite the large new boots (which I had taken the precaution of carrying as far as Camp Four to keep them dry) I could feel the cold penetrating my feet. Constant wiggling of my toes didn't seem to be having any effect, so I stopped, took off my boots and stockings, and massaged my lower limbs in the shelter of my *pied d'éléphant*, an undertaking rendered somewhat complicated by the strong wind.* Couzy and Schatz had halted to imitate me a short way above. Trail-breaking was getting progressively easier, and presently it became no more than a matter of cramponning up hard snow on a regular slope of thirty to thirty-five degrees. Camp Five, pitched at the foot of a short rock step, seemed a mere stone's throw away, yet for all our efforts it never appeared to get any closer. I could feel the insidious onset of cold again, so I forced the pace in order to have time to attend to my feet before the others arrived. Rébuffat, reasoning the same way, overtook Couzy and Schatz, but I kept up my lead without much trouble.

When I reached the tent it was half-buried, but I pushed my way into the small remaining space, and by the time Gaston arrived I was ready to yield it up to him while I started hacking out a platform for the second tent. Schatz,

* *Author's note.* Frostbite at altitude is not due solely to cold, but also to rarefaction of the air. This causes an increase of red corpuscles. The blood, thus thickened, clogs easily in the capillary vessels.

whose motto is 'never say die', gave me valuable help in this heavy task. We had nothing to work with but our ice axes and our mess tins. The wind-hardened snow was almost as tough as ice, and on such a steep slope a very deep step had to be cleared before there was room to erect a tent. At 24,500 feet, where the smallest effort is enough to make one out of breath, this navvy's work was just about the limit. After every ten blows with the axe I felt as if I was about to spew up my lungs, and when I stopped the blood pounded in my ears. It would take a good thirty seconds to recover from the feeling of suffocation and to let my pulse slow down a little. At this rate we would never get finished, so I decided to go to the limit. At times I would force so much that a black veil began to form in front of my eyes and I fell to my knees, panting like an overdriven beast.

However I refused all help from the Sherpas and insisted that they should start down at once. This was the least we could do. The storm had risen, visibility was steadily getting worse, and it was essential that our devoted companions should get back to Camp Four before the tracks were completely covered. Couzy had now come to our aid and the platform was growing rapidly. Finally we improved the rather too rudimentary one left by our forerunners, pitched the new tent, and re-erected the original one in which Rébuffat had just succeeded in getting life back into his feet. The discomfort of this hurriedly installed camp was augmented by the fact that we had only three air mattresses and one pressure cooker. Couzy and Schatz crammed themselves into one tent, Rébuffat and I into the other.

But what were Herzog and Lachenal up to? Since they had left their tent here they must be making a bid for the still-distant summit. Time went by without our seeing anything. Outside the furies of the storm were in full cry, and we began to get seriously worried. It would soon be too late for anyone to get back to Camp Four, and we would be forced to sleep three in tents already too small for two persons. Couzy and Schatz, who were obviously suffering from altitude sickness, therefore decided to start on down and go as far as they could. No sooner had they gone than I moved bag and baggage into their tent and, according to habit, began to get busy with the cooking, which consisted of melting water for Ovomaltine and Tonimalt.

As time went by we became more and more anxious. I kept on sticking my head out of the tent to see if I could see anything, but there was nothing but the pitiless blizzard. At last my straining ears heard the unmistakable scrunching of footsteps on snow, and I threw myself out of doors just in time to greet Maurice, who was alone. With his beard and his clothing all strangely coated in rime and his eyes shining, he told me of victory.

I seized him by the hand, only to find to my horror that I was shaking an icicle. What had been a hand was like metal. I cried out: 'Momo, your hand is frostbitten!' He looked at it indifferently, and replied: 'That's nothing, it'll come back.' I was surprised that Lachenal was not with him, but he assured me that he would arrive at any moment and then crawled into Gaston's tent. I began to heat up some water. Lachenal still hadn't arrived, so I questioned him again. All he knew was that they had been together a few moments before entering camp.

Putting my head out of doors, I fancied I could hear a cry coming from some way off. Then the raging wind carried a faint but unmistakable 'Help'. I got out of the tent and saw Lachenal three hundred feet below us. Hastily I dragged on my boots and clothes, but when I came out of the tent again there was nothing to be seen on the bare slope. The shock was so terrible that I lost my self-control and began to cry, shouting in desperation. It seemed that I had lost the companion of the most enchanted hours of my life. Overcome with grief I lay in the snow unconscious of the hurricane that howled around me. Suddenly the thing occurred for which I had not dared to hope. A gap in the clouds showed him still on the slope, but much lower down than I had remembered. Without even waiting to put on my crampons I launched out on an audacious glissade, shooting down the steep slopes at the speed of a racing car. The surface was so crusted by the wind that I had considerable difficulty in stopping.

Lachenal had obviously had a long fall. I found him hatless, glove-less, axe-less and with only one crampon. With staring eyes he called out:

'I peeled. My feet are frozen stiff up to the ankles. Get me down to Camp Two quickly, so Oudot can give me an injection. Quick, let's get going.'

I tried to explain the mortal danger of a descent without rope or crampons in the dark and the hurricane, but his fear of amputation was such that, when he heard me starting to argue, he suddenly grabbed my ice axe and started running across the slope. His single crampon impeded him, however, and he crumpled onto the snow weeping and screaming:

'We must get down. I've got to have some injections or I'll be ruined for life. They'll cut off my feet.'

I forced myself to reason with him, to explain that there was no hope but to spend the night at the camp, but he didn't want to listen. Thus we carried on a sort of deaf man's dialogue for some minutes, while the gusts cut the snow across our faces like a whip. Finally he gave in. Puffing and panting I hacked furiously away at the slope, while he followed on all fours, at the end of his tether.

As soon as we were back in the tent I tried to unlace his boots, but everything had gone as hard as a block of wood and I had to cut the leather with a knife before I could get them off. My heart sank at the sight of the feet inside, white and utterly insensible.

Annapurna, the first eight-thousander, was climbed, but was it worth such a price? I had been ready to give my life for the victory, yet now it suddenly seemed too dearly bought. But this was no time for meditation—I must act, and quickly.

So began a night more deeply dramatic than any ever described in fiction. Seated on packages of food which had to serve as insulation in the absence of an air mattress, I rubbed and whipped* till I was out of breath. When I missed my aim and my blows landed on still living parts Lachenal would cry out in agony. Every so often I would stop and make hot drinks for the two invalids. From the other tent came sounds of Rébuffat going through the same processes for the benefit of Herzog. The hours crawled by and sometimes I would fall asleep at my work and collapse on top of Lachenal, always starting up again with a new burst of energy. As I toiled away my friend told me the story of the assault.

The tent had almost collapsed under the weight of snow the night before, and in the morning they had been forced to set out without even a hot drink. The higher they climbed the farther away the summit seemed as cold and fatigue took their toll, but at last they had got there. Those moments when one had expected a fugitive and piercing happiness had in fact brought only a painful sense of emptiness. He could remember nothing of the descent except the fall and being resigned to death as he bounded madly down the slope, followed by the unexpected and inexplicable stop and the return to life and fear and suffering.

I listened to him in silence. The willpower and sacrifice of my friends had crowned all our efforts and dangers. The action of the hero had fulfilled years of dream and preparation. Those whose work, undertaken in the service of a pure ideal, had made it possible for us to set out, were rewarded. And with what typically French panache Herzog and Lachenal had set the coping stone in this great arch of endeavour, showing the world that our much-decried race had lost none of its immortal virtues!

Outside, the hurricane had risen to unheard-of heights, threatening to tear the tents from their moorings. Snow had filled up the gap between them

* *Translator's note.* It should perhaps be noted that this treatment, then considered the best remedy for frostbite, is now thought harmful. No friction or violence should be used, but body warmth should be applied to the frozen part.

and the slope, and was now pushing us gradually towards the edge. In spite of everything we could do to shake it off it continued to encroach in a most worrying way. But my night's work had not been in vain. Lachenal could now move his toes, and the horrid pallor of the evening before had given place to a healthy shade of pink.

Having heard no signs of life for some time, I called to our companions in the other tent. They had dropped off to sleep, utterly worn out. Dawn was approaching, and to our bitter disappointment the storm did not abate as usual. Was our wonderful luck giving out on us at last? It was the first time in two months that the normal afternoon blizzard had not died down during the night. Was it the vengeance of the goddess Annapurna at the desecration of her shrine, or simply the more mundane but redoubtable arrival of the monsoon? Whichever it was we had to get down fast. Tomorrow we should only be weaker and the mountain in worse condition.

I began to dress Lachenal for the fray, but immediately came up against the problem of footwear. His feet were too swollen to be squeezed into his boots. It would be a cruel fate for him to wade through the snow in stockinged feet when I had only just succeeded in getting rid of the frostbite, and anyway how would we fasten his crampons? He would never be able to keep his footing on the hard-frozen slopes without them. We might be able to lower and tow him at first, but we would never manage it once we got to the traverses. What a silly-sounding but insoluble problem!

At first I could not think of any way out of it, but suddenly I had an inspiration: my own boots were two sizes larger than his, and would now fit him perfectly. No sooner had I thought of this than I realised the implication, and a shiver ran through me. If he wore my boots I should have to wear his, too small and hacked about with a knife. Without a doubt it would then be my turn to get frozen, yet try as I might I could think of no other solution. The weight of destiny crushed me for a moment or two. To sacrifice a portion of one's own body seemed somehow more horrible than death, but in every fibre of my being I felt the duty more urgently than instinct itself. To give way would be dishonour, a crime against the name of friendship. There was nothing else for it, and with the feelings of a soldier going over the top I hauled off my second pair of stockings and stuffed my feet into the new instruments of torture.

The spirit of action now possessed me completely. Foreseeing the worst, I crammed some food and a sleeping bag into my sack, calling out to Herzog and Rébuffat to do the same. I also intended to carry a tent. Four of us, taking turns with two sleeping bags in such a tiny space, ought to be able to resist the cold for a long time. Outside it was still blowing an icy gale, and we had trouble doing up our crampons. As Lachenal had lost one of his the day before I had to be content with the remaining one. But where was my ice axe? In my haste the previous evening I had forgotten to put it away carefully, and now it was nowhere to be found. As Lachenal had also lost his during his fall we only had two left between the four of us, and Gaston and I took over these as of necessity. I wanted to fold up the tent, but the first pair had already started off down the slope. The gale was still at its height but it had stopped snowing for the moment and visibility was not too bad, so Lachenal, more impatient than ever, tugged at the rope and bellowed:

'Hurry up! What the hell do you think we're going to do with a tent? We'll be at Camp Four in an hour.'

Suddenly I felt a wave of optimism. We ought to be able to see far enough to find the way back through the seracs without going wrong. In the upshot I let him have his way. We should just have to take our chances. It was up to luck now.

We ran down the first couloir of hard snow easily enough, and the difficulties only began when we reached the first seracs. The wind had fallen and it had begun to snow in huge flakes, making it difficult to see a man at fifty feet. It was impossible to recognise a thing. An awful feeling of being lost came over us, the full gravity of our situation appearing in all its horror. In these conditions we hadn't one chance in twenty of finding Camp Four B, but it was Hobson's choice—we just had to keep on trying while there was any daylight left. Tomorrow, if there were any survivors after a bivouac without equipment, they would be in no fit state to help themselves, and only the return of fine weather could possibly save them.

We wandered backwards and forwards for hours and hours, constantly thinking we had found a way out of the maze only to meet each time with the same bitter disappointment. The flakes fell thick and fast, building up so quickly on the ledges that you could see it happening. It was getting harder and harder to break the trail; we sank in up to the thighs, then to above the waist, though fortunately the light powder was not too difficult to pack down. I was amazed at my own reserves of energy. Rébuffat took regular spells at the job too, showing a great deal of courage. His legendary stubbornness worked wonders, and I well remember how, after I had retreated from a particularly trying bout with a steep, loose slope, he patiently advanced up it inch by inch until he had won. Sometimes we would sit down in discouragement, and I would take advantage of the respite to remove my boots and rub my numbed feet back to life. Though ready for death, I had no wish to survive mutilated.

Herzog followed his leader without a murmur, but Lachenal gave me more trouble. Convinced we were wasting our energy to no purpose, he wished for no more than to dig a hole in the snow and wait there for fine weather. To get him to budge I had to haul on the rope and curse him roundly. Personally I had reached the stage of complete detachment. In perfect consciousness of what I was doing, but without any sensation of fear, I crossed zones that were ready to avalanche and wandered happily in my one crampon over steep ice slopes, surprising myself by the manoeuvres I was able to perform. The object of all these peripatetions was to find the narrow exit on the left of the seracs which alone gave access to Camp Four, but unfortunately the cloud distorted everything and upset one's judgement to such an extent that one might have passed by it a hundred times without recognising it. In case anyone happened to be at Camp Four B we periodically shouted for help. We had now eaten practically nothing for twenty-four hours, yet our energy was amazing for men who had lived and worked for several days at an altitude of over twenty-three thousand feet. Did we owe this miraculous state of affairs to the drugs which Oudot insisted on our taking regularly?

While we fought for our lives time had gone by unnoticed, and now, suddenly, it was almost night. The essential thing was to find a crevasse which would shelter us from the rising wind. I therefore began to explore the various holes which surrounded us, and in the meantime Rébuffat and Herzog made one last effort to reach a landmark we thought we recognised. There seemed to be nothing but bottomless abysses or tiny hollows round which the wind howled unimpeded. I had already given up the search as a bad job and was trying to deepen a hollow with the ice axe when there came a terrible cry from Lachenal just behind me. I jumped around, but he was nowhere to be seen, a fact explained by the presence of a small round hole in the snow from which issued a muffled voice assuring me that he had accidentally fallen into the very place we needed. A twelve-foot jump down proved that he was telling no more than the truth. We were in an ice cave the size of a small room and perfectly sheltered from the wind. It seemed almost warm by comparison. After a certain amount of arranging we managed to settle down in relative comfort. I hauled out my sleeping bag, only to learn immediately that the other pair, overexcited at the prospect of leaving our wretched camp that morning, had neglected to bring theirs.

I was absolutely perished by the cold, and the soft touch of the down-filled bag sent waves of warmth along my limbs. With the brute selfishness to which men return in moments of suffering I slid it up round me, carried away on a tide of voluptuous bliss. Beside me my friends sat freezing in silence, huddled up against each other. I soon began to feel my disgusting egoism, however, and after some contortions Herzog, Lachenal and I all managed to squeeze our lower portions into the providential bag. Little memory remains of that terrible night. I only know that the constant struggle against the cold, the cramps that racked me and the intermittent bouts of rubbing my friends' hands and feet kept me so busy that I had no time to think of anything else. Perhaps this was just as well, since I knew that only fine weather could save us. Yet hope springs eternal, and so we concentrated all our energy on surviving until daybreak. There would be time to think of dying after that. After hours of resistance sleep and exhaustion finally overcame me.

I awoke chilled to the marrow. A faint light seemed to be filtering through to our cavern, but I could not distinguish anything in particular. I was trying to understand what was wrong when suddenly there was a heavy shock just above us and a mass of snow fell on top of me. I realised at once that an avalanche had passed overhead, demolishing part of our roof. We were not buried so much as lightly covered, and a few shakings and flailings soon brought us back to the fresh air, whereupon it became plain what my trouble had been: I was partly snow-blind. Gaston was in the same condition. Well, so what? The first thing was to have a look outside and find out what the weather was like.

Our equipment had been scattered all over the cave, so we had to grope for it under the snow. Gaston was the first to find his boots and climb up into the daylight. We shouted up questions about the weather, but he could only reply that there was a strong wind blowing; otherwise he could see nothing. I found my boots next, but was so blind I had to get Lachenal to help me put them on, which he was too impatient to do properly. In the end I had to use all my strength to force my feet into these clogs of ice. As I emerged from the cave sharp gusts buffeted me, and overhead all seemed grey and misty. Judging that the weather had not improved I therefore gave myself up to despair. There seemed no further hope.

Lachenal was yelling his head off behind me, so I turned to give him a hand up. He was still in stockinged feet, having been unable to find his boots. No sooner was he up than he started bellowing again: 'It's fine! It's fine! We're saved! We're saved!'—and ran off towards the end of the trough in which our cave was situated. Out of all this verbal delirium I at least managed to gather that the sun was shining, and that my ophthalmia was responsible for my not being able to see it. This condition had been provoked by taking off our goggles to see better in the previous day's storm, through which the rays had nevertheless penetrated sufficiently to do damage.

Down in the cave Herzog the realist was still sifting through the snow for our gear. I hoisted up successively two pairs of boots and several rucksacks, then it was his own turn. Unfortunately he could do little to help himself with his poor frozen hands, and for all my natural strength and professional technique I could not haul his 180 pounds on my own. Several times he slid back, but finally, by a supreme effort, I succeeded in getting his head and shoulders sufficiently far over the edge for him to seize my legs. As he lay there gasping it was his turn to feel a moment of despair, and he said: 'It's all over, Lionel. I'm finished. Leave me and let me die.' I encouraged him as best I could, and in a minute or two he felt better.

Presently we found our companions sitting in the sun at the top of an impossible three-thousand-foot drop. Lachenal, now completely hysterical, was shouting and semaphoring in the direction of Camp Two, which he claimed he could see at the bottom of the slope. I handed him his boots and crampons, then tried to fit on my own single one, but as I could hardly see I naturally fumbled a good deal. Gaston and I tried to put on Herzog's boots with much the same sort of results, while Lachenal, instead of helping us, lost control of himself even further, screaming: 'Quick, quick, hurry up, we're saved.' It took half an hour to get Maurice equipped, and it was only done thanks to the discovery of a knife which enabled us to cut up the boots still more than they were already.

An interrogation of those who could still see produced the result that Lachenal said we should now head to the right, Maurice to the left, without either of them showing much conviction. What was one to do? Were we really to die in full view of our powerless friends at Camp Two? Obviously we were still far from saved. Maurice and Louis were frostbitten and exhausted; Gaston and I had lost our sight. In such circumstances there was little we could hope to do, and the fine weather had been nothing but a cruel deceiver. Why could we not just have been buried once and for all in the crevasse? The situation came home to me in all its dramatic intensity.

And just as in an old-fashioned film script, this was the precise moment at which the miracle occurred. From somewhere apparently not far away on our left came sounds, though at first none of us dared to believe the evidence of our senses. But there was no getting away from it, help was on its way. Suddenly Schatz emerged from behind a serac fifty yards away: I could just make out a dark patch moving against the whiteness of the snow. As we were thus plunged back into the world of the living I realised that I had not felt anything in my hands or feet for several hours. What on earth would I do if they had to be amputated? Nothing really mattered to me beyond my work—I must save myself while there was still time. I ran off along Schatz's track like a madman and threw myself into the tent at Camp Four B just as Couzy had finished getting ready. I asked that the others should be taken down right away and that someone should return for me when possible, the next day if necessary.

The sound of the descending parties gradually faded away and I was left alone in the oppressive silence of great altitudes. I rubbed and beat my hands and feet for hours. Probably they were not as bad as I had feared. After a time the circulation came back and their rather greeny whiteness gave place to a fine healthy pink, but the pain was so great that I could not restrain myself from groaning out loud. Time went by without my realising it and I was too absorbed to reflect that I was alone, a minute speck on the immensity of the mountain, and that I was utterly dependent on those who had promised to return for me. If one of the avalanches I kept hearing should sweep them away my fate would be a slow death from starvation which, in my blind state, I could do nothing to avoid.

But presently there came a sound of words and of feet crunching the snow, and I heard the friendly voice of Schatz railing:

'It's all right, Lionel. Don't worry. Angtharkay and I are coming.'

Despite my raging thirst I was ready to start down at once, but Marcel did not want to until he had made the heroic effort of searching in our crevasse for the camera and films we had left there. He was so long away that Angtharkay had time to melt me several billies of snow, and I began to get seriously worried in case he had fallen into a crevasse himself. At last he returned, however, triumphantly brandishing part of the films, and we started on down without any further delay.

From now on we were withdrawing our necks which had been stuck out so far, at times, that they had been in danger of getting broken. We had to push our luck once or twice more, but it stayed with us right to the end. Not the least of its miracles was our safe return down these slopes of thick new snow, surrounded on all sides by avalanches. Camp Four was carried away the exact moment that two Sherpas had left it. Herzog, Panzy and Aïla were actually caught in one and only saved because a snow bridge broke under Herzog so that he fell into the underlying crevasse and the rope held over the edge.

And so, as the dream faded, we returned to earth in a fearful mix-up of pain and joy, heroism and cowardice, grandeur and meanness. In time we came to the first main road and its traffic. I was weighed down with sadness that it should all be over. Now we should have to face the world again.

In the epilogue to his book *Annapurna*, Maurice Herzog expresses something of the underlying meaning of such an adventure:

'Men often talk of an ideal,' he says, 'as an end which is never attained. But we did attain Annapurna. Our youthful minds did not go astray among the fictional prospects conjured up for the imagination of young people. For us the mountains formed a natural background where we played on the frontiers of life and death, and in doing so found the freedom we had sought without knowing it, one of the ultimate needs of our natures. As a mystic might worship an ideal of the divine we looked up to the beauties of the mountains. The Annapurna we approached in spiritual poverty is now the treasure on which we live; a different life opens before us. There are other Annapurnas in the lives of men.'

Eleven years have gone by since 3 June 1950, when our combined efforts rose momentarily to the height of our ideal. Looking back, it is interesting to ask which of us have in fact found other Annapurnas.

It seemed only too probable that Herzog would survive as a mere shadow of the brilliant athlete and intellectual he had been. His constitution was permanently weakened, and he was forced to undergo serious amputations. Though he will never be able to climb again, in the old way, he has surmounted all his ordeals and redirected his energies into new fields. His inborn instinct for men and affairs has enabled him to become not only a director of industry but a highly active president of the Club Alpin Français. Quite recently he has become a leading reorganiser of the various national institutions governing sport and youth services.

Lachenal, by tragic contrast, died before finding any compensating fulfilment. Would he have found one in time?

In five years he had to submit to no fewer than sixteen operations, an ordeal he faced with astonishing courage. In the end he recovered sufficiently to work as a mountaineering instructor, but he could never recover his genius. This curtailment profoundly changed his character. Once he had seemed magically immune from the ordinary clumsiness and weight of humankind, and the contrast was like wearing a ball and chain. This slower kind of mountaineering no longer gave him the old feeling of moving in a fourth dimension, of dancing on the impossible, and he sought desperately to rediscover it elsewhere.

His driving soon became a legend (though, like all legends, it was much exaggerated) and every day his audacity and sense of timing would enable him to perform incredible feats. Once behind the wheel he seemed possessed, and would push any engine to the limit of its possibilities. I have driven with quite a number of notorious drivers, and if some of them perhaps showed more judgement I have never known one to equal him for daring and natural skill. Obviously he ran terrific risks, but once again his sphere of being seemed to be at the very edge of the technically possible. That he survived four years of this kind of thing has always seemed a miracle to me.

Many people naturally and rightly criticised his behaviour, but those who saw in it a taste for exhibitionism were quite mistaken. Lachenal's passion for speed bore no relation to vanity. It was a drug to some imperious inner need of his nature. I have often seen him about to set out in his Dyna, and asked: 'Where are you off to?' He would reply: 'Nowhere. Just a drive'. Nobody ever heard of most of his exploits, which he indulged in for the sheer joy of the thing.

It has been written that driving became a sort of outlet for his 'frenzy for life'. This judgement is at least half-true, but I think the word *frenzy* is too strong, and I knew him perhaps as well as anyone. Certainly his bubbling vitality could sometimes burst its banks like a mountain torrent, but he was very far from being one of those restless personalities who never know a moment of calm. Most of the time he was a peaceable, jovial character, fully sensitive to the harm and the poetry of life. What he really sought in the intoxication of speed was escape from the human condition which he now felt so heavily. Once he had poised over the fall of cliffs with the lightness of a bird, and it hurt him to be transformed into a blundering animal like the rest of us. Behind the wheel of his car he seemed to recapture those instants of heavenly grace.

As a mountaineer Lachenal was a genius. The mountains had given him a field of action for his extraordinary gifts, and, as Alain de Chatellus has remarked: 'Few professions are big enough for a man like that.' Outside the mountain world he was like an eagle with clipped wings, ill-adapted to the humdrum life of society. He was a person who could turn his hand to any trade, yet who never mastered a technique apart from climbing; who was intelligent, but insufficiently educated to become an intellectual; who was exceptionally clever with his hands (indeed he was cobbler, tailor, carpenter, mechanic, architect and mason all rolled into one), yet not really a craftsman. Ill-prepared, therefore, for struggles other than those of the mountains, it is difficult to see where he would have found a way of life in which his character could grow to its full richness. He realised this in a confused way, and it hurt him. Its outer manifestations were his eccentricity and bitter wit.

Yet wisdom seemed to be coming with the years. Already he was driving less madly, and it had begun to look as though he would soon resign himself to being a man like any other. The affectionate father he had always been was getting the better of the panther of the snows. All the signs pointed to his ending up as a comfortable, well-known local citizen, looked on by all with affection and respect. Fate, however, had decided otherwise. One autumn morning when the air was cool off the mountains and the sun shining on the snow, he went and dragged a companion out of bed, carrying all before him as in the great days. Up on a glacier where thousands of skiers glide unharmed every season he let himself go, revelling in the thrill of speed and the plumes of powder snow kicked up by his skis in passing. Suddenly a hidden crevasse opened under him, and in an instant the man who had defied death so often that he seemed immune was no more than a broken bundle of bone and flesh.

In a section bulletin of the Club Alpin I wrote an obituary which I will reproduce here, conscious that it repeats a good deal that I have already said, because it seems to me to sum up his climbing life:

> How can I hope to conjure up in words his frank, piercing gaze, which was yet liable to flame up at any moment into an expression of perfect, if sometimes slightly malicious, joy? How can ink and paper reanimate one who was life itself? Lachenal was born at Annecy, where he passed a somewhat disorderly youth but showed early signs of the sharp intelligence, subtle humour, inventive mind and passionate taste for physical exercise which were the most obvious marks of his character. He was attracted to mountaineering from the very beginning, and quickly showed his exceptional talent. He joined Jeunesse et Montagne in 1941, and it was not long before he was promoted to be an instructor in skiing and mountaineering. After the Liberation he became a guide and instructor in the Chamonix valley, and it was here that we met for the first time. We were attracted to one another by our common passion for the great climbs, and before long we formed a team of unusual unanimity. For the next five years every instant of spare time from our work as guides was spent on some big ascent, despite the accumulated fatigue which weighed on our shoulders.
>
> The list of climbs we achieved together is too long to be enumerated here, but the most important were the fourth ascent of the north spur of Les Droites, the fourth ascent of the Walker Spur of the Grandes Jorasses, the second ascent of the Eigerwand, and the seventh of the northeast face of the Piz Badile. Although Lachenal did most of his big climbs in my company he also did a number with other companions, and a few with clients. Among these was the third ascent of the north face of the Triolet with the guide André Contamine. Lachenal was by far the most talented climber I have

ever met, and I would go so far as to say that at the height of his career his quality amounted to genius. If a few have equalled and even surpassed him in the field of pure rock climbing, and also, though more rarely, of pure ice climbing, no one has ever equalled him on the overall complex of them both, which makes up the terrain of greater mountaineering, and especially the great north faces.

His virtuosity is shown not only by his list of climbs but by the fabulously rapid times in which he did them. I could go on for pages about the ascents he did in half or even a third of the previously best time. Perhaps the most astonishing of all are the Badile, climbed in seven and a half hours as opposed to nineteen hitherto; the north face direct of the Aiguille du Midi in five and a half hours from the Gare des Glaciers to the actual summit, despite the fact that I had to beg thirty minutes' rest in the middle of the climb to eat and get my breath back; and finally his extraordinary double ascent of the east ridges of the Dent du Caïman and Dent du Crocodile, both in one morning, which he did with André Contamine. They completed this almost unimaginable feat by returning to Montenvers by the beginning of the afternoon.*

It would be a great mistake to imagine that Lachenal broke records with the actual object of doing so. Nothing could be farther from the truth. It was just something that happened naturally, almost against his will, because he climbed like lightning, because he was more dextrous than anyone at rope management, and because he had a sort of hypnotic effect on his companions which made them surpass themselves. Above all, perhaps, the records fell because he loved the feeling of etherealisation, of liberation from the laws of gravity, which a perfect mastery of climbing technique can bring. Perfectionism was almost an obsession with him: he liked everything done in a quietly impeccable way, and of course, in the case of mountains, this meant climbing them in the minimum time.

The fact that Lachenal never in the whole of his life did a single first ascent is quite characteristic of his approach to climbing.** The ascents he liked best were the really grandiose ones, regardless of the number, of times they had been done, because by contrast with shorter climbs of extreme difficulty they gave him what he really

---

* *Publisher's note.* Less than twelve hours' return from Envers des Aiguilles.

** *Translator's note.* Except, of course, Annapurna.

sought in the mountains: grandeur, technical and aesthetic perfection, and self-surpassment.

In 1950 he was selected for the French expedition to Annapurna. One of the pair who reached the summit, he came down from the mountain covered in the somewhat fugitive glory of our sport, but physically mutilated. The courage he showed in overcoming his infirmities was beyond all praise. He accepted all his operations and subsequent adaptations in the most stoical way, and it had begun to seem that after five years he had almost made up the leeway. In spite of his shortened feet he might soon have returned to the greatest ascents, but fate decided otherwise. He who had dominated the mountain completely was not destined for any partial mastery.

As Maurice Herzog has written: 'Not only his deeds will remain in our memories, but also his great gusts of laughter, his joy in action, and the sheer likeableness he radiated.'

Our veteran, Marcel Ichac, has succeeded brilliantly in his career. The film he made of our adventure, though necessarily not quite complete, attracted thousands of viewers both at lectures and on the commercial circuits. This film and Maurice Herzog's book between them went a long way towards popularising the sport of mountaineering; so much so, in fact, that latterly it has been possible to raise the money for other national expeditions in the Andes and Himalayas. Thus our success made it possible for many other climbers also to realise their dreams.

After a few years in which he was involved in lesser enterprises, Ichac took the major gamble in 1958 of producing, for the first time in the history of the cinema, a full-length feature in which the mountains were more than a backcloth and mountaineering more than a popular myth. This time mountaineering was the real subject of the film. It was called *Les Étoiles de Midi*. No doubt some of my readers have admired its thrilling story and superb photography. I was lucky enough to be Ichac's main collaborator, not only in so far as I played the lead, but also in choosing the majority of the scenes, directing the team of porters and guides in their complex manoeuvres, and in some small measure advising on the script, so that I am in a position to give an opinion on the various problems we encountered.

Our budget was less than half what is normal for such a long and ambitious feature. The whole undertaking therefore had something of the character of an adventure from start to finish, and right up to the very last day success was not assured. To have overcome such material difficulties at the same time as the technical and artistic ones seems to me to add still more to the stature of Ichac's achievement. *Les Étoiles de Midi* may have its weaknesses, but the praise it received from the toughest critics and the large audiences it attracted proved its overall value. For Ichac it was a tremendous success, only achieved by desperate risks and hard work—a genuine 'other Annapurna'.

Oudot, our brave doctor, was also to know a destiny out of the ordinary, but an untimely death prevented him from reaching the summit of his career. An experienced clinical surgeon, he was pursuing researches in the cardiovascular field, and had already risen to national eminence. Some of his discoveries marked notable steps forward, and he had just brilliantly passed the extremely difficult *concours de chirurgien des hôpitaux de Paris* which opened the gateway to the professorship he desired. All this time he continued to visit Chamonix regularly, and it was in the course of one of these visits that he skidded into an oncoming vehicle while travelling at high speed on a wet road, causing an appalling accident in which several people lost their lives and others were seriously injured. Jacques died a few hours later, and French surgery and mountaineering lost one of their leading figures.

In many ways Rébuffat seems to me to have had the most remarkable success of us all. Born into a lower-middle-class family of reduced circumstances, he was forced to leave school after the primary stage. When I first knew him at the age of twenty he was disciplined yet ungainly, affable yet shy, even a bit dull—in other words a perfect average Frenchman, undistinguished either for good or for bad qualities. Only his apparently crazy mountaineering ambitions, which were apt to slip out in the course of conversation, gave any sign that he might blossom into anything other than the office clerk he had begun as, or the physical education teacher he was studying to become.

Under this unremarkable exterior, which tended to be accentuated by an odd listlessness of gesture, Rébuffat concealed the industrious stubbornness of an ant, the decisiveness of a Napoleon, intelligence, and an amazingly accurate power of intuition. Motivated by his unlimited enthusiasm for the mountains these qualities made him, in spite of limited physical endowments, the greatest guide of his generation.

In fact, curious as it may seem, greater mountaineering calls much more for mental than for physical qualities. A careful study of alpine history shows that the greatest climbers have rarely been physically favoured by nature, whereas many athletes who seemed born for the job have never become anything more than brilliant performers on small training crags. This is simply a reflection of the fact that success in any sport, no matter how simple, always requires real intellectual and moral capacity over and above the necessary physical aptitude. In most of them, however, the physical side remains preponderant to the extent that you rarely if ever get a champion who has not shown unusual giftedness from the outset. Perhaps this supreme predominance of the mind over the body is the main distinction of mountaineering over other forms of athletic activity, and gives it an added moral value.

One year after Annapurna, Rébuffat had one of the most remarkable Alpine seasons ever known. Having had the initial luck to be engaged by 'the' client capable of doing the greatest climbs, he made ascents of the Walker (thus becoming the first man to do it twice and the only guide to have done it in a professional capacity up to the present) and, a few weeks later, the Eigerwand, despite a violent storm on the way up. He and Paul Habran thus became the first men to have done the two greatest Alpine climbs in one season. After such exploits it would have been natural to expect him to attack the last great problems of the Alps or higher and harder summits overseas, but he did nothing of the sort. His successes in 1951 were practically his swan song, and thenceforward his life took quite a different orientation, doubtless for family reasons.

From this time on he guided spasmodically, and only on classic routes, most of his methodical energy being diverted into other channels. By virtue of a staggering capacity for work he succeeded in simultaneously practising several professions with considerable success despite a complete lack of training. At one and the same time he was a commercial director of a large business, an alpine writer of style and inspiration whose works ran frequently to several editions, a talented mountain photographer, a popular lecturer, and a promising film producer.* If family and social success is the right end of the mature man, Rébuffat has without any doubt won the greatest of all his victories in attaining it.

Francis de Noyelle, the young diplomatist who was our interpreter and transport officer, occupied a rather special position in our team. A good companion in fair weather or foul, he was popular with us all, but although he had done a few easy climbs he was not, strictly speaking, a mountaineer. He enjoyed travelling but was in no way hagridden by any desire for adventure. Son of an ambassador, the traditions of his service were not such as to encourage flights of fancy. In the event he has pursued an active and no doubt interesting life in his chosen profession, visiting many parts of the world and advancing steadily towards a position of importance.

Schatz, our athletic draper-physicist, has shown both brilliance and originality in his subsequent career. Less than a year after the expedition he got married and gave up regular climbing, spending the next few years in

---

* *Translator's note.* On, it is fair to add, some of the hardest climbs in the Alps.

expanding his family business. To all appearances he had become a settled and prosperous businessman when, at over thirty, he went back to doing research. His wife supervised a large part of his commercial interests while he himself worked like a galley slave, rapidly becoming so highly qualified that he took part in the perfecting of the first French atomic bomb.

Couzy likewise had a career of distinction, but, contrary to what his intellectual capacities might have led one to expect, as a mountaineer rather than as a mathematician. When he was killed by a falling stone on an unclimbed face of the Roc des Bergers in November 1958, he already had one of the greatest alpine records of all time. There was nothing in his outward appearance to foreshadow such a destiny; indeed he was gentle, thoughtful and meticulous. His unusually wide culture sprang from an enthusiasm for philosophy and the arts quite as great as for scientific research, though as a graduate of the Polytechnique and the École Supérieure d'Aéronautique he held an important post in military aviation.* Happily married to a charming wife and father of four children whom he adored, he seemed bound for every form of social and intellectual success once the adventurous instincts of youth had been appeased.

But Jean was not made for the rat race of this world. He was a sort of saint, an idealist tormented by visions of the absolute. Whatever the nobility of his aims and objects, no man can become what society calls a success without a certain element of practical cunning. Couzy was the complete opposite of a Lorenzaccio:** he could only march straight forward. Perhaps he might have become a great research worker (had he not been accepted for the École Normale Supérieure?), but laboratory life repelled him. Like the knights of olden times, he was possessed not only by an ideal but also by an intense need for physical action. Climbing, as his friend Schatz has penetratingly written, 'gave his inner riches a means of expression'.

He was lucky in that his work left him more leisure than most, and above all the possibility of arranging it to suit his own convenience. Naturally this was a major factor in his alpine development. But how far was it really accidental? Despite his very genuine interest in aviation, it was possible to suspect that Jean had chosen his career partly for the freedom it gave him, and the more so because he had turned down lucrative offers from private industry.

* *Translator's note.* Admission to the École Normale Supérieure and the Polytechnique is a sign of the highest intellectual eminence in France. Their graduates constitute an elite in the national life.

** *Translator's note.* A devious character in a play of the same name by de Musset about Florentine life.

For fifteen years he made the most of this freedom, and his huge volume of achievements illustrates with the clarity of a graph how an inflexible will is an even more important element of success than luck.

Muscular and with tremendous stamina under his almost frail appearance, he was an accomplished athlete. Unshakeable health and the digestive system of an ostrich were further assets on big climbs. A certain lack of manual dexterity handicapped him, by contrast, in his earlier days; and on mixed ground, where no technique or intelligence can make up for instinctive neatness of gesture, he always remained slow and ill at ease. But he never let this lack of natural agility stop him from attempting and overcoming the greatest difficulties, and by means of thought and application he eventually made up for it. On rock, in particular, he became a past master.

Jean accepted every sacrifice necessary to acquire and maintain his class. He took regular daily exercise, shunned all excess, and never let a weekend go by without training on the rocks of Fontainebleau or the Saussois whatever the weather. In his view the best training for climbing was climbing, but though he loved these gymnastic outcrops he never considered them as an end in themselves. Proud though he was to be one of the best 'rocknasts' of 'Bleau' and 'Sauss', he would always head for the Alps or the Pyrénées as soon as the weather report was hopeful, often borrowing an aeroplane from his club in order to get there quicker. These three-day trips from Paris account for his accumulating in under fifteen years what has been called 'the most varied and complete list of climbs ever assembled'. Thanks to his unflagging enthusiasm he was thus able 'to scale the steepest Dolomite faces, from the Marmolada to the Cima Ovest di Lavaredo; the toughest rock routes in the range of Mont Blanc, from the Aiguille Noire de Peuterey to the Grandes Jorasses; the most difficult ice climbs from the Triolet to the Dent d Hérens'.

If Couzy already deserved to be known as a great climber by the number of hard routes he had repeated, his own first ascents put him among the ranks of the really outstanding. Together with his partner René Desmaison he became one of the last great conquerors of the Alps. He disdained the fiddling new climbs on which some people try to found cheap reputations, and sought for lines which by their scale and elegance would equal or surpass those of the past. Among his dozen or so important innovations I would quote particularly the direct route on the northwest face of the Olan and the first winter ascent of the west face of the Dru, the latter of which marked the beginnings of a new era in its own extreme kind of mountaineering.

With the evolution of tactics and equipment the Alps had become too restricted a field of action for one who combined creative vision with his strength, skill and determination. Only the world's highest summits could now enable him to give of his full measure. At the time of Annapurna he had still been too young to play a decisive part, but on the Makalu reconnaissance in 1954 (which also climbed Chomolonzo) he was the most dynamic and efficient member of the whole team, and the same applied to the successful Makalu expedition of the following year.*

I was lucky enough to be his almost constant companion in the course of these two adventures. We led a hard life at close quarters, and it was during this time that I came truly to know and like him. On those far-off mountains, where man will never be master, one is not drawn on by the prospect of confronting exceptional technical difficulties; it is more a question of braving loneliness, lack of oxygen, wind and cold over a period of months. This austere contest strips off every pretence and lays bare the deepest weaknesses of a man's character. It was in precisely such circumstances that I was able to measure Jean's true worth. He was a hero who had found his proper place.

In his intelligent and sensitive obituary, Schatz cites the final assault on Chomolonzo, of which I was a witness, as best illustrating Couzy's personality. Looking back I agree with him that in this secret trial by combat our friend showed his quality still more than on the most desperate faces in the Alps, and it is with this recollection that I would like to leave him. I can however add one or two details which seem to me to enhance the value of his performance. Throughout the whole of the previous night we had been battered by the most violent tempest I have ever known in the Himalayas. Our tent seemed likely to rip in two at any moment, and some of the seams did in fact yield under the sledge-hammer blows of the wind. At dawn the temperature was minus twenty-seven degrees Centigrade inside the tent. The wind had abated somewhat, but ninety-mile-per-hour gusts still blew us off our feet every so often. Psychological conditions were hardly more favourable, and personally I had no thought but to get down out of it all as quickly as possible. Only Jean's magnetic personality constrained me to follow him like one condemned to the scaffold. There were tears in the Sherpas' eyes when they saw us preparing to set out, so little hope had they of seeing us again!

'Lionel is fully in agreement', says Schatz, 'in attributing the initiative for this adventure to Jean. The reconnaissance had ended in the virtual certainty of success on Makalu the following summer, but to him such a result seemed to be returning empty-handed. Three miles of icy ridge away lay the giant Chomolonzo without whose head Jean was unwilling to sound the retreat.

* *Publisher's note.* Chomolonzo: 7,796 metres, or 25,584 feet. Makalu: 8,490 metres, or 27,854 feet.

Surely no Himalayan summit of such stature has ever fallen so quickly and surely as this one, on which they stood that same noon.

'How Jean's eyes burned when he showed me the photographs, and what modesty he displayed in carefully explaining that the weather report was favourable, the snow in good condition, in fact the whole thing just a matter of going through the motions! There is a particular grandeur in reducing such deeds to a simple scrutiny of the evidence, in seeking excuses for such happy inspiration. Jean was entire. That was the secret of his comportment in the face of danger—for he was without physical fear and always acted as, on mature reflection, he had decided to act—and no doubt the secret of his life.'

| 8 |

Mountain Ranging

When I disembarked at Orly in July 1950, bearded, astonished at the hysteria of the crowd, and carrying my mutilated friend in my arms, it seemed the end of an episode that was never likely to be repeated. It certainly never occurred to me that a new pattern had been created in my life. Perhaps, one day, I will find the time and the energy to give a detailed account of the second part of my career, but in this already overlarge book I must be content with a brief summary.

It soon became clear that our exploit had excited an interest far exceeding our wildest dreams. The press, that tyrant of modern times which can make and unmake heroes and legends to its own convenience, gave us the sort of publicity normally reserved for the amatory adventures of film stars and kings. The novel and dramatic aspect of the story, together with its triumphant outcome, made for just the sort of sensationalism on which the public is fed, while the general ignorance of geography caused many to think that we had climbed the highest mountain in the world instead of just the highest so far. Some of our renown, indeed, was probably founded on precisely this confusion.

Deliberately ignoring anything so difficult to understand as teamwork, the papers proceeded to transform Herzog into a national hero, concentrating all their attention on him as a kind of fabulous Big White Chief. The rest of the expedition, including Lachenal, were relegated to the position of mere accessories. Slightly later, in order to renew flagging interest, they picked on me, blowing me up as a sort of cross-grained Hercules with a heart of pure gold. Since then I have been preceded by this awful reputation wherever I go.

The Eigerwand had taught me the transitory nature of journalistic glory. I was in a hurry to get back to the things that really mattered, and I did not wait for the round of victory celebrations. Less than a week after our arrival I was climbing again. Still suffering a bit from cumulative fatigue, I managed nevertheless to guide a client on the first complete traverse from the Col des Hirondelles to the Col du Géant, a two-day expedition across all the points on the summit ridges of the Grandes Jorasses and Arête de Rochefort. It was a remarkably fine summer, and I had more clients than I could cope with. The fatigue continued to build up in my muscles as I forced myself to carry on. By the end of August I was very near exhaustion, but after a few days' rest I felt fit enough to consider doing some amateur climbing again.

In mid-September I decided to have a try at the west face of the Aiguille Noire de Peuterey with Francis Aubert, the young friend who had been in Canada with me the winter before. This was a rock climb which had not often been done at that time, and which had acquired a reputation for extreme difficulty. We crossed the Col de l'Innominata at dawn. The descent to the Fresnay glacier on the other side is not difficult enough to require putting on the rope, and in the half-light each followed his own path. Francis noticed that he had got slightly off route and climbed a little way back towards me. I was in the process of giving him some directions when suddenly a large jammed block came out on top of him. For a moment he fought to heave it aside, then peeled off into the three-hundred-foot gulf beneath, and I was left alone on the mountain.

Several times I had had to carry down the bodies of men who had fallen a long way in climbing, and during the war comrades had been killed at my side, so that I thought myself pretty well hardened to such sights, but I was wrong. Crazed with grief I called and called to my friend. There came no answer but the sound of the wind.

This experience left me badly shaken for several months, and for the first time I began to doubt. Were the mountains worth such sacrifices? Was my ideal no more than a madman's dream? I made the resolution never again to leave the reasonable, well-worn trails of traditional guiding.

Despite my two years' absence, the École Nationale de Ski et d'Alpinisme invited me to rejoin it as an instructor for the winter. Canada had been an interesting and fruitful experience, but the actual skiing had been disappointing. Throughout my stay there I had dreamed constantly of great hills and long descents. Now I could resist them no longer, and although it meant giving up important material advantages, I decided to stay at Chamonix. Gradually the delights of skiing and competition began to soothe and overlay the memory of the Innominata tragedy. By the time spring came my old longing for action had utterly taken possession of me again. All my wise resolutions of the autumn were thrown to the winds, and I dreamed of nothing but new adventures.

Precisely at this moment came exciting news. Réné Ferlet and some of my friends in Paris were getting up an expedition to one of the most notorious mountains in the Andes, the FitzRoy peak. This Matterhorn of the south was already well known in France, and pictures in the mountaineering journals had shown it to be a great cone of granite rising in majesty for thousands of feet out of the surrounding wastelands of Patagonia. Several expeditions of proven climbers had already attempted it in vain.

Despite its relatively low altitude of 11,319 feet, none of these expeditions had even succeeded in passing the pedestal on which the mountain stands. So far as they could tell, the final step of some 2,500 feet was likely to prove as difficult as the hardest climbs in the Alps, but the real obstacle would be the Patagonian climate. One would be lucky to get a few consecutive fine days even in summer, and the ascent would be rendered extremely dangerous by the bitter cold, the verglas and the sudden, violent hurricanes. These terrible weather conditions had exhausted and discouraged the earlier expeditions even before they reached the foot of the climbing proper.

From the first moment I heard of it I was carried away with enthusiasm for Ferlet's venture. All my old passion for the great climbs came back with a rush. FitzRoy, after all, was the type of the ideal summit such as I had not yet found in the Alps or the Himalayas. Annapurna had given me the excitement of travelling in new lands, the joy of exploration, and almost too much of a good thing when it came to sheer adventure, but the actual climbing had been a disappointment. Tough and thrilling as it was, Himalayan mountaineering, on this mountain at least, seemed something different in kind from 'alpinisme', which I think of as an essentially individual experience almost like artistic creation. On the world's highest mountains the scale is such that no man can hope to succeed solely by his own efforts. Victory is only secured by a collective undertaking, bringing into play considerable technical resources, and in my eyes the whole business becomes more military than artistic.

My dream, then, was to tackle mountains which would give harder and more complex problems than the Alps, but remain within the scope of a normal rope of two men. The FitzRoy was obviously tailored to my requirements, and no sooner had I heard of Ferlet's project than I wrote asking him if I could join his party, to which he kindly agreed.

With Patagonia being situated in the southern hemisphere the seasons are of course all inverted, and there was no need to set out until the following

December. Although there were some months to be passed before going into action I was by no means short of something to do, since the F.F.M. had begun to sponsor lectures illustrated by Ichac's film. They were a prodigious success. Outside the Salle Pleyel over one hundred thousand people queued up for one lecture alone out of the forty that were given. In the main provincial centres large crowds milled around the box offices and many people had to be turned away for lack of places.

Herzog and Lachenal, still heavily bandaged, presided over most of these evenings, but all the rest of us did our share too. Some showed quite unexpected talent as speakers, but it has to be confessed that although their sincerity and spontaneity were attractive, the intellectual level of the lecturing was not very high. This in no way affected their success, however, and the crowds continued to bring down the roof. It was hard to tell if they were mesmerised by the grandeur and nobility of the deed, or by the large-scale publicity!

My work at the École Nationale left me little time to take part in this great effort to collect funds for future French expeditions. I went up to Paris for the 'first night', of course, and somewhat later I gave a few lectures in villages around Chamonix at Maurice Herzog's request. My beginnings as a lecturer were rather comic—indeed the first attempt practically amounted to slapstick.

I had set off from Chamonix after the day's skiing was over, and with no more respite than a good meal was pushed onto the platform in front of the crowd. All I had to do was to give a short briefing on the Himalayas with the aid of some coloured slides, then provide the commentary to Ichac's film. I had no notes, had done no homework, and had not seen the film since the first night a month previously. Needless to say I had the wind up badly despite a certain amount of practice in public speaking in Canada, and was mainly relying on the goodwill of the public in order not to be hissed.

I forgot half of what I wanted to say during the introduction, but, to my surprise, the applause broke out like a hailstorm. Then came the slides. I was expecting the same ones that had been shown at the Salle Pleyel, but these turned out to be a set I had never even seen, and just to cap matters the operator had neglected to arrange them in logical order! First came an unexpected photo of Annapurna, but it was not too difficult to think of some appropriate comment. The next slide showed some gorgeous Nepalese girls. It took me a moment to absorb the shock, then by a rapid piece of mental acrobatics I found a connecting theme, and said loudly:

'When it comes to beauty, Nepal has everything. High in the sky rise the most beautiful mountains in the world, while down in the valleys the traveller meets so many of these ravishing creatures that it is hard to force oneself to go on.'

The third shot showed a lorry on the road. I felt as though I was going mad and broke out in a cold sweat, nevertheless I managed to find some far-fetched connection. The fourth was a view of Dhaulagiri, and, recovering my confidence, I explained about our preliminary reconnaissance of that mountain. It was at this moment that the fifth slide appeared: it showed a high diver in the air!

In my panic I could find no possible link between this and the previous views. As the first shock wore off, however, I realised that diver looked just like me, and rather than stand there stupidly saying nothing I blurted out:

'Ladies and gentlemen, this muscular, graceful athlete with the lean brown frame is none other than myself.'

After a moment of silence there came a great roar of laughter. The pictures continued to turn up in lunatic order, but this success had given me the confidence to play the clown. The evening turned into a kind of Himalayan *Hellzapoppin'*, with the public rolling in the aisles. At last we came to the film. There could be no mistake now, and I remembered Rébuffat's excellent advice: 'Let the pictures speak for themselves.' I therefore simply threw in a relevant or explanatory remark from time to time.

After it was all over I expected a row from the promoters, but on the contrary they were delighted. There was nothing but congratulations and 'My dear fellow, what an original commentary', 'How funny you are', or 'You've given us a most wonderful evening.'

I didn't know in those days that such remarks are not intended to be taken too seriously, but even so I think they exaggerated a bit!

A few weeks later I gave some lectures in central France. The first took place at Thiers. I arrived very late as a consequence of a breakdown, carrying the 16-mm projector which Lachenal had handed over to me the day before. I was counting on finding a trained operator on the spot to work it, but due to faulty liaison Paris had not informed the local section of the Club Alpin that one would be needed. The hall was already full and people were beginning to stamp their feet, so I asked to see the operator at once. Everyone was amazed.

'What, you don't work the machine yourself?'

'I haven't the remotest idea how it works', I replied with complete sincerity.

There was a complete panic. Nobody knew how to make the machine go. Should they refund the entrance fees? But really, that would be altogether too bad for the prestige of the C.A.F. I decided to take a chance on starting the introduction while they were tinkering with the projector. Presently I received a discreet message to spin it out as long as I could, as an expert was on the way. After I had finished all the slides I started telling stories, but presently I ran out of inspiration. Things were going from bad to worse when suddenly the lights went out and the title appeared on the screen, only to disappear at once, leaving the hall in darkness again. For some unknown reason nobody turned the lights on. I tried to tell more stories, but the public's patience was at an end. People were stamping; somebody called out 'Refund'; others were booing. Everything was going wrong when suddenly a ray of light shot through the room and some of the credits appeared on the screen. The audience heaved a great sigh of satisfaction which filled my harrassed soul with a warm glow of gratitude. No sooner had I felt this than the light went out again.

'This time', I thought, 'it's the end.' I felt utterly crushed and ashamed. The lights went on and the crowd rose to go. Before they had reached the door the lights went out for the last time, the film appeared on the screen, and contrary to all expectation the whole thing ran through without any further hitch.

When the skiing season was over the Himalayan Committee asked me to undertake a series of lectures lasting a month, which I accepted the more willingly on account of a good expense allowance and salary. My few experiences during the winter, however, had given me no idea of what I was letting myself in for. The promoter, obviously more concerned with his profits than with the convenience of the lecturer, had arranged a programme of almost impossible density. Apart from the regular evening lecture to an adult audience I also had to give one and sometimes two morning sessions to schools. In addition I had to work all the projection apparatus myself, suffer numerous parties, banquets and receptions, and, of course, drive my old Renault from place to place. Sometimes I had to cover considerable distances, since the programme had been dictated by (sometimes rather odd) commercial considerations rather than geographical ones. Thus I had to speak one day at Grenoble, the next at Annecy, and the one after at Valence.

I was neither physically nor mentally adapted to such an unhealthy and nerve-wracking life. By the time I got back to Chamonix I was more exhausted than if I had done three climbs on the run, and determined never to repeat the experience. Not for one moment did I imagine that in fact I was to spend years driving up and down the country, trying daily to flog up enough enthusiasm to inspire the public with adventures that, to me, had become desperately boring through over-repetition.

Summer found me back at my guiding, and in September I had time to do some climbing for my own pleasure. A period of bright, calm weather enabled me to do the west face of the Aiguille Noire de Peuterey for which I had set out, with such tragic results, the year before. This very steep, sometimes over-hanging face was considered one of the two or three hardest climbs done on granite before the war, and had only just been surpassed by Walter Bonatti in his ascent of the east face of the Grand Capucin.

Guiding turned out not to have been very good training for these rock-gymnastics. In the hardest places I felt close to my limit, whereas my young companions, who had practised every week on the short but exceptionally difficult limestone crags around their hometowns, were astonishingly at ease. The importance of the right sort of preparation for this extreme form of mod-ern mountaineering, at least for anyone not naturally gifted as a rock gym-nast, was driven home to me. The long 'artificial' pitch also made me realise the tediousness of this mode of climbing, especially if prolonged over several pitches or even hundreds of feet.

On my return from this incursion into the domain of the *sestogradisti* I was more than ever convinced that if mountaineering was to develop into anything other than a mere technique it would have to be conducted on a vaster, more complex terrain than the mountains of Europe. Progress in tech-nique, training and equipment had made the climber too efficient; as in many another field, technique was in the process of killing adventure. For those who sought to define their own nature in the combat of man against the mountain there would soon be no solution but the desperate ways of the solo climber and the winter mountaineer.

The details of the expedition continued to take form during the summer, but Ferlet was having a lot of trouble over funds. Although an ascent like the FitzRoy only costs about a quarter as much as a major Himalayan undertak-ing, it was still touch and go whether we should succeed in getting away. There was plenty of money in the coffers of the Himalayan Committee, thanks to the Annapurna book and film, but it was earmarked for a possible French expedition to Mount Everest, and they were unwilling to sponsor the FitzRoy trip in its entirety. They did, however, give us a big grant, which was made up by the Paris section of the C.A.F., other bodies of the same kind and private donors; but for all this we were still far from making ends meet.

Ferlet therefore asked each member of the team to make a large personal contribution, Magnone immediately turned in the old jalopy which repre-sented his worldly wealth, and I devoted the majority of my savings to the cause. Unfortunately some of us, like Jacques Poincenot, had hardly two beans to rub together, and we were still far from achieving our target. We had almost begun to despair when the Languedocian climber Dr Azéma offered to make up the balance on condition that he could join the party. By running up a few debts here and there it was now possible for us to go.

This new adventure proved both tougher and more thrilling than I expected. The Argentine people greeted us with an enthusiasm and a touching kindness no longer to be met with in our ageing Europe. General Péron received us in person and made no object of upsetting several ministers of state in order to help us. It was rather like living in a fairy tale. Despite our shortage of cash our journey into Patagonia was transformed into a millionaire's holiday.

For all that, difficulties appeared even before we reached the base of the mountain. Floods and the malignity of an old gaucho kept us waiting around for our pack ponies for over a week. The FitzRoy is less than 125 miles north of Cape Horn, so notorious for its storms, and the climate is as rigorous as that of arctic Norway. Great ice caps descend right down to the waters of the Pacific Ocean. The summer is short and offers few periods of fine weather. We were not particularly early, and every day lost, therefore, might cost us the victory. In order to compensate as far as possible for the wasted time Jacques Poincenot and I set off on a reconnaissance. We were light-heartedly crossing a swollen torrent when he was swept away and drowned. He was a perfect companion and a prodigious climber, and his sudden disappearance dealt us a cruel blow. For forty-eight hours, indeed, we debated seriously whether to pack up and go home. After a few days we recovered our spirits and carried on, seriously weakened, however, by the loss of one of our best members.

For three weeks we exhausted ourselves battering our way forward against hurricanes of over 125 miles per hour. Camp One was torn to shreds by the violence of the gusts, and we were obliged to dig ice caves in the glacier in order to find shelter. Every day we had to renew the trail from camp to camp, sinking into the snow over our knees at every step. Despite all this we were able, by dint of desperate efforts, to set up three camps and considerable dumps of food and equipment.

The route, though long, was not too difficult as far as Camp Two, but the thousand feet before Camp Three were another matter. This stretch turned out to be a wall of mixed rock and ice worthy of an Alpine north face. In order to get up and down it safely with heavy loads we had to equip the whole section with fixed ropes.

Nobody lived in this region but for a few sheep farmers, so porters were unobtainable. We were therefore forced to hump more than a ton of necessities on our own backs, a third of it to the top camp. There was never any respite

from the wind, whose gusts were sometimes strong enough to knock us off
our feet and bowl us along helplessly for several yards, and this, combined
with the cold, the snow, and the discomfort of living constantly in damp grot-
tos in the ice, made the experience the most exhausting I have ever known.

Nor did the psychological climate make our task any easier. We had been
warned all about the atmospheric conditions we were likely to meet in lower
Patagonia, but the reality surpassed even our worst imaginings. Never had
we known circumstances so unfavourable to the idea of climbing. Hope
had almost disappeared under the continual assault of weather infinitely
worse than anything we had ever known in the Alps. 'Hope springs eternal'
says the old proverb, and without it our struggles and sacrifices were extremely
hard to bear.

To tell the truth I never quite knew just how deeply my companions were
afflicted by loss of faith in our ultimate success, but the general debility of
some and the occasional bouts of discouragement which assailed even the
best left room for little doubt that morale was dangerously low. As for myself
I fought on without much hope, more for the principle of the thing than anything else, in order to have no regrets; and also, doubtless, for the pure joy of
giving myself in action without other justification than itself.

Our plan was to make the last camp as comfortable as possible, to stock
it full of food, and to wait there for a fine spell. At last all was ready, and a
group of three took possession. This consisted of Guido Magnone, a power-
fully built Parisian, well known as a rock climber; Georges Strouvé, our film-
photographer; and myself. Strouvé was to remain in camp, taking pictures and
keeping an eye on things, while Guido and I went for the summit. No sooner
had we settled into our icy residence than an exceptionally violent storm blew
up which kept us there for five days. We were just starting to run out of spirit
for our cookers when a lull enabled us to flee down to Base. After our sojourn
in the upper world, the simplicities of trees, grass, warmth and fresh food gave
us a more intense pleasure than anything known to all the potentates of the
east combined.

The storm continued for two days more, the snow coming right down to
Base Camp at a mere 2,625 feet. During the afternoon of the third day, however, the sky suddenly cleared and became as radiantly fine as at the height
of an Alpine summer. Next morning was just the same, and hope flooded
back into us. Despite new snow up to the waist we ploughed upwards so
buoyantly, taking turns with the trail-breaking, that we reached Camp Three
the same day. When we crept out of the cave at dawn the cold was bitter and
the sky threatening, but we attacked nonetheless. The climbing was extremely

difficult from the very beginning, railing for plenty of pitons, and Magnone also forced a very severe free pitch. By seven o'clock in the evening we had climbed no more than four hundred feet out of the wall's total of two thousand five hundred.

As planned, we descended to camp for the night, fixing ropes as we came down to speed the next attempt. At dawn there was not a cloud in the sky and the air was utterly still. Fate was with us at last: we must strike and strike hard.

In order to climb as fast as possible we decided on daring tactics. We packed a large number of pitons in order not to waste valuable minutes taking out the firmest ones, and to make up for the weight of all this ironmongery we cut food and drink to the minimum, carrying only a cape and a down jacket each for the bivouac. Despite the fixed ropes it was four hours before we passed our limit of the previous day, whereupon movement became slower still. The difficulties were extreme, calling for much artificial climbing, and one pitch alone took us over five hours. When darkness fell we had climbed about half the face. The night, which was perforce spent on a narrow, outward-sloping shelflet, was particularly trying for want of adequate nourishment and protection.

Next day the technical difficulties diminished somewhat, but at the same time the rock was more iced-up and we had to climb in crampons. The routefinding was complicated and the weather was starting to look threatening once more. There could be no shadow of doubt that if the storm rose to a climax while we were on the wall our retreat would be cut off, and unless it abated we should be doomed to death from starvation and cold. I was so impressed by the reality of this menace that I lost courage and wanted to turn back while there was time, but Magnone's iron resolution won me over. I accepted the enormous risk and the ascent continued. We had almost completely run out of pitons when at last the difficulties eased, and at four o'clock in the afternoon we reached the summit.

The clouds which had dappled the sky since morning had thickened and were now drifting around the crags, but by an extraordinary piece of luck the wind was late in rising. Our descent was a rout. Eighteen rappels took us back to the top of the fixed ropes, at which point the storm finally broke. Immediately the snow began to fall, the wind constantly increasing in violence, but fortunately we now had something to hold on to and it did not take us long to reach the foot of the face. At ten o'clock in the evening we fell exhausted into the arms of our friends at Camp Three.

In 1956, after other experiences of a similar kind, I wrote in the *Annales du G.H.M.* as follows:

Of all the climbs I have done, the FitzRoy was the one on which I most nearly approached my physical and moral limits. Technically speaking it is doubtless slightly less extreme than some of the climbs which have been done on granite in the Alps of recent years, but a great ascent is more than the sum of its severe pitches. The remoteness of the FitzRoy from all possibility of help, the almost incessant bad weather, the verglas with which it is plastered, and above all the terrible winds which make climbing on it mortally dangerous, render its ascent more complex, hazardous and exhausting than anything to be found in the Alps.

I have still found no reason to make me change my mind, and the ascent of the Cerro Torre, a more difficult neighbour of the FitzRoy, by Toni Egger and Cesari Maestri, seems to me the greatest mountaineering feat of all time. The end of the expedition was one long party. Our ascent was given star billing by the Argentine government, and for nearly three weeks there was a continual round of receptions and banquets, accompanied by considerable popular enthusiasm. The Andean Mountain Club of Mendoza and the Argentine army even invited us to climb Aconcagua, which at 21,991 feet is the highest summit in the Andes.*

Set on foot in four days, without any time to acclimatise to the altitude, this extremely easy ascent almost ended in disaster. Each member of the party in turn was so overcome by mountain sickness that they had to give up, but I managed to preserve our honour by reaching the summit (though only with great difficulty) with Paco Ibanez, the likeable young Argentine officer who had been with us in Patagonia. The whole idea had been to get acclimatised for an attempt on the unclimbed southeast ridge of the mountain, plus possibly a reconnaissance of the south face. This vast wall was obviously a magnificent objective for a future expedition. Unhappily, on the descent, we found a party of Chileans almost asphyxiated by lack of oxygen. The rescue was long and exhausting, and one of them later died. These various peripatetions cost us much time, and we decided to return straight home to France without trying the ridge.

Hardly had I returned to Chamonix than a new opportunity came my way. My Dutch clients Kees Egeler and Tom De Booy, both professors of geology at the University of Amsterdam, were going to Peru to carry out some research, and had decided to prolong their stay in order to attempt a couple of

* *Translator's note.* The height of this mountain is disputed.

large peaks. Reckoning that a party of two would not have much chance, they asked if I would come as their guide. The FitzRoy had shown me what a perfect playground the Andes were, and although I was fully aware that the Peruvian mountains were quite different from those of Patagonia, there seemed no reason why they should not be just as good in their own way. Nothing could have pleased me more than the idea of returning.

In this area, I realised, it would not be a question of scaling acrobatic rock walls so much as high, ice-mantled peaks, sometimes so steep that no one had yet found a way of getting up them. I knew too that the generally stable climate of the old Inca 'Empire of the Sun' would facilitate our task, but that on the other hand the rarefaction of the air at over eighteen thousand feet would make every movement far more of an effort than at Alpine levels. But these new problems, far from deterring me, seemed an added attraction.

Egeler, De Booy and I had climbed together so much in the Alps that we were already close friends, and this was another attraction. I had often had occasion to appreciate their courage, enthusiasm, sense of humour and comradeship, and in fact had rarely met climbers with whom I felt so much in sympathy, so that one way and another I was overjoyed to accept their invitation.

Our main objective was the Nevado Huantsan, a fine peak of 20,981 feet which happened to be the highest unclimbed summit in the central Andes. It looked as though this would be taking on a great deal for a party of three with limited equipment, due to the length and difficulty of the route. In order to get acclimatised and acquire some notion of local conditions, therefore, we decided to have a shot at the more modest Nevado Pongos (18,733 feet) first, which despite considerable difficulties in its upper portions, was climbed in a day and a half from base camp. For me this was something of an achievement, since, thanks to air travel, I took only eight days from Paris to the top of Pongos, of which the journey from Lima accounted for four.

Huantsan proved to be quite a different kettle of fish. Our first attempt failed, very nearly ending in tragedy. We were retreating down through the night when De Booy, seized with cramps after a false move, let go the rappel rope and fell twenty-five feet free, then shot down a steep ice slope more than two hundred feet high. By one of those miracles which occasionally occur in mountaineering he fetched up on the glacier virtually unhurt.

After a few days' rest and a spell of bad weather we had too little time left to envisage the classic method of building up a succession of camps. The mountain would have to be stormed and revolutionary tactics were the only hope. Having found a good route and placed a second camp at around eighteen thousand feet, we decided to go straight for the summit from there, carrying with us everything we would need for a week.

At first our sacks weighed over fifty pounds. With such a load on one's back it was both exhausting and delicate to traverse the narrow, corniced ridges, where we were constantly forced off onto steep ice slopes on one side or the other. After a first night in the tent the going got easier and our sacks lighter. We crossed the north peak, 20,013 feet high, and descended into the saddle separating it from the principal summit. On the third day the mountain was finally vanquished after some very difficult ice climbing. It took us another two days to retreat back down the mile and a half of ridge to Camp Two, so that we had been absent for five days altogether. The porters, convinced that we had met with an accident, had packed up and gone home!

In two months from the time I had left I was back in Paris, reaching Chamonix the following day. Forty-eight hours later I was bivouacking with two British clients at the foot of the Pillars of Fresnay on Mont Blanc, and the day after we did the third ascent of this very difficult route.

This short expedition to Peru is one of my happiest memories. Despite the daring shapes of the peaks with their huge cornices and elegant ice pendants we had not been through any experiences intense or dramatic enough to rival those of Annapurna, nor had we conquered any adversary so redoubtable as the FitzRoy. We had not even done anything especially notable from a technical point of view. Yet, though I might easily have become blasé through too-frequent adventure, I had in fact returned home radiantly happy, aware of having lived through moments of hitherto unequalled quality.

With little equipment, with no other aid than that of cowardly porters, always ready to steal or to desert, the three of us had ventured out into a savage, semi-deserted range, peopled only by a few Indians reduced to the state of beasts by four centuries of subjection. Tiny and alone in the midst of this frozen world we had fought our way past every obstacle to our chosen goal in the limited time available. The very meagreness of our means safeguarded the proportions of the peaks and restored difficulties to their true value, giving us back mountain adventure in its original purity, as known to Whymper and the pioneers.

On the ridge of Huantsan, without a support party or means of communication, we had been in the truest sense cut off from the world, a rope of three friends linked together for better or worse. Nothing but our common ideal impelled us towards the unknown summit. The utter silence, the remoteness from all human concerns, the friendship without reserve, all gave to our conquest a flavour more piercing than that of other, more celebrated victories.

Nor had the climbing been the only satisfaction derived from this voyage. As had happened before in Nepal, the old Inca empire had shown me another world, another point of view, a new kind of poetry. I marvelled at the land's richness in contrasts and extremes, its people at once colourful and dirty, splendid and crude, ecstatic alike in happiness and sorrow, hospitable yet dishonest, artistic yet drunken and dull. As I returned to the kind soil of France I retained a heavy sense of nostalgia for that country of high relief where adventure still lurks at the roadside, and to return became one of my most constant dreams. As with so many of my young dreams, four years later this one came true with greater richness even than I had imagined. Against all expectation, the first adventure was father of the second.

Up to 1952 I had hardly taken a photograph, let alone a film. At the time we did the Walker and the Eiger Lachenal and I were such purists in matters Alpine that the thought of profiting from our adventures never even crossed our minds. The most elementary cameras seemed fussy, cumbersome objects, liable only to spoil our pleasure, and in point of fact we never took a single photo during the five years of our partnership. My point of view had changed little by the time of the Annapurna and the FitzRoy expeditions. We had specialist photographers with us—it was up to them. I had come to climb mountains. On the FitzRoy I was at such a pitch of tension that I several times told Strouvé to go to hell when he wanted me to pose or to climb down a few feet so he could film me, and it was largely my fault that we took no camera with us on the final assault.

Somewhat later, on Aconcagua, we spent quite a lot of time kicking our heels. For lack of anything better to do I asked Strouvé to show me how these mysterious gadgets worked, took a few photos, and even carried a light cine-camera to the summit. On my return to Paris I was quite surprised to see how well the pictures came out. It then dawned on me at last that, contrary to what I had so stupidly supposed, photography was a straightforward technique rather than an occult art. About the same time I began to realise that our expedition films were and would always remain priceless souvenirs of some of the greatest days of my life.

In setting out for Peru I felt rather sad to think that for lack of a professional cinematographer we would have no record of our adventures. My friends had an ordinary camera and even an old movie camera as well, but they had little experience and less film, added to which the movie camera was too heavy and fragile for high mountain use. A few days before leaving, I had a violent and inexplicable impulse to try making a film myself. Being practically without funds, I borrowed one hundred thousand francs* from a friend, and with it bought 1,300 feet of Kodachrome in magazines which would fit the light camera we had had in Patagonia.

That same evening I met a friend, the well-known film-photographer J. J. Languepin. Hearing of my purchase he threw up his hands.

'What on earth are you hoping to do? Even if you only take at sixteen per second you haven't enough there to make anything worthwhile. Anyway, without experience you'll only make a mess of it.'

I could only reply with some embarrassment:

'Oh, you know how it is, it's just to have something to look back on and show my friends.'

After a moment or two's thought his rather glassy stare relaxed into his normal kindly expression.

'Come round and see me tomorrow morning', he said. 'I'll give you a few hints. After all you're no dimmer than the next man, and with a bit of luck you might just bring back something interesting.'

Throughout the expedition I followed his advice as closely as possible. I forced myself to carry the camera all the way up the final ridge of Huantsan and, what is more, to use it, despite the wind and cold. Skilfully edited by Languepin and augmented by the pictures taken in the valley with the Dutch camera, the film eventually amounted to nearly forty minutes. Needless to say, it was far from being a masterpiece. Many of the shots were clumsy or imperfect, yet in a simple way it gave quite a complete idea of our adventure. In particular the shots taken on the final assault were something new at that time. They were not all very spectacular, but for the first time audiences could see for themselves the authentic actions of climbers on a difficult peak, and several persons competent to judge thought that the film might interest the general public.

Without expecting profits in any way comparable with those of the Annapurna film, it seemed that one might earn enough to finance another expedition to Peru, and I began to follow the idea up excitedly. The promoter was interested, but thought the film too short. He therefore suggested shooting another feature on climbing in the Alps in order to complete the programme. At this point I thought of making a film on ski mountaineering. Skiing was a much more popular sport than climbing, and it seemed that in this way we might attract larger audiences. My own experience in both departments would make the whole thing relatively easy, or so I reasoned. As usual, the

* *Translator's note.* Then equivalent to approximately one hundred pounds sterling.

problem was money. To make a good film, even on 16 mm, is very expensive, and I had next to nothing. Fortunately various firms in the ski business promised aid in return for publicity in the credits, and by borrowing left and right I finally realised enough to make a beginning.

The plan was to feature the descent of extremely steep slopes, several of which had recently been done, but on reflection I decided to limit the field of action to the north face of Mont Blanc which, though less difficult than some others, had never been skied down. In the event, the filming turned out quite an adventure in itself. We were several times cut off by bad weather in the Vallot hut, at 14,304 feet. The weeks went by, and our cinematographer, Jacques Ertaud, had to leave to fulfil another contract. Luckily Georges Strouvé was able to take his place.

Hardly had he arrived when, in the course of filming a connecting shot, I misjudged a turn and fell over a seventy-foot ice wall, at the foot of which I went head over heels down the slope, only managing to stop myself a few yards from the edge of a precipice. As I got to my feet a pain in the back told me I had done something to my spine. Fine weather chose this moment to arrive, but in spite of a slight dislocation of one vertebra I managed to finish the film. Bill Dunaway, an American friend, accompanied me on the descent, and Strouvé, with the help of Pierre Tairraz, was able to shoot nearly all of it.

The film was mildly humorous in tone. It turned out most satisfactorily, winning first prize at the International Festival of Trenta, and against all expectation *La Conquête du Huantsan* obtained the second. The lectures given with the aid of these two films never attracted vast crowds, but they more than repaid the time and trouble that had gone into their making. Thanks to the sums thus realised I was able to return to Peru in 1956, with my Dutch friends, for an even more wonderful adventure than our first.

With two successful expeditions, 1952 was a particularly splendid year for me, but 1953 was rather difficult by way of contrast. After the painful experience of finishing off *La Grande Descente du Mont Blanc* my back was extremely stiff, and although the pain was quite bearable it was annoying, making guiding rather a problem. By the time September came round I was so far from trying any big climb as an amateur that I had to consult my father in his professional capacity at Aix les Bains.

My hope of participating in another French Himalayan expedition began to materialise during the autumn. After the conquest of Annapurna the French Himalayan Committee was in a position to apply for an attempt on Mount Everest, but unfortunately fate was to decide otherwise. In 1951 a

British party had explored the Nepalese side of the mountain, which up to then had never been reconnoitred by any European. On their return they declared that, contrary to what had always been supposed, there was a distinct possibility of climbing the mountain by this face.

As a consequence of this discovery several nations asked the Nepalese government for permission to attempt the mountain. After a long series of negotiations it was decided that the Swiss should attack in 1952, the British in 1953, and the French in 1954.

Despite the shortage of time the Swiss succeeded in organising a powerful expedition, but, unluckily from their point of view, the lack of a light and efficient oxygen apparatus brought the assault party, consisting of Raymond Lambert and the Sherpa Tenzing Norgay, to a halt at just under twenty-eight thousand feet. This was a remarkable achievement in itself and gave every hope for a future success, but the actual altitude was no greater than that twice attained by the British before the war on the north ridge. After this third trial it seemed highly probable that there was a physiological ceiling at around this level. If men as tough and well trained as Lambert and Tenzing could not take another step, it was no more than logical to conclude that the air no longer contained sufficient oxygen to support life.

The British made the most of their two years' respite. With the aid of a great deal of money they organised a truly enormous expedition, consisting of no less than thirteen Europeans and forty Sherpas, all under the command of a high-ranking officer. Thanks to the huge scale of the supporting pyramid and the efficiency of the open-circuit oxygen apparatus which enabled them to breathe a mixture of air and oxygen comparable to what one might find at around twenty thousand feet, the giant of the earth succumbed almost without a struggle. This victory marked the end of an era which had lasted more than thirty years, and was a turning point in the evolution of mountaineering.

The highest mountain in the world had been climbed. For the man in the street, mesmerised by the altitude figures and ignorant of the true impulsions, there was nothing more to be said, nothing more to be sought but gold and the Abominable Snow Man. This decline of popular interest meant that henceforward it would be far more difficult to finance expeditions by the support of the press, the cinema and governments thirsty for prestige. For mountaineers, however, the conquest of Everest was rather the beginning of a new era. The most difficult mountains still remained to be climbed.

Now that the culminating point of the globe had been attained, several countries considered trying the three or four summits which approached it in height, and a rather stupid international competition began, to get permission

Southwestern Nepal (Elevations are in metres.)

to attempt them. The Italians, after exerting considerable pressure on the Pakistani government, obtained authorisation to try K2, the second highest mountain in the world (28,351 feet).

France might perhaps have obtained permission for an attempt on Kangchenjunga which, at 28,166 feet, was scarcely lower than K2, but since a British party had already made a reconnaissance which seemed to offer definite hopes of success the Comité de l'Himalaya very sportingly stood down.

Two possibilities remained: either the fourth highest mountain in the world, Lhotse (27,973 feet), or the fifth, Makalu (27,854 feet). The first was a few feet higher, but properly speaking it is no more than a southern outlier of Everest, and three-quarters of the route had already been pioneered by the Swiss and the British. The element of exploration would therefore largely be lacking from its conquest, rendering the exploit less striking. Makalu, by contrast, was a magnificent, isolated peak in the heart of a wild region. Two lightweight parties had looked at its western flank and had returned impressed by its apparent difficulties. Even the approach march seemed to offer considerable problems, and everyone who had seen the mountain, especially from Everest, seemed to be in agreement that it would be the toughest nut of all the eight-thousanders. Its beauty and the interest promised by its ascent, both from the technical aspect and from the point of view of exploration, made it the automatic choice.

A request was therefore sent to the Nepalese government, but the reply came that for 1954 permission had been granted to an American expedition. Falling back on Lhotse was then considered, but on maturer reflection it was decided that the American team was too inexperienced to represent a serious threat, and that Makalu would be attempted in 1955. In order to have the maximum chance of success the committee took the wise decision to send out a reconnaissance beforehand, in the short period of fine weather between the end of the monsoon and the onset of winter, with Jean Franco as its leader. His job did not permit him to carry out the whole of the ungrateful task of preparation in person, so Lucien Devies asked Guido Magnone and me to take over a large part of it. Jean Couzy was charged with perfecting the oxygen apparatus, based on the English Everest model, but to be lightened if possible.

Makalu is some 1,250 feet lower than Everest. On level ground this sounds no distance at all, but at high altitude it makes a very considerable difference. Apart from the progressive rarefaction of the air, it means an extra camp with all that this implies of extra bulk and organisation the whole way down the mountain. There seemed little doubt, therefore, that we could envisage a lighter expedition than the English had taken to Everest; but on the other hand it looked as though the steep, rocky summit cone of Makalu might very well be much more difficult.

To attack a rock face at such an altitude was in fact a new and daring conception, posing many problems, the solution of which was likely to be hazardous. Our intention was to take a smaller, less cumbersome party than the Everest one, but, if possible, still more efficient. In order to accomplish this it was decided to do away with all preconceptions and, without neglecting the lessons of the past, to think out each problem again from first principles.

From April to June 1954, Franco, Magnone, Dr Rivolier (the expedition's doctor), Couzy and I all toiled like ants to devise new oxygen apparatus, clothing and camping gear that would be lighter, stronger, warmer and simpler than those used hitherto; new methods of packing; light, nourishing and appetising rations for high altitude; and some original tactics into the bargain. By the end of June everything was ready for the reconnaissance. In addition to those already mentioned the party included the guides Pierre Leroux and Jean Bouvier, both of urban origin. Since we were not to leave until the beginning of August, I had a month in which to fulfil some engagements with a few of my best clients.

We were naturally in a state of some anxiety about the progress of the American attempt on 'our' mountain, but at last the news of its failure came through. For reasons that I fail to understand their attack had been launched against the southeast ridge, hardly the most favourable of routes to judge from our aerial photos. They duly ran into enormous difficulties and were forced to retreat before even getting very high.

At the same time we learned that a New Zealand expedition, led by Hillary, which was in the district with permission to attempt certain seven-thousanders, had also raided Makalu. Seeing the Americans getting nowhere on the southeast ridge they went for the more reasonable-looking northwest face, but were stopped at around twenty-three thousand feet by smooth slabs and a wall of ice.

The results of these two attempts were hardly enlightening. On the contrary, the checkmating of the New Zealanders at only twenty-three thousand showed that we were likely to run into serious difficulties much sooner than we had expected. The importance of reconnaissance before launching an attack on such a complex mountain was thus doubly emphasised.

The approach march, which took place in the thick of the monsoon, was trying and difficult due to the incessant rain. Floods rendered many of the

The Makalu Massif (Elevations are in metres.)

fords unusable so that long detours had to be made to find primitive bridges. It took us twenty-four days of hard labour to reach the foot of Makalu's impressive west face, where base camp was set up. In spite of the heat, the wetness, and the onslaught of countless leeches, I found constant sources of delight as we marched along. The country was far wilder than any we had seen in 1950. Everything I loved about Nepal was still present. With a few local variations there was the same luxuriance of nature, the same smilingly philosophical inhabitants, all the charm which had won my heart forever at first sight.

Before getting to grips with Makalu the whole team went through a stage-by-stage course of acclimatisation and 'fittening' which had extremely satisfactory results. Several of the surroundings peaks were climbed, thus enabling us to get excellent views of the whole of the Nepalese flank of the mountain. It soon became obvious that the only reasonable course was to follow a spiral route from the foot of the northwest face to the north-northwest ridge (this being the route attempted by the New Zealanders) and thence onto the north face, the upper part of which, however, we could not see. It was the one great unknown quantity, and to judge from the aerial photographs it might well be steep and rocky.

It did not take us long to set up three camps, the last of which, at around twenty-one thousand feet, became Advanced Base. Camp Four was pitched on a shelf in the middle of an ice wall two thousand feet higher up. Soon after this Leroux and Bouvier succeeded in forcing the barrier which had checked our predecessors and installed Camp Five on a saddle of the north-northwest ridge at about 24,600 feet. So far the weather, though cold and windy, had remained fine. These hard but bearable conditions now began to deteriorate, a gale blew up, and at Camp Three the temperature never exceeded minus twenty degrees Centigrade.

In such circumstances mere survival became a battle, but the reconnaissance of the north face was carried on all the same. During one lull Franco and I, with two Sherpas, had the luck to make the ascent of the 25,162-foot peak at the far end of the north-northwest ridge, known as Kangshung, or Makalu II. From this point we were able to see a good part of the north face of Makalu proper. It appeared feasible, but a bar of seracs and the final rocky wall were obviously going to be serious obstacles. The steepness of the whole face would entail a severe risk of avalanche in snowy weather, such as is normal in spring. Since we could only see three-quarters of the face it was plain that we would be able to form a better opinion from the summit of Chomolonzo, a higher and more northerly peak linked by an easy ridge to the ice plateau below Camp Five.

During the days which followed, first Bouvier and Leroux, then Couzy and Magnone tried to get onto the north face to look for the beginning of the route, but despite the unchangingly blue sky the wind, now risen to hurricane force, compelled them to return to Camp Three. Life had now become absolutely infernal. Franco therefore decided to raise the siege and asked Couzy and I to try and bring down the tent and equipment from Camp Five. Tormented at the thought of once more leaving the Himalayas without a big peak to our name we asked him for permission to try Chomolonzo if the wind happened to drop a little. This 25,590-foot summit stands out well on its own: so much so, in fact, that a German expedition had once thought of taking it as its primary objective. Thus its ascent would be a notable scalp, quite apart from the fact that it would give us a perfect view of the north face of Makalu.

At Camp Five we found the tent blown down and somewhat torn. In the circumstances it was a miracle that it hadn't been blown away altogether. The temperature was approximately minus thirty degrees Centigrade and the gale was still in full swing, making repairing and repitching an atrociously painful business. No sooner were we inside than it rose to a hurricane worthy of Patagonia. The col on which the camp was situated acted like a wind tunnel, and some of the gusts were certainly in excess of ninety miles per hour. Fortunately we had pitched the tent end-on to their direction, and as it was highly aerodynamic in shape it stood up to the battering beyond all expectation. Each burst would force it down until it seemed to be shrinking, but as soon as the strain relaxed it would spring up again with a sharp report. Some of the seams started to give, but a few safety pins staved off disaster. We were in a state of extreme tension for several hours, and our three Sherpas were quite grey with fear, yet one grows used to anything in time and in the end we slept, fully dressed and shod, like soldiers in the front line.

At dawn the wind fell to about half its previous force. Couzy was still determined to have a try at Chomolonzo, and his dynamic energy carried the day in the face of the supplications of the Sherpas and my own total lack of enthusiasm. A long descent down gentle slopes took us to a col at about 23,650 feet which was the beginning of the Chomolonzo ridge. Setting our oxygen flow at four litres a minute we began to trudge up the ridge, which was technically easy. The wind had recovered its original violence, and it was impossible to stand upright before the gusts, but the hard snow, the lack of difficulty and the excellence of our oxygen sets made it possible to go on. We progressed by a series of charges like soldiers in attack. As soon as a gust died down a little we ran uphill as hard as we could go until the roar of the next gust could be heard coming, whereupon we huddled down with our backs to the storm, forcing our ice axes into the snow for purchase.

Just as we were approaching the summit the intense cold, which was certainly close to minus thirty-five degrees, froze up the valves on our oxygen sets. Fortunately we were able to shelter behind a cornice while we fixed them, but from then on we had to keep one heavily gloved hand constantly over our face masks in order to stop the rime from reappearing.

The summit was eventually reached at about noon. From here we could see the whole of the north face of Makalu. It was obviously climbable, and one could even trace out the exact line of probable ascent.

Our return to Camp Five was somewhat dramatic. On the way down, we ran out of oxygen. The going immediately became much more trying, but we did not worry unduly because we were certain of finding two full bottles which we had left on the col planted upright in the snow for easy location. When we reached this extensive snow saddle, however, they were nowhere to be seen. Thinking that the wind must have blown them over, we poked around for a long time among the sastrugi.* All this was very tiring, and I began to feel like a fish out of water for lack of oxygen. Couzy was all for climbing up to Camp Five without it, but I felt so feeble that I preferred to go on searching. Finally I despaired, and had just resigned myself to trudging after Couzy when I found the bottles, knocked over and half-buried in the snow. Less than two hours later we were celebrating with the Sherpas, who had given us up for lost.

Once the hot drinks had been swallowed and the tent folded away it was high time to flee these inhuman surroundings. The presence of fixed ropes at all the difficult places enabled us to get back to Camp Three soon after nightfall. It was one of the toughest and most intense days I had ever known, rendered particularly memorable by Couzy's display of inflexible willpower. Today, as I write about it, it still seems among my most wonderful.

The wind and the post-monsoon cold made the Makalu reconnaissance a trial of endurance, but the complete success of the following spring was undoubtedly due to it. We had found the line of least resistance and proved the value of our new equipment, especially the breathing apparatus.

Less than a month after our return to France we had to start preparing for the expedition proper. There followed an exhausting succession of weeks in the swarming ant's nest of Paris, miles of bumph, hours of argument and irritation at F.F.M. headquarters. A few details of our equipment and quite a lot of our organisation had to be modified in the light of experience. The team was reinforced by the addition of André Vialatte and Serge Coupé, and the number of Sherpas was very nearly doubled. We had thus developed a veritable eight-thousander machine, which worked perfectly in practice.

On our return to Nepal we benefited from a long spell of clear, calm weather, and the conquest of the mountain almost turned into a textbook exercise. There was no need for any searching. The teams relayed each other like a well-trained corps de ballet, five camps went up in practically no time at all, and a ton and a half of food, kit and oxygen bottles were stockpiled at Camp Five. Thanks to these reserves and the almost uninterrupted system of fixed ropes linking it to Camp Three, this advanced outpost became a place where one could remain in comfort and safety, secure in the knowledge that one could retreat in any weather.

* *Translator's note.* Dunes of snow formed by the wind.

Franco chose Couzy and myself for the first assault. We left Camp Five with three hand-picked Sherpas, and after traversing some steep snow slopes which the heavy frost had made safe we found an unexpectedly easy way through a bar of dangerous seracs. Camp Six was installed at around 25,600 feet, after which the Sherpas went back down, leaving us alone in our eyrie. In spite of a temperature of minus thirty-three degrees Centigrade inside the tent, a slow rate of oxygen enabled us to spend a reasonable night.

We left camp at seven o'clock, and less than two hours later reached the foot of the rock wall which had looked so formidable from our previous distant viewpoints. This was at about 26,900 feet. In the event the face turned out to be steep but far less difficult than we had expected. The shattered granite offered plenty of holds and, no doubt due to the force and frequency of the wind, there was astonishingly little snow or verglas. We switched the oxygen flow to maximum, and an hour's climbing at what would have been a rapid pace at half the altitude brought us to the final ridge. Three-quarters of an hour later, having surmounted one genuinely difficult step on the way, we stood on the pointed summit of the fifth highest mountain in the world.

The disconcerting facility with which we had vanquished this giant, to which I had devoted a year of my life, came as a slight anticlimax. Shortly after our return, while the feelings I experienced at that moment were still fresh, I was to write the following words:

> Victory must be bought at the price of suffering and effort, and the clemency of the weather combined with the progress of technique had sold us this one too cheaply for us to appreciate it at its true value. How far it all was from the proud ecstasy I have sometimes felt as I hauled myself onto some more modest summit after a life-and-death struggle. In my dreams I had foreseen it all quite differently: coated thickly with frost I was to have crawled the last few yards to the top with my final strength, worn out from the mortal combat to which I had given my all. Instead I had got here not only without having to fight, but almost without fatigue. There was something disappointing about such a victory. And yet . . . I stood at last on the perfectly formed summit of the noblest of all the great peaks. After so many years of perseverance and toil, so many mortal risks willingly accepted, the wildest of all my dreams had come true. Was I completely stupid, to be feeling like this? Madman, for whom there is no happiness but in desire, rejoice for once in reality, exult in this moment when, half-borne up by the wind, you stand over the world.

Drink deep of infinity: below your feet, hardly emerging from the sea of cloud that stretches away to the horizon, armies of mountains raise their lances towards you.

Like a wound-up spring the mechanism which had raised us load by load and camp by camp to the summit continued to function. The same evening, Franco, Magnone and the sirdar Gyalzen took our place at Camp Six, going to the top in their turn the next day. The following day Bouvier, Leroux, Vialatte and Coupé made the third ascent. For the first time in the history of mountaineering a whole expedition had reached the summit of an eight-thousander, a spectacular demonstration of our mastery of the situation.

Analysing these events in a remarkable article, Jean Franco prophetically concluded:

> In our hearts we felt a little bit let down. Given the perfection of our tools and the continuity of our good luck, one might even have wished for a slightly tougher adversary. Be that as it may, the ascent of Makalu, in its comfortable security, will always remain one of the happier pages in Himalayan history.
>
> Just as, in our over-explored Alps, the last and hitherto forbidden routes are being climbed amid the overthrow of classical traditions, the Himalayas are yielding up their last eight-thousanders. The Golden Age of the highest range on earth will only last a few years. The ascent of lesser-known summits by routes of extreme difficulty, however hazardous they may seem today, will then begin. There are 'Aiguilles Vertes' waiting beside the 'Monts Blancs', and 'Drus' beside the 'Vertes'. It looks as though the weapons are forged.

It was even so. In 1957, following our example both as to equipment and to methods, a Swiss expedition made the first ascent of Lhotse with amazing ease, simultaneously bagging the second ascent of Everest into the bargain. All but one of the eight-thousanders have now fallen,* and if some of them, like Dhaulagiri, gave their conquerors a good deal of trouble, this was primarily because the latter lacked financial resources really adequate to the job in hand. The Himalayan 'Drus' began to succumb at the same time. By a particularly striking irony the Muztagh Tower, once considered the type of the unclimbable, was conquered in the same year by two different parties attacking from opposite flanks.

* *Translator's note.* Gosainthan [Shishapangma], which is in Tibetan territory.

We had no professional cinematographer with us on Makalu. Coming after Annapurna and Everest it seemed unlikely that we would succeed in attracting really large audiences with another Himalayan epic. Nevertheless, if we could film the arrival on the summit and a fair amount of the more exciting parts of the climb, it might interest enough people to pay its way. Filming of this sort could only be carried out by members of the assault parties themselves, however, and the expense of a professional was therefore hardly justifiable. In the end it was decided to trust the job to an experienced amateur.

Since I had done a good deal more filming than anyone else in the party Franco asked me to take on the responsibility. My films on Huantsan and Mont Blanc had given me a certain reputation and understanding, but personally I was still uncomfortably aware of my lack of mastery. However, I did have a couple of more or less original ideas in my head which I was anxious to put into practice, and in spite of the extra work and responsibility involved I accepted Franco's proposition.

It was obvious to me that the photographer could not hope to be present every time something interesting happened, and I therefore asked Franco, Leroux and Magnone to carry a light camera with them the whole time. They shot numerous sequences, and thanks to their collaboration I was able to bring back a complete and interesting record of the expedition right from the Indian frontier to the summit of Makalu.

Convinced that the life and customs of the Sherpas and other Himalayan peoples would be of wide interest, I asked Franco, on our return to Base Camp, for permission to go off and film in the Sola Khumbu valley. Magnone and several Sherpas came with me, and we had a wonderful trip. Three days' march over a couple of twenty-thousand-foot cols took us to the tiny capital of the Sherpas, Namche Bazar. At last I could observe our happy, faithful companions in their natural surroundings. For two days there was a continual round of singing, dancing and brotherly libations of buttered tea and millet beer.

At this point word came that a religious festival was about to begin at the monastery of Thami, situated half a day's journey from the Tibetan frontier at an altitude of around 14,500 feet. Such a chance was not to be missed, and in the event its interest exceeded even our expectations. The splendour of the costumes, the strangeness of the symbolic dances, the monstrosity of the masks, the barbaric and disconcerting music of the giant horns, the whole seen and heard against a background of savage mountain grandeur, gave a sensation of witnessing scenes from another planet. The monks gave us complete freedom to film as we wished, and as Magnone was also able to record the music on tape we produced a most unusual documentary, which had a considerable success. After being much applauded at lectures it was transferred to 35 mm and commercially distributed in numerous countries.

The festival came to an end, and it was time to think about getting back to the outer world. An unbelievable path over a twenty-thousand-foot col took us through to the lower hill country in three days, whence a week's forced march brought us to Kathmandu. This raid into the most beautiful part of the Himalayas had enabled me to broaden my knowledge of Nepal, and, still more than the approach marches to Annapurna and Makalu, had given the feeling of living in another age. But the loveliest dreams come to an end, and now we had to plunge back into the swarming furnace of India.

The lectures given in Germany and the Low Countries by my friends Egeler and De Booy, plus those I had been able to give in France during my periods between expeditions, had now put sufficient funds into the coffers of the Dutch Foundation for the Exploration of High Mountains for them to envisage another trip to Peru in 1956. As with the previous one, the majority of its time was to be spent on research into the formation of certain kinds of rock, and only two out of its total duration of six months could be devoted to mountaineering.

It seemed to me rather silly to go so far for such a short time, so I decided to prolong my stay by making a film on the life and customs of the country, and also by getting up a second, private expedition to follow on the first. With this in mind I began to contact some of my better-off climbing friends. On hearing of my project, however, Lucien Devies suggested that I abandon it in favour of a French national expedition to attempt one of the three or four unclimbed Peruvian 'six-thousanders', which appeared to be more difficult than anything so far attempted at that sort of altitude. It was a wonderful proposition and I accepted it at once. We quickly settled on the Nevado Chacraraju, a magnificent summit of 20,046 feet.

The mountain had been explored before the war by two powerful Austro-German expeditions, and since 1945 had been selected as main objective by several American parties as well as another German one. None had been able to discern a weak point anywhere in its defences, since all its flanks are festooned with almost vertical columns of ice over a height of more than 2,500 feet. Its appearance is so discouraging that all of them had turned away on reaching its foot, without even a real try. Some, and not the least among them, had gone so far as to declare it impossible, and the leader of one American team had written publicly that the mountain 'would require siege or suicide, or probably both.' Erwin Schneider, one of the most famous prewar Austrian mountaineers, who had been among the first to reconnoitre the peak, wrote that he was unable to advise me which side to attack it from, since 'none of the faces appeared to offer any serious hope whatever.'

Everyone who had seen Chacraraju was full of praise for its beauty, and all seemed in agreement that it would be one of the finest objectives one could choose. The rock climbing seemed likely to be of a standard rarely attempted at such altitudes, and the ice work more difficult than anything normally found in the Alps. These opinions plus the splendid photos we had been able to obtain convinced us that Chacraraju was much the most interesting unsolved problem in the central and tropical Andes, and an ideal object for our expedition. The project having been officially adopted by the Himalayan Committee, set to work. I had to see to all the preparations entirely by myself and at the same time help my Dutch friends get ready for the earlier expedition, which we had been planning now for four years.

After three months of paperwork everything was in readiness. I landed in Cuzco in April, where I was met by Egeler, De Booy and the surveyor Hans Deckhout. A few days later the brilliant young Genevan climber Raymond Jenny, who had been invited to join us, arrived from Bolivia, where he had been earning a living for the last six months as a skiing and climbing instructor.

This expedition was to take place in the Cordillera de Vilcabamba, 625 miles southeast of the Cordillera Blanca which contains Huantsan and Chacraraju. Since none of its summits exceeds 20,341 feet it will be seen that the range as a whole is noticeably lower. The massif projects into the endless Amazonian jungles like the prow of a vast boat, condensing all their humidity on its icy flanks and so receiving a quantity of precipitation that makes climbing difficult. By way of compensation, however, the area was comparatively little explored. So far only one major peak had been climbed. This was Salcantay, ascended by a Franco-American party some years previously.

After a training period, during which we did the first ascent of the very difficult Veronica (19,029 feet) in a neighbouring range of mountains, we went for the second highest peak in the chain, Soray. The exact height of this summit, which is also known as Humantay, has never been properly determined, but is in the general region of twenty thousand feet. It had been reconnoitred by several expeditions and seriously attacked by an Italo-Swiss team, and to judge from their comments it was likely to be an extremely difficult proposition.

All the faces of Soray are exceptionally steep, but the north face, although made up of a succession of ice and rock walls, has the advantage of being

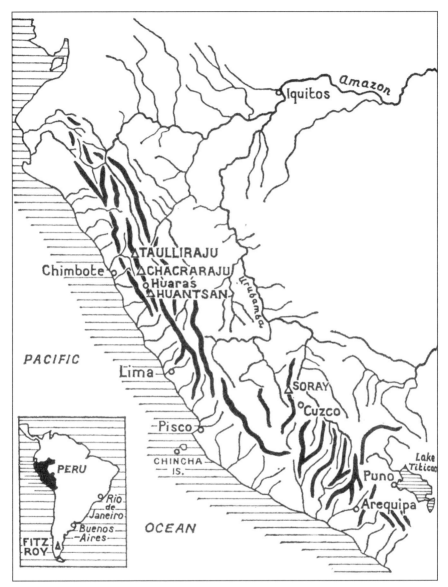

Map of Cordillera de Vilcabamba in Peru

shorter and more open to the sun; thus it was by this face, in spite of grave danger from toppling seracs, that we chose to attack. Parts of the ascent involved very delicate ice climbing, but the mountain fell more quickly than we expected. For something to do in the few weeks that remained we therefore decided to try the second ascent of Salcantay.

Two victories in succession, both won at the charge between spells of bad weather, had put us on exceptional form. Our morale was equal to anything. The giant of Cuzco was treated with no more respect than an ordinary Alpine peak. Several days of rain and snow having confined us to base camp, we were beginning to run short of time, and resolved to attack without any preliminary reconnaissance at the first sign of a clear spell. Whereas our predecessors had spent nearly three weeks putting up camps and hundreds of feet of fixed ropes, our ascent followed the Huantsan model in being done all at once. The first day took us to five hundred feet below the top. After an uncomfortable bivouac with four of us crammed into one two-man tent we reached the top early the following morning. Except for one short rappel we descended entirely on crampons, getting back to base towards midnight.

Inasmuch as it was bigger and better equipped, this second Dutch expedition had been slightly less of an adventure than the first, but in its own way it had been a complete success, both from a sporting and from a human point of view. In less than two months we had climbed three high and difficult mountains. Bad weather had often made the conditions trying in the extreme, but nevertheless we had worked together in an atmosphere of unreserved friendship that I have never known on more ambitious expeditions, where you always get certain individuals behaving in a difficult way due to a secret desire to arrive first at the summit.

Another factor in our favour had been the location of the range, dividing the equatorial forest on one side from the cradle valleys of Inca civilisation on the other. We had thus been forced willy-nilly to travel across some of the most fascinating country anyone could possibly imagine. Once again, as in the Himalayas, I had been completely won by a combination of mountain splendour with the outlandish charm of a people whose ancient customs had been preserved almost intact through a feudal society. Around Cuzco, whence the Quechua Indians once set out to conquer 'The Empire of the Sun', the strangeness of manners and costumes is sometimes even greater than in central Asia. The most world-weary of men could not help but be struck by the monumental remains of lost civilisations. When my Dutch companions went back to their scientific investigations I therefore spent some while making a film on Quechua life until it was time to meet the incoming French expedition in Lima.

A week later we were circling Chacraraju, looking for a possible way up. The north face looked the most favourable, but it took us five days to whip forty recalcitrant mules up to the thirteen-thousand-foot mark, where we established a well-supplied base camp. Thenceforward our assault followed more or less Himalayan lines. With the aid of three energetic mestizo porters we put an advanced base beyond a labyrinth of seracs, at around 16,750 feet, some six hundred feet from the base of the wall. Even taking turns with the work it took us three days to rig the first thousand feet with fixed ropes. There was a serious risk of falling ice on this part of the climb, and the rock climbing in some places was so difficult that we had to have recourse to artificial means. Only at the third attempt did we succeed in pitching a bivouac camp, on a narrow platform hacked out of the ice wall, at approximately 16,750 feet. On the following day the leading pair cut their way up another 750 feet of over sixty-degree ice, installing fixed ropes as they went.

A period of bad weather now drove us back to base. On 30 July we all went up to the bivouac camp with heavy loads of food and equipment, and next morning the assault began two hours before dawn. The fixed ropes enabled us to reach the previous highest point just after first light, whence some difficult rock pitches soon led us to the foot of a vertical ice groove with a small overhang in the middle of it. Since the ice was too soft for the use of ice pegs it took more than an hour's delicate progress to overcome the obstacle. Another 130 feet of very severe climbing brought us to a broad snow terrace three hundred feet from the top. From here the last part of the climb looked so awkward that we decided to attack without waiting for a rest. Four rope's lengths of continual step cutting then led me to the hitherto untrodden summit at five o'clock, and a few minutes later all six members of the assault party were shaking hands on its constricted dome.

The 'impossible' Chacraraju had been climbed at last, but in spite of the size and quality of the team, the quantity of equipment and the methodical tactics deployed against it, the battle had been long and hard. Eleven hours had been required to overcome the last 2,500 feet, seven of which were on the face itself. The last six hundred feet had been rendered doubly severe by the altitude, and some of the ice pitches had been harder than anything that any of us had ever seen before.

It was a moment of supreme happiness. From every point of the horizon the great ice and rock peaks of the Cordillera Blanca, flaming with evening colour, seemed to salute us. Below our feet the shadow of our mountain stretched out over the desolate hills of the Altiplano like a giant arrow. The grandeur of the moment sang in me . . . yet how cold the wind blew on this ridge, how small and far away our base camp. Without a tent or so much as a sleeping bag, a bivouac here would be absolutely infernal.

After a short discussion we took a vote. The majority preferred to climb down through the night by the light of our head torches and so, after innumerable rappels, we got back to the bivouac camp at seven o'clock the next morning, twenty-six hours after leaving it. We were too exhausted to carry on, and it was not until the following day that we got back to the flowers and grass of the valley.

After our hard-won victory over Chacraraju our thirst for adventure was largely appeased for the moment. The east peak of the mountain,* slightly lower but certainly more difficult still, seemed rather too grandiose a project to occupy the three weeks that remained to us, and we settled instead for Taulliraju (19,127 feet). We had frequently admired this mountain's haughty bearing, and its ascent promised the double attraction of being difficult but reasonably short.

Although the real climbing on Taulliraju is only about 1,600 feet in extent, it turned out to be at least as trying as Chacraraju, and perhaps even more strenuous. There was no ice pitch as difficult as the notorious ice groove, but one magnificent granite slab proved certainly as hard as anything ever done at such an altitude on rock. Some very delicate ice climbing was nevertheless called for before we got the first thousand feet fully equipped with fixed ropes. Then, after a short break in the weather, the attack was launched on 17 August. Although there remained little more than six hundred feet beyond the top of the fixed ropes it was obvious that we would not get up and down in one day, and we therefore carried equipment for a relatively comfortable bivouac, including sleeping bags and two minute tents, one weighing a pound and a half, the other two pounds.

The fixed ropes enabled us to reach our previous highest point by nine o'clock. From there on we had to climb on the left flank of the east ridge, where we were forced to spend much time and energy clearing away the deep, soft snow. Even the sufficiently suggestive photos we brought back give no real idea of the toilsomeness and danger of our advance. The floury powder lay at an angle of over sixty degrees. Once a section of it gave way, but fortunately I was held on the rope by Sennelier after a fall of thirty feet. Each rope's length took over an hour, and it was not until three o'clock that we emerged from an ice overhang back onto the crest of the ridge, at the foot of a superb slab of granite, fully a hundred feet high. Sennelier led this pitch and fixed a rope on it for the following day.

Despite cloud and intermittent snowfall, we were up and doing by eight o'clock on the morning of 18 August. A fine ice pitch followed the slab, after which we found ourselves condemned to the left side of the ridge again with its tedious flailing and delving and stamping. Finally an ice tower gave us

---

* *Translator's note.* Climbed in 1962 by a party including Terray.

some delicate cramponning to reach the summit at two o'clock. More than fourteen hours' climbing time had been necessary to surmount six hundred feet. Never, perhaps, in the whole history of mountaineering, had the ascent of a peak been such sheer hard work. Another night was spent in our tiny tents, attached in an incredible position to the bottom of the slab. On the nineteenth we reached the glacier and staggered off in the direction of Camp One after a fast of over twenty-four hours.

My companions now went home to France, but I stayed on in Peru for another two months. Living like a mestizo, travelling in trade trucks and sleeping in huts, I shared the life of the Indians as I toured the south of the country to finish the film I had begun on the Quechuas. A passion to record the violence and poetry of life on film took complete possession of me, and in constantly analysing things to arrive at their essence, in seeking the most striking images, the acuity of my senses became doubled, so that I experienced forms of beauty with an intensity I had never known before. When I at last resigned myself to return to Europe, at the end of October, I was gorged with beauty and adventure.

In less than seven years I had taken part in seven distinct expeditions, spent twenty-seven months overseas, done approximately 180 ascents in the Alps, given nearly seven hundred lectures and driven over ninety-four thousand miles! My wife and friends were all astonished that after such an effervescent existence I felt not the least bit tired; and to tell the truth I was rather surprised myself. To be quite honest I had often felt it was time to stop before my luck turned—but these were times when I could not sleep for nervous fatigue, or when I had got back to the valley exhausted after over-prolonged exertions. At such times I would typically dream of a quiet life, divided between the soft warmth of my own fireside and the love of nature. No sooner had I pulled myself together, however, than I would start to ponder on the past. The circumstances of daily life would start to seem petty, ugly and monotonous, until the memory of my more intense hours began to obsess me. I would find myself burning with desire to experience others as ardent, and once again I would hurl myself into the great game.

1957 looked as though it was going to be a more peaceful year, since there were no expeditions in the offing until 1958; but unfortunately it was upset by painful events which everybody knows about and on which I will not dwell.*

* *Translator's note.* The author refers to the New Year rescue attempts on Mont Blanc.

My summer was given up to guiding, and I did a number of serious climbs. With Tom De Booy, for example, I made the fifth ascent of the north face of the Grosshorn in the Bernese Oberland. This is considered one of the steepest ice faces in the Alps, but despite unfavourable conditions we got up its more than three thousand feet in ten and a half hours. On a day of threatened storm in 1955 we had climbed the north face of the Triolet, which is slightly less high but still harder, in exactly five hours. If one compares these times with those of my ice climbs in the Peruvian Andes one cannot help but be struck by the difference. The greater altitude does not entirely account for it. The intrinsic difficulty of the Andean peaks is also very much greater; so much so, in fact, that since I got to know them the ice faces of the Alps have felt like training grounds.

After our triumph on Makalu and the successes of the Muztagh Tower and Chacraraju one might have been pardoned for supposing that the French were well prepared to make a step forward in the art of climbing the apparently most inaccessible mountains. The reader may wonder whether there was much left worth attempting after so many formidable six-, seven- and eight-thousanders, and whether the tool had not once again become too perfect for the job. In fact this was far from being the case. There were and are numerous peaks far harder than anything yet attempted relative to their height and latitude. In particular there exists a huge field of action among the many difficult summits of barely less than eight thousand metres, which combine technical severity with great height and all its attendant problems.

True to its pioneering doctrines, the Himalayan Committee now accepted Jean Franco's advice in formulating a project of unheard-of audacity, namely the ascent of Jannu, the most spectacular of all the unclimbed peaks. This granite tower, rising in two successive vertical tiers to a height of 25,295 feet, appeared to be the most impregnable of nature's remaining fortresses. A light reconnaissance party led by Guido Magnone went out in the autumn of 1957 to examine the possibilities. They returned with a series of wonderful photographs, showing a gigantic face interrupted only with overhanging seracs and walls of rock. This, it seemed, was the easiest side of the mountain . . .

Our friends' eye of faith had picked out an unbelievably daring line through this vertical obstacle course. No single section of it looked unclimbable in itself, but the sheer length and continuity of the difficulties were out of all proportion with the most grandiose ascents so far done. It was roughly equivalent to climbing three Chacrarajus one on top of another. This meant more than a step forward—it meant a veritable jump.

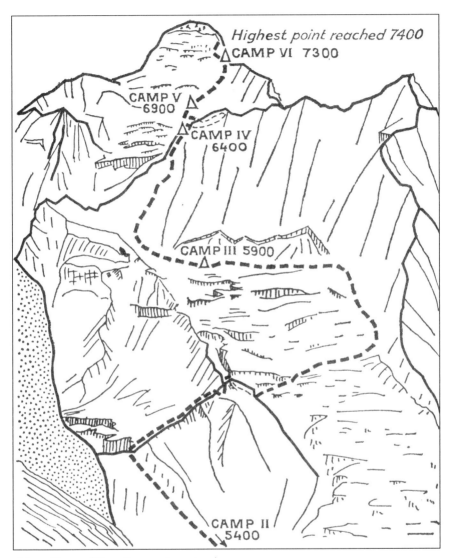

Map of Jannu (Elevations are in metres.)

The Committee hesitated somewhat before the risks involved, but the money was in the coffers, the tool was whetted, and once the idea had been formed it swelled like a mountain torrent, sweeping away all prudence and tradition from its course. An expedition to Jannu was decided on, but in order to get the right men and equipment together it was postponed until 1959.

My time being my own in 1958, I was able to accept Ichac's offer to join him in his great project of shooting a full-length feature film about mountains, a project which we carried out in five months of continuous filming on the faces and glaciers of the Mont Blanc massif. This feature to which I have already referred, was called *Les Étoiles de Midi.*

When the expedition to Jannu finally took place, it fully lived up to our expectations. The line envisaged by the reconnaissance party turned out to be too dangerous, on account of continual ice avalanches, for us to have any hope of getting up it without a disaster, but by a stroke of luck we found an alternative. This was much less exposed to objective risks, but it was very difficult and above all extraordinarily roundabout. It meant first of all scaling the defences of a 21,982-foot satellite peak, then rejoining the mountain proper at the base of its final tower by means of a daring ridge-traverse.

The first part of the ascent was scarcely less difficult than that of the most redoubtable Peruvian peaks. Eight European climbers and seventeen Sherpas rigged the mountain with six camps, 150 ice pitons, and over 6,500 feet of fixed rope. In the hardest part, between Camps Three and Four, heavy loads had to be backpacked on more than forty occasions. Yet in spite of all this unprecedented effort the summit was not conquered.* About nine hundred feet from the top a last crag proved too much for the assault party.

It would be both long and boring to analyse the reasons for this failure. There were a number of contributing factors, and every member of the team would probably emphasise one or another according to his temperament. Personally, I think one can only say that our ambition exceeded our abilities. Climbing is before everything else a gamble, even on the Himalayan scale, and if it lost its element of hazard it would lose its own nature. 'It is obvious that the risks and doubts must increase in proportion to the technical difficulties', as Lucien Devies has said. We had deliberately chosen difficulty on a gigantic scale, thereby reducing our own chances. Even before setting out we had reckoned that the odds on getting up Jannu were no better than 30 percent. We had gambled and lost. Nothing could be more natural.

The level and continuity of the difficulties, the length and complexity of the route, the state of the weather and the element of luck all combined to take up too much time. When we eventually reached our highest point the season was almost over and we were too short of material necessities to finish out with a reasonable margin of safety. The mountain had had the last word, though there had not been much in it. With a slightly bigger organisation and a little more luck the spirit of man would once again have triumphed over the insensate forces of nature.

* *Translator's note.* It was climbed by the 1962 party led by Terray.

There was no disagreement when we got back to Paris: we would just have to try again. The experience we had now acquired should suffice to tip the scales in our favour. Our enthusiasm persuaded the Himalayan Committee to arrange for a new attempt in 1961, but various circumstances combined to delay it until 1962. Jean Franco felt that he was beginning to get old for this kind of thing, and at his request the leadership was entrusted to me, a heavy responsibility which I only accepted after a good deal of hesitation.

In a few days' time I shall be forty years old. Twenty years of action on the mountains of the world have left me with more energy and enthusiasm than the majority of my younger companions, yet I am no longer altogether the same person who once rode roughshod over men and the forces of nature to victory on the Walker, the Eiger, the FitzRoy and Chacraraju. So many years of trial and danger change a man in spite of himself.

Shortly after our return from Jannu I was crossing the Fresnay glacier with a client when we were surprised by an avalanche of seracs. My companion was killed and I was buried under fifteen feet of ice. At that moment it seemed as though the insolent luck which had hitherto walked by my side had abandoned me at last, but in fact, by one of the most amazing miracles in the history of mountaineering, I emerged without a scratch. Imprisoned under a block of ice in the bottom of a crevasse, I managed by a series of contortions to reach a knife which I had by sheer chance left in my pocket. With its aid I was able to reach a cavity in the debris which, once again, had formed close to me by the merest luck. With an ice piton and my peg hammer I then carved out a gallery towards the light. Five hours later I reached the fresh air. This stay in the antechambers of death, where yet another companion was lost at my side, ripened me more than ten years of successful adventures.

In every adventure, whatever my nominal capacity, I have marched with the van. On expeditions or in the Alps, I have accepted every risk and responsibility with a tranquil mind. If I have sometimes led others into danger I have never hesitated to stand at their side. Today my willpower is no longer quite so inflexible, the limits of my courage not so far out. In the assault on the most redoubtable bastion ever invested by a group of mountaineers will I still be a captain leading his shock troops in the last charge, or will I have changed into a general who waits in fear behind the lines while his men advance into action?

And after Jannu, what? Will there be anything left to satisfy man's hunger for transcendence?

326 ~ CONQUISTADORS OF THE USELESS

There can be no doubt that others will tackle peaks less high, but harder still. When the last summit has been climbed, as happened yesterday in the Alps and only recently in the Andes, it will be the turn of the ridges and faces. Even in the era of aviation there is no sign of any limitation yet to the scope for the best climbers of their day.

My own scope must now go back down the scale. My strength and my courage will not cease to diminish. It will not be long before the Alps once again become the terrible mountains of my youth, and if truly no stone, no tower of ice, no crevasse lies somewhere in wait for me, the day will come when, old and tired, I find peace among the animals and flowers. The wheel will have turned full circle: I will be at last the simple peasant that once, as a child, I dreamed of becoming.

| 9 |

Postscript

Towards the end of this book it must have seemed to the reader that my personality was changing, that the springs of my energy were gradually drying up as a result of too-numerous adventures and incessant activity, that the philosopher was gaining the upper hand over the man of action. The tone of the last pages gives an impression that, in accepting leadership of the second Jannu expedition, I was thinking of it as a sort of swan song to be followed by progressive retirement into a more peaceful way of life.

Nothing could have been farther from the truth: 1962 was in fact the most active and important year of my whole career.

No sooner had I finished writing *Conquistadors of the Useless* in July than I began the guiding season. In September I went to Paris to undertake the enormous administrative burden of organising a large-scale expedition. Everything was going well when, in November, a ledge gave way under me while climbing on the Saussois (a limestone crag some 120 miles southeast of Paris) and I fell thirty feet, breaking six ribs and perforating the pleura. The doctors at the hospital condemned me to bed for a month. It seemed that if I was lucky I might be able to go with the Jannu expedition as far as base camp, but that any idea of taking part in the assault was out of the question.

No doubt this was a correct prognosis for a typical social security subscriber, but a guide's life is not like that. Three days later I spent four hours dictating letters, and five days after that I left the hospital altogether, against all the best advice, to take up my task again in spite of a good deal of pain.

Despite the delay caused by this accident, the expedition was ready on schedule. Bigger and better equipped than its predecessor, it set out for the mountain at the beginning of March. Base Camp was pitched on the nineteenth. The team of ten climbers and thirty picked Sherpas was technically very strong, and armed with the previous year's experience they carried out the attack with such address that Camp Six was set up by 18 April, a full fortnight in advance of our most optimistic predictions.

At first I was so fatigued from the accident and the weeks of overwork that I could only coordinate and direct, but as the days went by I began to feel better. As soon as Camp Three had been pitched I began climbing again, and by 15 April I was once more happily at the front of one of the assault teams. Two days later I led and fixed ropes up a large part of the steep ice face between Camps Five and Six. On the 26th, although my oxygen apparatus was not working properly, I was able to lead for most of the barrier of rock slabs that had stopped us the year before. Twenty-four hours later four of my teammates finally reached the summit which so many Himalayan mountaineers had thought inaccessible, and in the next couple of days seven other Sherpa and French climbers, including myself, stood on its ideally pure point.

We got back to France at the beginning of June, and less than a month later I was on my way to Peru. This time our objective was the redoubtable east peak of Chacraraju, a dream I had been cherishing for six years. From the summit of the west peak in 1956, which is some three hundred feet higher, we had been able to pick out every detail of this apparently unclimbable arrowhead of rock and ice. So formidable did it seem that after our success on the higher summit we abandoned the idea of attempting it, and fell back instead upon the more modest Taulliraju.

Shortly afterwards I was to write: 'The east peak of Chacraraju will call for the undivided attention of an extremely strong party.' This proved to be no exaggeration, for subsequently several expeditions of various nationalities which had gone to Peru with the mountain as their express object retired discomfited at the mere sight of it. Our group, of which the leadership had been confided to me, was organised by Claude Maillard and contained several highly expert climbers, of whom the best known was perhaps Guido Magnone. By virtue of my previous Andean experience, and the fact that I was still in excellent trim from the Jannu expedition, I was able to remain in the forefront of operations for three weeks without intermission. Our route up the east face and northeast ridge was both severe and sustained. The last couple of thousand feet in particular were extreme, mainly on ice but also occasionally on rock, and this at an altitude where even the fittest of men are somewhat handicapped. Naturally, it was a very slow business, and on certain days the party in front would not succeed in surmounting two hundred feet. The route was in fact so tortuous that we had to fix 6,500 feet of rope to climb a vertical height of only 2,500. Lengthy and exhausting as the task was, it brought its reward on 8 August when five of us attained the delicate ice fretwork of the summit. The following day, thanks to our fixed ropes, I visited it a second time with our film photographer, Jean-Jacques Languepin, and four more of the party reached it within the next twenty-four hours.

1962 held yet another adventure in store. After ten years of groundwork my Dutch friends Egeler and De Booy had succeeded in getting afoot an expedition to the Himalayas, and by mid-September I was on my way to join them in Nepal. As always, their aims were both sporting and scientific, the climbing group consisting of five Dutch mountaineers led by myself. Our objective was Nilgiri, a fine mountain of 23,950 feet close to Annapurna, whence we had seen it in 1950.

I caught up with them at the end of September, after a long forced march, at the last village before the mountain. After some rapid reconnaissances we decided to attack the north face. This was consistently steep and looked difficult in its central part, but it was sheltered from the prevailing winds and relatively safe from objective hazards. Some serious rock obstacles were swiftly overcome, and Camp Two was installed on a terrace just under twenty thousand feet. Our lack of Sherpas obliged all of us to undertake some heavy portering work to stock the camp as quickly as possible. Above, our way lay up and across a very steep ice slope, an obstacle it took us no less than six days to surmount and equip with fixed ropes despite its mere 1,200 feet. Camp Three was eventually placed on the final ridge at around 21,300 feet. The last lap offered no particular difficulty, and we climbed it in a little over half a day. It was on 26 October, a day of icy gales, that the three brothers Van Lookeren Campagne and the Sherpa Wongdi stood with me on the summit, gazing across at the north face of Annapurna.

The first ascent of Nilgiri was not in the same class as those of Jannu and Chacraraju East, but it was quite serious enough for all that; and it was the first time in the history of mountaineering that one man had led three major expeditions to success in the course of one year, in three distinct ranges and on two continents.

THE ASCENT OF
MOUNT HUNTINGTON

IT WAS WHEN I SAW some of Bradford Washburn's superb photographs in an alpine periodical that I realised what a magnificent field of activity the Mount McKinley chain would be for enthusiasts for 'big-scale' climbing. I began at once to brood upon the possibilities of climbing one of its summits. Thus, from 1955, I was in communication with Bradford Washburn as well as Bob Bates, Fred Beckey and other American mountaineers.

It very soon became apparent to me that, although some very great routes were still to be opened up on McKinley, Foraker and even Hunter, nevertheless all the really important peaks of Alaska had already been done.

This was a serious obstacle to bringing a French expedition into being. In fact, in France it is extremely difficult to focus interest in the first ascent of a face, no matter how fine and difficult it might be. Luckily, thanks to the photos sent me by friendly American climbers, it seemed that despite its quite modest altitude Mount Huntington was a very fine summit, both spectacular and difficult, and perfectly worthy of justifying an expensive transatlantic trip.

I was much occupied with other projects for the next few years. Each autumn I felt a real sense of relief when letters from America informed me that Huntington was still unconquered. After our success on Jannu in 1962, the expeditions committee of the Fédération Française de la Montagne put major enterprises to one side and concentrated on objectives of relatively low altitude but presenting some major technical difficulties. Mount Huntington fitted into this framework exactly and 1964 was ideal for an attempt. Thus my Alaska project became a national undertaking directly organised by the

F.F.M., and in the event of a rapid success on Huntington, we also had freedom to attempt another climb—the south face of Mount McKinley or the 'Moose's Tooth'.

On 28 April 1964 Jacques Soubis and I disembarked at Anchorage airport with about a ton and a half of equipment and foodstuffs. On 5 May the six other members of the expedition arrived and on the next day the picturesque Fairbanks train took us to Talkeetna. It was raining when we arrived and the streets of this minute village were made practically impassable by mud and melting snow. Luckily, after twenty-four depressing hours of waiting the weather cleared. It was now the job of the famous 'bush pilot', Don Sheldon, to deposit us on the Ruth Glacier, exactly at the foot of the northeast face of Mount Huntington.

The mountains were as big and majestic as the finest Himalayan peaks. Unfortunately, the thermometer stuck resolutely at about minus twenty-five degrees Centigrade and the wind was raising enormous swirls of powder snow. In such conditions, setting up base camp took place in the heroic circumstances of a polar expedition.

I recalled my experiences of Patagonian storms and was haunted by the idea that this wind, which was already blowing so strongly, could turn into a hurricane, capable of carrying our tents away. Prudently, I had an igloo built in which we could take refuge in case of need.

The weather stayed clear, but very cold and windy. We planned to attack the steep glacier slope that led to the northwest arête.

A first party began its ascent in a couloir threatened to some extent by a barrier of seracs; the snow was fearfully deep, and the men sank into it to mid-thigh, so that progress was very slow. As they moved forward the climbers cleared the route and equipped it with fixed ropes to make later trips safer and quicker. The four exhausted men reached the foot of the terminal couloir and, having established a depot for equipment, descended at once.

Next day (10 May) Paul Gendre, Marc Martinetti, Maurice Gicquel and Jacques Batkin were the first to leave. They carried only light loads so as to climb quite quickly and thus have the time to ascend and equip the last couloir. Jean-Louis Bernezat, Sylvain Sarthou, Jacques Soubis and I followed, carrying what were virtual mule loads.

We ascended the first couloir slowly, dragging ourselves up the fixed ropes with the help of jumars, those metallic grips with a spring clip which, once placed on the rope, block themselves perfectly when pulled upon, but slide effortlessly when pushed upwards.

The wind blew in biting squalls and the first party's track was already almost effaced. Soubis led; his face taut with the struggle, he stamped the deep snow with all the surliness of a southerner. Suddenly I heard an anguished cry and almost simultaneously the whole central part of the couloir began to slide away. I realised in a flash that a sheet of wind slab had just broken loose. Luckily Jacques had been able to keep his grip of the fixed rope and Jean-Louis, Sylvain and I were at that moment on the edge of the couloir so that the avalanche passed within a few inches without throwing us off balance.

It took us a few minutes to recover from the excitement and discuss the event. But we all knew that, although the conquest of a great summit can produce moments of excitement and happiness unequalled in the monotonous materialistic life of modern times, it can also produce moments of great danger. To seek out danger is not the object of high mountaineering, but it is one of the experiences that have to be endured in order to deserve the pleasure of raising oneself for an instant above the state of 'crawling larvae'.

Bending under our loads we set out again on the route to the summit. After about six hours we joined the first group on the arête. Overlooking an immense rock face nearly seven thousand feet high, the whole northwest ridge of Mount Huntington was revealed to us. Edged with cornices that were sometimes gigantic, and sometimes carved with all the delicacy of lace, this arête seemed very much larger than we had imagined. It rose towards the summit in four distinct steps.

The small shoulder on which we stood was quite suitable for setting up a camp, but there was no protection from the wind. At such a spot, in the event of a hurricane, life could be hell and there would be a risk, especially, of the tents being torn away. Without hesitation, I decided that we must dig a cave.

We set to work without delay. The snow turned out to be very hard and had to be cut with ice axes. The work had progressed slowly and late in the afternoon we were forced to go down to Base Camp.

The next day we set off again very early, carrying enormous sacks. The wind had fallen and, the track remaining good, we got to our destination about ten in the morning. By working all day like madmen we succeeded in digging a cave deep enough for four of us to sleep in. After a rough night, Martinetti, Gicquel, Soubis and I attacked the arête. For more than an hour and a half we followed a long and relatively easy crest, and at last reached the first big step.

Thirty yards over a slope of hard ice led us to the foot of a forbidding wall. At first Martinetti and Gicquel climbed a hard ice pitch. Soubis and I followed, placing the fixed ropes and enlarging the steps.

After two rope lengths hardly less difficult we came to a halt at a rock wall some sixty feet high. Gicquel passed into the lead. The holds were all more or less covered with snow, so it was with great difficulty that he climbed to the bottom of an overhang which he overcame with the help of seven or eight pitons. But he emerged onto a verglas-covered slab and, lacking crampons, could climb no further and descended. I jumared up to the high point and finished the pitch. Soubis joined me and we continued along the corniced arête. Luckily the ice was covered with a thin film of hard snow, then, despite the steepness of the slope, I was able to climb two more rope lengths without step cutting.

On our return to Camp One we found the cave considerably enlarged by the rest of the party. This time there was room for six of us to stretch out and only Sarthou and Batkin went down to Base Camp.

When I went out at about one in the morning to inspect the weather, it was snowing and the wind was blowing violently. There was nothing to do but return to the warmth of my duvet. During the hours that ensued the weather did not improve and we stayed all day in the cave.

Our life there began to be organised: to the right of the entrance was the cooker and shelves of provisions; on the left was the sleeping accommodation where we could all stretch out on a carpet of plastic foam. Since in order to see clearly we were obliged to leave the door open, the temperature inside remained around minus eight to minus ten degrees Celsius, which detracted somewhat from the comfort of this excellent hotel!

During the following night the snow stopped but a polar cold prevailed which a strong wind made almost unbearable. Despite these conditions, four of us left at about 3:30 a.m. With the help of the fixed ropes, we soon regained our high point. From there a delicate traverse on the west face and the ascent of a couloir chimney led us to the snow saddle that separated the first and second steps. Seen from a distance the second step had looked very forbidding, but at close range it was even less attractive ... it was a horribly steep ice slope, the whole upper part of which was of black ice.

This proved the key pitch of the ascent of Mount Huntington and only succumbed after an enormous amount of step cutting. After another night in the snow cave Batkin, Sarthou, Soubis and I arrived early to work on this obstacle. I attacked at once. The bergschrund was quickly crossed and although the slope above was very steep, it was covered with good hard snow and was climbed quickly. An almost vertical step forced me to traverse diagonally to the right. After a few yards I came upon solid ice, but what ice! It was as smooth as a mirror and as hard as glass. I have never met ice like it. In accordance with the technique taught me by my master, Armand Charlet, I progressed methodically, holding my axe in both hands and cutting big but widely spaced steps. It is certainly the only way to make long hours of step cutting possible without excessive fatigue.

Every ten yards or thereabouts I fixed an ice peg, to which I attached the six millimetre line which I drew along behind me and which served after-wards as a fixed rope. The threaded pegs, which are usually so easy to use, refused to penetrate the Huntington ice. Fortunately I had some tubular pegs too and, by hammering them furiously, I was able to drive them in firmly.

All would have gone well if it had not been so cold and especially if the wind had been less violent. I had never made a difficult climb in such conditions! The wind tore at my face and I was ceaselessly unbalanced by the gusts. My feet were icy in spite of the Himalayan gaiters and felted boots.

A bulge, which for several metres sloped at an angle of about seventy degrees, slowed my progress for a moment. At last, at the extremity of the rope, I reached a rock where I was able to stop quite conveniently. Sylvain quickly joined me—his fine, clear blue eyes showed his joy but he was too frozen to smile.

About thirty yards of verglassed rocks led us to the base of an extremely steep slope of glittering dark-green ice.

After forty yards of the roughest spell of step cutting that I have ever experienced, I was able to reach a small rock islet. The slope was now a little less steep. Sixty feet above me I saw the edge of the arête which seemed covered with usable snow. We could have continued but our supply of fixed rope was now exhausted and, moreover, we were worn out by the really inhuman wind and cold. With one accord we let ourselves down the ropes.

The next day the weather was clearer but still as icy and windy. Gicquel, Martinetti, Gendre and Bernezat took their turn but were literally paralysed by the cold and did no more than complete the ascent of the Second Step and climb some sixty feet of the Third. Huntington was valiantly defending its virginity!

Determined to try to carry off a great coup, Soubis, Batkin and Sarthou and I set out at 2:30 a.m. to renew the attack. We pushed along at top speed and it was scarcely more than 8:30 when we reached the last equipped point. Using snow stakes, I was able to overcome a vertical wall of near twenty feet by artificial means, and after an easy slope I was slowed down by a very steep section of hard ice. But above it the snow became easier and at about ten o'clock we reached a sort of small dome which formed the summit of the Third Step.

The weather was no better than on the preceding days, but this time my morale was steely and I was determined to endure the worst in order to get as high as possible.

When the squalls momentarily dispersed the clouds, I saw the part of the arête we were about to attack. It was almost horizontal, but punctuated by a long series of saw teeth which we called 'the lace'. From here it seemed not too formidable and we reckoned that if we found good snow we should only need two or three bouts to reach the Fourth Step. For a moment I glimpsed the possibility of reaching the summit that very day!

Thus enthused I began the descent towards the ensuing gap. To my left a small crevasse had formed between the cornice and the mountain. To my right was an ice slope that plunged into the abyss of the west face. Like a tightrope walker I balanced along the narrow crest that marked the boundary of the crevasse and the slope.

Suddenly the slope broke away under one of my crampons; I lost my balance for an instant and to avoid falling into the crevasse I sprang a little to one side. Had I not done the same thing in the Alps many times? Unfortunately the ice was too hard and my crampons did not grip. Without being able to make a movement to save myself, I found myself slipping down the slope. I tried desperately to check my fall, but the face was as slippery as an ice rink and I slid away towards the abyss.

At last I felt a savage blow and at the same moment a horrible pain in my right elbow. I found myself hanging by the thin line which I had been trailing behind me for the second man to arrange as a fixed rope. Two snow stakes tied to the top of my sack had passed over my shoulder and then under my right arm, which was turned backwards in an unbearable position. Not without difficulty I succeeded in extricating myself and regaining my feet. Then, using the jumar in my left hand, I began a painful reascent up the steep ice bulges down which I had fallen back towards the arête.

Then I saw Soubis begin to come down towards me, looking rather stupefied. I shouted to him to wait for me. Soon I was beside him. He had not realised what had just taken place. At the moment of my fall he was not belaying me, but peacefully arranging the strap of one of his crampons. He had been very surprised when the bundle of rope which he had put down in front of him had suddenly reeled off at top speed, though he had not guessed the cause. We then realised the lucky chance which had prevented us from making 'the great leap' together. At the moment of my slip the second party had just fitted the thin 'Menaklon' line to a stake that had been firmly planted in the snow. Only this thin line had stopped my fall and prevented Soubis from being dragged off behind me.

Surely luck had been with us in our accident; nevertheless, my elbow had been severely sprained and my arm was horribly painful. I was deeply annoyed: I now knew that I would never get to the top of Huntington and this seemed to me most unfair. I had worked for months to have those unparalleled minutes of joy and excitement, and now I was to be cast aside like a useless beast.

The descent was done slowly, but with the help of the fixed ropes I was able to move reasonably well.

For me the accident was catastrophic, but the expedition was not going to stop for that. By nine the next morning four men had already reached the scene of my fall and it seemed they had a good chance of getting to the summit. In order to find snow, they tried to pass along close to the edge of the arête, but they had scarcely begun to climb the first point of the 'lace' when a large piece of cornice crumbled into the Ruth Glacier. Another few inches and Gicquel would have gone with it.

The wind blew and it was very cold. The arête was interrupted endlessly by short but vertical walls of ice, and progress was extremely slow.

Soon Martinetti complained that the ophthalmia which he had contracted two days earlier was worsening rapidly. His sight was almost gone and he suffered intolerably. Once again we were forced to descend, but this time we had gained only a few score yards and the party's morale fell hopelessly.

At Camp One that evening we held a council of war. After a brief discussion we argued that the 'lace' had turned out much more difficult than we had thought, and because the last step was not at all an easy walk the final stage on Huntington would still require a few more days. To avoid losing time in coming and going along the crests, we decided to set up a second camp at the foot of the Second Step.

At an early hour the six fit men descended to Base Camp to get more provisions and equipment. Unfortunately, a storm blew up in the afternoon and they could not climb back the same day.

Martinetti and I remained alone in the cave—a sad couple: he completely blind, me with a crippled arm. It was with great difficulty that I did the cooking and helped my comrade who could do practically nothing for himself.

Outside the snow fell ceaselessly: our comrades at Base Camp (with whom we talked by radio) told us that on the Ruth Glacier more than a metre had fallen in twenty-four hours. Thus we remained blocked for two long days.

To pass the time I tried to read, but I did not succeed. I was very depressed and very uneasy. I had read somewhere that big storms in this massif can last for eight or ten days. Now we had almost no provisions or fuel, and without doubt we were going to be forced in the midst of the storm to descend the evil slope that separated us from Base Camp. With almost two metres of new snow that would be ideal terrain for an avalanche.

During the twenty-five years that I have climbed among all the mountains of the world I had seen too many such avalanches begin beside me, or even over me, sometimes in the most unpredictable places. At the very idea of becoming involved on that slope I felt an animal-like fear.

At dawn on the third day the storm had ceased, but the sky was still very cloudy and the temperature rose. We had to descend quickly before the fog came back and the snow warmed up. Martinetti had practically regained his sight and I was able to use my arm a little. In the first couloir the snow had slid and we went quite quickly, but lower down an exhausting struggle began. We plunged in up to our bellies, and sometimes to the waist; the fog surrounded us and we could see only for a few yards; many landmarks had disappeared and it was very difficult not to lose the proper route. Moreover, the fear of seeing the whole slope move and of feeling oneself carried away helplessly plunged us into miserable anxiety. Luckily, the snow remained very cold, which lessened the danger a great deal. Eventually we reached the last couloir: here the new snow had already slipped off and we had only to let ourselves down the fixed ropes. Soon we were able to greet our comrades.

On the next day, at dawn, the wind was very violent, but the sky was limpid blue; my seven companions climbed up again to Camp One with heavy loads of provisions and equipment. Their plan was to send a party out onto the arête, and on the same day to pitch Camp Two, from which they would be able to launch the final assault on the summit.

Throughout the morning, very depressed, I watched my friends ascending. In all my life I have rarely felt so alone and unhappy: I had not even the courage to prepare a meal. During the night I scarcely slept, but in the morning I had reached a decision: I would rejoin my comrades and try to follow them to the summit. Certainly, my arm still gave me great pain, but by using the jumar with my left hand, I should be able to make progress.

At seven I made contact with Soubis and asked him to wait for me, which he agreed to do with pleasure. I took quite a long time getting ready. The track was still good but I was heavily laden and I made quite slow progress. The bergschrund that barred the upper part of the route held me up for a long time as it was very wide and overhanging. With only one arm I was not able to drag myself up with the jumar. Finally, thanks to an étrier, I succeeded in getting through though only after a desperate effort.

It was after five o'clock in the evening when I emerged upon the arête. Soubis and Gendre welcomed me with friendly smiles, which gave me great comfort. I was exhausted and hungry, and I simply had to regain my strength before going on.

While I was eating, my two friends told me that after many hours of step cutting Gicquel and Martinetti had succeeded in reaching the foot of the Fourth Step, while Batkin, Bernezat and Sarthou had been able to set up a rudimentary but adequate Camp Two.

We started off again at six o'clock but the weather had changed: it was snowing a little and the wind was blowing strongly, continually raising enormous and blinding swirls. Knowing the instability of the weather in this massif, we went on nevertheless. I had recovered my morale and energy and thanks to Soubis, who helped me a lot, I was able to haul myself up the fixed ropes without slowing our progress too much.

The higher we rose the greater became the intensity of the storm and when we reached Camp Two at eleven o'clock we were in the midst of a real hurricane.

While six men packed into a four-man 'Makalu' tent as best they could, Soubis and I shut ourselves up in a minute bivouac tent which was soon almost completely buried under the snow. We spent a heroic and splendid night struggling to feed ourselves and get a little rest.

In the morning we had to surrender to facts: the storm raged on and it was impossible for all eight of us to remain there waiting for good weather. We had not enough room, nor provisions, nor fuel. I decided that Batkin and Sarthou, who until then had done most of the less spectacular jobs, should remain so as to try and reach the summit at the first clearance. Then we started down the route to Camp One. The storm was diabolical, but we were now so used to the cold and the wind that this struggle with the elements seemed to us like an exciting game.

The next day (25th May), when we emerged from our cave, the weather was very moderate. The wind had almost fallen and the snow had stopped; on the other hand, Huntington was completely hidden by heavy clouds.

At ten o'clock when we resumed radio contact with our two comrades, we learned with surprise that they had set out very early and that, despite the wind, they had just reached the foot of the Fourth Step.

Mount Huntington Route Map

At noon, further contact told us that Batkin and Sarthou had surmounted a last difficult wall and were about to attack the terminal ridge. The wind, snow and fog hindered them a great deal, but their morale was steely and they were fully determined to reach the summit at all costs.

We lavished them with encouragement but also with advice to go carefully. Following their progress by radio was wildly enthralling; we were all in a state of extreme excitement. Eventually, at 4:30 p.m. Sarthou's voice, trembling with emotion, told us that for several minutes Batkin and himself had been standing on the top of Mount Huntington.

We jumped for joy and hugged one another like brothers. We experienced one of those moments of simple happiness which show their real meaning in mountaineering. I begged my two comrades to descend carefully and every two hours I made contact with them. The two men were tired and the wind had so filled their tracks that they had great difficulty in finding their steps again. In such conditions the descent was very slow and difficult. And they did not regain the camp until well after midnight.

Despite systematically equipping the route with fixed ropes, it still required twenty-three hours of almost uninterrupted effort to complete the final day of climbing on Mount Huntington. I think that in its very simplicity this figure shows very well how arduous and difficult the struggle had been.

Gendre, Martinetti, Gicquel, Bernezat, Soubis and I set out at 2:30 a.m. The weather was extremely cloudy, but the wind had fallen entirely and the temperature had eased a great deal.

At six we passed Camp Two, where our two comrades wished us luck. Then the climb was resumed at top speed. Fortunately, the tracks had not been filled up and I had become so used to using my left arm that I was able almost to keep up with the first two ropes.

At last we attacked the elegant 'lace' and I understood why so much time had been taken in overcoming it: We continually ran up against walls of ice that were quite short but vertical or even overhanging.

Now and again we exchanged yodels and shouts of delight. After so many difficult and dark days we had a marvellous feeling of liberation. We felt strong and light, and this ascent from crest to crest seemed like a triumphant gallop.

Eventually at 11:30 we were all together on the narrow summit. Unfortunately, the sky remained very cloudy and we had not a single glimpse of the great mountains that surrounded us. Delight showed, on every face: we were all shouting and singing, and it was in a festive atmosphere that we went through the traditional rites that mark the conquest of a peak.

But soon we had to start the descent. Suddenly I felt sad and distressed. I know, certainly, that a mountaineering victory is only a gesture in space, and for me, after the Himalayan and Andean peaks, Huntington was only another summit. Nevertheless, it was sad to leave that crest!

On this proud and beautiful mountain we had spent many ardent and noble hours in brotherhood. We had ceased for several days to be slaves and had truly lived as men. To return to slavery was hard . . .

LIONEL TERRAY'S CLIMBS AND EXPEDITIONS, AND OTHER ACHIEVEMENTS

SYMBOLS:

§ first ascent of mountain or route
+ expedition doctor

1933

Chamonix area. First alpine season. Trip to Couvercle Hut with guide. Ascent of Aiguillette d'Argentière with an older cousin who was working at the École Militaire de Haute Montagne. They also did Clochetons de Planpraz, the southeast face of the Brévent, the Grands Charmoz and the Petite Aiguille Verte.

1934

Vercors. Dent Gérard in Trois Pucelles by the 'Grange Gully'. Climbed with his friend Georgette and five others (one of whom was more experienced). This developed into a minor epic with Terray soloing the 'Sandwich Crack' to assist the leader in hoisting his second up the 'Dalloz Crack'. Later Terray tried the route again with Michel Chevalier but failed. **Chamonix area.** Second guided alpine season doing classic easy routes.

1935

Won prizes in regional ski competitions in Dauphine.

Aiguille du Grépon. Traverse via Mummery Crack, with Alain Schmit and a pushy guide who hoisted them up the climb—an efficient demonstration of brutal guiding.

1937

Won first ski championship. Reclimbed Grange Gully (Trois Pucelles) with a schoolmaster (G.H.M. member) in better style.

1939

Did well in national skiing championships in the Pyrénées and another competition in Provence during illicit absence from his school in Chamonix. Expelled, having already been moved from two other schools after similar incidents. Took part in further ski contests and earned some money as a ski instructor.

1940

Aiguille du Moine. Ascent of southwest ridge with Robert Michon (G.H.M.), an ex-soldier who sought him out after the end of hostilities in the north. This climb reignited Terray's climbing interests after years of skiing. They went on to do a series of classic routes during the summer including the north ridge of the Chardonnet and the Cardinal.

1941

Third in national ski championships.

Joined 'Jeunesse et Montagne'—a cadre of young outdoor instructors (with a military and mountain flavour) based at Annecy. In this Terray first met the Marseilles climber Gaston Rébuffat who had ambitious designs on great north faces. Both were later seconded to a climbing instruction unit at Montenvers commanded by André Tournier.

Dent du Requin (Mayer/Dibona), **Aig. du Grépon** (east face) with Gaston Rébuffat.

1942

Married Marianne Perrollaz (whom he met at a ski championship), and rented a farm in Les Houches. Gaston Rébuffat worked as their farmhand for a period.

Aiguille Purtscheller. West face § plus other climbs with Gaston Rébuffat (6 May).

Col du Caïman. North flank §, with descent by Pointe Lépiney and down the south ridge of the Fou, with Gaston Rébuffat (26 Aug.)—an epic and (for Terray) inspirational ascent, with difficult glacier work and an ice runnel to the col (c. Scottish 4).

Joins Groupe de Haute Montagne.

1943

Aiguille du Peigne. New line on west face of summit tower § (left of the Lépiney Crack) with René Ferlet (2 Aug.). Terray later had a close escape on this climb when he dropped his equipment at a critical point.

Aiguille des Pèlerins. West ridge § with Édouard Frendo and Gaston Rébuffat (10 Oct.).

1944

Meets Louis Lachenal in Annecy.

Pain de Sucre. East-northeast spur § (2 Aug.) with Gaston Rébuffat.

Aiguille des Pèlerins. North face—L/H route § (10 Aug.) with Gaston Rébuffat. Later to become an important winter climb (§ Rouse and Carrington, Feb. 1975).

Pointe Chevalier. East face § (11 Aug.) with Gaston Rébuffat.

Following Liberation (Aug.) Terray joined Compagnie Stéphane (ex Maquis) newly incorporated into the Chasseurs Alpins. In this largely independent unit Terray saw eight months of army service, with action on the Italian frontier near the Dauphiné.

Col de Peuterey. North face § as a new approach to the Peuterey Ridge with Gaston Rébuffat and the brothers Gérard and Maurice Herzog (15 Sept.).

1945

Transferred by Captain Stéphane to École Militaire de Haute Montagne, Chamonix.

Petit Dru. North face (via Allain Crack—HVS) with Jacques Oudot (15 Aug.).

Aiguille Verte. Couturier Couloir with J. P. Payot, followed by Lachenal and Lenoir.

Aiguille du Moine. East face (Aureille/Feutren), second ascent with Louis Lachenal.

Qualifies as a guide and is accepted into Compagnie des Guides de Chamonix.

Aiguille des Pèlerins. Grutter Ridge—difficult step direct § with Jo Marillac.

Aiguille Noire. South ridge with Jo Marillac.

1946

Les Droites. North spur with Louis Lachenal, André Contamine and Pierre Leroux in eight hours (one hour down to Couvercle) (4 Aug.).

Grandes Jorasses. Early repeat of the Walker Spur with Louis Lachenal (10–11 Aug.) with a variant trending into the Central Couloir § from above the Grey Tower.

Argentine. Second ascent of Grand Dièdre with Tomy Girard.

Bietschhorn. Southeast ridge and down north ridge with Louis Lachenal.

Matterhorn. Furggen ridge with Lachenal, Tomy Girard and René Dittert.

1947

Aiguille Verte. Nant Blanc face (Charlet/Platenov) with Louis Lachenal (31 May).

Eiger. North face (1938 route). A publicised second ascent with Louis Lachenal—bivouacs in Swallow's Nest and at the top of the Ramp (14–16 July).

Aiguille de Blaitière. West face (Allain/Fix). Second ascent with Louis Lachenal, Louis Pez and Joseph Simpson (20 Sept.).

Becomes an instructor at l'École Nationale d'Alpinisme (Director: Jean Franco).

1948

Moves to Quebec to run a hotel ski school, teach instructors and coach the state team—a comparatively lucrative posting lasting from Nov. 1947 to spring 1949.

1949

Mont Blanc. Brenva Face (Route Major) with Jean Gourdain (27 July).
Grand Capucin. (1924 route) with Tom de Lepiney.
Grandes Jorasses. Tronchey Arête second ascent with Jean Gourdain (31 July–1 Aug.). Piz Badile northeast face with Louis Lachenal in seven and a half hours (9 Aug.).

1950

Annapurna. § April–June via the north face—the first eight-thousand-metre peak to be climbed. Maurice Herzog (leader), Louis Lachenal, Lionel Terray, Gaston Rébuffat, Jean Couzy, Marcel Schatz, Jacques Oudot+, Francis de Noyelle, Marcel Ichac with Ang Tharkay (sirdar), Pansy, Sarki, Adjiba, Aila, Dawa Thondup, Phu Tharkay, Ang Dawa and others. After investigating several possibilities on Dhaulagiri during April, the party moved to Annapurna. After attempting the northwest spur they took the northern glacier route. Herzog and Lachenal reached the summit (3 June, without oxygen) but mishaps turned the descent into a survival struggle involving Terray and Rébuffat (support team). Herzog and Lachenal were severely frostbitten. *Annapurna* by Maurice Herzog (Cape, London, 1952; Dutton, New York, 1953); *Carnets du Vertige* by Louis Lachenal (Guerin, Chamonix, 1994).
    Aiguille Noire. September—a west face attempt was aborted after Terray's companion, Francis Aubert, was killed whilst descending (unroped) below the Col de l'Innominata.

1951

Aiguille Noire. West face early repeat with Raymond Emeric.

1952

FitzRoy (or Chalten). § René Ferlet (leader), Marc Azéma, Guido Magnone, Lionel Terray, Louis Dépasse, Francisco Ibañez (liaison officer), Louis Lliboutry, Georges Strouvé and Jacques Poincenot. There was an early tragedy when Poincenot, a talented rock climber, drowned during a hazardous river crossing (rumours that this might not have been the true cause of his death appear to be apocryphal). From Camp Three (an elaborate snow cave) Magnone and Terray tackled the southeast buttress utilizing several hundred feet of fixed rope and 118 pitons or wedges. There followed a final two-day summit push. Complex and difficult, the climb has proved less popular than the 1968 Californian route, or the 1965 Super-Couloir.*

Aconcagua. The FitzRoy party then tackled this peak but (as most were not acclimatised), only Terray and Ibañez reached the summit, in the process assessing the southeast ridge and south face (climbed in 1954 by another French expedition). Note: Ibañez (presumably briefed by Terray) mounted and led the 1954 Argentinian Dhaulagiri expedition. He returned from his summit push frostbitten but failed to withdraw quickly for treatment. He died of gangrene after his feet were amputated in Kathmandu.

Nevado Hauntsán § and **Nevado Pongos** § (Cordillera Blanca) by Lionel Terray with his clients and friends Tom De Booy and Kees Egeler.**

Mont Blanc, R/H Freney Pillar. With Godfrey Francis and Geoffrey Sutton.

Filmmaking: Terray shot his first movie footage in the Andes and then made the film *La Conquête du Hauntsán* (with J. J. Languepin). He also made *La Grande Descente du Mont Blanc* (with Georges Strouvé and Pierre Tairraz). Both films won prizes at the Trento Festival.

1954

Makalu. August–October: a reconnaissance expedition (to identify the correct route and try out new equipment) with Jean Franco (leader), Lionel Terray, Jean Couzy, Jean Rivolier, Pierre Leroux and Jean Bouvier. Makalu La § was reached by Leroux and Bouvier (15 Oct.) and probes made on the north face to approximately 7,800 metres.

* *Source: The Conquest of FitzRoy by M. A. Azema (Deutsch, London, 1957).*

** *Source: The Untrodden Andes by C. G. Egeler and T. De Booy (Faber, London, 1954).*

Kangchungste § (Makalu 2) was climbed by Franco, Terray, Gyaltsen Norbu and Pa Norbu (22 Oct.) and **Chomo Lonzo** § by Terray and Couzy (c. 30 Oct.)—both ascents were made with their highly effective new oxygen equipment.*

1955

Mont Blanc Massif. Louis Lachenal dies in a ski accident—he fell into a crevasse whilst descending from the Vallée Blanche to the Mer de Glace.

Makalu. § April–May: first, second and third ascents by an expedition led by Jean Franco, with Lionel Terray, Jean Couzy, Guido Magnone, Pierre Leroux, Jean Bouvier, Serge Coupé, André Vialatte, André Lapras+, Michel Latreille, Pierre Bordet, Gyaltsen Norbu (sirdar), Aila, Panzy, Mingma Tenzing, Ang Bao, Ang Tsering and others. Ascents were made by Couzy and Terray (15 May), Magnone, Franco and Gyaltsen Norbu (16th May), and Bouvier, Coupé, Leroux and Vialette (17 May).**

1956

Pic Soray § (Cordillera Vilcabamba)—by the north face; **Nevado Salcantay**—second ascent and **Nevado Veronica** § (Cordillera Urubamba), by Lionel Terray, Kees Egeler, Tom De Booy, Hans Dijkhout and Raymond Jenny.

Chacraraju § (Cordillera Blanca). First ascent (by north face, with much fixed rope) by Lionel Terray (leader), Maurice Davaille, Claude Gaudin, Raymond Jenny, Robert Sennelier and Pierre Souriac (31 July). Also involved was Maurice Martin. The same six also climbed **Taulliraju** § (by the north-east ridge on 13 Aug.). Both routes, with hard ice climbing and tough rock pitches, are amongst the most difficult in the Andes.

1957

Mont Blanc. January: Rescue bid to save the students François Henry and Jean Vincendon (beleaguered during a traverse of Mont Blanc begun on 23 Dec. 1956). They had been placed by rescuers in a crashed helicopter on the Grand Plateau. Terray and others—all unofficial rescuers—(approaching

---

* *Source: Makalu* by Jean Franco (Jonathan Cape, London, 1957).

** Ibid.

from the Grands Mulets on foot) were forced to retreat (1 Jan.). Further helicopter rescue bids failed and efforts were officially ended in good weather
conditions on 3 Jan. because of fear of further crashes. Terray and others were
highly critical of the failure of the Chamonix Mountain Rescue to initiate an
effort on foot when the alarm was first raised on 26 Dec.*

Wetterhorn. Northwest face with Kees Egeler and Tom De Booy.

Eiger. Rescue bid on the north face to reach the injured Claudio Corti
and Stefano Longhi, marooned in different positions high on the face. Two
other climbers who had disappeared were later found to have been avalanched
whilst descending the west face. A multinational team, directed by Robert
Seiler, Eric Friedli and Ludwig Gramminger, set up a winch/cable system on
the summit. Alfred Hellepart recovered Corti, but Terray's attempt to reach
Longhi was foiled when the cable jammed. Terray with Gramminger, Friedli,
Mauri, Cassin, Schlunegger, De Booy and others then lowered Corti down
the complex west ridge.

Grosshorn and **Triolet** climbed by their north faces with Tom de Booy
(two of several classic Alpine ice faces which Terray did with his Dutch
clients De Booy and Egeler).

1958

Pointe Adolphe Rey. East ridge direct § with Robert Guillaume.

Grand Capucin and other locations: filming Marcel Ichac's *Le Étoiles
de Midi.*

Jean Couzy killed in rock fall on Crête des Bergers, southwest face.

1959

Jannu (Kumbharkama). After reconnaissance in 1957 (by Magnone, Bouvier,
Leroux and Gyaltsen Norbu) the southern glacier approach was tackled by Jean
Franco (leader), Lionel Terray, Robert Paragot, Guido Magnone, Maurice
Lenoir, René Desmaison, Jean Bouvier, Pierre Leroux, James Lartizien+,
Jean-Michel Freulon, Philippe Dreux and Wangdi (sirdar) plus other sherpas.
They climbed the complex southwest ridge to 310 metres below the summit.**

Piz Badile. Northeast face with Suzanne Valentini (9 Aug.).

* *Source: The Tragedy on Mont Blanc* by René Dittert (*Mountain World* 1958/59, pp. 9–19).

** *Source: At Grips with Jannu* by Jean Franco and Lionel Terray (Gollancz, London, 1967).

1960

Obergabelhorn. Northeast face with Kees Egeler and Tom De Booy.

1961

Terray fell when ledge collapsed on the cliffs of Le Saussois. Broke ribs.

1962

Jannu (Kumbhakarna). § South glacier southwest ridge. The summit was reached by René Desmaison, Paul Keller, Robert Paragot and Gyaltsen (27 April). The climb was repeated (28 April) by André Bertrand, Jean Bouvier, Paul Leroux, Yves Pollet-Villard, Jean Ravier, Lionel Terray (leader) and Wangdi (sirdar). Also involved were Maurice Lenoir, René Vernadet (cameraman), Guy de Haynin+, Philippe Dreux and Jean-Marcel Rémy. Bottled oxygen proved crucial to success on this difficult route.*

Chacraraju Este. § July: first ascent by Lionel Terray (leader), Guido Magnone, René Dubost, Jacques Soubis, Paul Gendre. Also involved: Claude Maillard (organiser).

Nilgiri. § September/October—the first ascent of the 23,950-foot western satellite of Annapurna by a route up the north face by Peter, Paul and Holger Van Lookeren Campagne, Lionel Terray and Wangdi (19 Oct.). Also involved: Tom De Booy and Kees Egeler.

1964

Mount Huntington. § Lionel Terray (leader), Paul Gendre, Jacques Soubis, Jacques Batkin, Marc Martinetti, Maurice Gicquel, Sylvain Sarthou, Jean-Louis Bemezat tackled the sustained and stubborn south ridge, aided by an ice cave at its base and much fixed rope. Terray had a big fall high on the route (when unbelayed) and was only arrested on a thin line he was trailing for fixed rope. On 26 May, after eighteen days of struggle in bitterly cold conditions, the summit (12,240 feet/3,731 metres) was reached by Batkin and Sarthou and, in more benign weather, by the six other members of the party (27 May).

* *Source: At Grips with Jannu* by Jean Franco and Lionel Terray (Gollancz, London, 1967); *Total Alpinism* by René Desmaison (Granada, London, 1982). Note—Wangdi is incorrectly spelt Wongdi in official accounts.

1965

Gerbier: Arc de Cercle Crack. The roped bodies of Lionel Terray and Marc Martinetti were found below this difficult 400-metre rock climb in the Vercors, suggesting a fall while they were moving together (roped but unbelayed) on the easy upper section.

MOUNTAINEERS BOOKS is a leading publisher of mountaineering literature and guides—including our flagship title, Mountaineering: The Freedom of the Hills—as well as adventure narratives, natural history, and general outdoor recreation. Through our two imprints, Skipstone and Braided River, we also publish titles on sustainability and conservation. We are committed to supporting the environmental and educational goals of our organization by providing expert information on human-powered adventure, sustainable practices at home and on the trail, and preservation of wilderness.

The Mountaineers, founded in 1906, is a 501(c)(3) nonprofit outdoor activity and conservation organization whose mission is "to explore, study, preserve, and enjoy the natural beauty of the outdoors." One of the largest such organizations in the United States, it sponsors classes and year-round outdoor activities throughout the Pacific Northwest, including climbing, hiking, backcountry skiing, snowshoeing, bicycling, camping, paddling, and more. The Mountaineers also supports its mission through its publishing division, Mountaineers Books, and promotes environmental education and citizen engagement. For more information, visit The Mountaineers Program Center, 7700 Sand Point Way NE, Seattle, WA 98115-3996; phone 206-521-6001; www.mountaineers.org; or email info@mountaineers.org.

Our publications are made possible through the generosity of donors and through sales of more than 600 titles on outdoor recreation, sustainable lifestyle, and conservation. To donate, purchase books, or learn more, visit us online:

MOUNTAINEERS BOOKS
1001 SW Klickitat Way, Suite 201 • Seattle, WA 98134
800-553-4453 • mbooks@mountaineersbooks.org • www.mountaineersbooks.org

The Legends and Lore Series honors the lives and adventures of mountaineers and is made possible in part through the generosity of donors. Mountaineers Books, a nonprofit publisher, further contributes to this investment through book sales from more than 600 titles on outdoor recreation, sustainable lifestyle, and conservation.

We would like to thank the following for their charitable support of Legends and Lore:

FOUNDERS CIRCLE

- Anonymous
- Tina Bullitt
- Tom and Kathy Hornbein*
- Dianne Roberts and Jim Whittaker
- William Sumner
- Doug and Maggie Walker

SUPPORTERS

- Byron Capps
- Roger Johnson
- Joshua Randow
- Jolene Unsoeld

With special appreciation to Tom Hornbein, who donates to the series all royalties earned through the sale of his book, Everest: The West Ridge.

You can help us preserve and promote mountaineering literature by making a donation to the Legends and Lore series. For more information, benefits of sponsorship, or how you can support future work, please contact us at mbooks@mountaineersbooks.org or visit us online at www.mountaineersbooks.org.

MOUNTAINEERS
BOOKS